Fodor's EXPLORING

CALIFORNIA

FODOR'S TRAVEL PUBLICATIONS, INC.

NEW YORK • TORONTO • LONDON • SYDNEY • AUCKLAND

WWW.FODORS.COM

Published in the United States by Fodor's Travel
Publications.
Published in the United Kingdom by AA Publishing.

Fodor's is a registered trademark of Random House, Inc.

ISBN 0–679–00703–2
ISSN 1525-4380
Fifth Edition

Fodor's Exploring California

Author: **Mick Sinclair**
Revision verifier: **Carole Harley**
Revision editor: **Lodestone Publishing Limited**
Front cover silhouette: **David Vance/Image Bank**
Top inset: **Richard Cummins/Corbis**
Cover design: **Tigist Getachew; Fabrizio La Rocca**
Cartography: **The Automobile Association**

Special Sales
Fodor's Travel Publications are available at special
discounts for bulk purchases (100 copies or more) for sales
promotions or premiums. Special editions, including
personalized covers, excerpts of existing guides, and
corporate imprints, can be created in large quantities for
special needs. For more information contact your local
bookseller or write to Special Marketing, Fodor's Travel
Publications, 280 Park Avenue, New York NY 10017.
Inquiries from Canada should be directed to your local
Canadian bookseller or sent to Random House of Canada,
Ltd., Marketing Department, 2775 Matheson Blvd. East,
Mississauga, Ontario L4W 4P7.

Printed and bound in Italy by Printer Trento srl

How to use this book

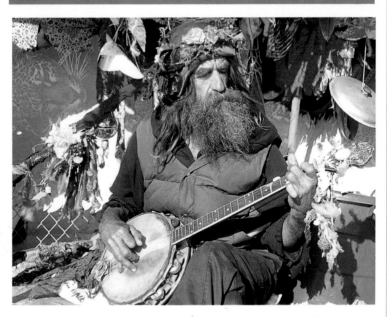

ORGANIZATION

California Is, California Was
Discusses aspects of life and culture in contemporary California and explores significant periods in its history.

A–Z
Breaks down California into regional chapters, and covers places to visit, including walks and drives. Within this section fall the Focus On articles, which consider a variety of subjects in greater detail.

Travel Facts
Contains the strictly practical information vital for a successful trip.

Accommodations and Restaurants
Lists recommended establishments throughout California.

ADMISSION CHARGES
Standard admission charges are categorized in this book as follows:

Inexpensive	under $7
Moderate	$7–$13
Expensive	over $13

ABOUT THE RATINGS
Most places described in this book have been given a separate rating. These are as follows:

▶▶▶   **Do not miss**

▶▶   **Highly recommended**

▶   **Worth seeing**

MAP REFERENCES
To make the location of a particular place easier to find, every main entry in this book has a map reference to the right of its name. This includes a number, followed by a letter, followed by another number, such as 176B3. The first number (176) indicates the page on which the map can be found, the letter (B) and the second number (3) pinpoint the square in which the place is located. The maps on the inside front cover and inside back cover are referred to as IFC and IBC, respectively.

Contents

**Mick Sinclair has
explored California
from its mountaintops
to its desert floors. He
is the author of several
guidebooks to the
state and has also
written guides to other
U.S. regions and cities,
including Florida, New
York, Chicago, and
Miami.**

My California

Simply put, California has everything. You can surf and
ski on the same day, climb mountains, explore deserts,
dine in chic restaurants among famous faces, or sample
life in a rural community little changed in appearance
since the Gold Rush. The California landscape that
encompasses volatile features such as geysers and sulfur
vents, and is regularly stirred by earthquakes (usually
too small to cause damage), also includes the serene
beauty of Yosemite Valley and no fewer than 264 state
parks giving protection to 1.4 million acres of pristine
land. The coastline, too, has the power to thrill, with the
beach-and-surfer dominated southernmost third and the
scenic drama of the bluffs and cliffs that lie farther north.

The discovery of gold made California independently
wealthy and stimulated an independence of mind that has
lasted into the present. Today's Californians include
individuals pushing back the boundaries of everything
from new technology to adventure sports, and a multitude
of cultures and creeds that continually reshape the
demography of the U.S.'s most populous state.

California has been the apple in the eye of travelers for
500 years. Seventeenth-century Spanish explorers, the
"forty-niners" of the gold rush, Hollywood hopefuls of
the 1920s, and the Asian immigrants of the 1980s are just
a few of those for whom the state has held the promise of
a new life and a brighter future.

While the social mixture can be stimulating—not least
for the opportunity to spread New Year celebrations over
several months (Asian celebrations follow the lunar
cycle) and sample the cuisines of the world without
leaving the neighborhood—it also contributes to the
stresses and strains of the state's infrastructure. At times
it threatens to erode California's tradition of support for
the underdog, as immigration issues move increasingly
to the center of state politics.

Yet lessons learned from the inner-city riots and the
widespread financial downturn of the early 1990s have
caused California to perform a remarkable self-
transformation. The state has reinvented itself, creating a
diversified economy and regaining enough social
cohesion to be once again a vibrant and welcoming place:
the California dream seems very much alive.
Mick Sinclair

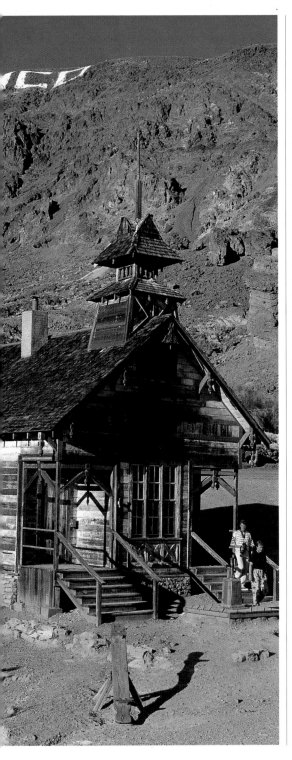

California Is
California Was

OREGON   IDAHO

Crescent City
Redwood National Park
Yreka
Mt Shasta 14163ft
Pit
Alturas
Cascade Range
Eureka
Cape Mendocino
Shasta Lake
Trinity
Redding
Lassen National Park
Susanville
Red Bluff
Coast Range
Quincy
Fort Bragg
Chico
Ukiah
Yuba City
Clear Lake
Point Arena
Auburn
Lake Tahoe
NEVADA
Santa Rosa
Napa
SACRAMENTO
Sierra
Point Reyes
Stockton
Sonora
Mono Lake
Oakland
San Francisco
Modesto
Yosemite National Park
San Jose
Merced
Bishop
Santa Cruz
San Joaquin
Kings Canyon National Park
Monterey
Salinas
Fresno
Independence
Mt Whitney 14495ft
Big Sur
Coast
Sequoia National Park
San Simeon
Santa Lucia Ra
Visalia
Death Valley
11050ft
Delano
Salinas
San Luis Obispo
Bakersfield
Ridgecrest
Range
Mojave
Santa Maria
Lancaster
Barstow
Desert
Needle
Lompoc
Santa Barbara
Sonora
Desert
Point Conception
Ventura
Pasadena
San Bernardino
Desert
Oxnard
Los Angeles
Anaheim
Palm Springs
Blythe
Long Beach
Salton Sea
Channel Islands
Oceanside
Escondido
Brawley
San Diego
(MEX)

PACIFIC OCEAN

CALIFORNIA

UTAH

ARIZONA

Colorado

0   100   200 km
0   50   100 miles

The golden state

Rarely has a region captured the imagination for as long or as strongly as California. Spanish explorers, the forty-niners, would-be film stars, and millions of tourists have all arrived in anticipation of finding America's promised land. Few of them have been disappointed, although California is never quite what people expect it to be.

California is a land of golden beaches only along the most southerly quarter of its 1,264-mile coastline; the rest is typified by bracing, pristine bluffs lashed by crashing ocean waves.

Inland California embraces parched deserts and snow-capped mountains, but also finds room for the lush valleys of the wine country and the lava landscapes of the far north.

The state's two major cities are poles apart. San Francisco is small and visually attractive, and it exudes a warm, cultured atmosphere. By contrast, brash Los Angeles, while never dull, struggles to justify its glamorous

Part of California's golden coast: a beach to the north of Malibu

image and gives new meaning to the word "sprawl."

California is far too diverse and complex—socially, geographically, and politically—to be defined by a single, simple image. Of 34 million Californians, surprisingly few were born in the state and barely half fit the traditional Anglo-American stereotype.

A flourishing New Age movement strengthens California's anything-goes reputation, while increased environmental protection is a product of many years of legislation. Yet California has plenty of conservatives, and Ronald Reagan's eight-year reign as state governor was far from unrepresentative of the state's political mind.

State Motto
eureka (I have found it)

State Song "I love you, California"

State Mineral gold

State Flower golden poppy

State Animal grizzly bear

State Bird valley quail

State Fish golden trout

State Reptile desert tortoise

State Insect dog-face butterfly

State Mammal gray whale

State Fossil saber-toothed tiger

Even before its European settlement, California was thought to harbor treasures beyond man's wildest dreams. The discovery of gold compounded this belief and set the state on the road to becoming a financial superpower, with a multitude of diverse industries underpinning an economy that would make today's California—if it were a country—one of the richest in the world.

END OF TRADITION California's long reliance on several key industries, particularly automobile production and aerospace research, was ended in the late 1980s by declining federal expenditure, national recession, and demographic changes. Simultaneously, Silicon Valley's computer industry hit a sharp decline, as did Hollywood's TV and film companies, locked into a downward spiral only compounded by the late 1992 L.A. riots that destroyed the city's tourist industry.

DIVERSE REVENUE By the late 1990s, however, California had made a remarkable recovery, deviating from traditional sources of income to create the most diversified economy in the state's history. Established areas such as film and computers boomed, but so did newer industries as varied as clothing and biotechnology. Tourism also rose, nowhere more so than in L.A. where visitors—up by more than 25 percent since 1990—spent over $10 billion annually. Overall, the state is creating around half a million jobs each year, and is the state's third largest employer.

Agriculture: a boon or a threat?

❏ Discovered in the 1860s, California's oil reserves continue to be lucrative. There are major wells in Los Angeles and in the Central Valley, although exploitation of offshore deposits was curtailed after a huge spill off Santa Barbara in 1969 caused widespread environmental damage. ❏

SILICON VALLEY From the 1970s, the development of the silicon chip turned computer whiz-kids into millionaire corporate executives overnight and made so-called Silicon Valley—a region south of San Francisco, long at the forefront of electronics research—the state's fastest-growing area.

The early 1990s stabilization of the computer industry led to recession in Silicon Valley. Now, though, the Valley is again drawing massive amounts of venture capital, around $3 billion annually, and opportunities created by multimedia and the Internet have created a new army of highly skilled software designers.

AGRICULTURE California's most reliable commodity is not film stars but farm produce. The Imperial and Central valleys produce half the fruit, nuts, and vegetables grown in the United States, a crop that is worth around $27 billion annually. Yet there is controversy surrounding the over-use of chemicals and the long-term ecological upsets caused by the conversion of desert to farmland.

Jogging, rollerblading, and skateboarding are wildly popular throughout the state, often in specially designated areas. So are cycling (including mountain biking), hiking and river rafting; toning one's physique in a health club or fitness center is a state ritual. The ocean and winter's snow-covered mountain slopes are other playing fields for this health and fitness orientated culture.

OCEAN SPORTS Although it may seem the most Californian of all the state's participant sports, surfing arrived from Hawaii in 1907 and did not capture the Californian imagination until the invention of lightweight surfboards in the 1950s.

Subsequently mythologized by the songs of the Beach Boys and the beach-blanket films of the early 1960s, surfing became a lasting symbol of the sun-kissed Californian beach life.

From the masses gathered at San Diego's Mission Beach to the hardy loners spotted off the rocky Central Coast, surfing has evolved into a subculture with its own barely penetrable language and customs. In some areas, local surfers actively deter outsiders from encroaching on the breakers they consider their own.

❏ Few of California's professional sports teams have roots in the state: the Rams moved west from Cleveland in 1946; the Dodgers arrived from Brooklyn in 1958; the L.A. Lakers were based in Minneapolis until 1960; the Oakland A's played in Kansas City until 1968. ❏

Scuba diving and snorkeling are pursued in numerous locations, especially along the central coast where the beaches are not crowded.

BEACH SPORTS Back on the sand, volleyball nets line many southern California beaches and anyone-can-join "pickup" games are common. If you play, don't expect mild exertion—sand is brutal on the leg muscles. You will soon appreciate the stamina of Californians who play beach volleyball professionally—they are the big-earning stars of televised tournaments held each summer.

WINTER SPORTS During the winter, many coast-dwelling Californians head inland. The 1960 Winter Olympics at Squaw Valley (near Lake Tahoe) gave many residents a sense of the magnificence of their own state's skiing. The winter resorts of Lake Tahoe and Mammoth Lakes are now major destinations for skiers and snowboarders, who are present in rapidly swelling numbers and who dazzle two-footed snow lovers with swooping downhill descents on their four-foot-long boards.

Although born in Hawaii, surfing has become inextricably linked with California

13

The price of more than a century of unrestrained growth has been the wreckage of California's ecosystems by the diverting of rivers and the decimation of forests, factors that have wrought havoc on the state's wildlife and created the worst air pollution in the country. From the founding of the Sierra Club in 1892 to the antipollution initiatives of the 1970s, California has led the country in encouraging environmental protection, but the greening of the Golden State is a far from settled issue: state bureaucrats, conservationists, and commercial interests regularly do battle in the courts.

AIR POLLUTION Twenty-five million vehicles and a cruel combination of geography and climate make smog a major Californian headache. Infamously bad in Los Angeles, smog also affects many southern areas, and Silicon Valley in the north.

Catalytic converters and the use of unleaded gas has had some effect, but attempts to encourage car pooling have been less successful. These include a multi-million dollar public transportation program in Los Angeles that over-optimistically hoped to wean 8 million drivers off their cars by the year 2000.

IN THE HOME Antismog measures also apply in the home. California's Air Resources Board has created a list of 2,500 household items, among them carpet cleaners, hair sprays, and disinfectants, that must comply with new safety standards by 2005. Detergents and face creams are among products currently being evaluated. The board claims that the targeted products daily release hydrocarbons equivalent to 500,000 car exhaust emissions.

NO SMOKING To improve air quality for staff and nonsmoking customers in California's licensed premises, it became illegal to smoke in bars, restaurants, and nightclubs from the first day of 1998. Although only 18 percent of Californians smoke, the new law was widely condemned by bar owners, fearing lost business; many kept polishing their ashtrays and turned a blind eye to customers who continued to smoke. In general, the ban has been more widely adhered to in upscale establishments. In 1996, San Francisco became the first local government to sue the tobacco industry to recover money spent treating smoking-related illnesses.

❏ California has more endangered, rare, or threatened species than any other state: 360 at the last count. ❏

Golden Gate Bridge

DANGER TO HABITATS Half a million people settle annually in California, and the demand for new homes causes fragile coastal and desert regions to disappear beneath tract housing and shopping malls. In some areas, residents have voted for higher taxes to ensure undeveloped land stays that way, and to maintain protected wildlife areas.

A stimulus to southern California's growth and the productivity of the Central Valley farmlands was the diverting of water from the state's northern rivers. Consequently, the Sacramento delta, the confluence of rivers from the Sierra Nevada mountains, and the San Francisco Bay underwent profound changes, adversely affecting migratory birds and fish stocks, and leaving inhabited land prone to flooding. Legal arguments rage over water rights, and droughts have led to rationing.

L.A. WATER Los Angeles finally got some comeuppance for the devious practices that brought the city its first fresh water supply via a 250-mile aqueduct, which stimulated its growth, when, in 1997, it was ordered to spend $300 million annually to improve the source area around Owens Lake in the Sierra Nevada. The Los Angeles Department of Water and Power is now required to reduce the amount of water taken and partially flood

California's surge of economic growth has an environmental price tag…

the lake to reduce the dust, laden with arsenic toxic metals, that makes the Owens Valley one of the most polluted places in the United States (see panel). In an unrelated incident, also in 1997, a toxic chemical used in the production of rocket fuel was found in the drinking water of three California counties, including Los Angeles.

FORESTS Ninety percent of California's redwood and Douglas fir trees have been chopped down since the gold rush. Even the federal protection of some strands of coastal redwoods and giant sequoias does not guarantee their survival—the felling of the forest leaves them exposed to erosion.

❏ Wind-borne dust from the dry bed of Owens Lake carries carcinogens such as nickel, cadmium and arsenic across an area housing 40,000 people, some 150 miles distant. A long-term plan to introduce shallow water, vegetation and gravel to the lake bed aims to bring the area into line with federal air quality standards by 2006. ❏

There is precious little evidence of it as yet on the state's governing bodies, but currently only 53 percent of Californians are white Anglo-Americans. In the future, there is expected to be no ethnic majority at all in the state, just several large ethnic minorities.

Military conflicts and eased entry restrictions brought substantial increases in Asian immigration into California from the 1950s, and the state's already established Hispanic population grew by more than 70 percent in the 10 years to 1992. Of 7 million new arrivals and births in California during the 1980s, 85 percent were Asian or Hispanic.

Meanwhile, migration from California to other US states reached record levels with 250,000, mostly non-Hispanic whites, departing for economic reasons in 1994. In the same year, international migration into California, increasing by 60 percent through the early 1990s, reached a record with 200,000 documented new arrivals, mostly from Asia or Latin America. Additionally, an estimated 125,000 settle illegally in California annually.

NATIVE AMERICANS Enduring removal from their ancestral lands since the time of the Spanish missions and with few recognized rights until the 1960s, California's Native Americans increased in number during the 1970s and 1980s and there are now around 200,000 living in the state. Despite being indigenous residents, Native Americans are the least conspicuous of all California's ethnic communities, not least the (approximately) 20 percent of them living on reservations.

❏ More people live in California than in Canada. ❏

BLACK AMERICANS Blacks of African descent were a significant element in some of California's earliest Spanish settlements, though the state's black population underwent its biggest expansion during the 1940s, when wartime heavy industry attracted labor from the rural and economically ailing Deep South.

Subsequently, sheer weight of numbers provided the electoral clout to put blacks into important positions in California political life, but not the economic power to regenerate the cheaply built housing projects that evolved into inner-city ghettos. In some instances, the arrival of Asians into black neighborhoods has caused resentment and violence among already established communities.

Simultaneously, California's uncertain job market is tempting some Californian blacks back to the Deep South.

Variety is the spice of California: Melrose Avenue, L.A.

16

Pictures of a diverse and lively culture from the Mission District in San Francisco

HISPANICS California's Spanish history is echoed in its place-names and street names, while its Spanish-speaking present is evident in the TV and radio stations catering to a Hispanic population now accounting for one in four of the state's inhabitants.

As early as 1945, Los Angeles had the biggest Mexican community outside Mexico; many more Mexicans crossed the border between 1951 and 1964, when the U.S. government encouraged the import of agricultural labor. Since then, the depressed Mexican economy, and trouble and strife throughout Central and (to a lesser extent) South America, have contributed, along with a comparatively high birthrate, to the growth of California's Hispanic numbers.

ASIANS Thirty-five percent of the Asian population of the United States lives in California, where Asians make up one in ten of the state's inhabitants and are projected to number 21 million by 2025.

California's earliest Asians were Chinese who arrived at the time of the Gold Rush. Many of these immigrants became laborers, some became merchants, and all experienced the racism that caused them to band together in Chinatown districts. The Chinese population did not significantly change until the repeal of anti-Asian immigration laws in 1965. After that year many

new arrivals left their traditional homes in Chinatown as soon as they could afford to in favor of homes in the suburbs. Those left behind tended to be the poor and elderly, those least able to integrate into U.S. society.

Following the first Chinese, Japanese laborers and farmers settled in California and laid the foundations of the state's prosperous agricultural industry between 1890 and 1910. After the Japanese attack on Pearl Harbor in 1941, their internment devastated an entire generation of Japanese Americans; among their children, who are increasingly adept at balancing two cultures, are success stories spanning most walks of Californian life.

❑ Approximately 30 percent of U.S. immigrants settle in California. If California were a country, it would be the 30th most populous. ❑

Koreans became a strong presence in parts of Los Angeles beginning in the 1950s; in the 1970s, following the fall of Saigon, 100,000 Vietnamese, Cambodians, and Laotians arrived in California.

In San Francisco, the Laotians and Vietnamese have been evident opening businesses in the Tenderloin district. Less happily, teenage Cambodians in Long Beach's "Little Phnom Penh" are integrating into American society by joining black and Hispanic street gangs.

From Marxist logging colonies to the ragbag of beliefs of the New Age movement, cults have been a mainstay of California life for decades and show few signs of abating.

Idealistic cooperative communities appeared as early as the 1880s, the largest being the 400-strong Kaweah Colony, who followed a Marxist plan for self-sufficiency that included a potentially devastating project to scythe down all the state's giant sequoia trees.

Oriental mysticism and arcane magic had stolen the cult spotlight from utopian politics by the 1920s, when the Krishnamurti Foundation was founded in Ojai, and the Rosicrucian Order built a home in San Jose, both of which still exist. In Los Angeles, inspired by a visit by English occultist Aleister Crowley, the Builders of the Adytum formed; their tarot-decorated temple continues to explore the mysteries of the Kabbala. Mount Shasta is thought by some to be inhabited by Lemurians, a race of highly advanced beings from a lost city of the Pacific.

In 1930, one G. W. Ballard claimed he had quenched his thirst while hiking on the mountain with what turned out be the Elixir of Life, handed to him by a youth who proceeded to reveal the secrets of the universe. Ballard responded by forming the I AM Foundation of Youth that, by the 1950s, was attracting 3,000 brightly robed believers to its ceremonies.

While Ballard was being enlightened on Shasta's slopes, mining engineer W. Warren Shufelt was producing a map of tunnels beneath Downtown Los Angeles that, he thought, were the home of an ancient race of "Lizard People," mentioned in Hopi Indian legends.

❏ Tales of "glowing humanoids" and three-fingered aliens buying supplies in local grocery stores have convinced some Californians that the Joshua Tree National Monument is a UFO landing site. ❏

In 1969, the Charles Manson "family" (see page 33) committed gruesome murders; in the 1970s, Jim Jones's California-based People's Temple moved to Guyana where Jones and 900 followers committed mass suicide in 1978. Another mass suicide took place in 1997, when 39 members of the Heaven's Gate UFO cult committed suicide in Rancho Sante Fe, near San Diego, believing that it was time to "shed their containers" and join a spacecraft behind the Hale-Bopp comet.

Have aliens gathered at Joshua Tree National Monument?

Cults might flourish in California but they are, by definition, of limited appeal. Of more lasting consequence is the state's unique ability to allow alternative approaches to life and living to be tried and tested before, in many instances, being adopted throughout the world.

ON THE NET Long at the front line of computer technology, California was among the first places in the world to begin exploring the possibilities of the Internet.

In unwitting anticipation of the worldwide information super-highway, many San Francisco cafés were linked by SF Net by the early 1990s, a method of communication through cyberspace with customers in other on-line cafés throughout the city.

Some of the Internet's most startling company success stories have been rooted in the Silicon Valley area around San Jose. San Francisco's many multimedia companies have brought an influx of future-obsessed "dot.com people" into the city.

MEDICINAL MARIJUANA As the effectiveness of marijuana to ease the pain of those suffering serious illness is increasingly recognized by the medical profession, California has led the way in enabling the illegal drug to become available to those who have medical reasons for using it.

From the early 1990s, a buyer's club in San Francisco sold marijuana to its 11,000 members with the tacit approval of the city authorities, and a statewide referendum in November 1996 led to the legalization of medicinal marijuana use within the state, even though its cultivation and possession remains illegal under U.S. law.

❑ A 1991 survey revealed 25,000 people claiming to be pagans or wiccans (practitioners of witchcraft) in San Francisco and the Bay Area. ❑

NEW AGE In the early 1960s, the Esalen Institute near Big Sur became the home of the human potential movement. Twenty years later, many of its tenets of self-discovery were echoed in the New Age movement, in full swing during the 1980s and an umbrella term that encompassed long-standing pursuits such as dream interpretation, astrology, and tarot reading with newer areas such as channeling, rebirthing, and belief in the powers of crystals. In August 1987, thousands of Californians participated in a "Harmonic Convergence" gathering on the slopes of Mount Shasta, to welcome the Age of Aquarius. By the 1990s, however, many Californians were beginning to regard the New Age as old hat.

19

Californians were among the first to benefit from the convenience of cyber cafés

Some 200 million years ago the area that is now California was consumed by the Pacific Ocean, with the western edge of the North American continent being defined by the mountains of what is now Nevada.

GEOLOGY Around this time, two of the 20 tectonic plates that form the earth's crust—the Pacific plate and the North American plate—began moving. The heavier ocean plate slid beneath the continental plate and caused buckling, which eventually created undersea mountain ranges.

MOUNTAINS One mountain group would become California's coastal ranges; another group, farther east, would become the Sierra Nevada mountains. The latter formed along an east–west geological fault line that caused the northern section to move slowly 60 miles west, becoming what are now the Klamath Mountains.

Pressure within the earth forced the mountains continually up, and they broke surface 25 million years ago.

PLAINS Because of the movement of the Klamaths, the Pacific Ocean continued to cover northeastern California until its sediments created a plain. As high temperatures in the earth's mantle forced the plain to fracture, lava flowed to the surface through fissures and solidified to become the Modoc Plateau.

The Coastal Ranges and the Sierra Nevada mountains had also trapped a section of the Pacific between them. This too filled with sediment and became the Central Valley.

DESERT Sixteen million years ago, the Sierra Nevada mountains became tall enough (though well short of their present height) to influence the weather. Blocking the passage of rain from the ocean, the mountains caused the land on their eastern side to become arid and evolve into deserts.

Over several ice ages, the most recent ending 30,000 years ago, glaciers smoothed the Sierra's granite peaks and carved great U-shaped valleys, such as the great valley in Yosemite.

❏ The first Europeans to experience a California earthquake were the members of the Portolá expedition of 1769. At the time, they were encamped by the Santa Ana River in what was to become Orange County. ❏

THE SAN ANDREAS FAULT
California's immensely varied landscapes lie on one of the world's most geologically active zones, part of the "Ring of Fire" that girdles the Pacific Ocean. Of hundreds of fault lines running across the state, the longest, and most famous, is the San Andreas fault, which runs for 600 miles and marks the meeting point of the Pacific and the North American plates.

The solid granite slopes of Yosemite National Park, carved and shaped by the passing of glaciers

Recent discoveries indicate that human habitation in the Americas may date much farther back than previously believed, but it is still widely accepted in scientific circles that the earliest North Americans arrived by crossing by a land link over the Bering Strait, between Alaska and Siberia, around 12,000 years ago.

Estimates suggest that at the time of European discovery 300,000 Native Americans lived in California (their forebears having settled around 6,000 years before), split into just over 100 groupings, each of which comprised several hundred people—communities too small to fit the usual definition of a tribe.

CULTURE AND BELIEFS Across the land, a host of different skills and belief systems developed. In central California, for example, the Maidus, Pomos, and Wintuns observed the Kukso cult, creating elaborate feathered costumes for use in dances and ceremonies, with the Pomos becoming renowned for their feathered basketry.

Farther south, the Chumash demonstrated advanced artistic skills with the most intricate of rock art, and the Gabrieleño followed a one-god

Preaching to Native Americans

religion and meted out severe punishment on any member who deviated from a strict moral code.

Despite these differences, and with food abundant for all (except those groups inhabiting the desert regions), there were none of the tribal wars that occurred elsewhere in North America, and trading between different groups was common.

❑ Believed to be the last surviving Yahi, "Ishi" (as he was named) was discovered in California's far north in 1911, and spent the next five years living in the anthropology museum of the University of California in San Francisco, passing on details of his people's culture before dying of tuberculosis as a result of his first cold. ❑

ARRIVAL OF THE EUROPEANS The talent that the Native Americans displayed for living in harmony with each other, and with nature, were not traits shared by California's European settlers, who considered the "Indians" barbarians, fit only for laboring tasks.

Although many of the first European settlers were guilty of mistreating the Native Americans, greater damage to the native population was caused by European-borne diseases, such as measles and smallpox, to which the indigenous people had no immunity, and by the enormous influx of land-hungry whites at the time of the gold rush, which resulted in most Native Americans being forcibly resettled on reservations.

An expedition in 1533 under the Spaniard Hernando Cortés is credited with making the first sighting of Baja (or Lower) California, a long peninsula that was mistakenly believed to be an island. This geographical error also applied to Alta (or Upper) California—what is now the state of California—for many years.

In 1542, the crew of Juan Rodríguez Cabrillo, a Portugese navigator in the employ of Spain, became the first to drop anchor off Alta California, pausing at what is now San Diego Bay and at the Channel Islands off Santa Barbara.

Not for another 25 years did a European set foot in California, and it was not a Spaniard but a Briton, Francis Drake. He landed at a site near Point Reyes (the actual location is a matter of dispute) in 1579, claiming California—which he named Nova Albion—for Queen Elizabeth I of England.

Without fixed settlements it was impossible for any territorial claims to be made firm, however. After Sebástian Vizcaíno landed at what he called Monterey in 1602, he toured the coast bestowing many of the bays and headlands with their enduring Spanish names. Vizcaíno's claims for the area's topography were less successful, though, and his cartographer was hanged for producing a wildly inaccurate map of Monterey Bay.

With a Jesuit mission established in Baja California in 1690 and Alta California discovered to be part of the North American mainland in 1742, the Spanish king ordered the construction of a north–south string of Franciscan missions across California, with Monterey becoming the province's administrative center. Ostensibly, this was a religious crusade to convert the Native Americans to Catholicism, but the building of the missions (fully described on pages 110 and 111), and four attendant presidios, each housing several hundred troops, was also intended to bring a social infrastructure to the region that, it was (rather optimistically) hoped, would deter any rival colonial power from intruding on California.

❑ The first European sighting of California's greatest natural harbor, San Francisco Bay, was made from land in 1769 by a Spanish expedition heading north from San Diego hoping to find an overland route to Monterey. ❑

23

Symbol of a religious crusade: San Diego Mission

Despite 21 missions and the base at Monterey, California remained sparsely inhabited, and it had barely been explored inland from El Camino Real, the route linking the missions from San Diego to Sonoma. Many of the missions—most of which were not completed until the early 1800s—became extremely prosperous, mainly by exploiting Native American labor on vast tracts of farmland grazed by imported cattle.

THE RUSSIANS During the mission period, a colony of Russian fur trappers had advanced into California from Alaska (part of the then-expanding Russian empire), seeking beaver and sea otter pelts. The Russians established Fort Ross, 60 miles north of San Francisco, in 1812. Through mutual necessity as much as anything else, the Russians and Spanish enjoyed friendly relations, neither side having the facilities to mount a serious challenge to the other.

THE BRITISH They had been plotting routes across Canada from the late 1700s, in the hope of locating the Northwest Passage to speed trade between Europe and Asia. They failed to find the Northwest Passage but did succeed in developing British influence in the area through the Vancouver-based Hudson Bay Company, and were ever-mindful of Drake's claim of California for the British crown as they mounted fur-trapping expeditions throughout the West Coast.

THE FRENCH Their interest in North America was growing, and they made several expeditions to California during the 1820s. A few citizens of the United States (whose ships were forbidden to land in California) also arrived.

THE CALIFORNIOS As conflicts between the European powers became focused on issues closer to home (namely the rise of Napoleon), a change of control in California

eventually came from those most directly affected by such a move: the Californios, the mostly California-born Mexicans, who took advantage of Mexico's independence from Spain to declare themselves under Mexican rule in 1822.

> ❏ Total livestock holdings of the California missions in 1828: 252,000 cattle, 268,000 sheep, 3,500 mules, 34,000 horses, 8,300 goats, 3,400 pigs. ❏

Russian stronghold: Fort Ross

In Mexico City, California was generally considered to be an unimportant outpost and the governing of the province was left to the Californios themselves. Through the distribution of enormous land grants, a handful of Californio families became prominent and organized life on the ranchos with themselves at the top of a feudal-type system.

Native Americans. In fact, the Californios simply seized the land for themselves.

Through the early decades of the 1800s, many U.S. citizens—some making the perilous overland journey, many more arriving after a three-month sea voyage around Cape Horn—arrived in California and acquired great influence by marrying into the leading families

The Pala Mission, San Diego

Like their Spanish predecessors, the Californios exploited Native American labor but, unlike the Spanish, they lacked agricultural skills. Rather than developing the land, the Californios were content to slaughter cattle and sell the hides to U.S. traders—who turned the hides into leather goods and sold them back to the Californios.

> ❑ "I am afraid we shall see a great deal of trouble in California this year. There are 7,000 or 8,000 emigrants from the U.S.A. expected." ❑
> —W.D.M. Howard, San Francisco merchant and landowner, 1846.

THE MISSIONS' INFLUENCE declined after Spanish rule, and their secularization was ordered by the Mexican government in 1834. This act provided for mission land to be split equally between Californios and

and displaying the entrepreneurial zeal that some Californios lacked.

As the expansionist doctrine of Manifest Destiny came to hold sway over U.S. foreign policy, California (and much of the present southwestern United States) was increasingly seen as a desirable acquisition.

The United States had made various illegal incursions into California, and even attempted to buy the province from Mexico by the time the Mexican War broke out in 1846, after U.S. actions in Texas. In June of that year, a group of U.S. soldiers took over a barely defended presidio in Sonoma and declared California an independent republic—the short-lived Bear Flag Republic. In July, there were unopposed U.S. landings at Monterey and San Francisco, and very soon every major settlement in California had the stars and stripes flying over its Spanish plaza.

The conclusion of the Mexican War allowed the United States to acquire California—also Nevada, Utah, New Mexico, and parts of Wyoming and Colorado—for $15 million, in a deal ratified in February 1848.

On January 24, 1848, just nine days before California was formally handed over to the United States, gold was discovered on the land of John Sutter, a European immigrant of the Mexican era, 50 miles east of his Sutter's Fort headquarters (the future site of Sacramento). Washed down from the Sierra Nevada, flakes of gold had accumulated in California's rivers over countless centuries and, to all intents and purposes, were there for the taking.

The news of the gold strike was delayed, however, as Sam Brannan, owner of the *California Star* newspaper, waited until May 12 (and until he had equipped his supply store at Sutter's Fort) before running down a San Francisco street waving aloft a vial of gold dust.

LINGERING DOUBTS Outside California, people continued to have doubts over the truth of the discovery of gold until December, when President James K. Polk not only

A 1905 prospector hits the trail

verified the existence of California gold but exhibited 230 ounces of it.

GOLD FEVER Destined to be one of the greatest population movements in world history, the Gold Rush began in 1849, increasing the size of California from 7,000 non-native inhabitants in 1848 to 100,000 four years later.

These figures would certainly have been much higher were it not for the fact that reaching California still required a marathon sea trip or a high-risk overland trek across mountains or deserts.

POPULATION BOOM A vast seaborne influx of men and mining machinery swelled San Francisco's population from 500 to 25,000 within two years (at one point, San Francisco Bay became blocked by abandoned ships whose crews headed for the gold-laden rivers), and inland river ports such as Sacramento and Stockton became major centers of population.

Other new towns were established on the bays and inlets of the north and central coasts, while scores of mining communities grew in the center of the gold-producing area (what eventually became known as the Gold Country), on the western slopes of the Sierra Nevada mountains.

❏ The biggest gold nugget found in California weighed 195 pounds. ❏

The Wells Fargo Museum, L.A.

Finding gold was the stuff of dreams, but more solid profits stemmed from feeding and housing the booming population: farming and lumber quickly became lucrative industries (this was the start of the decimation of the state's forests).

WILD TIMES Socially, the California of this time was the epitome of the fabled Wild West. The vast majority of its inhabitants were single males, and catering to their baser desires provided plenty of scope for unscrupulous entrepreneurs. San Francisco's Barbary Coast area (demolished in the 1940s) became infamous the world over for its prostitution, gambling, and drinking, yet it was only the largest and most notorious example of what was to be found in virtually every California community of the mid-1800s. What law there was tended to be upheld by vigilante groups, and in many towns the gallows saw frequent use.

END OF AN ERA Within three years, the Gold Rush was over. The river gold had quickly been picked clean, and company-owned mines provided the only access to the gold-bearing quartz still embedded in the Sierra Nevada hillsides. Those who had arrived seeking their fortunes either returned to the East or settled in the new towns along the coast.

Though no longer promising instant riches, gold mining continued to generate tremendous revenue—$81 million in the peak year of 1852—and was to have a lasting effect on California's development.

> ❏ The great migration into California included many European vintners aware of the grape-producing potential of the Napa and Sonoma valleys north of San Francisco, where the state's first winery was established in 1857. ❏

Because of the mines' wealth, California bypassed the usual transition period as a frontier territory and attained full statehood in 1850. Geographically distanced from the core of the conflict and too busy getting rich to worry about it, California was barely affected by the Civil War, which raged through the rest of the United States from 1864 to 1869. Attention focused instead on the construction of the State Capitol Building in Sacramento, which was completed in 1874 and which became a symbol of California's emergence as a self-reliant, economically powerful entity.

The gold rush had made rich men of California's shop owners and merchants, but one group of Sacramento storekeepers—Charles Crocker, Mark Hopkins, Collis P. Huntington, and Leland Stanford, later dubbed the Big Four—were set to become the wealthiest and most powerful men in the state by investing in what was to be the next key component in California's rapid development: the railroads.

Armed with the plans of an established railway engineer, Theodore D. Judah (who was later elbowed aside), the Big Four set about transforming the long-cherished dream of a coast-to-coast railroad link into reality and formed the Central Pacific Railroad Company in 1861.

BIG MONEY Playing on the U.S. government's fear of losing California to the Confederate States as the Civil War loomed, the Big Four extracted enormous subsidies for their transcontinental railroad project. For each mile of construction they received 12,800 acres of land and $18,000 in cash, more for building over difficult terrain.

POWER AND WEALTH Employing a host of scandalous schemes, the Big Four got the U.S. government to meet the entire cost of the railroad and bought themselves luxurious mansions in San Francisco's exclusive Nob Hill district.

After the transcontinental railroad was completed in 1869, the Big Four absorbed the rival Union Pacific Railroad to create the Southern Pacific Railroad and they then held a monopoly on trade routes across the state.

RESENTMENT AND RACISM Able to control the fate of entire communities, and with immense personal wealth, the Big Four wielded a level of political power unparalleled in California's history. There was much resentment of the rail barons, however, not least from the growing numbers of poor, who were feeling the effects of the post-Gold Rush depression by the late 1860s.

❏ Of the Big Four, it was Charles Crocker who oversaw the actual construction of the transcontinental railroad. Crocker, who weighed 250 pounds, allegedly stood on the freshly completed tracks "bellowing like a bull" at the laborers. ❏

SUPPORT The spread of poverty in northern California also spawned racism, directed in particular at the Chinese, who had provided the bulk

Knotts Berry Farm, Buena Park

of the labor force and who were obliged to seek support from one another in the Chinatown areas taking root in San Francisco and in numerous other communities around the state.

THE BOOM SPREADS SOUTH As northern California had been enjoying the prosperity unleashed by the Gold Rush, southern California had remained isolated and arid, inhabited by only a few thousand people, mostly divided between Los Angeles and San Diego, cities the Big Four considered too remote to be worth joining to their rail network.

When a rival company, the Santa Fe Railroad (later to be taken over by the Big Four), began pushing west through Arizona in search of an outlet on the Pacific, the people of southern California saw their chance.

THE RAIL RACE Tremendous competition developed between San Diego and Los Angeles to be first with a rail link. With its natural harbor, San Diego was the logical choice, but a subsidy (in effect a bribe) of $602,000 underwritten by the 5,000 citizens of Los Angeles swayed the balance, and the Angelenos were duly connected to the rest of the nation in 1886. San Diego acquired a spur line a year later.

There followed a vigorous advertising campaign promoting southern California as a Mediterranean paradise. This, together with absurdly cheap train fares (round-trip tickets from Kansas City for just $1), brought tens of thousands of people to the newly accessible region. In the property-selling frenzy that ensued, plots of southern California land increased tenfold in value within the space of a year.

❏ In 1899, the Los Angeles Police Department sought to improve their response time by forming their first bicycle squad. ❏

The railroad also boosted the trade of southern California's harbors, making San Pedro (in Los Angeles), San Diego, and Santa Barbara outlets for the agricultural products of the Central Valley and for the sweet, seedless oranges that had recently been introduced to southern California.

New communities took shape— Pasadena, Venice, and Hollywood (which was originally founded by two Methodists as a temperance colony); oil was discovered beneath Los Angeles in 1892, and, through the early years of the 20th century, what were to evolve into gigantic aeronautical and automobile industries got started.

LOOKING SOUTH While all of California had its share of earthquakes, the San Francisco Earthquake of 1906, which razed the city and caused fires to rage for three days, encouraged many in the depressed north to seek their share of the wealth that was now being generated in the state's booming southland.

THE EARTH—"I HOPE I SHALL NEVER HAVE ONE OF THOSE SPLITTING HEADACHES AGAIN."

After the 1906 earthquake

The prosperity of the mid- and late 1800s did much to foster the myth of California as the American promised land, but it was Hollywood—a placid farming community on the outskirts of Los Angeles that transformed itself into the center of the fledgling film industry—that was to present California as a latter-day Garden of Eden to the world at large.

EARLY DAYS In the early days of film, a monopolistic patent company, the Film Trust, had sewn up filmmaking on the East Coast, forcing aspiring directors to turn their attentions elsewhere. In 1907, William Selig's *The Count of Monte Cristo* became the first feature film to use a Los Angeles location, and news of the area's suitability for film production quickly spread.

Besides being too distant for patent laws to be enforced, southern California promised daily sunshine at a time when technical limitations made it necessary to shoot even indoor scenes outdoors. It also boasted a great stock of readily available natural backdrops that, with a few strategically placed props, could replicate almost any landscape in the world.

Nonetheless, once they had reached the West Coast, filmmakers and their entourages were not welcomed with opened arms. In the small California towns where hardworking settlers were carving out new lives for themselves, filmshoots disrupted

Cecil B. De Mille and Jesse Lasky, two greats from Paramount

business and the riotous behavior of the crews outraged the God-fearing locals.

Several L.A. communities banned filmmaking altogether and, with rents in downtown Los Angeles too high for impecunious moviemakers, many camera-wielding arrivals traveled eight miles west to the farming town of Hollywood, quickly turning disused barns into production offices and filling the streets with standing sets.

> ❑ One early Hollywood arrival was Cecil B. De Mille, who in 1913 completed the first western feature to be shot in the district, *The Squaw Man*. In the make-do spirit of the times, De Mille shared his office with a horse. ❑

Most early films were cheap one-reel Westerns, but by 1916 D. W. Griffith was employing 15,000 extras on the set of *Intolerance* and had re-created the Hanging Gardens of Babylon on Hollywood and Sunset boulevards.

THE BIG TIME Five years later, 100,000 Los Angeles residents were making a living from the movies, which were now grossing a billion dollars annually, and the best-known faces in the country were the screen stars, such as Douglas Fairbanks and Mary Pickford, ensconced in the new mansions of Beverly Hills.

As the fame of Hollywood spread, so did its notoriety. Sensation-seeking scandal sheets fed an eager public, and found plenty to fill their pages in the bars, clubs, and bedrooms of Tinseltown.

As one sordid revelation followed another, an initiative by top studio bosses to "clean up" Hollywood resulted in the Hays Code of 1930. It was a form of self-censorship limiting what could be shown on the screen (in force until the 1960s, when it was replaced by the ratings system).

THE STUDIO SYSTEM Formed as Hollywood's earliest producers banded together to create large companies such as Paramount, RKO, and Warner Brothers, this also exerted a tight grip on what made it onto celluloid by signing staff—including actors and actresses—to exclusive, long-term contracts.

The creative inertia inherent in this system was apparent by the 1950s, when a loosening of control enabled independent productions to thrive—particularly so during the 1960s and 1970s. Despite this, the major studios still carried considerable clout in deciding exactly what reached the screen, and by the 1980s there was a swing back toward carefully marketed big-budget blockbusters.

Through diversification into TV and music, the major film companies have retained a large slice of the world entertainment market and continue to be major California employers. This enables Los Angeles to justify its reputation as a stomping ground for budding actors, screenwriters, and directors—and the home of the stars—despite the fact that Hollywood has become a slum and most studios have moved to the suburbs.

❏ "It's not true I was born a monster. Hollywood made me one."
—Boris Karloff. ❏

Mann's Chinese Theater

Often to the amusement, and sometimes to the horror, of Americans living elsewhere, there has been an undertow of radicalism in California life since the Gold Rush. While it was lampooned for many years as the place to which all of America's nuts eventually rolled, radical California really got into gear during the 1950s and the 1960s with the beatniks, hippies and political protesters.

BIRTH OF THE BEATNIK Intent on breaking free from the conventions of American society, and variously inspired by bebop jazz, cheap wine, and Zen Buddhism, a small band of unconventional writers and painters began colonizing the Italian coffee shops and cheap rooming houses of San Francisco's North Beach during the mid-1950s. They called themselves "Beats" but were derisively dubbed "beatniks" by a local newspaper columnist mindful of the recent Soviet satellite, sputnik.

The fame of the Beats was confirmed when Allen Ginsberg's epic poem *Howl* was banned for obscenity in 1956, and when Jack Kerouac's breathless novel, *On the Road*, became the literary sensation of 1957. Devoted to constant travel, the Beats were actually much less of a California phenomenon than the subculture that succeeded them, the hippies.

The genesis of hippiedom was a mind-altering drug called LSD (lysergic acid diethylamide), being tested on volunteers at Stanford University through the mid-1960s. While teaching a writing course at the university, Ken Kesey (author of *One Flew Over the Cuckoo's Nest*) brought a supply of the still-legal drug to San Francisco, where it was enthusiastically consumed at multimedia events featuring live music and the first liquid light shows.

LSD was soon outlawed, but not before its ability to send the user on a quasimystical, psychedelic "trip" had been widely recognized, and it was soon under production in illicit laboratories.

FLOWER POWER The Victorian homes of San Francisco's Haight-Ashbury made ideal communal hippie pads, and by 1967 it seemed every disaffected youth in the United States had arrived there. Free concerts in Golden Gate Park were attended by tens of thousands of long-haired, painted-faced people, drawn to hear bands such as the Grateful Dead and Jefferson Airplane.

> ❏ "Women and men alike carried flowers and wore ribbons in their hair. There were more clean, long-haired males assembled in one place than at any time since the Crusades." ❏
> —Journalist Ralph Gleason describing 1967's Human Be-In in Golden Gate Park.

Flower children announce the "death of the hippie," 1967

As more addictive substances replaced LSD in popularity and Haight-Ashbury became squalid and overcrowded, hippiedom's slide from peace and love to horror was compounded by the activities of Charles Manson.

Recruiting his infamous 29-member "family" in Haight-Ashbury, Manson moved with them to a desert base to launch a series of grisly killings in Los Angeles, including that of film director Roman Polanski's pregnant wife, Sharon Tate. Manson was subsequently convicted of seven murders and frequently makes appeals for parole.

In their own ways, the Beats and the hippies both rejected the entire social order, but 1960s California also found the political establishment being challenged in (comparatively) more orthodox ways.

POLITICAL PROTEST Formed on the campus at Berkeley in 1964, the Free Speech Movement (see pages 84 and 85) was the stimulus for a decade of nationwide campus revolts and anti-Vietnam War protests. Meanwhile, the increasingly diverse ethnic makeup of what was fast becoming the nation's most populous state was not reflected in the white-dominated corridors of power, and discontent simmered in various quarters.

Anger erupted most dramatically in Watts (a depressed section of Los Angeles) in 1965, when the National Guard was called upon to quell a six-day battle that left 34 dead and caused $40 million of damage.

During the following year the militant Black Panthers formed, pledging themselves to armed struggle against the ruling classes.

STATE POLITICS The turbulent 1960s had mellowed by the following decade, when there was (at least some) assimilation of ethnic minorities into policy-making bodies. Simultaneously, state governor Ronald Reagan—nicknamed "Ray-guns" for his willingness to use force in response to protest—lost the election to Jerry Brown, a fourth-generation Californian who was viewed by many as the embodiment of Golden State wackiness.

❏ The formation of the National Farm Workers' Union by Cesar Chavez in 1962 brought about improved conditions for California's vast army of undervalued agricultural workers through a series of strikes and public-supported boycotts. ❏

Eschewing the governor's luxury mansion built by Reagan in favor of a simple apartment, and conducting a much-publicized romance with fashionable rock singer Linda Ronstadt, Brown imposed strict controls to reduce smog, decriminalized possession of marijuana, and set California on course to being the country's most environmentally aware region by the time he left office with an eye on the White House in 1983.

SAN FRANCISCO

0		1		2 km
0			1 mile	

- Bay Area Rapid Transit (BART) Stations
- 49 Mile Scenic Drive

GOLDEN GATE BRIDGE

Fort Point National Historic Site

Maritime National Historical
Fort Mason Center, African American
Historical & Cultural Society, Mexican Museum
and San Francisco Craft & Folk Art Museum

Crissy Field
Golden Gate Promenade

Marina Green Fort Mason

MARINA

LOMBARD STREET

Octagon House

Palace of Fine Arts & Exploratorium

Presidio Army Museum

PRESIDIO

PACIFIC HEIGHTS

Haas Lilienthal House

Baker Beach

China Beach

South Bay

Lands End

Point Lobos

Lincoln Park Golden Gate

PRESIDIO HEIGHTS

CALIFORNIA STREET

SEACLIFF

San Francisco Fire Department
Pioneer Memorial Museum

Palace of the Legion of Honor

Holocaust Memorial

Veterans Hospital

POINT LOBOS AVE

CLEMENT STREET

Duquette Foundation
Pavilion of St Francis

Japan

GEARY BOULEVARD

ARGUELLO BLVD

St Mary Cathedral

Cliff House

Seal Rocks

Sutro Heights Park

RICHMOND

TURK STREET

WESTERN ADDITION

MASONIC

University of San Francisco

DIVISADERO STREET

Alamo Square

Performing Library &

FULTON STREET

MH de Young Memorial Museum

Conservatory of Flowers

FELL ST

Ocean Beach

Dutch Windmill

Golden Gate Park

Stow Lake

Japanese Tea Garden

LOWER HAIGHT

Panhandle

HAIGHT ASHBURY

Buena Vista Park

14TH STREET

California Academy of Sciences

STANYAN STREET

Strybing Arboretum & Botanical Gardens

LINCOLN WAY

PARNASSUS AVE

Mission Dolores

JUDAH STREET

7TH AVENUE

BUENA VISTA

CASTRO

Mission

Dolores Park

SUNSET

19TH AVENUE

Twin Peaks

EUREKA VALLEY

CASTRO STREET

ORTEGA STREET

FOREST HILL

CLIPPER STREET

Sunset Reservoir

TARAVAL STREET

NOE VALLEY

PARKSIDE

DIAMOND HEIGHTS

Glen Canyon Park

GREAT HIGHWAY

SUNSET BOULEVARD

Pine Lake Park Sigmund Stern Grove

SLOAT BOULEVARD

PORTOLA DRIVE

925ft
Mt Davidson

San Francisco Zoological Gardens

ST FRANCIS WOOD

Glen Park

SAN JOSE AVENUE

Stonestown Shopping Center

GLEN PARK

City College of San Francisco

OCEAN AVENUE

Balboa Park

EXCELS

Harding Park

San Francisco State University

INGLESIDE

MISSION STREET

PERSIA AVENUE

Lake Merced

LAKE MERCED BLVD

SOUTHERN FREEWAY

Balboa Park

Golden Gate National Recreation Area

JOHN MUIR DRIVE

BROTHERHOOD WAY

OCEAN VIEW

GENEVA AVE

SKYLINE BOULEVARD

San Francisco City Limit

A B C

A BEAUTIFUL CITY Set on a small, hilly peninsula, San Francisco is an easy place to fall in love with. Since Gold Rush times, settlers from the far corners of the globe have arrived here. Their sheer diversity fosters the live-and-let-live attitude for which the city is renowned.

The city splits into a mosaic of tightly grouped neighborhoods. The Financial District and the Civic Center mark either end of Downtown, linked by the city's main artery, Market Street. North of Downtown, Nob Hill, Russian Hill, and Telegraph Hill are prime residential areas, yet they nestle close to the bustling streets and alleyways of Chinatown and the Italian-flavored North Beach. Fisherman's Wharf, to the north,

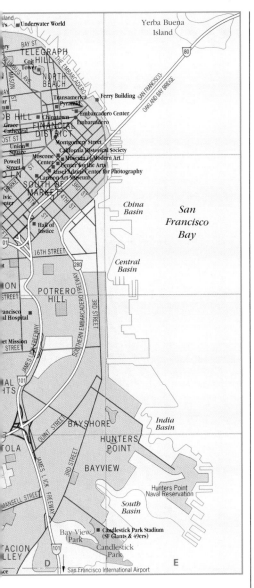

is the one place in San Francisco where tourists outnumber locals.

South of Market Street, up-and-coming SoMa borders the mostly Spanish-speaking Mission District, just west of which the Castro is a predominantly gay and lesbian area.

West of Downtown, Haight-Ashbury saw the rise and fall of flower power, and adjacent, the bucolic Golden Gate Park stretches almost to the ocean. North of Haight-Ashbury lies tiny Japantown and the broad streets of Pacific Heights, which lead on to the woodlands of the Presidio area, covering the city's northwest tip.

36

FESTIVALS
Hardly a week passes without some kind of festival happening in San Francisco. The highlights are the Chinese New Year, usually in February, celebrated with firecrackers and a three-hour dragon-led parade through Chinatown; the St. Patrick's Day parade in March; the Cherry Blossom parade in Japantown during April; the Bay-to-Breakers fun run across the peninsula in May; the Mission District Carnaval, also in May; and the Halloween parade along Castro Street in October.

Districts

▶ The Castro   *34C3*

San Francisco's most famous gay area, the Castro, is much changed from 15 years ago when its streets were a wild celebration of gay lifestyles. The city's raunchiest Halloween parades continue to happen here, but the success of the Castro's many gay-run businesses has instilled a sense of quieter respectability.

Few people could be left unmoved after visiting the **Names Project▶▶** (2362 Market Street; tel: 415/863–1966), where each grave-sized patch of a gigantic quilt represents one local victim of the AIDS virus—at present, the quilt has over 6,000 patches.

▶▶▶ Chinatown   *35D4*

Squeezed between the Financial District and North Beach, Chinatown is a riot of sights and smells, and holds banks, newspapers, and schools serving what is claimed to be the largest Chinese community outside Asia.

Dragon-tail-entwined streetlights and pagoda-style buildings overlook a ceaseless procession around the food stalls on Stockton Street and the herbalist shops, tearooms, bakeries, and gaily painted, century-old temples that fill numerous alleyways.

▶ Civic Center   *35D3*

Rightly regarded as the best beaux-arts grouping in the United States, the public buildings of the compact Civic Center are dominated by the dome of the elegant **City Hall▶▶▶**—raised in 1915 (see page 52)—and by hundreds of homeless people occupying their neat plazas.

▶ Downtown/Union Square   *35D4*

Downtown San Francisco encompasses the Civic Center, Tenderloin, and the Financial District, and holds the bulk of the city's hotels, big-name stores, and the well-known—though uninteresting—Union Square.

▶ Embarcadero Center   *35D4*

One of the best views of San Francisco is from the **Skydeck ▶▶** (tel: 888/737–5933) on the 41st floor of One Embarcadero Center, one of a group of four soulless high-rises housing offices, shops, and hotels between the Financial District and Chinatown.

▶ Financial District   *35D4*

Stride among the power-dressed power brokers of the Financial District to find out why San Franciscans dread the "Manhattanization" of their city, a condition exemplified by the sterile glass and steel corporate towers built here during the 1970s and early 1980s.

▶ Fisherman's Wharf   *35D4*

The base of a large fishing fleet until the 1940s, today's Wharf is almost entirely devoted to the tourist. T-shirts and trinkets are sold in every store, street stands do a brisk trade in overpriced sourdough bread and seafood, and the best among a glut of attractions are **Underwater World▶** (Pier 39; tel: 415/623–5300; 888/732–3483), and **San Francisco Maritime National Historical Park** (see page 41).

▶▶ Haight-Ashbury   34C3

Haight-Ashbury found itself at the forefront of the flower-power revolution of the late 1960s, when thousands of long-haired youths poured into what had been a declining middle-class neighborhood.

Haight Street, the area's main thoroughfare, still bears a distinct counterculture bias, even though the offbeat bookstores and wacky clothes shops are steadily being replaced by pricey restaurants and fashion boutiques as the neighborhood becomes increasingly gentrified.

▶▶ Japantown   34C4

Concealed behind Japantown's usually unexciting exteriors are the shops, temples, and social centers serving the city's Japanese community, only a small percentage of whom actually live here. Between Post Street and the Geary Expressway, the large **Japan Center▶** contains numerous outlets for quality Japanese arts and crafts, and several temptingly priced restaurants. Within the center, Kabuki Hot Springs (tel: 415/922–6000) offers a traditional Japanese steambath and shiatsu massage.

▶▶ Mission District   35D3

A Spanish-speaking enclave whose population is chiefly drawn from Central and South America, the Mission District also attracted some of the city's writers, artists and left-wing activists. Controversially, recent arrivals have been affluent new media folk, causing property prices to soar.

Other than Mission Dolores (see page 54), the draws are well-preserved Victorian houses and vivid street murals. To find the former, walk south from Mission Dolores and turn left along Liberty Street; for the latter, walk south from the corner of Mission and 24th Streets.

SAFETY
The closest San Francisco gets to being seriously seedy is the ten-block strip between Union Square and the Civic Center, where most of the city's homeless congregate and where prostitutes ply their trade from street corners. The Western Addition, a rough neighborhood between Haight-Ashbury and Japantown, is also best avoided after dark.

Looking north across San Francisco, with Alcatraz Island and Telegraph Hill's Coit Tower clearly visible

DASHIELL HAMMETT
The master of hard-boiled detective fiction, Dashiell Hammett, moved to San Francisco in 1920 to work for the Pinkerton Detective Agency. The booming but corrupt city made the ideal setting for his cynical investigator Sam Spade, and Hammett's writing reached a peak with *The Maltese Falcon* in 1930. Hammett's most productive years were spent at 1155 Leavenworth Street in Nob Hill. He departed to write film scripts in Hollywood, only to be imprisoned for refusing to testify during the anti-Communist witch hunts of the 1950s.

Two of the Mission District's many murals, reflecting the artistic traditions of the area's predominantly Hispanic population

▶▶ Nob Hill
35D4

In the late 1800s, California's first tycoons erected lavish homes on Nob Hill. Only one of the mansions survived the 1906 earthquake—it is now the ultraexclusive ivy-covered **Pacific Union Club▶** (1000 California Street)—and today's Nob Hill holds exclusive hotels and restaurants patronized by famous faces.

One place meriting a stop is the reposeful **Grace Cathedral▶▶▶** (1051 Taylor Street; tel: 415/749–6300), modeled on Paris's Notre-Dame. While ministering to the spiritual needs of its ultrarich congregation, the cathedral has—controversially—also sheltered the city's homeless in its basement.

▶▶▶ North Beach
35D4

Italians were the first to give North Beach a lasting style, arriving in force from the late 1800s and opening the first of the restaurants and cafés that make this the city's best place for pasta and pizzas, and for lingering over a cappuccino beside the seething Columbus Avenue.

During the mid-1950s, North Beach's (then) cheap rents, wine, and food made it the home of the first beatniks—so dubbed by San Francisco newspaper columnist Herb Caen. The most illustrious of these are remembered by street names in their honor and by their still-standing haunts, such as the City Lights Bookstore and Vesuvio, a café and bar. See the walk on page 50.

▶ Pacific Heights
34C4

A yuppie stronghold, Pacific Heights' Union Street—once the location of several dairy farms, and known as Cow Hollow—is packed with chic clothes shops and arts-and-crafts galleries. Close by are several landmark Victorian homes. These include the eight-sided **Octagon House▶** (2645 Gough Street; tel: 415/441–7512) and the **Haas-Lilienthal House▶▶** (2007 Franklin Street; tel: 415/441–3004), the only fully period-furnished house in San Francisco open to the public.

▶ Russian Hill 35D4

Most people stay in Russian Hill only long enough to photograph a section of **Lombard Street▶▶**, hailed as the crookedest street in San Francisco. Its descent between Hyde and Leavenworth streets is landscaped into a series of curves decorated by plants and bushes.

While in Russian Hill, find time for the **San Francisco Art Institute▶** (800 Chestnut Street), the oldest art school on the West Coast, with displays of student work, and an outstanding mural by Diego Rivera.

▶ SoMa 35D3

Through the 1990s, many of the disused warehouses and factories of SoMa ("South of Market Street") were transformed into a cultural complex of museums and performance venues, ringed by fashionable restaurants and nightclubs. At the core is **Yerba Buena Gardens**, five landscaped acres laced with walkways overlooked by the Museum of Modern Art (see page 43) and the $44 million **Center For The Arts**, staging film, music, and drama (tel: 405/978-ARTS). The Sony **Metreon**, (tel: 405/537–3400) is a state-of-the-art entertainment and shopping complex.

▶ Telegraph Hill 35D4

Telegraph Hill is a coveted address with some splendid modern residential architecture lining the steep streets that wind up to **Coit Tower▶▶▶** (Telegraph Hill Boulevard; tel: 415/362–0808), a memorial to the city's volunteer firemen, erected in 1933.

The tower is notable less for the views from its summit than for the outstanding Depression-era murals decorating its inner walls. Depicting scenes of Californian life of the time, the murals' militant symbols upset the authorities and delayed their unveiling for several years. After visiting the tower, get down from Telegraph Hill by way of the **Filbert Steps▶▶**, a steep and partially wooden walkway fringed by effusive vegetation.

CROOKED STREETS
Anyone will tell you that Russian Hill's Lombard Street is the crookedest street in San Francisco. But nearly as crooked, and much less crowded, is Vermont Street in the Potrero Hill area, just east of the Mission District. Vermont Street also has the distinction of being the only city thoroughfare that fire-engine drivers refuse to navigate because of its tortuous twists.

ANSEL ADAMS CENTER FOR PHOTOGRAPHY
One of the first cultural institutions to establish itself in SoMa was the Ansel Adams Center For Photography (250 Fourth Street, tel: 405/495-7000; www.friendsofphotography .org; open daily 11–5, and until 8 first Thu of the month. Admission: inexpensive/moderate.). The five galleries mix historical and contemporary work from photographers from around the world. The center is named after the celebrated landscape photographer Ansel Adams, who was born in San Francisco in 1902. One gallery shows changing selections of Adams's own work from among the 125 items he donated prior to his death in 1984.

A bird's-eye view across North Beach and Telegraph Hill to Fisherman's Wharf

San Francisco

CABLE CARS

Invented by Andrew Hallidie, the first cable car ran along Clay Street on August 2, 1873. A safer way of negotiating steep streets than horse-drawn wagons, the cable car also made possible the development of hitherto inaccessible high areas such as Nob Hill. By 1906, there were 600 cable cars in operation but that year's earthquake, and the subsequent rise of motorized transportation, conspired to render them obsolete. Preserved as a National Historic Landmark, the system in use today—mostly for the enjoyment of tourists— was improved by a $60 million facelift in 1982.

The U.S.'s only moving National Historic Landmark, cable cars provide public transportation in San Francisco along three routes

Museums and galleries

▶ African American Historical and Cultural Society 35C4

Building C, Fort Mason Center (tel: 415/441–0640)
African-American history and achievements in the San Francisco area and beyond are chronicled through archival material and paintings. An annex at 762 Fulton Street in the Western Addition holds more material.

▶▶ Cable Car Museum 35D4

1201 Mason Street (tel: 415/474–1887)
Giving a rather dull, pictorial record of the 120-year history of San Francisco's famous cable cars, and showing off some early examples, the museum also reveals the simple but clever engineering principle that keeps the cable cars working: each car is pulled along the streets by an underground cable that never stops moving.

▶▶▶ California Academy of Sciences 34B3

Music Concourse Drive, Golden Gate Park (tel: 415/750–7145)
Open: late May–early Sep 9–6; early Sep–late May 10–5
(1st Wed of month open until 8:45; free all that day)
Pitched at children and intended to stimulate an interest in the natural world, the California Academy of Sciences gets a D for its static exhibits on California ecology and the native cultures of the world, but an A-plus for the wide-ranging selection of marine life in the **Steinhart Aquarium▶▶▶**—from bloated Amazon Basin predators to the mysterious splitfin flashlight fish.

Elsewhere, the safe-quake exhibit, inside in the **Hohfeld Earth and Space Hall▶▶**, vibrates the floor with the same magnitude with which the earthquakes of 1865 and 1906 shook San Francisco's streets. Regain your balance by visiting the **Far Side of Science Gallery▶▶▶**, lined with the hilarious cartoons of Gary Larson.

An additional fee brings admission to the adjoining **Morrison Planetarium**, humorously billed as "California's largest indoor universe."

▶ Cartoon Art Museum 35D3

814 Mission Street (tel: 415/227–8666)
Changing exhibitions taken from a vast permanent collection trace the development of a cartoon or comic strip from the hand of the artist to the finished product.

▶▶ Chinese Historical Society of America 48C3

650 Commercial Street (tel: 415/391–1188)
An engrossing accompaniment to a walk through Chinatown, outlining the Chinese arrival in California, their labor on the region's first railroads, and their banding together for mutual support in the face of "Yellow Peril" racial hostility. Look, too, around the shows of the **Chinese Cultural Center▶**, on the third floor of the Holiday Inn, 750 Kearny Street.

▶ Exploratorium 34C4

3601 Lyon Street (tel: 415/563–7337 or 415/561–0360 info line)
The best place in San Francisco to amuse young minds with low boredom thresholds, the Exploratorium is a

single vast hall filled with 650 interactive exhibits designed to illustrate and explain the fundamentals of natural science and human perception. The exhibits, such as crackling tesla coils or coupled resonant pendulums, stand alongside the results of an innovative artist-in-residence program that produced *Tornado*, a reservoir of fog continually pulled upward in an inverted vortex, and Alien Voices, allowing two people in separate wooden telephone booths to speak to each other in a choice of 16 computer-altered voices.

The Exploratorium's most popular area (reservations necessary) is the Tactile Dome, a dark space that you can only leave by feeling your way out on hands and knees.

The Balclutha, *built to move grain between California and Europe, forms part of the Hyde Street Pier Historic Ships collection*

▶ Fort Point   34B4
Beneath Golden Gate Bridge (tel: 415/556–1693)
Finished in 1861 to protect the entrance to San Francisco Bay, Fort Point was never attacked despite becoming obsolete a year after its completion by advances in weaponry design. Some rooms within the three-story granite fortress store historical artifacts, and enthusiasts in Civil War uniforms give tours.

▶ Maritime National Historical Park   35D3
Polk and Beach streets (tel: 415/556–3002)
Back when Fisherman's Wharf was full of fishermen rather than tourists, ferries to Berkeley and Sausalito sailed from Hyde Street Pier, which now permanently moors several historic vessels. Among them are the 1890 ferry *Eureka*, once the world's largest passenger ferry,

A GHOST SHIP
On chilly nights when the Golden Gate Bridge is eerily shrouded in fog, look for a phantom clipper, the *Tennessee*, gliding through the waves. The two-masted vessel sank here over 100 years ago but is regularly sighted most famously in 1942 by several of the crew of a naval destroyer.

and the *Balclutha*, a square-rigged sailing ship that was launched in Scotland in 1886, which rounded Cape Horn several times before ending its days transporting Alaskan salmon. The National Maritime Museum, nearby at Aquatic Park, is rather staid, displaying mostly models of seagoing vessels.

▶▶ Mexican Museum   34C4
Building D, Fort Mason Center (tel: 415/441–0404)
Besides giving new Mexican-American artists a chance to break into the museum exhibition circuit, the Mexican Museum mounts outstanding shows on many aspects of Mexican arts and culture.

▶▶ M. H. de Young Memorial Museum   34B3
Tea Garden Drive, Golden Gate Park (tel: 415/863–3330)
There are few better places to observe how American art gradually turned away from European tastes and acquired a distinctive national identity. Works by many of the country's most influential artists are here, such as John Smibert, noted for his 18th-century society portraits, and Albert Bierstadt, whose 19th-century landscapes chronicled the settlement of the American West. Few pieces, however, are as entertaining as the room of trompe-l'oeil paintings, notably William Michael Harnett's *After the Hunt*.

In contrast to the theme of the de Young collection, the breadth and diversity of the **Asian Art Museum▶▶▶** (tel: 415/379–8801; *Open* Tue–Sun 9:30–5. *Admission: moderate.* First Wed of month open until 8:45, free all day), is almost too vast to comprehend. It is the small pieces that stick in the mind: the 15th-century votive *stele* from China, Japanese Netsuke—wooden toggles for boxes and pouches, fashionable during the 18th and 19th centuries—and a human thigh-bone trumpet from Tibet.

FREE ENTRY
The following museums all have free entry on the first Wednesday of the month: the California Academy of Sciences; the California Palace of the Legion of Honor; the M.H. de Young Museum; the Exploratorium. The Museum of Modern Art has free entry on the first Tuesday of the month.

42

The Egyptian-style main building of the M. H. de Young Memorial Museum

▶▶▶ Museum of Modern Art   35D3

151 Third Street (tel: 415/357–4000)
Open: late May–early Sep, Fri–Tue 10–6, Thu 10–9; early Sep–
late May, Fri–Tue 11–6, Thu 11–9. Admission: moderate
The centerpiece of the Yerba Buena Arts Center development that totally changed the face of SoMa during the 1990s, San Francisco's Museum of Modern Art opened in 1995. It is housed in an architecturally striking building, six storys high.

The second-floor galleries highlight painting and sculpture from 1900 to 1970, and include significant contributions from Europeans—among them Picasso, Braque, and Matisse. Amid many notable abstract expressionist canvases are works by Pollock and de Kooning, and the last completed work by Barnett Newman. A separate gallery houses works bequeathed by California abstract expressionist Clyfford Still. Over 100 works by Paul Klee are included in the collection of German Expressionists, and surrealism is represented by offerings from primary figures such as Dali and Ernst.

Complementing the painting are architecture and design exhibitions; the third floor houses photography from the likes of Man Ray and Moholy-Nagy.

▶ Museum of Money of the American West   49D3

400 California Street, Bank of California basement
(tel: 415/765–3434)
Stable currency was not a feature of pioneer-era California, and here you will see a variety of bills issued by different states before standardized laws were adopted.

▶ North Beach Museum   48B4

1435 Stockton Street, in the Eureka Savings Bank
(tel: 415/391–6210)
Temporary shows, often made up of the possessions of local people, illuminate the rise of one of San Francisco's most fascinating districts.

▶ Pacific Heritage Museum   49D3

608 Commercial Street (tel: 415/399–1124)
The exhibitions displayed here on the history of the countries of the Pacific Rim are varied and rarely uninteresting. On the lower level, the permanent displays recall the building's time as the city's original mint, established on the heels of the Gold Rush in 1854.

▶▶▶ Palace of the Legion of Honor   34A4

34th Avenue at Clement Street, Lincoln Park (tel: 415/863–3330)
Open: Tue–Sun 9:30–5; first Sat of month until 8:45.
Admission: moderate
Modeled on its namesake in Paris and erected in memory to California's dead of World War I, the Palace of the Legion of Honor, on a bluff overlooking the ocean, makes an architecturally imposing showcase for San Francisco's major collection of fine art.

Amid a rich endowment of paintings and decorative arts spanning several centuries, and the Achenbach Foundation's excellent collection of graphic art, it is the superb collection of Rodin sculptures, including the accomplished *Victor Hugo*.

FREE MEDIA
Each week the *San Francisco Bay Guardian* and *SF Weekly* provide excellent city-wide news, views, and events listings. You will find the papers distributed on street corners and in many shops and restaurants. Also free, the monthly *North Beach Now* covers goings-on in the North Beach area, and the biweekly *Bay Times* serves the city's gay and lesbian community, as does the weekly *Bay Area Reporter*.

43

A Thinker, from the original cast, is among the selection of Rodin sculptures at the Palace of the Legion of Honor

San Francisco

HILL TALK
"When you get tired of walking around San Francisco you can always lean against it."— Transworld Getaway Guide, 1975–76.

Though the sign outside claims it to be the oldest building in San Francisco, the 1776 Commandante's Quarters at the Presidio contains few original sections

▶ Performing Arts Library and Museum   *34C3/35D3*

401 Van Ness Avenue, Room 402 (tel: 415/255–4800)

As a prelude to an evening at the ballet or opera, take a peek at these changing exhibitions relating to San Francisco's performing arts heritage. The displays include vintage costumes, photos, posters, and programs galore.

▶ Presidio Army Museum   *34C4*

Corner of Lincoln Boulevard and Funston Avenue (tel: 415/561–3319)

Housed in a one-time military hospital in an 1863 building with verandas, the Presidio Army Museum charts the growth of San Francisco's military garrison, from its Spanish beginnings through its role in two world wars to the present. Alongside the massed uniforms and insignia lies an excellent display on the city's 1906 earthquake, and outside are two of the "refugee cottages," which were rented to homeless survivors of the catastrophe for $2 a month.

The museum is just one building of the 1,480-acre **Presidio**, founded by the Spanish as a military base in 1776 and owned by the Sixth Army until being de-commissioned and given to the National Park Service in 1994. Many early buildings remain (within an easy walk from the museum); the **military cemetery▶** holds graves dating back to the Civil War and is the subject of a park ranger-led tour on Saturdays.

▶ San Francisco Craft and Folk Art Museum   *34C4*

Building A, Fort Mason Center (tel: 415/775–0990)

Always worthwhile shows of curious arts and crafts: from California decoys to mythical African figures.

▶ Wells Fargo History Museum   *49D3*

420 Montgomery Street (tel: 415/396–2619)

In the 1840s, Wells Fargo ran the first stagecoaches between the eastern and western United States, transporting people, gold, and mail thousands of inhospitable miles. An 1860s stagecoach suggests the discomfort of public transportation, and much more in the museum represents the banking wing of the company.

Over the last decades, San Francisco's fabled tolerance of unconventional lifestyles has helped to make it the home of the largest and most assertive gay and lesbian communities in the world.

Many gay men landed in San Francisco toward the end of World War II after being discharged from the U.S. military in disgrace for their homosexuality—or suspected homosexuality. Unable to face the stigma awaiting them at home, most stayed in the city, socializing in a network of discreet bars and clubs.

Gay rights The radicalism of the 1960s, and anger fueled by continued police raids on gay-patronized establishments, brought many gays to the streets to proclaim their sexuality and to demand their civil rights. Simultaneously the Castro district began changing from a working-class Catholic area to an almost exclusively gay neighborhood.

As the Castro's fame spread far and wide, gays from all over the country moved into the district, their sheer force of numbers making the gay vote of crucial concern for aspiring city politicians. Many liberals running for public office adopted the gay rights agenda, and in 1977, Harvey Milk, who ran a camera store on Castro Street, became the country's first out-of-the-closet public official.

Slow integration Homophobia was by no means eradicated, however. A year after his election, Harvey Milk and the city's gay-supportive mayor, George Moscone, were assassinated. The light sentence of five years' imprisonment passed on Dan White, the right-wing politician who committed the double murder, so incensed the gay population and large numbers of heterosexuals as well that 50,000 people took part in a mass protest. It culminated in police cars being overturned and

City Hall being attacked in 1978's "White Night Riot."

Several decades of standing up and being counted have left San Francisco's gays—and, to a lesser extent, lesbians—with a unique level of integration into mainstream city life.

AIDS Tragically, the impact of AIDS has perhaps been felt more powerfully here than anywhere else in the western world. Yet the crisis has revealed hitherto unknown reserves of community solidarity and has provided a new focus for political activity.

Gay culture is an established part of the San Francisco community

Walk

Looking around Chinatown

See map on pages 48–49.

Begin at the Chinatown Gates at the corner of Bush Street and Grant Avenue.
Since 1970, the **Chinatown Gate** has made a less than imposing entrance to Chinatown's main street.

Walk north along Grant Avenue, pausing at the corner of California Street.
At 600 California Street, the **Old St. Mary's Church** was the first Catholic cathedral on the West Coast, blessed in 1854.

Turn east off Grant Avenue onto Commercial Street for the Chinese Historical Society of America.
At 650 Commercial Street is the **Chinese Historical Society of America** (see page 40).

Turn left onto Kearny Street, turning left again after one block onto Clay Street and cross onto Waverly Place.

Chinatown's distinct style

Here are many Chinatown buildings such as the 1852 **Tien Hou Temple**, on the top floor of Nos. 123–129.

Exit Waverly Place turning left onto Washington Street and then left onto Stockton Street.
Crowded **Stockton Street** is where the city's Chinese community buys its fresh meat, fish, and vegetables.

From Stockton Street, take any street to Grant Avenue, a block east, and then return to the Chinatown Gate.

● **Stroll** *Entering Golden Gate Park (see page 56) on John Kennedy Drive takes you past the ivy-covered McLaren Lodge, now the park headquarters and formerly the home of John McLaren, a Scot who spent 50 years cultivating the park, and on to the colorful blooms and luscious palms which surround the Conservatory. Just ahead, Tea Garden Drive branches left, running between the California Academy of Sciences and the M. H. de Young Museum (see pages 40 and 42 respectively), and the wistful Japanese Tea Garden with its statue of Buddha, cast in 1790. A short walk farther on, two bridges cross Stow Lake to the foot of Strawberry Hill, the highest point in the park.*

BANK OF CANTON
OF CALIFORNIA

The Financial District

See map on pages 48–49.

Begin at the Federal Reserve Bank at 101 Market Street.
Using computer simulations in the **Federal Reserve Bank** lobby, you can rearrange the country's finances.

Cross Market Street and walk west along Pine Street to the corner of Montgomery Street for the Bank of America building.
At the foot of the Bank of America building, a severe black granite sculpture has earned the nickname "Banker's Heart."

Continue north along Montgomery Street for the Wells Fargo History Museum.
At 420 Montgomery Street, this museum documents the rise of the Wells Fargo company (see page 44).

Continue three blocks north along Montgomery Street for the Transamerica Pyramid.
The city's tallest structure, the 853-foot-tall Transamerica Pyramid, at 600 Montgomery Street, displays mildly diverting works of art on its lobby-level walls.

Continue north along Montgomery Street, turning right onto Jackson Street for Jackson Square.
Around Jackson Square, many buildings that predate the Financial District's high-rises by a century or more have been restored.

From Jackson Square, walk west along Washington Street and return to Montgomery Street.
Throughout the year, the City Guides conduct hour-long walking tours around particular places of interest, including City Hall, Coit Tower, Nob Hill, Japantown, and the Mission District murals. For more details, call 415/557–4266.

● **Stroll** *From Mission Dolores walk south along Dolores Street to Liberty Street, turning left for the heart of the Liberty Hill Historic District, filled by late 19th-century buildings.*
From the end of Liberty Street, walk north along Valencia Street and turn right onto Twentieth Street. At the corner of South Van Ness Avenue, Tribute to Carlos Santana *is among the biggest and boldest of the Mission District's many murals.*

Begin at Aquatic Park, just west of Fisherman's Wharf.
Nearly four miles of breezy waterside walking, the Golden Gate Promenade covers a tiny section of the Golden Gate National Recreation Area, leading

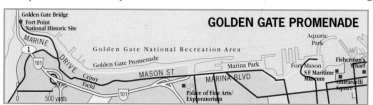

GOLDEN GATE PROMENADE

Golden Gate Promenade

over the hills of Fort Mason (see page 53) and past the flashy yachts that are tethered alongside the marina, by the old Presidio military base (see page 44), finally concluding close to Fort Point (see page 41) at the foot of Golden Gate Bridge (see page 54).

San Francisco

SAN FRANCISCO

TELEGRAPH HILL

Coit Tower

LOMBARD

North Beach Playground

St Peter and St Paul Church

GREENWICH

FILBERT

Washington Square

NORT

UNION

RUSSIAN

Fugazi Hall

North Beach Museum

GREEN

HILL

Ina Coolbrith Park

VALLEJO

VALLEJO

BROADWAY

JACK KEROUAC STREET

BROADWAY

BROADWAY Tunnel

Columbus Tower

PACIFIC AVENUE

Buddha's Universal Church

Chine Cultu Cent

Powell - Hyde Line

Cable Car Museum

Tien Hou Temple

Portsmouth Square

WASHINGTON

Chinese Historical Society of America

NOB

Kong Chow Temple

COMMERCIA

CHINATOWN

HILL

Old St Mary's Church

SACRAMENTO STREET

Huntington Park

California   Street Line

St Mary's Square

Grace Cathedral

Powell - Mason Line

Powell - Hyde Line

Masonic Auditorium

PINE

Chinatown Gate

BUSH

SUTTER

Marines Memorial Theater

POST

Union Square

Showcase Theater

0   100   200 m
0   100   200 yards

GEARY

Curran Theatre

American Conservatory Theater

48

Walk

A journey through North Beach

See map on pages 48–49.

Begin at Jack Kerouac Street, on the 1000 block of Grant Avenue.
Named after one of the Beat Generation's brightest lights, **Jack Kerouac Street** marks the transition from Chinatown to North Beach.

Take a few strides north to the corner of Columbus Avenue and Broadway.
With strip joints nestling alongside jazz and other music clubs, the area around the **corner of Broadway** and **Columbus Avenue** is the scene of some of the city's lewdest and loudest nightlife—as it has been for decades.

Walk north along Columbus Avenue for the City Lights Bookstore.
At 261 Columbus Avenue, the **City Lights Bookstore** became the first paperback bookshop in the country when it opened in 1953; its owner, poet and painter Lawrence Ferlinghetti, published many works of the best of the Beat writers, beginning with Allen Ginsberg's controversial poem, *Howl*, in 1956. Facing City Lights across Adler Place, **Vesuvio** is another beatnik-era survivor.

Continue north along Columbus Avenue for Washington Square.
Overlooked by the twin spires of the Romanesque Church of St. Peter and St. Paul, **Washington Square** has amateur art exhibitions each weekend, and elderly Chinese practice the slow, artful exercises of Tai Chi every morning.

Cross Washington Square and walk south along Grant Avenue.
From here to Broadway, **Grant Avenue** has some of the area's best-priced restaurants, many funky shops, and some venerable R&B clubs.

Continue south along Grant Avenue and return to the starting point, Jack Kerouac Street.

The Octagon House, in the Union Street area of Pacific Heights

Given a week or a weekend in San Francisco, there are endless permutations of places to go and things to see. The following itineraries will give you a balanced look at the city.

Week's itinerary

Day one Explore the Financial District and Chinatown on foot (see pages 46 and 47). Lunch in North Beach. Take a cable car north to explore both Fisherman's Wharf and Fort Mason, or take a journey by bus to Golden Gate Bridge.

Day two Take a cable car to Nob Hill, explore the area and adjoining Russian Hill on foot. Lunch on Union Street. Walk south through Pacific Heights to Japantown.

Day three Travel by BART to Berkeley and explore the town and university campus. Lunch on Telegraph Avenue. Take BART to Lake Merritt for the Oakland Museum. Return by BART to the city.

Day four Visit Alamo Square, and continue to the Haight-Ashbury area. Lunch on Haight Street and spend the rest of the day exploring Golden Gate Park.

Day five Tour Alcatraz in the morning (see page 80). Have lunch in North Beach. During the afternoon, explore Telegraph Hill and walk along the Embarcadero to Embarcadero Center.

Day six Sail across the bay and spend the day at Sausalito or Tiburon.

Day seven Tour the Civic Center and walk south into SoMa for lunch on Folsom Street. Visit the small museums and factory outlet shops in SoMa, or take a journey by bus into the Mission District.

Weekend's itinerary

Day one Spend a day following the blue and white seagull signs marking the 49-mile Scenic Drive. The route is designed to take in all the major areas and points of interest in San Francisco. A map of the drive is available free from most hotels and tourist information offices.

Day two On the second day, walk around Chinatown (see page 46), and take a bus to Golden Gate Park for a picnic lunch by Stow Lake. Visit the Academy of Sciences (ideal for children) or the M. H. de Young Memorial Museum and Asian Art Museum. Or simply walk around the park.

NOT "FRISCO"
You will know you are talking to a Bay Area resident if they refer to San Francisco as "the city." You will know you are talking to a tourist if they call the city "Frisco."

TAI CHI
Visit Washington Square or Huntington Park on any morning and you will see dozens of people engaged in slow-motion movements. Tai Chi is based on coordinated, carefully balanced rhythmic movements that use all the body's joints, ligaments, and muscles, and help to regulate blood flow.

With Alcatraz Island in the background, one of the city's pleasure cruises leaves Fisherman's Wharf for a tour of San Francisco Bay and the Golden Gate

San Francisco

San Francisco City Hall, its dome visible across much of the city. Behind the three large central windows is the mayor's office

Buildings

▶ Buddha's Universal Church   48C3
720 Washington Street (tel: 415/982–6116)
Built by donations from its congregation, Buddha's Universal Church welcomes the public every Sunday to its free lectures and tours of the church, whose symbolic design culminates in a rooftop lotus pool.

▶ The Cliff House   34A1
1066–90 Point Lobos Avenue (Visitor Center
tel: 415/556–8642; Restaurant tel: 415/386–3330)
Plans are underway for major renovations at Cliff House.
The seven-story "French-château-on-a-rock," erected by wealthy one-time Populist city mayor Adolph Sutro in 1896, remains the most famous of several Cliff Houses that have occupied the headland site since 1853.

Just to the north, ruins are all that remain of the 1896 Sutro Baths, where up to 24,000 people at a time could swim in a lavish three-acre complex of saltwater tanks beneath a massive glass dome—for just 10¢ a day.

▶▶▶ City Hall   35D3
Civic Center, Van Ness Avenue,
between Grove and McAllister streets (tel: 415/554–6023)
Free tours given seven days a week go to South Light Court
Easily the city's most opulent building and the centerpiece of the Civic Center's grouping of often exquisite public buildings, San Francisco's 1915 City Hall was conceived by the young architectural firm of Brown and Bakewell,. The firm was headed by former students of the influential École des Beaux-Arts in Paris, who decided they had nothing to lose by submitting the boldest, grandest scheme they could think of, which was budgeted at a then-astronomical $3.5 million. Marble, granite, gold inlays, and sumptuous arches are the building's characteristics.

Time-lapse photography reveals the volume of night-time traffic along Columbus Avenue, running between North Beach, Chinatown, and the Transamerica Pyramid. To the left, Café Tosca is thought to be one of the city's oldest bars; to the right are Chinese restaurants

▶ Columbus Tower   48C3

Corner of Kearny Street and Pacific Avenue
Bought and restored by locally based film director Francis Ford Coppola in the 1970s, the flat-iron Columbus Tower dates from 1905. With the towering Transamerica Pyramid nearby, Columbus Tower adds considerable character to the view from North Beach toward Chinatown.

▶▶ Ferry Building   49F3

Eastern end of Market Street
Until the construction of the city's bridges, the turn-of-the-century Ferry Building was the emblem of San Francisco—also its tallest structure—and the landing point for tens of thousands of commuters who made the daily voyage across the bay. A greatly reduced number of sailings still depart from the rear terminal.

▶▶ Fort Mason   34C4

West of Fisherman's Wharf, across Van Ness Avenue
In 1796, the Spanish garrison based at the Presidio (see page 55) built a battery on this bluff overlooking the bay. It became a U.S. Army command post from the 1860s, and 80 years later was the embarkation point for over a million soldiers headed for war in the Pacific. The fort remained under military ownership until becoming part of the Golden Gate National Recreation Area in 1972.

Some Victorian buildings on the hilltop are still used by the military, while the former hospital serves as the headquarters of the Golden Gate National Recreation Area (of which Fort Mason is a part; see page 56).

At the foot of the bluff, several converted warehouses house the **Fort Mason Center▶▶** (tel: 415/441–3400) which includes the African-American Historical and Cultural Society (see page 40), the Mexican Museum (see page 42), and the San Francisco Craft and Folk Art Museum (see page 44).

MAJOR EARTHQUAKES
On April 18, 1906, an earthquake measuring 8.3 on the Richter scale, and a three-day fire that followed it, destroyed much of the city, leaving 3,000 dead and 300,000 homeless. Increased earthquake awareness and strict building codes helped prevent a similar catastrophe when a 6.9 earthquake struck the city on October 17, 1989. Eleven were killed and 1,800 lost their homes.

The Golden Gate Bridge seen from the west side, overlooking the inlets holding Baker Beach and China Beach

BRIDGE SUICIDES
The Golden Gate Bridge found instant popularity as a suicide stop, the first fatal jump into the cold waters and fast currents of the bay taking place just three months after its opening. Over 900 people are known to have leapt to their death from the bridge and the true figure is probably over a thousand. In 1993, phones linked directly to suicide counsellors were installed on the bridge for would-be jumpers.

▶▶▶ Golden Gate Bridge 34B4
US 101 (tel: 415/921–5858)
24 hours cars and bikes; 5 AM–9 PM pedestrians
Inexpensive toll southbound only
Named for the bay it crosses rather than its color (a reddish orange, the color most visible in fog), the Golden Gate Bridge is a remarkable artistic as well as engineering feat. Its construction defies the currents and depth of the bay, and the simplistic designs look entirely at home in a stunning natural landscape.

Designed by Joseph B. Strauss (although controversy still ensues as to whether Strauss was genuinely responsible for the bridge's form), the bridge was completed in 1937 at a cost of $35 million (a sum paid off in tolls by 1971). Almost two miles long, with towers as high as a 48-story building, it is still among the world's largest suspension bridges. The bridge can be crossed by car or on foot, though the wind and rumble of traffic tends to upset contemplation of the views.

▶▶▶ Mission Dolores 34C3
320 Dolores Street (tel: 415/621–8203)
Open: daily 9–4. Admission: inexpensive
Originally titled Mission San Francisco de Asís to honor the patron of the Franciscan order, Mission Dolores was completed in 1791. It was the sixth of the 21 Spanish missions that spread the length of California.

Thick adobe walls have enabled the mission to withstand earthquakes and years of neglect, and to become the oldest building in San Francisco—even the original bells and various other artifacts that arrived from Mexico by mule remain.

Behind the atmospheric chapel, with frescoes on its walls, a museum houses a small collection of early mission items. A courtyard leads to the cemetery, where over 5,000 Castonoan Indians—many of them victims of European diseases—are buried in unmarked communal graves.

▶▶▶ Palace of Fine Arts
34C4

Baker and Beach streets

A collection of dreamy beaux-arts structures grouped around an immense rotunda, Bernard Maybeck's Palace of Fine Arts was intended as a temporary contribution to the city's Panama-Pacific Exposition of 1915. At the Expo's conclusion, public feeling staved off the planned demolition and a well-heeled local resident funded a total restoration during the 1960s.

▶ Presidio
34B4

Main Gate on Lombard Street, junction with Lyon Street

Across the 1,500 acres of hills and woodlands that cover the northwest corner of the city, a Spanish Presidio (or garrison) was founded in 1776. Until being decommissioned in the 1990s, the area served as the base for the U.S. Sixth Army, but has long been freely accessible to the public and a couple of its buildings are noteworthy. The **Officers' Club▶** (on Moraga Avenue) is still partly walled by Spanish-era adobe; across Pershing Square, the 1857 Old Station Hospital, holding the Presidio Army Museum (see page 44), is the oldest complete building on the base. More about the Presidio can be found at the Visitor Center on Montgomery Street (tel: 415/561–4323)

▶▶ Rincon Center
49F2

101 Spear Street (tel: 415/243–0473)

Enter the spacious indoor plaza of the Rincon Center at lunchtime and you will find snack-munching office-workers and the gentle music of a fountain and a pianist in a dinner jacket. This modern building has enclosed the delectable art-deco form of the 1940 Rincon Annexe Post Office Building. A series of controversial **murals▶▶** by Anton Refregiar, grittily portraying several murky moments in San Franciscan history, make for stimulating viewing on the post office walls.

▶ St. Mary's Cathedral
34C3

Corner of Geary and Gough streets

In a city better known for its Victorian architecture, St. Mary's Cathedral is a forceful piece of modern design by Pietro Belluschi, completed in 1971 at a cost of $7 million. The open-plan cathedral can seat 2,500 people and was built to replace the previous St. Mary's, which served as the city's Catholic Cathedral from 1891 until being destroyed by fire in 1962.

55

Forming the shape of a Greek Cross, towering paraboloids give St. Mary's Cathedral a 190-foot-high ceiling. Inside, they also help eliminate the traditional divisions between apse, nave, transept, baptistry, and narthex

With the Financial District to the rear, Alamo Square's "Painted Ladies," built in the 1890s, contribute to one of San Francisco's most reproduced photographic juxtapositions

SAN FRANCISCO'S TWINS
San Francisco is twinned with 14 cities: Abidjan, Assisi, Caracas, Cork, Esteli, Haifa, Ho Chi Minh, Manila, Osaka, Seoul, Shanghai, Sydney, Taipei, and Thessaloniki.

GGNRA
Created in 1972 to limit commercial development, the Golden Gate National Recreation Area safeguards nearly 70 square miles of mostly coastal terrain, embracing much of the city's northern and western edges and extending across the bay to the rugged Marin County Headlands. There are several museums, as well as the blustery Coastal Trail between Lincoln Park and the Golden Gate Park.

Parks and gardens

►► Alamo Square — 34C3
On the crest of a hill between the Western Addition and Pacific Heights, Alamo Square's eastern side is faced by six "Painted Ladies," Victorian homes with the modern city skyline for a backdrop.

►► Aquatic Park — 34C4–35D4
Beach Street
A grassy area with a concrete bandstand close to Fisherman's Wharf and the historic ships of Hyde Street Pier, Aquatic Park is mostly used by walkers and joggers.

► Baker Beach — 34B4
Access from Lincoln Boulevard, Presidio
Breezy mile-long Baker Beach is a pleasant place to pass half a day; enthusiastic anglers spend considerably longer.

► Buena Vista Park — 34C3
The name means "good view," and that is precisely the reward for scrambling through the twisted mass of Monterey pine and California redwoods filling this very steep park, encircled by graceful Victorian mansions.

► China Beach — 34B4
Near Seacliff Avenue
A small and marvelously secluded beach hemmed in by bluffs. It is named for the Chinese fishermen who once camped here. Though often cold, the calm waters make China Beach one of the few places in San Francisco where swimming is safe. The lifeguard post is occupied during the summer months.

►►► Golden Gate Park — 34A3–C3
Park Headquarters, 501 Stanyan Street (tel: 415/831–2700)
City parks rarely come any better or bigger than Golden Gate Park, which extends for more than three miles between Haight-Ashbury and the ocean. Large enough to hold a polo field, soccer fields, a golf course, ten separate lakes, and a couple of major museums, the park

also has several busy roads; pedestrian crosswalks make life safe for walkers.

A **Dutch windmill▶**, a **Japanese tea garden▶ ▶ ▶** (Tea Garden Drive; tel: 415/752–4227. *Admission: inexpensive*) and a large assortment of enigmatic statuary are unexpected features.

▶ Mission Dolores Park   *34C3*

18th and 20th Church and Dolores streets
Often bathed in sunshine when the rest of the city is shrouded in fog, Mission Dolores Park is a few blocks from the Dolores Mission and makes a fine place for a picnic when exploring the Mission District.

▶ ▶ San Francisco Zoo   *34A2*

Sloat Boulevard (tel: 415/753–7080)
Founded in 1889, San Francisco Zoo has benefited from a major renovation, swapping its cages for detailed re-creations of its inmates' natural habitats. Another welcome addition is the excellent **Primate Discovery Center▶ ▶**, which explains more than you will ever need to know about such creatures—many of whom swing merrily from the branches of the zoo's artificial rain forest. Koalas, penguins, pygmy hippos, and leopards are among the zoo's other residents, while the tarantulas, black widows, and scorpions of the insect zoo are creepy in every sense.

▶ Sutro Heights Park   *34A3*

Point Lobos Avenue and Great Highway
Scattered with ruined statuary, this covers the former estate of Adolph Sutro, one of the leading figures of his time (see page 52). On a bluff above the Cliff House, the park is great for sunset watching.

WHAT'S IN A NAME?
There is no beach in the North Beach, no statue of George Washington in Washington Square, and no square in Jackson Square.

TWIN PEAKS
The nearly 1,000-foot-high dual summits of Twin Peaks give unmatched views of San Francisco and beyond. The first Spanish arrivals named these humps of high ground *Los Pechos de la Chola*—Breasts of the Indian Girl—and they're easy to locate by looking for the Sutro TV Tower, which is nearby on Mount Sutro.

57

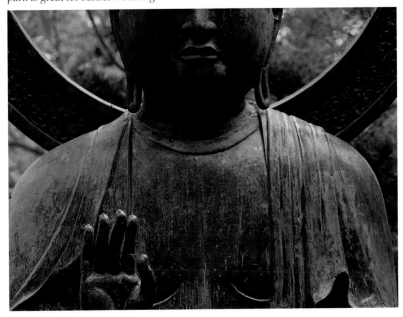

Statue in Golden Gate Park's Japanese tea garden

Excursions

From hikes in untamed hills to wine-tasting amid the state-renowned vineyards, you have many day-tripping options out of San Francisco. Most can be undertaken on public transportation or by car; you can also use one of the tour operators listed opposite.

Suggested Routes
Coast Seaside towns seldom come more picturesque than **Sausalito**, an eight-mile ferry ride north of San Francisco, where scores of expensive hillside homes rise steeply above a waterfront lined by enjoyable cafés, galleries, and shops.

Many high points in San Francisco give views of the strikingly barren headlands of **Marin County**, directly north across the bay and forming part of the **Golden Gate National Recreation Area (GGNRA)**. A network of hiking trails winds over them, passing through sheltered valleys to isolated beaches, and there are other routes leading to the shady redwood groves of **Muir Woods**.

Traveling by BART east from the city brings you to **Berkeley**, its famous university, and the more industrialized **Oakland**, noted for the restaurants of its Chinatown area and the outstanding Oakland Museum of California. Both make a pleasurable day's break. Further descriptions are on pages 76, 77 and 83.

Scenery One hundred and sixteen miles to the south of San Francisco, California's one-time capital, **Monterey** (see page 99), and the mission town of **Carmel** (see page 92) stand on either side of the scenic Monterey Peninsula, and within easy reach of Big Sur (see page 92),

A typically wild and rugged section of Golden Gate National Recreation Area, which fills 76,500 acres of San Francisco's coastline. It was created in 1972 by an amalgamation of city parks, private land, and formerly military-owned areas

rightly acclaimed as the most photogenic portion of the entire central coast.

Wineries are found all over California, but the major center of production is the so-called Wine Country (see pages 244–255), occupying the verdant valleys of **Sonoma** and **Napa**, beginning 50 miles north of San Francisco. Many wineries are open for tastings, and balloon rides above the valleys are widely available.

A more unabashed tourist attraction is **Six Flags Marine World**, 30 miles northeast of the city close to Vallejo, where exotic animal species fill a 160-acre park, and where tigers, lions, sea lions, and dolphins are expertly trained to entertain.

Tour Operators and Special Tours

Blue and Gold Fleet (tel: 415/773–1188). operate daily crossings to Oakland from Pier 39 in Fisherman's Wharf and from the Ferry Building, and in summer (less often in winter) to Angel Island. Daily crossings to Vallejo operate from Pier 39, and from Pier 41 to Sausalito, Tiburon, and Vallejo. There is a catamaran service to Six Flags Marine World. Blue and Gold also operate coach trips further afield to Muir Woods, Napa and Sonoma valleys, Monterey and Carmel, and Yosemite National Park.

California Wine Tours (tel: 415/434–8687) offers coach tours to the wine-producing Napa Valley.

A Day in Nature (tel: 415/673–0548). Half-day naturalist-led tours of the Marin Headlands and Muir Woods, and full-day tours to the Napa Valley.

Golden Gate Transit Ferries (tel: 415/923–2000). operate frequent crossings daily to Sausalito and Larkspur from the Ferry Building.

Golden Gate National Recreation Area Any GGNRA visitor center will supply maps and general information. GGNRA's headquarters is at Building 201, Fort Mason (tel: 415/556–0560).

Gray Line (tel: 415/958–9400). operate excursions by bus to Monterey and Carmel, Muir Woods and Sausalito, and the Wine Country.

Great Pacific Tour Co. (tel: 415/626–4499). offer excursions by minivan to Monterey and Carmel, Muir Woods and Sausalito, and the Wine Country.

Haight-Ashbury Flower Power Walking Tours (tel: 415/863 1621). Visit the landmarks of 1960s Haight-Ashbury on a two-hour stroll.

Red & White Fleet (tel: 415/447–0597 and 800/229–2784). operate sight-seeing cruises on the bay and coach tours to nearby places of interest such as Muir Woods, the Wine Country, and the Monterey peninsula.

San Francisco Helicopter Tours (tel: 800 400–2404) give a bird's-eye view of the city and points beyond.

GUIDED WALKS
As well as the San Francisco walking tours described on pages 46, 47, and 50, there are many other guided walking tours that typically cost $20–30. One of the most popular is the **Chinatown Adventure Walk** (tel: 800/3281–9255). On this walk you explore the sidestreets of Chinatown, and visit with local traders. There is an optional lunch—expect dim sum.

The **Victorian Home Walk** shows you the city's Victorian homes and their architecture (tel: 415/252–9485); similar homes are featured in the **Haight-Ashbury Flower Power Walk**, though only for their role in Haight-Ashbury's hippie 1960s. To discover gay history and landmarks, join the **Cruisin' the Castro** walk (tel: 415/550–8110).

Some of the city's best walks cost nothing and are operated by **City Guides** (tel: 415/557–4266). Itineraries include City Hall, Haight-Ashbury, Nob Hill, Sutro Heights Park, and Pacific Heights.

Ghirardelli Square (below) is housed in a former chocolate factory

Shopping

Vast shopping malls, a common sight in other cities, are not much in evidence here. However, San Franciscans can be enthusiastic shoppers and every neighborhood has a street worth browsing.

Predictably, it is mostly tacky tourist fare that fills **Fisherman's Wharf**, although the shops and galleries filling two converted factories—**The Cannery** (2801 Leavenworth Street) and **Ghirardelli Square** (900 N. Point Street)—are entertaining places to wander around and can turn up unexpected finds, such as fine crafts.

If you are shopping for more interesting souvenirs, fruitful territory might be the Chinatown section of Grant Street, where dozens of places display unusual items, from carved jade figures to cheap toys. While in Chinatown, drop in at the Ten Ren Tea Company (949 Grant Avenue), where many fine imported brews can be sampled at the counter.

Investigate the neighborhood's herbalists, such as Chung Chou City (898 Stockton Street) or Fung Yun Wah (868 Jackson Street).

For more mainstream buying Classy stores of Macy's, Neiman-Marcus, and Saks Fifth Avenue stand within a credit card's throw of one another beside Union Square. If you have time to visit only one such emporium, though, make it **Nordstrom's** (865 Market Street), where spiral escalators whisk you between fashionably stocked floors.

For those with eyes bigger than their bank accounts, the windows to watch are along Maiden Lane. Among this street's stylish boutiques, **Chanel** (No. 155) has three floors laden with the French company's finest products, and **Candelier** (No. 60) displays candles and candle-holders in countless unusual shapes.

Take a peek also at the nearby **Gump's** (135 Post Street), an institution among the city's swells for its fine crystal and world-class jade and pearls—all at world-class prices.

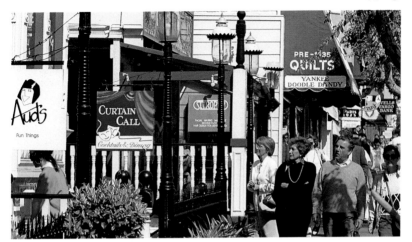

The toughest antiques hunt This could well end amid the historic brick buildings of Jackson Square, a number of which have ground-level shops stuffed with European 18th- and 19th-century furnishings, Turkish rugs, and fine Asian tapestries and decorative pieces. The price tags can often be steep, but well-heeled, knowledgeable collectors should find the varied selection tempting.

There is more that is old among the stores of Haight-Ashbury. Much of the clothing here is salvaged from decades past, or imported: Aardvark's (1501 Haight Street) carries some great gear of yesteryear; more of the same fills Held Over (1543 Haight Street), and the slightly pricier Wasteland (1660 Haight Street). For mindblowing day-glo T-shirts, try Positively Haight Street (1400 Haight Street).

In the same neighborhood, Revival of the Fittest (1701 Haight Street) recycles and re-creates American household knickknacks of the 1940s and 1950s, Curios & Candles (289 Divisadero Street) turns crystals and semiprecious stones into pricey talismans, and Pipe Dreams (1376 Haight Street) has giant rolling papers and waterpipes. Haight Street is also the place to find a wide variety of used CDs and records: try Recycled Records (No. 1377).

In a city of bookworms, you will discover plenty of bookshops in which to browse and buy. Nationally known chain stores such as Barnes & Noble and Borders are well stocked with the latest titles, often at reduced prices.

Specialty bookstores include Forever After (1475 Haight Street), with a tremendous stock of used volumes on all subjects; City Lights (261 Columbus Avenue), carrying the definitive range of writings by and about the Beat Generation, plus political and general titles; The Sierra Club Bookstore (85 2nd Street, 2nd Floor; tel: 415/977–5600) has a tremendous stash on natural California and is a recommended stop for hikers and walkers; William Stout Architectural Books (804 Montgomery Street) has an unmatched inventory of what its name suggests.

Defined by chic boutiques, antique shops, and fashionable restaurants, the section of Union Street between Gough and Fillmore streets is the main shopping strip of Pacific Heights, one of the city's wealthiest areas

DISCOUNT SHOPPING
Well within the range of the average pocket are the numerous factory outlets occupying former warehouses in the SoMa area. Cruise the multistore complex of Yerba Buena Square (899 Howard Street) where many top companies discount their damaged or discontinued lines. The bargains can be tempting. Elsewhere, Esprit (499 Illinois Street) is one of the major names in California casualwear.

San Francisco

FISHERMAN'S WHARF EATING
While visiting Fisherman's Wharf it is wise to limit your eating to snacks from the seafood stalls on the street and preserve your appetite for a meal in more inspiring surroundings.

Food and drink

Food and drink are major preoccupations in this city, and its restaurants offer everything from downhome American fare to cuisines culled from every corner of the globe. For Californians with cultured palates—or just big appetites—San Francisco is much less about bay views, cable cars, and the Golden Gate Bridge than it is about eating.

Prices Fierce competition helps keep prices low, and all but the most exclusive restaurants are well within the range of the majority of travelers. Even the tourist-packed eateries of Fisherman's Wharf are not the gastronomic wastelands that they could be. Despite claims to the contrary, though, comparatively little of what is offered in the area's seafood restaurants comes from local waters.

Although San Francisco is serious about its food and restaurants, the atmosphere of most eateries is casual. Men almost never require a tie and they can usually get away without even a jacket.

Italian The streets of North Beach, just south of Fisherman's Wharf, are jammed with Italian restaurants offering authentic regional cuisine from every inch of this Mediterranean country and providing excellent value. A simple fresh pasta dish is unlikely to cost more than $10, and even three-course dinners for less than $25 are not unknown.

North Beach dining is no secret, however, and for evening you should plan to dine early (before 7) to avoid crowds. Earlier in the day, you will have no problem finding a cozy niche inside one of the neighborhood's many atmospheric cafés, where you can linger over a cappuccino and a light Italian lunch and dessert, to your heart's content.

Crab During its mid-November to June season, look for Dungeness crab, which many Italian restaurants serve as

62

One of the oldest and most popular of North Beach's many Italian restaurants, Fior d'Italia has occupied the same site since 1886

the centerpiece of a seafood dish called *cioppino*. The same creature turns up in Chinese restaurants, deliciously flavored with ginger and garlic.

Chinese This type of food has long been a feature of San Francisco, and Chinatown is its culinary hotspot, despite the fact that many of the top Chinese chefs have departed for other areas—notably the Richmond district, just west of Pacific Heights, where Clement Street in particular holds many Asian restaurants of merit.

Within Chinatown, cooking styles reflect the diverse ethnic backgrounds of recent immigrants: besides Cantonese (and variations on it such as Hakka and Choazhou), Hunan, and Szechuan fare, unusual Vietnamese-Chinese and Peruvian-Chinese dishes enliven many menus.

The best way to sample Chinatown's food is inside one of the large and lively dim sum restaurants, which cater mostly to a local Chinese clientele and usually open between 11 and 3. Only in Hong Kong are you likely to encounter a bigger variety of dim sum—pastries and dumplings filled with seafood, meat, and rice and noodles.

Pointing is the surest way to get what you want, as the dishes are wheeled on trolleys in front of diners. If, as is likely, you are not sure what you are looking at, ask the waiter or waitress for advice or simply select whatever looks interesting. When you have finished, the bill is determined by the number of empty dishes on your table. Many dim sum restaurants serve regular Chinese dinners in the evening.

Other Asian and Far Eastern For Japanese food aim for Japantown's Japan Center and you will come across several dozen reasonably priced Japanese restaurants and sushi bars.

Many Thai and a lesser number of Indian restaurants are well established in San Francisco. Particularly hot and spicy dishes are usually helpfully marked as such on the menu.

Among the gritty fast-food joints of the Tenderloin (be careful, as it is not the safest area in the city, see page 36), dozens of small Vietnamese, Laotian, and Cambodian cafés have appeared, providing exotic, spicy food at giveaway prices.

The Empress of China— a San Francisco favorite

DIM SUM DISHES
Popular dim sum dishes in Chinese restaurants include *Jow Ha Gok*, shrimp turnovers; *Siu Mai*, steamed meat dumplings; *Cha Siu Bow*, barbecued pork inside buns; and *Gee Cheung Fun*, rolls of rice and noodles.

WALK WITH A WIZ
If you can't tell a geoduck clam from a pig's knuckle, take a stroll through Chinatown—it's best on a busy Saturday morning. Or sign up with native San Franciscan Shirley Fong-Torres, whose Wok Wiz Chinatown Tours stop at a medicine shop, a tea room, a dim sum restaurant, and a food market (tel: 415/981-8989).

San Francisco is well-stocked with bakeries selling delicious fresh snacks

GIMME SOME DOUGH
Sourdough bread is the food most often associated with San Francisco, though it is said to have originated in the French Basque country. In the 1850s, Gold Rush miners toted the uncooked dough to the Sierra foothills to forestall starvation—and sourdough became a sobriquet for the miners themselves. Now, just about every San Francisco baker worth his salt makes a version of the sharp-smelling bread.

Contemporary fare Elsewhere around town, particularly on Union and Fillmore streets in Pacific Heights, some of the city's more innovative restaurants are blazing a trail with contemporary American cuisine—modernized variations on regional American dishes that bear the nutritional and esthetic imprint of California cuisine (see page 78), which itself has largely faded from fashion.

French The city's more traditionally inclined and the longer-established power brokers don suits and head for the upper-crust restaurants of Nob Hill, noted for their classic French food.

Latin American Much more down to earth than the city's expensive restaurants—and usually with much more filling food—are the innumerable low-priced Mexican and other Latin American food outlets crammed into the Mission District. These range from dirt-cheap hole-in-the-wall takeout stands to fully fledged restaurants where the food is tasty and well priced and the service is swift and cheerful—they're Brazilian, Guatemalan, El Salvadorean, Chilean, Peruvian, and beyond.

Bohemian For a meal in the company of the city's artists, writers, lesser media celebrities, and full-time nightclubbers, try any of the restaurants and cafés along Haight-Ashbury's Haight Street or SoMa's Folsom Street. Many of these serve no more than basic, filling American food—such as massive omelets and huge sandwiches—but do so in bizarre settings with a carefully cultivated bohemian atmosphere.

Tea and coffee A growing band of hotels in San Francisco has taken up the practice of serving afternoon tea, which usually features a good range of real teas and snacks such as scones and pastries.

In North Beach, the rich aroma of roasting coffee beans regularly drifts across the streets. Certainly, there is no better place than a North Beach *caffè* to down an invigorating espresso. Many of the city's hundreds of cafés are patronized by serious coffee drinkers, alert to bean type and nuances of flavor.

Alcohol California's wines are world-renowned, but the best of them rarely make it outside the state. Dining in San Francisco, the biggest city in close proximity to California's wine country, affords you the best opportunity to sample the widest range of California wines at very reasonable prices.

The most popular derive from the Cabernet Sauvignon (red) and Chardonnay (white) grapes. You will also find fine examples of other varietals and blends, including reds from Zinfandel, Shiraz, Merlot, Pinot Noir, Sangiovese, and Nebbiolo, and whites from Sauvignon Blanc, Riesling, Gewürztraminer, and Viognier.

Many but not all restaurants serve alcohol; in those that do, a glass or two of **California wine** makes a nice accompaniment for a meal. To mix your alcohol with a view, try sampling one of San Francisco's rooftop hotel cocktail lounges (see page 66).

Irish coffee's debut Irish coffee (allegedly) made its first appearance in the United States in 1952 in San Francisco, at the Buena Vista Café, Fisherman's Wharf (2765 Hyde Street).

American brew Beer-lovers are in for a treat in San Francisco. Alongside the usual wines and spirits, most bars stock the products of the area's many micro-breweries: beers whose body and flavor—and strength—are well worth sampling.

Anchor Steam Beer is among the most widely found of the local brews in San Francisco, but there are many more and their names are often chalked up on a board above the counter.

Smoking A new state law decrees that smoking is now barred in all enclosed public spaces, so that means most restaurants. If they have an outdoor terrace, you may be permitted to smoke there, but check first.

ANCHOR, AWEIGH
During the Gold Rush, some 150 years ago, breweries flourished in San Francisco. The only one that remains from that era, the Anchor Brewing Company, makes Anchor Steam Beer, and six other beers, plus whiskey, and gin in limited quantities. "Steam" was a local nickname back then for beer made in a hurry; the word is now part of the Anchor trademark. You can tour the brewery by appointment (tel: 415/863–8350).

A damp morning brings plenty of customers to Fisherman's Wharf's Buena Vista Café

Nightlife

For a major city, San Francisco's nightlife is surprisingly small-scale and friendly, with little evidence of the social snobbery and price-hiking that goes on down the coast in Los Angeles.

What's on The free weekly papers, the *San Francisco Bay Guardian* and *SF Weekly* (see page 43), are the best sources of nightlife listings.

The main ticket agency is BASS (for bookings, or recorded information tel: 510/762–2277), which has outlets all over the city. TIX, on the Stockton Street side of Union Square (open Tuesday to Thursday 11–6; Friday and Saturday 11–7; tel: 415/433–7827), offers half-price, day-of-performance tickets for selected performing arts shows.

Watering holes Affable and socially very diverse, cafés and bars are found all over the city, with the greatest concentration in North Beach, The Mission, and SoMa districts. You should also plan to spend a few daylight hours at one of the rooftop cocktail lounges, which provide views along with the (usually expensive) drinks. Top of the tops is the Carnelian Room, on the 52nd floor of the Bank of America Building at 555 California Street.

Classical music, opera, and ballet San Francisco enjoys a deservedly strong reputation for its classical music, opera, and ballet. Major performances by the **San Francisco Symphony**, based at the Louise M. Davies Symphony Hall, 201 Van Ness Avenue (tel: 415/864–6000), take place from September to May, with many special shows in summer.

The **San Francisco Opera** has a star-studded September to December season at the War Memorial Opera House (tel: 415/864–3330). In summer, the **Pocket Opera** (tel: 415/575–1100) mounts lesser-known operas in smaller venues (which change from year to year).

Rated among the world's best, the **San Francisco Ballet** performs from February to May at the Opera House, 301 Van Ness Avenue (tel: 415/865–2000), returning for special Christmas performances.

Theater Between October and May, there is drama at the Geary Theater, 415 Geary Street (tel: 415/749–2228), from the respected **American Conservatory Theater**, and throughout the year at the tiny Magic Theater, Building D, Fort Mason Center (tel: 415/441–8822). More in the mainstream, Broadway hits are performed at the Curran Theater, 445 Geary Street (tel: 415/551–2000).

The witty and raucous *Beach Blanket Babylon* is the longest running theatrical show in San Francisco, a revue popular since the early 1970s; see it at Club Fugazi, 678 Green Street (tel: 415/421–4222).

Comedy Cutting-edge comic Lenny Bruce got arrested in San Francisco in the early 1960s. The gags of today are unlikely to bring police raids, but the city still has a fair number of lively comedy clubs. The longest established

Evening rush hour: the Ferry Building in the middle distance, once the tallest structure in the city, is dwarfed by Financial District towers; the lights of Oakland are visible across the bay

66

is Punch Line, 444 Battery Street (tel: 415/397–7573). In keeping with the city's offbeat nature is the more alternative performance space of **Mock Café**, 1974 Valencia Street (tel: 415/641–0235). The venue hosts open-mic nights, satirical shows, and description-defying multi-media events.

Completed in 1923, the Castro Theater is a popular venue for cult movies

Cinema Each spring, the popularity of the San Francisco Film Festival confirms the city's love of good movies. Besides many first-run complexes, such as the eight-screen Kabuki Center, corner of Post and Geary streets (tel: 415/931–9800), there are a number of cinemas that screen rarely seen cult and arthouse films: the Castro Theater, 429 Castro Street (tel: 415/621–6120), the Roxie, 317 16th Street (tel: 415/863–1087), and the Red Vic, 1727 Haight Street (tel: 415/668–3994).

Jazz, rock, and R&B Many of the top U.S. and international bands include the city on their tours. Major venues for contemporary sounds are the Paradise Lounge, 11th and Folsom streets (tel: 415/861–6906), and the DNA Lounge, 375 11th Street (tel: 415/626–1409).

On the local live music circuit, it is R&B that pre-dominates and sounds best at rough-and-ready venues like The Saloon, 1232 Grant Street (tel: 415/989–7666). For the novelty value alone, show up at one of the early evening shows at Brain Wash, 1122 Folsom Street (tel: 415/861–3663)—a combined bar and laundromat.

The best of the mainstream jazz clubs are Slim's, 333 11th Street (tel: 415/522–0333), and Up & Down Club, 1151 Folsom Street (tel: 415/626–2388).

Dance Clubs San Francisco's club scene is varied and extremely changeable. Most venues have a different theme each night, and are located in SoMa. A geographical exception is the Bahai Cabana (1600 Market Street; tel: 415/626–3306), which holds captivating salsa and world beat nights.

JOKES, JAZZ, BREAST IMPLANTS
These days, North Beach is best known for its restaurants, but from the 1950s its comedy clubs showcased cutting edge comics such as Lenny Bruce and Mort Sahl. The jazz clubs of the time, based in local cellars, hosted wild nights of bebop that inspired the Beat movement. Another pioneer was Carol Doda, whose silicon-implanted breasts starred in the nation's first topless show, at the Condor Club in 1964. The event is remembered by a wall plaque at 300 Columbus Avenue.

There's no shortage of accommodations in the city; some hotels, like the Marriott, are hard to miss

68

BEYOND THE CITY
Spending a night across the bay provides an enjoyable change of pace and scenery. Several hotels perch on the Sausalito hillsides. None are cheap and most are full at weekends, but they offer a chance to stroll the quaint village after the day-trippers have departed. A stopover in Berkeley encourages a leisurely gourmet meal in one of the town's award-winning restaurants without the need to dash back to the city.

HIDDEN EXTRAS
Be warned that quoted prices for accommodations rarely include the city's 12 percent "transient occupancy" tax, which guests have to pay.

Accommodations

From fax-equipped suites in marble towers to four-poster beds in wood-framed Victorian mansions, places to stay in San Francisco are as abundant as the hills and as varied as the views. In fact, this is one of the best places in California to find affordable and atmospheric alternatives to chain hotels and motels.

Making a reservation is always a good idea, but is only essential during the busiest period—summer and early fall, when prices are around $10–$20 higher than during the rest of the year.

The **San Francisco Visitors and Convention Bureau** (see page 71) publishes a free guide to lodgings, with copious listings and room rates, and its office stocks many leaflets detailing individual properties.

Hotels In a city that is small and easy to get around, precisely where you stay is of minor consequence. Most large hotels are close to Union Square, and there is a group of newer chain hotels close to Fisherman's Wharf. But it is a smart move to avoid these congested areas in favor of the more characterful residential areas.

The luxurious "grand hotels" of Nob Hill pride themselves on pampering their guests, often with complimentary newspapers and magazines, and drinks and snacks laid out for guests to help themselves, though the price (starting at around $200 and rising swiftly) will deter all but the most wealthy visitor.

A better bet are the so-called "boutique hotels" ($80–$140), several of which are situated between Nob Hill and Downtown. These are small hotels with attentive staff and a limited number of rooms in what used to be an affluent family home. The fittings and fixtures are carefully chosen to add period charm, breakfast is included, and often complimentary wine or sherry is served in the afternoon. Reservations are advised.

Broadly similar to the boutique hotels, many rambling Victorian homes throughout the city have been refurbished and converted into bed-and-breakfasts. Widely fluctuating prices ($60–$190) reflect the fact that both the individual properties and the rooms within them vary greatly: some rooms may be small with a shared bathroom; others might be large and equipped with a whirlpool and CD player.

It is the very lack of hotel-like standardization that is part of the appeal of B&Bs, however, and describing one's room is a favorite topic at breakfast, usually a hearty affair served around a communal table.

The enormous popularity of B&Bs means that you should make a reservation early, especially if arriving in summer or staying over a weekend. Use one of the special agencies such as Bed & Breakfast California, P.O. Box 2247, Saratoga, CA 95070 (tel: 408/867–9662 or 800/872–4500).

Budget accommodations While prices are generally above what you will pay elsewhere in the state, and campsites are nonexistent, San Francisco is good news for travelers on tight budgets, with dozens of privately run hostels and guesthouses, plus two Hostelling International properties, offering dormitory beds, single rooms, and double rooms.

The hostels include the 160-bed San Francisco International Hostel at Fort Mason (tel: 415/771–7277), one of the largest youth hostels in the United States; others are across the city.

Many impose a three-night maximum stay during the busy summer season, and some may impose a curfew. Reservations are essential July through October, and advisable November through June at HI-San Francisco-Downtown in Union Square (tel: 415/788–5604). For more information take a look at the HI website: www.hiayh.org.

GAY AND LESBIAN ACCOMMODATIONS
Wherever they stay in this tolerant city, gay and lesbian travelers are unlikely to encounter discrimination. Indeed, a number of hotels and bed-and-breakfasts, particularly in the Castro area, are staffed by and cater specifically to gays and lesbians.

69

One of seven luxury hotels on Nob Hill, the Mark Hopkins Hotel opened in 1926 and occupies the site of the mansion of early California railroad mogul Mark Hopkins

Practical points

Listings of recommended San Francisco accommodations begin on page 266.

Arriving by air San Francisco's airport (tel: 650/761–0800) is 14 miles south of the city. Links into the city are generally quick and reliable.

A number of companies, such as Super Shuttle (tel: 415/558–8500), and Lorrie's Airport Service (tel: 415/334–9000) run minivans from the traffic island directly outside the terminal's upper (departures) level. The information desk on the airport's lower (arrivals) level can supply a full list of operators and prices, usually around $15 to any city address.

Alternatively, the SFO Airporter (tel: 415/495–8404) bus runs every 20 minutes (5 AM–11 PM) between the airport—departing from the blue column outside the lower level—and the main hotels around Union Square.

Routes KX and 292 of the local SamTrans bus service (tel: 800/660–4287) are cheaper but slower, and baggage (on the KX) is limited to one small item. The buses depart from marked stops outside the airport's upper level.

Airline phone numbers American (tel: 800/433–7300); British Airways (tel: 800/247–9297); Delta (tel: 800/221–1212); Northwest (tel: 800/225–2525); United (tel: 800/241–6522); USAir (tel: 800/428–4322); Virgin (tel: 800/862–8621).

Arriving by train Arriving by train (tel: 800/872–7245 for information; www.amtrak.com) in San Francisco means disembarking at the gleaming terminal at Emeryville, across the bay, and continuing into the city aboard one of the free shuttle buses that meet arriving passengers.

Arriving by bus Greyhound buses (tel: 800/231–2222; www.greyhound.com) to San Francisco stop at the Transbay Terminal, 425 Mission Street.

Car rental In a city that is so easy to walk around and served by an excellent public transportation system, you

TAXI FARES
Only for three or four people sharing the cost are taxis from the airport to the city financially worthwhile. Fares are likely to range from $28 to about $35.

The wavy lines on the side of this San Francisco bus spell "MUNI," the name of the city's transportation authority, derived from "San Francisco Municipal Railway"

will not need a car. If you are traveling further afield, however, you may want to rent one (see pages 257–258); all the main firms have desks at the airport and offices around the city.

Alamo (tel: 800/327–9633)
Avis (tel: 800/331–1212)
Budget (tel: 800/527–0700)
Hertz (tel: 800/654–3131)
Thrifty (tel: 800/367–2277)

Parking Local law requires a car's front wheels to be turned toward the curb when parked, to prevent the vehicle from rolling down the street.

Climate San Francisco enjoys mild weather year-round, with temperatures seldom above 70°F (21°C) or below 40°F (4°C). Stiff breezes often whip in off the bay, however, and fogs are a regular feature, liable to make the city feel cooler than it actually is. Play it safe by bringing a warm sweater or jacket even in summer, and in winter, be prepared for chilly evenings, when a coat is essential.

Travelers with disabilities All public buildings are wheelchair accessible and have adapted toilets for people who use wheelchairs; most buses can "kneel" to the curb, and all BART stations have elevators between street and platform levels. Information on other facilities can be obtained from the Disability Co-ordinator, Mayor's Office of Community Development, 10 United Nations Plaza, Suite 600, San Francisco, CA 94102 (tel: 415/252–3158).

Doctors Two hospitals with 24-hour emergency rooms are **San Francisco General Hospital** (1001 Potrero Avenue, tel: 415/206–8000) and the **Medical Center** at the **University of California, San Francisco** (500 Parnassus Avenue at 3rd Avenue, near Golden Gate Park, tel: 415/476–1000).
The **Downtown Medical Center**, 450 Sutter Street (tel: 415/362–7177), offers same-day appointments and is open 6 AM–6 PM. If you need medical treatment in your hotel, try the **A-Traveler Medical Group**, 490 Post Street, Suite 225 (tel: 415/981–1102), who offer around-the-clock service and also have a walk-in health care service.

Information For free maps and brochures, or for more general information, stop into the Visitor Information Center, located on the lower level of Hallidie Plaza near the corner of Market and Powell streets (tel: 415/391–2000; www.sfvisitor.org; *Open* Mon–Fri 9–5, Sat and Sun 9–3).

Pharmacies Several **Walgreen** drug stores have 24-hour pharmacies, including those at 498 Castro Street (tel: 415/861–6276) and 3201 Divisadero Street at Lombard Street (tel: 415/931–6417). Also try the Walgreen on Powell Street near Market Street (135 Powell Street, tel: 415/391–7222; *Open* Mon–Fri 8–9, Sat 9–5, Sun 10–6. AE, MC, V).

EMERGENCY NUMBERS
Dial 911 for fire, police, or ambulance. Other emergency numbers include the Rape Crisis Hotline: 415/647–7273 or 821–3222.

FREE MUSEUMS
To save money, avoid the rain, or simply to enjoy something for nothing, San Francisco has several major museums offering free admission on certain days (see page 42). The following are always free:
Cable Car Museum (page 40)
Chinese Cultural Center (page 40)
Chinese Historical Society (page 40)
Fort Point (page 41)
Museum of Money of the American West (page 43)
North Beach Museum (page 43)
Presidio Army Museum (page 44)
Wells Fargo History Museum (page 44)

71

SAN FRANCISCO'S FOG
Visitors underestimate San Francisco's infamous fog at their peril. Particularly during the summer, fog rolls in from the ocean and engulfs much of the city in a blanket of white. The fog usually burns off by midday but in the morning expect cool temperatures and restricted views.

One of the city's most popular sports: jogging

72

HEALTH
For a doctor or dentist, look under "Physicians and Surgeons" or "Dentists" in the Yellow Pages. Alternatively, call Visitors' Medical Services (tel: 415/353–6566) for referral to a doctor, or the San Francisco Dental Office (tel: 415/777–5115) for a dentist. Hospitals with 24-hour emergency rooms are San Francisco General, 1001 Potrero Avenue (tel: 415/206– 8000) and Davies Medical Center, Castro and Dubuce Streets (tel: 415/565–6060).

Newspapers Both the city's daily newspapers, the morning *San Francisco Chronicle* and the evening *San Francisco Examiner* (combined on Sundays), are the obvious places to find local and state news, although they tend to be thin on national and foreign coverage.

The widely found *L.A. Times* and *New York Times* are better for hard news from further afield and make a better read, and for city features and events listings, the free papers detailed on page 43 are the prime source.

Also worth flipping through are the free tourist magazines such as *San Francisco Quick* and the *Bay City Guide*, found in most hotels.

TV and radio Affiliated to national networks, the main San Francisco TV channels are 2 KTVU (FOX); 4 KRON (NBC); 5 KPIX (CBS); 7 KGO (ABC); and 9 KQED (PBS). Many hotels also offer selected cable TV channels. A multitude of radio stations cover the AM and FM frequencies.

Participant sports Like most Californians, San Franciscans are enthusiastic participants in outdoor activities, and visitors will find a whole range of physical pursuits.

Cycling The city has two excellent signposted bike routes, one through Golden Gate Park, the other crossing the city to the Golden Gate Bridge. Bike rental costs start at $20 a day, and outlets are plentiful along Stanyan Street.

Golf There are public 18-hole courses at Lincoln Park (tel: 415/221–9911) and Harding Park (tel: 415/664–4690), and a pitch-and-putt nine-hole course in Golden Gate Park (tel: 415/751–8987). Rates range from $23 to $28 at Lincoln Park to $10 to $13 at Golden Gate Park, all per person.

Hang-gliding Constant breezes make San Francisco a popular place for hang-gliding; the 200-foot-high cliff at Fort Funstan, near Lake Merced, is the main venue.

Sailing and parasailing You will get the best views of the city while bobbing about on the bay. Numerous companies operate yachts and other small craft from Pier 39 in Fisherman's Wharf. If you want a rush of adrenalin along with the views, contact Sausalito Bay Adventures, 85 Liberty Ship Way, Sausalito (tel: 415/331–0444), who offer powerboats and a captain to tour the bay highlights or take a more adventurous route to the ocean.

Spectator sports Tickets for most major sport events are available through BASS Ticketmaster (tel: 510/762–2277) and the outlets mentioned below.

Baseball During the April to September baseball season, the San Francisco Giants draw crowds to Pacific Bell Park in China Basin. Tickets are available at the stadium box office (tel: 415/467–8000).

Football The city's football team, the San Francisco 49ers (tel: 415/656–4900), also play at 3-Com Park.

Baseball and basketball Further professional sporting action takes place across the bay, with the Oakland A's baseball team and the Golden State Warriors basketball team, who appear at the Oakland Coliseum and Oakland Coliseum Arena, respectively (tel: 510/762–BASS).

Public transportation San Francisco's famous **cable cars** are tourist attractions rather than a practical way of getting around. They operate on two routes between Downtown and Fisherman's Wharf, and another between Nob Hill and the Financial District. Tickets can be bought from self-service machines.

More useful are the **buses** and **streetcars** run by MUNI (tel: 415/673–6864). Exact change ($1) is necessary on buses, and a single-journey ticket with free transfers is valid for two changes of route within 2 hours.

If you are using public transportation a lot, a MUNI Passport will save money; these are valid on all MUNI services for one, three, or seven days. MUNI routes are shown in the phone book, and at most bus stops.

The state-of-the-art **Bay Area Rapid Transit (BART)** (tel: 415/989–2278 or 510/464–6000) system is chiefly of use for crossing the bay to Berkeley and Oakland. Fares range from $1 to over $4 according to distance traveled; tickets can be bought from self-service machines at BART stations.

Taxis can be ordered by telephone but are usually easy to hail in the street. The cost includes the flag charge, $1.70, when the meter starts running, plus $1.80 for each mile of the journey. Scores of cab companies are listed in the phone book.

Few can resist a ride on a cable car

THE BAY AREA

— see Drive
page 79

74

CONTRASTS From the wild hills of Marin to the high-tech suburbia of Silicon Valley, the Bay Area encompasses a host of contrasting communities with only their proximity to San Francisco Bay in common. The area is by no means dull, but there is no single spot justifying a long-term stay and it is ideally examined on day-trips from San Francisco.

In the East Bay, backed by steep hills holding rustic homes and covered by a great number of parks, life in Berkeley (for all but devoted gastronomes, who know it as the birthplace of California cuisine) revolves around a world-famous university campus, noted as much for its student politics as for its breakthroughs in nuclear physics. Neighboring Oakland is enjoying a revival of its fortunes, and tempts passersby with one of the state's best museums and an immense tidal lake.

MAIN ROUTES Along the 55-mile-long peninsula stretching south from San Francisco, Highway 1 charts the coast (see pages 90–101) while Highway 101 keeps to the bayside of the peninsula's central mountains, passing tree-shrouded foothill communities before hitting the dense suburbia filling Santa Clara Valley, now better known as Silicon Valley, home of high-tech industries and San Jose—the fastest growing U.S. city.

Stanford University is the outstanding sight here, although Silicon Valley's towns are at pains to polish up whatever historical remnants and natural areas they possess to make themselves attractive to visitors whose interests extend beyond microcircuitry.

North from San Francisco, the green spaces of Marin County were partly colonized two decades ago by San Francisco's original hippies, whose inner-self explorations developed into the New Age pursuits of Marin's more recent, much better bankrolled, arrivals.

Marin is best tasted as part of a loop around San Pablo Bay, on the inland side of which lie several small towns of historical interest on the scenically appealing Carquinez Straights. The wild and scenically spectacular Point Reyes area is covered in the North Coast chapter (see pages 240–241).

The Bay Area

76

*Previous page:
Fireworks over the San
Francisco-Oakland Bay
Bridge*

*Berkeley students stroll
around Sproul Plaza,
overlooked by the
Campanile and by the
distant hills that hold the
university's science
laboratories*

▶ Angel Island   74B4

Native Americans hunted seal and otter from the banks
of Angel Island long before its discovery by the Spanish
in 1775. The island—the largest in San Francisco Bay—
was used in various ways by the U.S. government,
including as an arrival point for Asian immigrants,
before becoming a state park. Walking trails cross the
tree- and scrub-covered island, and the wind-sheltered
beaches at Ayala Cove (landing point for Fisherman's
Wharf ferries) and Quarry Point are perfect for picnics.

▶ Benicia   74C4

In the frenzy of the Gold Rush years, a deepwater harbor
enabled the town of Benicia to keep pace with San
Francisco in the race to become California's number one
port. It even enjoyed 13 months as state capital from
1853, and the **Benicia State Capitol Park▶** preserves the
handsome Greek Revival building in which state
business was carried out. The **Fischer-Hanlon House▶**, a
renovated Gold Rush hotel beside the park, is also open
for tours by arrangement (tel: 707/745–3385). In the
nearby **Benicia Arsenal▶** building, local artisans have
studios and shops.

▶▶ Berkeley   74B4

Beginning with the Free Speech Movement of the early
1960s, student activity on the campus of the **University of
California at Berkeley▶▶▶** (Visitor Information
Center, 101 University Hall, 2200 University Avenue; tel:
510/642–5215) has brought one of the country's top
educational establishments a reputation for radicalism.
The university began as a Christian college in the 1850s;
it was taken over by the state of California in 1873.

   Stalls dispensing literature and views on any number
of controversial topics are common on campus, and

Berkeley has one of the most left-leaning local governments in the country. But these days revolt against authority seems the last thing on the minds of the 30,000 students, most of whom earnestly pursue their studies with an eye on the job market.

Berkeley is easy to reach by BART from San Francisco, and the campus is within easy walking distance, directly east of the station. Devote most of your time to the campus, as only the well-stocked bookstores and lively restaurants along **Telegraph Avenue**▶▶ are of interest elsewhere. For more on Berkeley's militant past, see pages 84–85.

Once the scene of anti–Vietnam War protests, **Sproul Plaza**▶▶, close to Berkeley's Bancroft Way, is jammed by milling students and makeshift stalls manned by ecological and political activists. The 200-foot-high **Campanile**▶▶ (to the right), modeled on the bell tower of St. Mark's in Venice, has been a landmark since 1914. Immediately north, safeguarding the university's rare books, the **Bancroft Library**▶ also has a small museum of Californian history. The adjoining **Le Conte Hall** is where physicist Robert Oppenheimer labored over plans for the first atomic bomb.

Farther north, across University Drive, is the 1907 **Hearst Mining Building**▶. Beneath its impressive rotunda the building displays mineral collections and exhibits on mining in California. The **Hearst Museum of Anthropology**▶, on Bancroft Way (to the south), holds an intriguing stash, including much from Native American cultures; and across Bancroft Way is an architectural tour de force—the imposingly modern **University Art Museum**▶▶ (2626 Bancroft Way; tel: 510/642-0808), which has an impressive permanent collection and regularly stages exhibitions.

▶ Fremont · 74B2

If you are passing through Fremont, you might be tempted by the 1797 **Mission San José de Guadalupe**▶ (43300 Mission Boulevard), although a $5 million rebuilding has left the mission looking far grander than it ought to.

A better stop is the **Ardenwood Historic Farm**▶ (off Highway 84), whose animals, gardens, and shops re-create local rural life around the turn of the century. Between August and April, thousands of migratory birds also pass through Fremont, some of them using the **San Francisco Bay National Wildlife Refuge**▶▶ (1 Marshlands Road; tel: 510/792-0222) as a food stop.

▶ Hayward · 74B3

Eight miles south of Oakland, Hayward's **Historical Society Museum**▶ (22701 Main Street; tel: 510/581-0223) charts the growth of this sizable residential community from its origins as a supply stop on the gold mine route. A peek into the spacious rooms of the **McConaghy House**▶ (18701 Hesperian Boulevard; tel: 510/278-0198) shows how the town's wealthy enjoyed life during the late 1800s, and a leisurely hour can be passed strolling among the native Californian vegetation artfully arranged in the **Japanese Garden**▶ (22372 N. Third Street).

THE BIRDMAN OF ALCATRAZ
The Birdman of Alcatraz, murderer Robert Stroud, had his last taste of freedom in 1909, aged 19. It was at Leavenworth jail in Kansas that Stroud began keeping and studying birds, and wrote the highly regarded *Stroud's Digest of the Diseases of Birds*. The "Bird Doctor of Leavenworth" was transferred to Alcatraz in 1942, leaving his birds behind. A biography of Stroud, published in 1955, first coined the phrase "Birdman of Alcatraz," which was later used as the title of a 1962 film about Stroud, starring Burt Lancaster.

77

MARIN'S CIVIC CENTER
Arguably the greatest, and certainly one of the most influential architects of the 20th century, Frank Lloyd Wright erected 25 buildings in California, none of them more instantly striking than the 1957 Marin County Civic Center, a buff- and blue-colored concrete and steel creation linking three hilltops just east of Highway 101 on the northern edge of San Rafael. The architect's first government commission, it was also the last job he undertook before his death in 1959.

ACRES OF ORCHIDS
Eight miles south of San Francisco, the laboratories of Acres of Orchids (1450 El Camino Real) experiment with the gene pool of the much-loved plant. Free tours pass through the greenhouses, and around a lush garden filled with more types of orchid than you ever imagined possible.

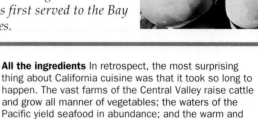

In no part of California is eating taken more seriously than it is in and around San Francisco, and it was in the upscale restaurants on Berkeley's Shattuck Avenue—an area known as the "gourmet ghetto"—that California cuisine was first served to the Bay Area's salivating foodies.

PIZZA: CALIFORNIA STYLE

Outlets of California Pizza Kitchen, now a nationwide chain, bake pizzas in brick ovens and serve them with exotic toppings such as goat's cheese, duck, or lobster.

78

CALIFORNIA AGRICULTURE

California's fertility helps make fresh produce a regular feature of the meal table. During the 1920s, the diverting of a northern river to irrigate the 400-mile-long San Joaquin Valley, which runs through the center of the state, enabled it to become one of the world's most agriculturally productive regions. Together with the more southerly Imperial Valley, the San Joaquin Valley enables California to grow more food than 90 percent of the world's nations.

Date cultivation near Palm Desert in the Coachella Valley near Palm Springs, one of the world's major date-producing regions

All the ingredients In retrospect, the most surprising thing about California cuisine was that it took so long to happen. The vast farms of the Central Valley raise cattle and grow all manner of vegetables; the waters of the Pacific yield seafood in abundance; and the warm and sunny climate makes fresh fruit available year-round. For decades, the ethnic diversity of the state's inhabitants has made international and regional American cuisines widely available and well known.

A unique blend In the late 1970s, Berkeley's top chefs began crossing the borders of international cuisine, juxtaposing methods of preparation, flavoring, and styling, using whatever local produce was in season. In some cases, animals were reared and a range of vegetables grown to the exact specifications of a particular restaurant, and chefs bought seafood directly from individual fishermen.

A matter of taste Coming to the fore just as healthy eating was becoming a national preoccupation, California chefs selected ingredients for their nutritional balance, appealing to the digestive tract as much as the taste buds. And the artful presentation of food on the plate was also important.

Although the fame of California cuisine spread far and wide, the highly valued individuality of each chef prevented any single dish—which might be anything from grilled pigeon breasts to red snapper in peanut sauce—from becoming uniquely associated with California cuisine.

The rise of California cuisine was matched by the rise of the celebrity chef, none more illustrious than Wolfgang Puck, credited with inventing the "designer pizza" and owner of several renowned restaurants in California, including Postrio in San Francisco and Spago in Los Angeles.

Marin County, the North Bay, and the East Bay

See map on page 74.

Leave San Francisco on the Golden Gate Bridge, entering Marin County on Highway 101 and shortly exiting for Sausalito.
A picturesque and very upscale "artist's colony," **Sausalito**▶▶ is a pleasant bayside town of steep, narrow streets and a strollable—though very commercialized—waterfront area.

Return to Highway 101 and drive north for two miles, exiting for Tiburon.
Another affluent bayside community, placid **Tiburon**▶ boasts the **Richardson Bay Audubon Center and Sanctuary**▶, which offers bird-watching from an effortless and rewarding nature trail.

Return to Highway 101 and drive north for six miles to San Rafael.
The seat of Marin County, **San Rafael** holds a 1949 replica of an 1817 mission chapel and the architecturally significant **Marin County Civic Center**▶▶.

Continue north on Highway 101, after nine miles reaching Novato.
In **Novato**, a dairy-farming town named after a Hookooeko Indian chief, the **Marin Museum of the American Indian**▶ details local Native American prehistory and culture.

Leave Highway 101 and drive 20 miles east on State Road 37 to Vallejo.
The large shipbuilding town of **Vallejo** is mostly visited for the Six Flags Marine World theme park located on its outskirts (see page 87), although the **Naval and Historical Museum**▶ merits a quick look.

Drive south from Vallejo, crossing the Carquinez Strait on Highway 80 and landing at Crockett. Turn left to follow the Carquinez Strait Scenic Drive as far as Port Costa.
This winding hillside route brings views over several local parks and across the strait to California's one-time capital, Benicia (see page 76).

Return to Crockett and head south along Highway 80 for Berkeley.
The university town of **Berkeley**▶▶ is described on pages 76 and 77.

Take any road south from Berkeley for Oakland.
A major East Bay community with an outstanding museum, **Oakland**▶▶ is described on page 83.

Return to San Francisco on Interstate 80, crossing the Bay Bridge.

Sausalito's waterfront district

Angel Island (see page 76) might be the largest of San Francisco Bay's islands, Treasure Island (see page 88) may have the best views, but the lump of granite known as Alcatraz is by far the most famous—or most infamous.

High security A mile and a half north of Fisherman's Wharf, Alcatraz (whose Spanish name means "Pelican") became the most feared U.S. place of incarceration from 1934, when "incorrigible" criminals—those deemed beyond salvation and considered too dangerous to be held in conventional jails—were moved to this top-security, strict-discipline penitentiary. Its most notorious residents were Al Capone, Machine Gun Kelly, and Robert Stroud—the so-called "Birdman of Alcatraz"—see panel on page 77.

At Alcatraz, work was regarded as a privilege and had to be earned by a prisoner through good behavior. There was one guard for every three inmates, and any prisoners who did escape from their cells were faced with the prospect of crossing the freezing, swiftly moving waters of the bay to freedom.

Although stays at Alcatraz averaged nearly 10 years, inmates were denied access to newspapers, radios, and TVs, and 80 percent of them never received a visitor. Only 36 of the 1,576 convicts imprisoned here ever attempted escape: all but five were recaptured within an hour; of those five, nothing was ever heard again.

Change of use The costs and problems of running an island prison, and the severity of the regime, led to Alcatraz's closure in 1963. After a period of Native American occupation, Alcatraz became part of the Golden Gate National Recreation Area, in 1972 throwing open its once tightly guarded doors to the curious public.

Most of the semiruined prison buildings—the cellblock, the mess hall with its tear-gas cylinders fixed to the ceiling, and the prison hospital—can be toured, and there is a small museum and a short documentary film. It is also worthwhile taking the audiocassette tour, which carries a terse commentary by former Alcatraz guards and inmates.

Frequent crossings between Pier 41 on Fisherman's Wharf and Alcatraz are operated by the Blue & Gold Fleet (tel: 415/705–5555 or 800/426–8687 for tickets; 415/773–1188 for boat schedules and information. *Admission: moderate*), though you should reserve a few days in advance during the summer.

An Alcatraz prison cell

▶ Los Altos and Los Altos Hills 74A1

Set deep in Silicon Valley, the relaxed communities of Los Altos and Los Altos Hills offer a pleasing escape from modern technology with the pioneer-era relics gathered at the **History House Museum**, 51 S. San Antonio Road (tel: 650/948–9427. *Admission: inexpensive*).

▶ Los Gatos 74A1

Sumptuous homes fill the hillsides and lanes of Los Gatos, 16 miles west of San Jose, whose owners sometimes emerge to scour the pricey shops and boutiques of the **Old Town▶** (on University Avenue) for antiques. Other pastimes include visiting the art and nature displays of **Los Gatos Museum▶** (4 Tait Avenue), and riding the **Billy Jones Wildcat Railroad▶** in Oak Meadow Park.

▶ Martinez 74C4

When he wasn't blazing a hiking trail through California's backcountry, Scottish-born naturalist John Muir lived in comfort in Martinez, in a 17-room house built by his father-in-law in 1882. Known as the **John Muir National Historic Site▶▶** (4202 Alhambra Avenue; tel: 925/228–8860) and kept as it was at Muir's death in 1914, it is well worth a visit. Be sure to catch the free film show, which reveals Muir's crucial role in the presentation of the country's wilderness areas—particularly Yosemite and other sections of the Sierra Nevada—and in the creation of national parks and forests.

The Martinez Adobe, built in 1849, and occupied for a time by Muir's daughter, shares the site and has displays on Mexican life in early California.

▶ Menlo Park 74A2

Many Californians bury their noses once a month in the pages of *Sunset*, a magazine devoted to the stylish upkeep of gardens, homes, and lifestyles in the western United States, and whose own experimental gardens, kitchens, and offices can be visited in Menlo Park, north of Palo Alto. Also in town, a group of elegant Spanish-style buildings set across a 3-acre garden holds the **Allied Arts Guild**, where several crafts studios are open to the public.

The John Muir National Historic Site, Martinez

81

LIVERMORE VALLEY
Top-secret weapon research is one of the main sources of employment in the Livermore Valley, 48 miles east of San Francisco, site of the Lawrence Livermore National Laboratory. Since the end of the Cold War, however, the research emphasis has tilted in favor of peaceful applications. More noticeable on the approach to Livermore are the hundreds of windmills spread across the hillsides, using the almost constant wind to produce low-cost energy.

It may lack the majestic peaks of Yosemite or the mysterious landscapes of Death Valley but, as natural regions go, San Francisco Bay is one of the most ecologically important places in California—and one of the most threatened.

BAY STATISTICS
At low tide, the surface of San Francisco Bay covers approximately 450 square miles. The greatest depth of water is 216 feet, although slightly more than 70 percent of the bay is less than 12 feet deep. Since the arrival of the first American settlers, the bay's shallowness has encouraged "landfill," the filling in of its edges to create new land for building.

82

Delicate balance The bay forms a huge estuary, with much of its 100-mile shoreline lined by cordgrass, an important oxygen- and nutrient-producing plant. In the bay's marshes, microscopic marine creatures thrive and provide food both for migratory birds—beneath whose flight path the bay stands—and, once the tiny organisms are swept out to sea, for large sea dwellers, including the celebrated (and enthusiastically watched) California gray whales, who pass by the bay on their annual journey between the frozen Arctic Ocean and the warmer waters off Baja California.

Damage There are two main causes for the damage to the bay's subtle ecology: increased urbanization, which has led to 75 percent of the marshland disappearing beneath new housing districts and industrial sites; and the diverting of the Sacramento and San Joaquin rivers to the farms of the Central Valley, which has severely reduced the amount of fresh water tempering the salty environment of the bay.

Conservation measures In the mid-1960s, continued lobbying by concerned citizens forced the state government to create the San Francisco Bay Conservation and Development Corporation, which first stopped the pumping of raw sewage into the bay, and then introduced new laws in order to restrict landfill practices.

Nonetheless, the decline of the bay has been slowed rather than halted, despite marshland reclamation projects and the requirement for any new landfill project to be matched by an area of equal size being returned to the water.

Currently, groups such as Save The Bay and the San Francisco Estuary Institute are focusing attention on the toxic substances that are building up in the bay, destroying its vital wetlands.

Another ongoing problem is the thirst of expanding Southern California—a region without its own water supply—which places ever-greater demands on the bay's freshwater rivers.

A nature refuge and ornithological research center, Marin County's Audubon Canyon Ranch

Further information More about the bay and its ecology can be gleaned at San Mateo's Coyote Point Museum (see page 88), Palo Alto's Baylands Nature Interpretive Center (2775 Embarcadero Road), the Environmental Education Center of the Don Edwards San Francisco Bay National Wildlife Refuge (at Alviso, on the northern edge of San Jose), and at Hayward Regional Shoreline (eastern end of San Mateo Bridge, close to Hayward), a major marshland reclamation project.

►► Oakland 74B4

Oakland may lack the fascination of San Francisco and the academic renown of Berkeley, but this blue-collar city is an ethnically varied, mixed-income community with spacious parks, a huge lake, and a successful re-development of its waterfront area. **Jack London Square►**, a bayside complex of shops and restaurants named for the writer who spent part of his life here, is where ferries from San Francisco berth. Nearby is the **USS *Potomac*►** (tel: 510/839–8256. *Open* Wed and Fri 10–2, Sun 11–3. *Admission: inexpensive*), the homely yacht used by president Franklin D. Roosevelt as the "floating white house". A mile north, **Lake Merritt►** is popular for yachting and water sports and is overlooked by the evocatively restored 1876 **Camron Stanford House►►** (1418 Lakeside Drive; Wed 11–4, Sun 1–5). The excellent **Oakland Museum of California►►►**, 1000 Oak Street (tel: 510238/2200; www.museumca.org. *Open* daily 10–5. *Admission: moderate*) chronicles the state's art, history, and natural history over three floors.

A bust of Jack London commemorates the opening of Oakland's Jack London Square, though the area holds little of substance to remember the San Francisco-born writer

►► Palo Alto 74A2

Affluent Palo Alto is the site of **Stanford University**, founded by railroad magnate Leland Stanford in 1885. Long viewed as the conservative counterpart to radical Berkeley, Stanford reputedly earns $5 million a year in royalties on its inventions. Romanesque sandstone buildings sit at the heart of the campus, the nicest being the mural-decorated **Memorial Church►** on the Main Quad. The quad is also a pickup point for free shuttle buses across the 9,000-acre campus, best appreciated from the observation level of the **Hoover Tower►**.

"Must sees" include the Asian and Egyptian collections of the **Cantor Art Gallery►** the **Rodin Sculpture Garden►**, where an eight-ton *Gates of Hell* is the most imposing of several pieces by Rodin, and the **Stanford Linear Accelerator Center►►**, located in the hills two miles from the main campus, tours of which (appointment only; tel: 415/926–2204) are conducted by students.

MOUNT DIABLO
The highest point in the Bay Area, moody Mount Diablo is well named as Devil's Mountain. Spanish soldiers reported seeing a mysterious figure taking the side of the Indians during battles around its slopes, and another group believed they had encountered Satan himself when a Native American shaman appeared. From the 3,849-foot summit you will see (fogs permitting) the Pacific and the Sierra Nevada mountains 200 miles east.

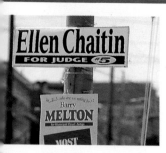

California is much less a hotbed of revolution than the world at large often seems to think it is. The only time complete social upheaval was seriously on the Californian political agenda was during the nationally turbulent years of the 1960s, and it was the Bay Area that saw the bulk of the action, with student unrest and violent agitation by the Black Panthers and the Symbionese Liberation Army.

84

REPUBLIC OF BERKELEY
The Berkeley campus may have a history of radical politics, but the administration of Berkeley itself is acknowledged as the most left-wing in the U.S., often nicknamed the Peoples' Republic of Berkeley. Over recent years, community legislators have passed laws aimed at improving the lot of disabled, gay, and homeless citizens, and changed Columbus Day to Indigenous Peoples Day, drawing attention to the negative impact of the arrival of European settlements on the Americas.

Organized student revolt This began in Berkeley during the autumn of 1964, when the university authorities attempted to halt fundraising activities and the distribution of political leaflets on the edge of campus by citing a clause in the state constitution requiring the university to be free of religious or sectarian influence.

Fronted by Mario Savio, the resultant Free Speech Movement (FSM) arranged student sit-ins and protest rallies and an occupation of Sproul Hall, which led to the largest mass arrest in California's history as police dragged 750 students from the building.

Eventually the university powers softened their attitudes, forced to heed student demands for participation in the running of the university.

The success of the FSM in encouraging student activism across the country laid the foundations for the massive anti–Vietnam War demonstrations of later years, when Berkeley was again the state's focal point of dissent. The civility of the FSM actions had become a very distant memory by 1968, though, when several days of rioting took place after the police blocked a student march along Telegraph Avenue.

More violence Berkeley saw more violence in 1969 when a pocket of university ground earmarked for development was turned—by the spades of a disparate bunch of radicals—into People's Park, an open space intended for community use. To take possession of the park (which for many years provided a refuge for the area's homeless), the county sheriff and the National Guard fired tear gas and buckshot, causing the death of one bystander and blinding another.

The Black Panthers While Berkeley was a center for student activity, Oakland was the birthplace in 1966 of the Black Panthers, who advocated self-determination for America's blacks by any means necessary. Although founded by Bobby Seale and Huey Newton, the Black Panthers' best-known figure was their minister for information, Eldridge Cleaver.

Influenced to varying degrees by Malcolm X, Karl Marx, Che Guevara, and Mao Tse-tung (one way the Panthers raised money was through buying 20¢ copies of Mao's Little Red Book in San Francisco's Chinatown and then reselling them to Berkeley's students for

$1 each), the Black Panthers dressed in a uniform of black jackets, black berets, and dark glasses.

Described by the FBI as the gravest threat to domestic peace as their message spread across the country, the Black Panthers were far smaller in number than their publicity suggested. Following shoot-outs with police and the imprisonment of many of its members (including Cleaver who, while on parole, stood as a U.S. presidential candidate for the Peace and Freedom Party), the Oakland Panthers grew increasingly less militant, devoting their time to local community projects and canvasing black support for the Democratic Party.

Cleaver, incidentally, who went underground in 1968 and moved to Cuba, Algeria, and then France, reappeared in the U.S. in 1975, declaring himself a born-again Christian.

The SLA The demise of the Black Panthers did not mean the end of armed insurrection in the Bay Area, however. By killing an Oakland schools superintendent with arsenic-coated bullets for his plans to instigate surveillance of high-school students, the Symbionese Liberation Army (SLA), an underground revolutionary group, announced their presence in 1973.

The following year, the SLA kidnapped the heir to the Hearst publishing fortunes, Patti Hearst. The ransom for her return involved a program of food distribution to California's poor, following which Hearst announced that she had decided to join the organization.

After a bank raid, six SLA members were killed in Los Angeles and in 1975 Hearst herself was arrested in San Francisco and sentenced to seven years' imprisonment. Now she is a Connecticut housewife.

Since then, the emphasis of Bay Area politics has largely switched toward community and ecological issues. The Berkeley campus has been quiet—perhaps a mark of the lasting achievements of the FSM—while, as in San Francisco, the clearest gains have been made by the Bay Area's gay and lesbian communities.

WOMEN EMPOWERED
In 1992, the unprecedented election of two women—former San Francisco mayor Dianne Fienstein, and Barbara Boxer—to represent California in the Senate reflected the ascent of women to positions of power within the state. In the Bay Area, achievements of the women's movement have been many, and it came as no surprise in the early 1990s when the San Francisco-ruling Board of Supervisors had a female majority, including two out-of-the-closet lesbians.

85

Bobby Seale, co-founder of the Black Panthers, speaks to students in 1968 during the height of the movement's fame

JAMES LICK'S OBSERVATORY

Atop Mount Hamilton, 19 miles east of San Jose and reached by a twisting road, the 36-inch telescope of the Lick Observatory has been scanning the heavens since 1888—less efficiently since urbanization filled the sky with smog. The observatory was created with the money of James Lick, whose body lies here, an eccentric Gold Rush-era millionaire who believed there was life on the moon. Open daily, the observatory conducts an informative interpretive program each Friday evening (tel: 408/274–5061 for details).

86

The architectural anomaly that is Winchester Mystery House—said to be haunted

►► San Jose   74B2

The rise of personal computers during the 1970s and 1980s boosted the population and economy of San Jose. Through the 1990s, the Internet revolution continued the upward trend. A mixture of public and private money has turned the heart of San Jose, the third largest city in California, into a user-friendly environment, with a light-railtrack system for pollution-free commuting and rows of sycamore trees for beautification. The **Children's Discovery Museum of Science►** and the **Tech Museum of Innovation►►** display, as their names point out, the area's best known activities.

Less likely sights stud the periphery of San Jose. Within the sphinx- and hieroglyph-decorated Rosicrucian Park (1342 Naglee Avenue), a re-creation of an avenue from ancient Thebes leads to the **Rosicrucian Egyptian Museum** (tel: 408/247-3636), whose collection includes everyday objects from ancient Egypt. Close to Interstate 280, the **Winchester Mystery House** (525 Winchester Boulevard; tel: 408/247–2101) is extraordinary—160 rooms, with stairways leading to ceilings, corridors leading nowhere, and doors opening on to walls. Its construction was financed by Sarah Winchester, heir to the weaponry fortunes. Sarah believed she would die if the house was completed, so work continued for 38 years until her death in 1921.

Other local discoveries include the **Chinese Cultural Gardens**, inside Overfelt Gardens (Educational Park Drive); the Japanese Friendship Garden and **San Jose Historical Museum** in South Kelley Park (1600 Senter Road; tel: 408/287–2290).

► San Leandro   74B3

Just south of Oakland, San Leandro once had a large Portuguese farming community but is now a residential and manufacturing base, of note for **Casa Peralta►** (384 West Estudillo Avenue) an 1897 home that can be toured.

The pick of California's theme parks are in the south of the state, close to Los Angeles (see pages 160–161), although there are a couple of major parks in the Bay Area, not to mention several places to put on a bathing suit and splash around when the temperature soars. The parks have a range of dramatic rides based on TV shows and movies, marine and African wildlife and some spectacular water slides.

Paramount's Great America▶▶

(tel: 408/988–1776). Close to Santa Clara between highways 101 and 237, Paramount's Great America fills 100 acres with daredevil roller-coaster rides and all-action simulations, some based on Paramount's most popular film and TV shows, and some simply designed to terrify.

Most spectacular are Invertigo, a suspended coaster that rises 138 feet before a spine-tingling plummet; Drop Zone, with a 224-feet freefall descent, and A License To Thrill, with participants cast in the role of super-spy James Bond. Alongside are calmer items such as Martian jokes and songs of Jetson's Space Blast as well as gentle rides intended for small children. A day is ample to see and do everything.

Six Flags Marine World▶▶ 2001

Marine World Parkway, near Vallejo (tel: 707/643–6722; www.sixflags.com. *Admission: expensive*) combines an oceanarium, a wild animal park, and a theme park where whales, dolphins, sea lions, and sharks can all be seen, as well as Bengal tigers swimming in a pool. There are elephant rides, bird shows, giraffes, and butterflies, plus Batman and Robin in a waterborne stunt show. The park has its share of thrill rides, too. These range from Monsoon Falls, a boat trip featuring a sudden 55-foot drop, to a selection of roller coasters, which include the corkscrew, double flips, and topping the twist loop of the 55mph Kong,

the three looping inversions on the backwards-running Boomerang.

Raging Waters If you are in San Jose when the sun beats down, cool off at **Raging Waters▶** (Lake Cunningham Regional Park, off the Capitol Expressway), a 14-acre park where everything involves getting people wet.

Much the same applies if you are in the Livermore Valley, where four twisting flumes make up the Rapids Waterslide, part of the **Shadow Cliffs Regional Recreation Center▶** (two miles east of Pleasanton on Stanley Boulevard).

A dolphin show at Marine World

FILOLI

Of several rambling mansions secreted in the foothills and forests of the Bay Area, only the Filoli Estate, a 43-room dwelling with exquisitely landscaped gardens, is likely to be familiar—it was the Carrington estate in the top TV soap, *Dynasty*. You will find it on Canada Road in Woodside (tel: 650/364–2880 for a guided tour).

TREASURE ISLAND

A manmade island in San Francisco Bay, created for the 1939 Golden Gate Exposition, Treasure Island was taken over by the U.S. Navy. The Treasure Island Museum details the history of the navy, although a stronger reason for making the ferry crossing from Fisherman's Wharf might be the fantastic views of the Golden Gate and Bay bridges and of San Francisco itself.

The Bay Bridge, seen from Treasure Island

▶ San Mateo   74A3

With computers, diaramas, and films, San Mateo's four-story **Coyote Point Museum▶▶** (Coyote Point, Peninsula Avenue; tel: 650/342–7755) presents an exceptionally informative account of the intricacies of—and the threats faced by—the natural life of San Francisco Bay. The museum, designed to blend in with its wooded surroundings, also exhibits a functioning beehive and an industrious colony of termites, while the tranquility of the bayside setting—interrupted only by the jets flying in and out of nearby San Francisco airport—makes it a good place for a picnic.

San Mateo is the seat of San Mateo County, whose past can be traced in nearby Redwood City at the **San Mateo County Historical Museum▶** (777 Hamilton Street; tel: 650/299–0104; Old Courthouse of Redwood City).

▶ Santa Clara   74B1

A fast-growing but largely uninteresting community just north of San Jose, Santa Clara evolved around Mission Santa Clara de Asís, founded in 1777 but survived only by a replica of its third (1825) church within the grounds of Santa Clara University.

The university's **de Saisset Museum▶** has objects from the original mission, and an illuminating collection devoted to California's indigenous cultures and the impact of European settlements. Most visitors pass right through the town, however, headed for the Great America theme park (see page 87).

▶ Saratoga   74A1

James D. Phelan, one-time U.S. senator and three-time mayor of San Francisco, lived comfortably in Saratoga, nestling in the lower slopes of the Santa Cruz foothills west of San Jose. Since 1930, Phelan's 19-room **Villa Montalvo▶▶** (15400 Montalvo Road; tel: 408/741–3421), with terraced gardens, arboretum, and bird sanctuary, has been a retreat for writers and painters. Numerous cultural events take place in the villa's theater.

If Saratoga's wealth becomes overwhelming, focus on higher things at the reposeful 15-acre **Hakone Gardens▶** (21000 Big Basin Way), landscaped along formal Japanese lines.

Though large parts of the Bay Area may be densely residential, an impressive area is wide-open countryside, where hiking trails, sedate lakes, and threatened wildlife all exist within an hour's drive of suburbia.

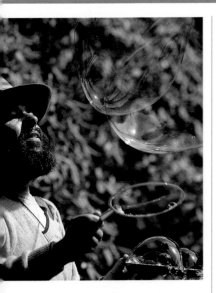

Bubble-juggling, Golden Gate Park

Big is beautiful On the hills above Berkeley and Oakland, the second-largest park system in the United States comprises 63,000 acres and divides into 43 separate parks. The largest and most popular section is **Tilden Regional Park▶▶** (off Grizzly Peak Boulevard; tel: 510/635–0138), where weekend crowds enjoy swimming in and sunbathing around Lake Anza, or honing their skills on the golf course and tennis courts. Others enjoy strolling in the botanical garden, as children amuse themselves riding a miniature steam train or vintage merry-go-round.

Peacefully pastoral Nice though it is, the recreational development of Tilden is at odds with the purely pastoral landscapes of the East Bay's other parks. **Wildcat Canyon Regional Park▶** borders Tilden

89

but its appeal is thoroughly rustic, with quiet hiking trails winding around a creek and across wooded hillsides.

From Wildcat Canyon, ambitious hikers can pick up the **Skyline National Trail▶▶** and thread their way south over 30 view-laden miles to the Anthony Chabot Regional Park, well known to local anglers for the bass and trout in its Lake Chabot and to wildlife watchers for the deer, raccoons, and bobcats resident in the neighboring **Redwood Regional Park▶**.

Landscapes are generally less dramatic directly south of San Francisco, although part-time lepidopterists should make a stop at **San Bruno Mountain Regional Park▶** (take the Brisbane exit off Highway 101), the last remaining habitat of the mission blue and a couple of other waning butterfly species. The Friends of Endangered Species lead free guided walks to see the butterflies, and to the sites of Native American significance within the park.

Elsewhere, earthquake enthusiasts might enjoy a close inspection of the San Andreas fault, the geological hiccup behind many of California's earthquakes, a section of which runs through the **Los Trancos Open Space Preserve▶** (seven miles southwest of Palo Alto, on Page Mill Road) and which is flanked by a walking trail.

❑ Oakland's Lake Merritt is the world's largest saltwater tidal lagoon. Canoes and a variety of boats can be rented for $4 to $10 per hour from the Sailboat House (tel: 510/444–3807). ❑

CENTRAL COAST NORTH

see Drive page 98

| 0 | 10 | 20 | 30 km |
| 0 | 5 | 10 | 15 | 20 miles |

LARGELY UNCHANGED Much of California's Central Coast, covering almost 400 miles between San Francisco and Los Angeles, has not changed a great deal since it was first sighted by seafaring Spaniards in the 16th century.

Pacific breakers continue to smash against the granite headlands, groves of towering redwood trees still smother many of the coastal valleys, and the colonies of honking sea lions and seals underscore the fact that, even today, it is nature that holds the upper hand.

Completing the sense of remoteness from the state's developed regions, the sole coastal road (Highway 1, also called the Coastal Highway) makes hair-raising crossings of deep canyons as it charts a winding two-lane course linking the area's scattered towns.

The first settlement of appreciable size is Santa Cruz, an affable university community noted for its eccentrics, left-wing politics, and the surfers who mass off its attractive beaches.

Fifty miles south, Monterey was California's capital for a period beginning in 1770 and documents the fact by keeping many of its historic buildings intact. The town also marks the edge of the Monterey Peninsula, a fist of forested granite jutting into the ocean, on whose southern edge sits the pretty—if heavily visited—village of Carmel.

A few miles inland from the coast, state parks cover many of the hikable hillsides, and out-of-the-way farming towns form the heart of what is sometimes called Steinbeck country, after the Salinas-born writer, John Steinbeck, one of many literary figures associated with the Central Coast.

BEYOND THE MONTEREY PENINSULA Big Sur comprises more than 70 miles of dramatic, wide-open country populated by barely a thousand souls, and brings the northern section of the Central Coast to an end on the outskirts of San Simeon.

Half Moon Bay pumpkins, harvested for Halloween

The pine-cloaked hillsides of Big Basin Redwoods State Park

92

GENDER-BENDING, FRONTIER STYLE
Born in New Hampshire in 1812, one-eyed Charley Parkhurst chewed tobacco with the best of them and piloted stagecoaches over a rough route through the Santa Cruz Mountains. Only on Parkhurst's death in 1879 was "he" discovered to be a "she."

▶▶▶ Big Basin   90A3
Boulder Creek, off Highway 236 (tel: 831/338–8860)
The first of California's state parks, Big Basin Redwoods State Park was created in 1902 to protect groves of 2,000-year-old redwood trees covering the ocean-facing slopes of the Santa Cruz Mountains, 25 miles south of Half Moon Bay. A simple self-guided walking trail leads around the biggest and best of the park's majestic redwoods, and 100 miles of hiking trails descend from the inland hills to secluded sandy beaches. There is hiking and horseback riding amid the 4,000 pristine acres of the Henry Cowell Redwoods State Park, close to Big Basin, and also an excellent self-guided walking trail through the Redwood Grove.

▶▶▶ Big Sur   90B1
Highway 1, Carmel–San Simeon
Coastal California reaches its scenic climax with Big Sur, a barely populated stretch between Carmel and San Simeon, where scrub-covered slopes and forested river canyons of the Santa Lucia Mountains meet the ocean.

Obscure tracks lead to hidden beaches, but even from the winding and dipping Highway 1, Big Sur cannot fail to impress. The **Henry Miller Memorial Library**▶ recalls just one of numerous writers and artists who have found inspiration here, and the Esalen Institute (see panel) further attests to Big Sur's mood-enhancing qualities.

▶ Bixby Creek Bridge   90B1
The largest of a series of tall, narrow bridges carrying Highway 1 across the canyons of Big Sur is the Bixby Creek Bridge, some 10 miles south of Point Lobos State Reserve, completed in 1932 and claimed to be the world's largest single-arch bridge.

▶▶ Carmel   90B2
Highway 1, south of Monterey
Visitor Information Center, upstairs on San Carlos between 5th and 6th Avenues (tel: 831/624–1329)
Founded by the Spanish and turned into an unconventional leafy retreat by turn-of-the-century San Franciscan bohemians, Carmel is a self-consciously quaint seaside town with about 5,000 wealthy residents (including ex-mayor Clint Eastwood) fiercely protective of their cottage homes and narrow streets, who have banned neon signs, traffic lights, and hot dog stands.

Carmel's lanes and courtyards merit a brief browse, although most hold only souvenir shops, pricey restaurants, and art galleries touting depictions of coastal landscapes. More deserving of time are the town's beach, the granite **Tor House**▶▶ (26304 Ocean View Avenue; tel: 831/624–1813), built by poet Robinson Jeffers, and the **Carmel Mission**▶▶▶ (3080 Rio Road; tel: 831/624–3600), where Junípero Serra, founder of California's earliest missions, died in 1784 .

▶▶ Castle Rock   90B4
Highway 35 (tel: 408/867–2952)
Rising high above coastal fogs and city smogs, the 3,600 acres of Castle Rock State Park offer rich pickings for backcountry fans. The mountain ridges, waterfalls, giant

boulders, and fantastic views cannot be fully appreciated without the requisite equipment and stamina for at least a day's heavy-duty hiking.

▶ Felton 90B3

A handy accommodations base when exploring the parks that lie around it, Felton, a mountain town five miles north of Santa Cruz, also boasts the century-old **Covered Bridge▶** spanning the San Lorenzo River valley, and two scenic railways: the Roaring Camp Big Trees Narrow Gauge Railroad, which navigates redwood groves on the way to Bear Mountain, and the Santa Cruz Big Trees & Pacific Railroad, which descends to Santa Cruz (both run daily in summer; less often at other times).

▶ Forest of Nisene Marks 90B3

By 1923, 40 years of logging had decimated 10,000 acres of forest inland from Santa Cruz. When logging finished, the land was purchased by a Danish immigrant family, who later put it under state protection. Hiking trails reveal young redwoods—proof of the forest's regenerative powers—and many remnants of the lumber industry.

93

▶ Half Moon Bay 90A4

Increasingly populated by wealthy refugees from Silicon Valley suburbia, the small oceanside town of Half Moon Bay maintains a picturesque main street, which has an old-fashioned charm. There are a number of Victorian buildings housing various cozy restaurants and several bakeries. Several miles of quiet, scenic beaches add to the town's appeal.

Just south of Half Moon Bay, the **Higgins Purisima Road▶** branches from Highway 1 to wind for eight miles through tiny, time-locked farming settlements, before rejoining the main highway.

Well-tended grounds, carefully preserved adobe buildings, and a handsome Moorish-towered church help make Carmel Mission one of the prettiest of California's missions

From turn-of-the-century bohemians to 1950s beatniks, writers and poets have long been a feature of the Central Coast. Inspired by fleeting visits or besotted enough to take up permanent residence, they have put the area's powerful landscapes to use as potent backdrops, or simply waxed lyrical about the region's natural splendor.

94

Steinbeck House in Salinas, now a lunch restaurant, where writer John Steinbeck was born in 1902

FESTIVALS
Anti-Steinbeck feeling in Salinas has subsided sufficiently for the town to mount a Steinbeck Festival in early August, with tours, films, lectures, and discussions relating to the author. Most events are based at the National Steinbeck Center (see page 96). Among the region's many other festivals, none is stranger than Half Moon Bay's Art and Pumpkin Festival throughout October.

Steinbeck No writer has had stronger links to the area than Salinas-born John Steinbeck, whose early jobs were as a ranch hand and fruit picker. Much of his work focused on California's forgotten people, such as the migrant farming communities around his hometown and the fish-cannery workers of nearby Monterey.

Of a prolific output during his peak years of the 1930s and early 1940s, one of Steinbeck's best-known books, *The Grapes of Wrath*, dealt with the plight of a Depression-era family arriving in California from the Dust Bowl of Oklahoma in search of the promised land but finding only an exploitative system of agricultural labor. It won the Pulitzer Prize but enraged the state's land barons, who branded Steinbeck a communist. In Salinas he was widely condemned as a traitor to his native town, and for many years, some local libraries refused to stock his titles. By contrast, Salinas now acknowledges the author with an annual festival and the displays of the National Steinbeck Center (see page 96).

Other famous names Long before Steinbeck was born, Robert Louis Stevenson arrived flat broke in Monterey in pursuit of Fanny Osbourne, a married woman from Oakland whom he had met in France; he married her the following year. Although he was in the town for only a few months during 1879, Stevenson was employed by the local newspaper and wrote two perceptive essays, *The Old Pacific Capitol* and *The New Pacific Capitol*, respectively contrasting Monterey's decline with San

Francisco's rise—and tramped the local coastline gaining inspiration for the landscapes which were later to appear in his famed *Treasure Island*.

From 1906, Carmel was home to an infamous, if comparatively short-lived, bohemian community led by romantic poet George Sterling. Many influential writers of the day—including Upton Sinclair, Mary Austin, and Jack London—joined him in what was then an idyllic, unheard-of coastal town. In 1926, Sterling published a biography of a longer-lasting Carmel resident, Robinson Jeffers. Born in Pittsburgh, Jeffers was a graduate in forestry and medicine who published his first volume of poetry in 1912 and moved to Carmel two years later.

Carmel's natural beauty and what Jeffers saw as the earthy purity of the local people kept him there. These things convinced Jeffers to abandon conventional poetry and devote himself to lengthy verses, likened to Greek epics, that used a wild, coastal setting in their explorations of human dilemmas.

Not content with constructing epic poems, Jeffers also constructed an epic dwelling, Tor House, using granite stones hauled up from Carmel Beach.

Henry Miller Given the salacious content of his 1930s novels, *Tropic of Cancer* and *Tropic of Capricorn* (denied publication in the United States until the 1960s), Henry Miller's 17-year presence in Big Sur, beginning in 1944, caused local speculation as to what debauched scenes were taking place in his secluded house.

In fact, other than an awful lot of writing, not much was taking place, although Miller's intensely personal narrative style had attracted fledgling Beat generation authors to him, who in turn became obsessed with Big Sur's landscapes. Miller wrote about the area in 1958's *Big Sur and the Oranges of Hieronymus Bosch*, while Beat author Jack Kerouac who liked its fiction potential but hated Big Sur's isolation loosely used Miller as the inspiration for his 1962 novel, *Big Sur*, a tale of a retired Beat idol seeking peace and seclusion.

ARTICHOKE QUEEN
Just north of Monterey, in Castroville, the self-styled "artichoke capital of the world", Marilyn Monroe was crowned California Artichoke Queen in 1947 at the Artichoke Festival. It is still held each September to celebrate the vegetable that provides the community with its main source of income.

95

Tor House, the Carmel home of Robinson Jeffers, completed in 1919 and occupied by the influential poet until his death in 1962

Seen from the aptly-named Ocean View Boulevard, waves crash against the rocky shoreline of Pacific Grove

OLDENBURG'S HATS
The California Rodeo is amusingly commemorated by *Hat in Three Stages of Landing*, a Claes Oldenburg sculpture in the gardens of Pacific Grove's Community Center (940 N. Main Street).

THOMAS DOAK
A sailor from Boston who jumped ship in then Mexican-owned California in 1816, Thomas Doak became the first U.S. citizen to settle in the region. Before marrying into the wealthy Castro family, Doak painted the reredos of Mission San Juan Bautista in return for room and board.

▶▶ Pacific Grove   90B2

A band of tent-carrying Methodists moved to the northern tip of the Monterey Peninsula in 1875, and the town that became Pacific Grove evolved into a fenced-in enclave of religious devotion and high moral virtue; its anti-alcohol laws were not repealed until 1969.

An abundance of shingle cottages gives this quiet seaside town a homey appeal. Monarch butterflies find Pacific Grove to their liking—tens of thousands of them migrate here from March to November to hang from pine trees (especially plentiful on Ridge Road), forming rippling flags of orange and black.

The **Museum of Natural History**▶ (165 Forest Avenue) has a good display on the butterflies. If visiting on a weekend, round off your tour with a stop at the 1855 **Point Pinos Lighthouse**▶▶ (Asilomor Boulevard, off Lighthouse Avenue; tel: 831/648–3116).

▶ Salinas   90C2

Author John Steinbeck was born in 1902 in Salinas, a down-to-earth town dominated by the agricultural industry and off the beaten tourist track despite being just 18 miles from Monterey. Steinbeck's birthplace and boyhood home at **132 Central Avenue** is now a restaurant but retains much of the appearance of the writer's time; very informal free tours are given during limited periods on weekdays; for details tel: 831/424–2735. A room of the **John Steinbeck Public Library**▶ (tel: 831/758–7311) displays photographs and manuscripts relating to the prize-winning writer, who featured the town and its problems in many of his books. Much more about Steinbeck, and his uncomfortable relationship with Salinas, can be found amid the interactive exhibits and temporary displays of the **National Steinbeck Center** (1 Main Street; tel: 831/796–3833), which is also the hub of the Steinbeck Festival, staged each August.

For many locals, however, Salinas is much less about John Steinbeck than the **California Rodeo**▶▶ (tel: 800/771–8807 or 831/775–3100), four days of ropin' and ridin' staged each July at the Rodeo Stadium on the northern edge of town.

Tear yourself away from the scintillating coastal scenery for even half a day and you will discover natural sights of no less beauty just a few miles inland, in the foothills of the Santa Cruz Mountains and in the untamed territory above Big Sur.

It is here, too, that you will encounter the southernmost strands of the coastal redwood trees; though slightly smaller than their counterparts farther north, they are still wide enough and tall enough to be the highlight of any backcountry ramble.

Wilderness The region's major parks are described elsewhere, but many smaller state- and locally-run tracts make the wilderness accessible. There is a particularly strong grouping close to the hamlet of La Honda, on State Road 84, between Half Moon Bay and Santa Cruz. The best of the bunch here is **Portola State Park►** (tel: 650/948–9089), a deep, rugged canyon lined by redwoods and firs, with trails leading up to the chaparral-covered higher slopes, and others winding through the thicker vegetation carpeting the forest floor.

Camping and hiking Thirty miles south of Monterey, Highway 1 passes through part of the redwood forest making up a large section of **Pfeiffer Big Sur State Park►►** (tel: 831/667–2315). There is an excellent program of ranger-led walks and hikes here, and views of the surf-pounded coast that are better than those from the coastal highway.

The main base for camping in the Big Sur area, the park—named after a family who settled the area from the 1860s, a time when Monterey was a four-day horse-ride away—is rarely short of customers, but the crowds can be left far behind as you follow one of the hiking trails, some of which cross into the Ventana Wilderness, a region of oak-cloaked gorges, scrublands, and even a few bristle-coned pines, which in turn feeds into the immense Los Padres National Forest.

Before setting out on foot, however, give due respect to the region's notoriously variable weather and remember that chilly fogs are a regular occurrence. It rains a lot, too, and if you get caught in a downpour, some solace might be found in the knowledge that the redwoods cannot grow without at least 40 inches of rainfall a year.

PICK-YOUR-OWN PRODUCE
The pick-your-own produce of the rich farmlands around Santa Cruz will improve the quality of the best-stocked picnic basket. Depending on season, large and juicy apples, strawberries, or raspberries will be among the crops that can be stuffed into your bag for a very modest sum. Look for the roadside signs, or drop into the Santa Cruz Visitor Council (701 Front Street; tel: 800/833–3494) for the free Country Crossroads brochure.

A park ranger introduces the intricacies of coastal ecology to youngsters at Monterey State Beach, just north of the peninsula

Drive

The Monterey area

See map on page 90.

From Monterey, drive 18 miles east on State Road 68 to Salinas.
Birthplace of the writer John Steinbeck and the home of the California Rodeo, **Salinas** is described on page 96.

Drive 15 miles north from Salinas on State Road 68 to San Juan Bautista.
With a impressive collection of 19th-century adobe buildings, **San Juan Bautista▶▶** gives a distinct taste of a bygone California (see page 100).

Drive west from San Juan Bautista on State Road 156, turn north onto Highway 101, and after three miles turn west on State Road 129 for Watsonville.
Famed for its apples, strawberries, and mushrooms, the small town of **Watsonville▶** has several streets of well-preserved Victorian homes.

Drive south from Watsonville, joining Highway 1 to reach Moss Landing.
A weather-beaten fishing village dwarfed by a gigantic power station, **Moss Landing** provides access to the **Elkhorn Slough Reserve▶** (1700 Elkhorn Road; tel: 831/728– 2822) where a four-mile boardwalk crosses wildlife-rich mud flats and marshes.

From Moss Landing, continue south on Highway 1 for 10 miles to Marina.
The sand dunes of **Marina▶** hold hardy shrubs and wildflowers, and hang-gliders soar overhead.

From Marina, continue south on Highway 1, turning west at Monterey for Pacific Grove to join the 17-Mile Scenic Drive toll road.
The **17-Mile Scenic Drive▶▶** loops through the **Monterey Peninsula**, passing the hilly peninsula's most photogenic sections.

Leave the 17-Mile Scenic Drive following signs for Carmel.
The pretty and affluent town of **Carmel** is described on page 92.

From Carmel, drive three miles north on Highway 1 to return to Monterey.

View along the 17-Mile Scenic Drive

In his 1945 novel Cannery Row, *John Steinbeck described the mean streets of Monterey at a time when the town—set on an impressive bay—was the world's busiest sardine processing center, annually canning 250,000 tons of the greasy creatures until stocks were fished to exhaustion.*

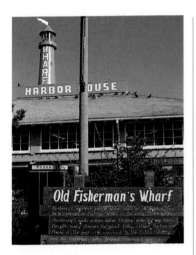

Fisherman's Wharf, Monterey

The former fish factories of Cannery Row are now occupied by trinket shops aimed at the town's 3 million annual visitors. Close by, Fisherman's Wharf, where ocean-going schooners once berthed, is full of seafood restaurants and snack bars.

History Make a short walk inland from these tourist traps, however, and you will discover well-preserved evidence of Monterey's crucial role in California's past. Settled by the Spanish in 1770, Monterey became capital of Mexican California in 1822, and gave birth to California's first state government in 1849.

New England seafarers who settled in Monterey adapted much of the town's Spanish Colonial architecture to what became the "Monterey style," typified by the 1835 **Larkin House▶** (corner of Jefferson Street and Calle Principal), a redwood-framed, porched adobe.

This antique-stuffed structure, and many other buildings nearby, comprise **Monterey State Historic Park▶▶▶** (20 Custom House Plaza; tel: 831/649–7118. *Open* daily, hours vary. *Admission: inexpensive*) a 7-acre area around Custom House Plaza.

If the magnitude of Monterey's 19th-century glories as a seaport still hasn't sunk in, tour the excellent **Maritime Museum and History Center▶▶▶** (5 Custom House Plaza; tel: 831/373–2469. *Open* daily 10–5. *Admission: inexpensive*) opposite Custom House Plaza.

Monterey's literary associations continue at the memento-filled **Robert Louis Stevenson House▶▶**

❏ The three-day Monterey Pop Festival in 1967 was the first large outdoor rock festival. It starred Jimi Hendrix, Janis Joplin, and local psychedelic stalwarts The Grateful Dead and Jefferson Airplane. ❏

(530 Houston Street), where the writer lived in the fall of 1879.

One place of absolutely no historical significance that should not be missed is the $40 million **Monterey Bay Aquarium▶▶▶** (886 Cannery Row; tel: 831/648–4888. *Open* Sep–May 10–6, Jun–Aug 9:30–6. *Admission: expensive*), a state-of-the-art facility cogently displaying and describing the ecology and the creatures of the ocean. Within a hundred galleries that replicate local underwater habitats lurk everything from octopuses to anchovies and seahorses to sharks.

A MYSTERY MAMMAL

The creature washed up on a Santa Cruz beach in 1925 was nearly 50 feet long, with its body tapering to a finlike appendage and with what looked like an elephant's foot sticking from its neck. One expert claimed the foul-smelling beast to be a plesiosaurus—a marine species believed to have become extinct 65 million years ago—and suggested it had been preserved by glacial ice. However, an official explanation held that the creature was a rare type of North Pacific whale, but this is still disputed.

▶▶ San Juan Bautista   90C2

Being an important stagecoach stop promised a rosy future for San Juan Bautista in the mid-1800s, but missing out on the railroad a few years later condemned the town to stagnation—and enabled many of its earliest buildings to survive intact into the present.

The town, three miles east of Highway 101, began in 1797 with one of the largest of California's missions, **Mission San Juan Bautista▶▶** (2nd Street at Mariposa Street; tel: 831/623–4528), in use ever since. **San Juan Bautista State Historic Park▶▶** (2nd Street; tel: 831/623–4881) has several 19th-century adobe structures, including the 1840 Castro House, the two-story Plaza Hotel, and the Plaza Stables' stagecoach memorabilia.

▶▶▶ Santa Cruz   90B3

Highway 1 and Highway 17, 74 miles south of San Francisco
Scores of congenial bars and restaurants, 30 miles of beaches, and a population spanning all income levels,

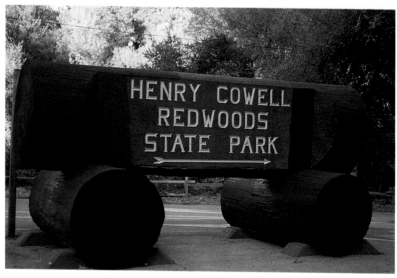

A sign points the way to Henry Cowell Redwoods State Park, where the tallest redwood tree reaches 285 feet. The park was once part of the ranch of Henry Cowell, who developed local limestone deposits and died in 1903

age groups, and political persuasions make Santa Cruz one of California's most instantly likable towns.

Since 1904 its major landmark has been the **Boardwalk▶▶** (tel: 831/426–7433), a beachside amusement strip with a vintage carousel, a 1924 roller coaster, and tacky charm in abundance.

Other interesting points of call are the **Surfing Museum▶▶** (in the lighthouse on W. Cliff Drive; tel: 831/429–3429), with surfers practicing in the ocean below, and the **City Museum of Natural History▶** (tel: 831/429–3773).

Do not expect to tour the **Santa Cruz Mission▶**: founded in 1791, it succumbed to disuse and earthquakes, and only a dull half-size model of it can be seen (at 126 High Street). And do not expect to find real mystery at the **Mystery Spot▶** (Branciforte Drive; tel: 831/423–8897), a patch of forest where distortions of perspective are cleverly disguised.

Anyone drawn to the Central Coast by the stereotypical picture-postcard view of sun-drenched Californian beach life is in for a surprise. You will find more sea lions than surfers, an ocean that is usually too cold and too treacherous to swim in, and a shoreline that has more coves and tidal pools than tanning torsos.

Natural beauty Few of the protected parks and beaches along Highway 1 will disappoint; those mentioned below reveal the Central Coast—whether with wildlife, geology, or classic coastal views—at its natural best.

Eighteen miles north of Santa Cruz, **Año Nuevo State Reserve▶▶▶** (Highway 1; tel: 650/879–0227) was set up in 1958 to protect the elephant seal, a sea mammal weighing up to three tons that had been hunted almost to extinction for its oil-rich blubber. Between December and March, thousands of the creatures waddle ashore here, and the males indulge in macho shows of strength prior to mating with 50 or so females. To join the large crowds of humans observing the noisy rituals, reserve a place on the three-hour ranger-led tour (tel: 800/444–7275).

Just south of Carmel, surf crashes against six miles of oddly shaped granite bluffs protruding from **Point Lobos State Reserve▶▶** (Highway 1; tel: 831/624–4909). Sharp eyesight might reveal sea otters feeding from the offshore kelp forest, while sea lions honk from Sea Lion Rocks. Spare a thought for the Monterey cypress tree, a species unique to the area that sprouts on granite peaks only to spend its life tormented by ocean winds.

In Big Sur, turn off Highway 1 about two miles south of Julia Pfeiffer Burns State Park (not to be confused with the inland Pfeiffer Big Sur State Park) for **Pfeiffer Beach▶**, whose sands are sheltered by an extraordinary multicolored rock formation situated just offshore.

Follow Pfeiffer Beach south and you cross into **Andrew Molera State Park▶▶** (Highway 1; tel: 831/667–2315) set around the lagoon marking the mouth of the Big Sur River. Sixteen miles of hiking trails run through the sycamores and maples.

ELEPHANT SEAL BIRTH
Once fertilized by a successful male, the egg of a female elephant seal does not move to the mother's uterus for between 10 and 14 weeks. This delay, part of an 8-month pregnancy, enables pups to be born on land rather than at sea, where their chances of survival would be far worse.

A section of Point Lobos State Reserve, bestowing protection to 1,250 acres of untamed coast just south of Carmel

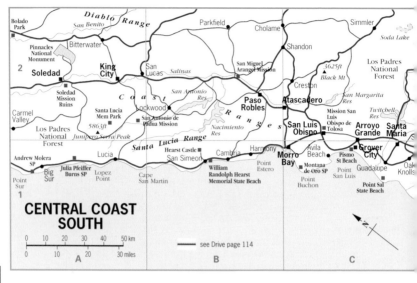

Oil platform off the California coast

ENDLESS BEAUTY Passing from the northern into the southern section of the Central Coast does not bring any immediate changes: crashing waves and jagged bluffs, and occasional quiet, secluded beaches, continue to dominate the view from Highway 1.

As a manmade introduction to the region, however, it is hard to beat Hearst Castle, a monument to incredible wealth—and incredible architectural aspirations—that sits dreamily on a mountain slope above the village of San Simeon, just beyond Big Sur.

San Luis Obispo grew up around one of the area's several Spanish missions and now draws most of its energy from a student population.

For picturesque settings, though, it is smaller towns like Cambria that rule the day, even if the numerous artists and artisans who have populated them are locked in permanent battle with the souvenir shops that are steadily encroaching into their serene, wooded valleys.

One of the richest and also one of the nicest looking towns in California is Santa Barbara, whose mission-style architecture enhances what is already an enviable setting beside a palm-fringed beach. Here the hedonistic southern California beach life announces itself for the first time on the Central Coast.

Thirty miles from Santa Barbara is Ventura, the region's southernmost town, which is only just spared the sprawl of Los Angeles. It is notable for a fine set of sands and a historic quarter, and provides an embarkation point for the Channel Islands National Park. This consists of volcanic islands free of human settlement that share this section of the ocean with oil rigs: a symbol of the Central Coast's struggle between commercial and ecological interests.

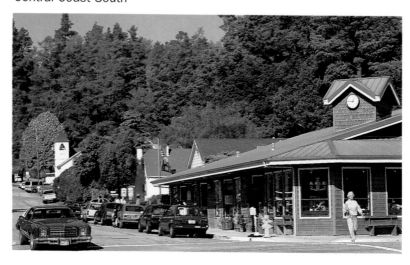

In sedate Cambria, shops offer a mix of Hearst Castle souvenirs and handicrafts produced by local artisans

JAMES DEAN'S LAST RIDE
Forty-seven miles east of San Luis Obispo, at the intersection of State Roads 41 and 46, 24-year-old teen idol James Dean was killed when his Porsche careered off the road on September 30, 1955. The actual site of the intersection has changed since Dean's last journey, but a memorial to the actor stands outside the Cholame post office.

A MISSION GHOST
On more than one occasion, guards at the Fort Hunter-Liggett military base have drawn their weapons only to see the suspected intruder vanish before their eyes. The apparition is thought to be the ghost of a headless Native American woman who roams the grounds of Mission San Antonio de Padua on horseback searching for her head, which her furious husband tore from her body as a punishment for her infidelity.

► **Cambria**   *102B1*
Great fun to explore despite its contrived Olde Worlde atmosphere and preponderance of half-timbered gift shops, Cambria lies about six miles south of Hearst Castle. It splits its time between pandering to tourists and providing the rural serenity that has inspired a community of artists, whose work can be seen in a dozen browse-worthy galleries.

Friendly and affordable restaurants are also a feature of the pine-shrouded town, and culinary overindulgence can be remedied by a lengthy stroll along the town's magnificent beaches: a scene of picturesque coves, broad sands, a large sea otter refuge, and seals sharing waves with surfers.

Just outside Cambria, **Nit Wit Ridge►** (on Hillcrest Drive) provides an anarchic counterpoint to Hearst Castle (see page 109). Beginning life in 1928 as a one-room shack, it became a wild and unwieldly mansion after generous applications of cement, seashells, glass, old car parts, and other bits and pieces and ultimately provided an unusual (not to mention eccentric) home for its enigmatic, unique creator.

► **Carpinteria**   *103E2*
Named by Spanish arrivals impressed with the woodworking skills of the local Chumash Indians, Carpinteria is a quiet coastal town between Ventura and Santa Barbara. It is worth a pause for **Carpinteria State Beach►** (tel: 805/684-2811) with its beckoning sands and—thanks to an offshore reef—some of the safest swimming waters along the entire coast.

► **Harmony**   *102B1*
Blink and you will miss Harmony, a minuscule privately owned town just inland from Cambria. Nearly all of its 18-strong population are either glassblowers, potters, or jewelry-makers, who sell their wares from roadside shops. In the fields around Harmony, Arabian horses are bred and trained on ranches still owned by the Hearst family.

▶ King City   102A2

There is a very worthwhile detour to be made from Highway 1 along the Nacimiento-Fergusson Road, which cuts dramatically across Plaskett Ridge in the Santa Lucia Mountains toward King City, a speck-on-the-map community on Highway 101.

Twenty miles southwest of King City stands **Mission San Antonio de Padua**▶▶ (tel: 831/385–4478), one of the most isolated and most evocative of the Californian missions. Authentic restoration of the buildings makes it easy to appreciate the mission lifestyle, but it is the secluded setting, in a quiet river valley, that really makes the place special. Oddly, although the mission sits miles from any urbanized area, it is inside the Fort Hunter-Liggett military base and you must go through a security check at the gates. If you have the chance, visit the second weekend in June, when the mission celebrates the feast day of San Antonio.

▶ Morro Bay   103C1

Some agreeable seafood restaurants cook up the daily catch of the fishing fleet in Morro Bay, a moderately interesting coastal town whose best feature is the volcanic hunk of Morro Rock, a near-vertical slab rising to 576 feet little more than a pebble's throw offshore, the last visible link in a chain of nine volcanic rocks between here and San Luis Obispo, nine miles south.

Morro Rock is a protected nesting ground for peregrine falcons, and climbing it—once a popular local pastime—is prohibited. You can visit the **Bay Aquarium**▶ (595 Embarcadero; tel: 805/772-7647), which holds minor marine displays and nurses injured otters and seals.

Just south of the town, Morro Bay State Park stretches around the flat coastal marshlands, home to an abundance of great blue herons. The ecological significance of the area is described at the **Museum of Natural History**▶▶ (Morro Bay State Park Road; tel: 805/772-2694) opposite the park's entrance.

105

Sailing craft in Morro Bay are dwarfed by the huge volcanic extrusion known as Morro Rock

Whether you are looking for palm-fringed beaches covered with bronzing flesh or you want to seek out secluded coves and spend hours discovering the secret life of the tidal pool, the southern section of the Central Coast has something to please.

CENTRAL COAST FISHING
Albacore, salmon, and rock cod are among the species that make the Central Coast a happy hunting ground for anglers. Fishing piers are plentiful, and rare is the coastal town that does not also offer guided fishing trips or run specialist sportfishing excursions to do battle with marlin. Prices for guided trips start at around $30 per day.

North–south split The coast has two distinct faces north and south of Point Conception (although the name has been anglicized, the local post office still uses the original Spanish form "Concepcion"). To the north, between San Luis Obispo and Santa Barbara, the predominantly rocky coast faces west, and fogs are prone to roll in off the ocean and fill the inland valleys. South of Point Conception, the coast faces south, and the beaches are generally better suited to sunbathing and surfing.

After you sample the opulence of the multimillionaire's castle (see page 109), the **William Randolph Hearst Memorial State Beach▶▶** (tel: 805/927–2035), close to San Simeon, is the ideal spot to rediscover life's simpler pleasures: a rustic fishing pier juts out from the quiet sands, which are fringed by eucalyptus trees and shaded picnic tables.

To the north The 1874 Piedras Blancas Lighthouse marks the edge of Big Sur (see page 92) and the start of the northern section of the Central Coast. A few miles in the other direction, the sands of **San Simeon State Beach▶** (tel: 805/927–2035) are broad but busy, especially in summer when the campground is usually full.

Heading south Six miles beyond Morro Bay (see page 105), the Estero Bay area has a trio of rewarding stops. You can swim at peaceful **Morro Strand State Beach▶**

One of several quiet beaches close to Morro Bay

(tel: 805/772–2560) (though there are no lifeguards), and the **Los Osas Oaks State Reserve▶** protects one of the longest surviving strands of handsome coastal oaks.

The biggest natural draw around Estero Bay, however, is **Montana de Oro State Park▶ ▶** (State Park Road; tel: 805/772–7434) whose Spanish name means "Mountain of Gold," and derives from a springtime bloom of wildflowers that turn the park's hillsides into a bright carpet of yellows and oranges.

The park's 8,000 acres encompass sandy beaches, tidal pools, and surf-pounded cliffs—around which seals, sea lions, and sea otters are commonly sighted—and reach inland to raccoon-infested river canyons, through which deer descend to spend the evening grazing on the coastal plain. Several trails snake through the most scenic sections of the park, and a four-mile loop trail climbs Valencia Point, a trek repaid by a stirring view of the coast—fogs permitting.

With a livelier time in mind Head for **Avila Beach▶**, 10 miles west of San Luis Obispo, whose beachside boardwalk is lined with bars and snack stands and where scores of surfers challenge the waves.

The surfers' presence helps make Avila Beach relatively lively at night—a striking contrast to sedate **Pismo Beach▶**, a coastal town a few miles south along Highway 101. Pismo State Beach is worth a look, though—it is well known to Californians for its Pismo clams, a succulent crustacean that has been hunted almost out of existence.

Magnificent sand dunes These are another feature of Pismo State Beach and they reach south, almost obliterating the diminutive community of Oceano. Propelled by wind and wave action, the dunes are ever moving and belie their forlorn appearance by performing an important ecological service, allowing numerous species of coarse vegetation to thrive, and providing a habitat for brown pelicans and California least terns, among other creatures.

The tallest dune reaches almost 500 feet high, but the most famous dune is the one where moviemaker Cecil B. de Mille buried the set of his 1923 film, *The Ten Commandments*. Since 1990, excavation has been underway in an attempt to salvage the evidence of one of Hollywood's greatest cinematic excesses. The set includes three-story-high pharaoh statues and the ten five-tonne statues that lined the film's Avenue of Sphinxes. As parts of the plaster-and-clay set become exposed above the dunes, they are steadily dissolved by storms and wind-propelled sand.

SANTA BARBARA BEACHES
A set of state beaches occupies the approaches to Santa Barbara. Thirty miles north of the town, Gaviota State Beach spreads across either side of Highway 101 and is enticing less for its sands than its trail inland, winding to Gaviota Hot Springs. Palm-lined Refugio State Beach, 12 miles ahead, is a nicer place to catch some rays and is linked by foot and bike paths to El Capitan State Beach, where seals and sea lions bask offshore alongside surfers.

107

CHANNEL ISLANDS NATIONAL PARK
Five islands off the coast between Ventura and Santa Barbara comprise the Channel Islands National Park, whose unique plant and bird life are staging a comeback after being devastated by California's first white settlers, who trampled over the islands hunting sea lions and seals. The islands have no tourist facilities and can be explored only on marked hiking trails. Trips are run by the Nature Conservancy, based in Santa Barbara (tel: 805/962–9111), and from Spinnaker Drive in Ventura (see page 115).

THE FIRST MOTEL
In 1925, a San Luis Obispo hotel owner renamed his property, at 2223 Monterey Street, the "Milestone Motel," thereby creating the world's first motel. As the affordable, mass-produced automobile changed the travel habits of millions, motels sprang up beside every busy highway and along the main approach routes to towns, becoming the most popular form of budget accommodation for travelers on the move.

The elegant shops of Ojai suggest the town's popularity with the well-heeled Californian weary of big-city life

THE MADONNA INN
Impossible to miss, beside Highway 101, San Luis Obispo's shocking pink Madonna Inn offers food and lodging to anyone who wants to put their tolerance of kitsch excesses to the test: the waterfall flushing the coffee shop's men's urinal is just the appetizer for 100 individually themed rooms.

▶ **Ojai** *103E2*

With its tennis courts, golf courses, luxury hillside homes, and a music festival, Ojai (pronounced "O-hi") has all the trappings of a rich country retreat but enjoys a more enduring reputation as a place where the mystically minded seek enlightenment.

The idyllic cvalley that the town occupies has long promised a spiritual Shangri-La (and did indeed provide the setting for Shangri-La in the 1937 film, *Lost Horizon*). The well-stocked library of the **Krishnamurti Foundation**▶ (1130 MacAndrew Road; tel: 805/646–4948)

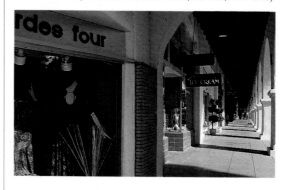

commemorates an Indian mystic who lectured here in the 1920s, while the similarly Eastern-influenced **Krotona Institute of Theosophy**▶ (on Krotona Hill; tel: 805/646–2653) also has a library packed with esoteric tomes. The landscaped grounds afford exquisite views of the valley's orange and avocado groves, and of the mountains that encircle the town.

Less ethereal matters are dealt with by the **Ojai Valley Historical Museum**▶ (109 S. Montgomery Street; tel: 805/640–1390). Housed in a former fire house, the museum is filled with entertaining paraphernalia.

▶▶ **San Luis Obispo** *102C2*

The 1772 **Mission San Luis Obispo de Tolosa**▶▶ (751 Palm Street; tel: 805/543–6850) sits at the heart of likable San Luis Obispo, 12 miles from the coast but within easy striking distance of Hearst Castle. If you are only passing through, try to do so on a Thursday evening, when the **Farmer's Market**▶▶ brings the whole town to Higuera Street to feast on barbecue.

The mission is not the most striking in California, but the historic plaza on which it stands is also the site of the **County Historical Museum**▶ (969 Monterey Street; tel: 805/543–0638), where the community's past is put on show, and the **Art Center**▶ (1020 Broad Street), determined to raise the profile of local artists.

Dominated today by the agricultural students of nearby Cal Poly, who often gather around the art-deco Fremont Theater (on Santa Rosa Street), San Luis Obispo in the late 1800s housed a large community of Chinese who were employed in railroad construction: the **Ah Louis Store**▶ (800 Palm Street; tel: 805/543–4332. *Open* irregular hours), now a gift shop, is a rare reminder of their presence.

In California, only Disneyland attracts more visitors than Hearst Castle, the former part-time home of publishing mogul William Randolph Hearst. Set on a hilltop above the village of San Simeon, Hearst Castle was built (but never officially completed) at an estimated cost, at today's prices, of $400 million.

Given the *San Francisco Examiner* by his father in 1887, Hearst went on to head a media empire that spanned newspapers, magazines, radio stations, and film studios. Aside from becoming phenomenally wealthy, Hearst also had incredible power to influence: most notoriously, he fanned the nationalistic fervor that led to the Spanish-American War in 1898.

After work began on Hearst Castle in 1919, architect Julia Morgan spent the next 28 years struggling with Hearst's constantly changing ideas and the five-ton wagonloads of Flemish tapestries, French fireplaces, Italian ceilings, Persian carpets, candelabras, and coats-of-arms Hearst collected from the great homes of Europe. Visiting the castle, it is impossible not to be struck by the incongruity of a would-be medieval palace sprouting on the rugged slopes of a California coastal mountain, or be less than awed by the sheer scale and extravagance of the place.

It is also easy to imagine the likes of Charlie Chaplin, Greta Garbo, and Clark Gable (friends of Hearst's long-time companion, actress Marion Davies) lurking amid the million-dollar classical statuary or admiring the lions and cheetahs that once roamed the grounds, enclosed in the world's largest privately owned zoo.

An informative visitor center lies at the foot of the hill on which the castle stands, and is also the starting point for tours.

HEARST'S LOSS; CALIFORNIA'S GAIN
Plagued in his later years by debts and astronomic tax bills, Hearst died in 1951 (ten years after his life had been the subject of Orson Welles's film *Citizen Kane*), and six years later the Hearst family donated the castle to the state in return for a $50 million tax write-off.

109

GUIDED TOURS
Three separate 90-minute guided tours visit different sections of the castle, while a fourth tour concentrates on the lavish gardens. All tours begin from the visitor center next to Highway 1. Reservations are essential, especially in summer (tel: 800/444–4445 reservations; 805/927–2020 general information. *Admission: expensive*).

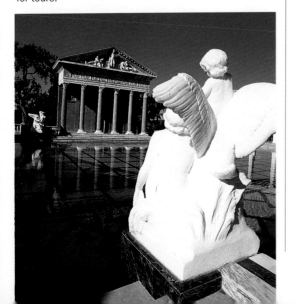

The Neptune Pool, the memorable first sight of opulent Hearst Castle for visitors arriving on guided tours

Some are beautiful and some are just ruins, but although they don't have many religious or historical treasures, all of California's 21 Spanish missions (plus five smaller branch missions, or asistencia), established between 1769 and 1823, offer a glimpse into the region's past.

JUNIPERO SERRA

Junípero Serra, the leader of Spain's Sacred Expedition into California, was born in 1713 on the Spanish island of Majorca and arrived in Mexico as a Franciscan missionary in 1749. Serra founded nine of California's 21 missions, and died at Carmel Mission in 1791. In the 1980s, the Vatican's decision to canonize Serra became a controversial issue within California, where many regard him as a major contributor to the destruction of native cultures.

San Diego Mission, founded in 1769, was the first Spanish mission in California, though poor irrigation led to its relocation

Historical significance Beginning at San Diego in the south and finishing with Sonoma in the north, the missions (each one a day's horse-ride from the next) played a crucial role in the development of the state—but you should be selective about which ones you visit if you want to discover more than a few dusty ruins beside the highway.

The southern portion of the Central Coast has some of the better examples: Mission Santa Barbara maintains a majestic presence in the town that grew around it; Mission San Antonio de Padua, near King City, survives in moody isolation; and Mission La Purisima Concepcion, near Lompoc, is so comprehensively re-created that you cannot fail to leave it without gaining some insight into the trials and tribulations of the mission times.

Origins The missions began when Spanish possession of what was then undeveloped Alta (or Upper) California was perceived as being under threat from Russia, active to the north, and the European settlers becoming established on North America's east coast.

The Spanish king dispatched a missionary party—the Sacred Expedition, led by Father Junípero Serra—to establish a series of missions across the territory. Their intention was to convert the indigenous population to Christianity while gaining their loyalty in any future colonial conflict; several missions were constructed side by side with a presidio—or fort—in which Spanish troops were barracked.

Effects on the native people Besides learning the rudiments of Spanish, the indigenous people were supposedly taught skills such as farming, building, blacksmithery, weaving, and winemaking. In reality their labor was exploited to further the wealth and self-sufficiency of the missions, many of which had vast landholdings and many head of cattle.

Few solid facts of mission life have been recorded, although reports of torture and other abuses of the neophytes (as the mission Native Americans were known) have greatly tarnished the benevolent façade that the Spanish sought to maintain.

It is certainly true that many Native Americans resisted the lure of beads and brightly colored clothes, used to tempt them into the missions, and in some cases they attacked the mission buildings.

Eventually, the mission system all but destroyed California's native cultures and caused the death of many thousands (thought to be half the indigenous population) through contact with European diseases, such as measles, to which Native Americans lacked immunity.

Some 88,000 Native Americans had been baptized and around 24,000 married in Catholic ceremonies by the time ownership of California switched to Mexico and the missions underwent secularization at the behest of the Californios (California-born people of Spanish or Mexican descent).

In theory, the neophytes were then allowed to live free, independent lives, but in fact many became the servants of the Californios, who grew rich by cultivating the former mission land which they usurped in its entirety, ignoring the Mexican ruling that half should go to natives.

Although the mission churches were usually maintained to serve as parish churches, other mission buildings—such as the workshops, priests' living quarters, and the outbuildings where the neophytes slept—were put to general public use, and during the early years of U.S. rule in California, some were functioning as saloons and hotels.

The mission buildings Always simple structures of tiled roofs and stuccoed adobe lightly decorated with Moorish designs, the missions endured earthquakes as well as decades of neglect, and not until 1903 was there any concerted effort to protect and restore their buildings.

All the missions are open to the public and each has a museum displaying at least a few original objects; some missions are still used by the Franciscan order of monks. Comparatively few original features remain, but the small mission chapels, often bathed in candlelight and decorated by frescoes painted by the neophytes, are charged with atmosphere.

Strolling the grounds can be rewarding, too, both for the well-kept gardens and for the somber feelings evoked by the cemeteries, where thousands of neophytes lie in unmarked graves beside ostentatious markers to their Spanish masters.

Mission Santa Barbara is one of the most impressive of California's missions

SERRA'S SUCCESSOR
Following the death of Junípero Serra, Fermín Francisco de Lasuén was chosen as his successor. Serra had envisaged the missions declining as the Catholicized native became self-supporting, but Fermín oversaw an expansion and strengthening of the mission system and replaced the simple churches with stronger, grander structures—many of which still stand today.

Walk

A tour around Santa Barbara

Begin at the County Courthouse, 1100 Anacapa Street.
The architecturally magnificent **County Courthouse** is described on page 113.

Walk southeast from the County Courthouse along Santa Barbara Street, turning right onto Cañon Perdido for El Presidio State Historic Park.
Several buildings form the **El Presidio State Historic Park**: on the north side of Cañon Perdido, the **El Presidio Chapel** is a detailed re-creation of a mission-era Spanish chapel; and across the street, the 1788 **El Cuartel adobe** is the second-oldest surviving building in California.

Return to Santa Barbara Street, walking one block southeast to De La Guerra Street for the Historical Museum.
The displays of the **Historical Museum** fill the gap between Santa Barbara's Spanish origins and its emergence as an affluent U.S. town.

Walk southwest along De La Guerra Street, turning right onto State Street and continuing to the Museum of Art.
On the corner of Anapamu Street,

Santa Barbara County Courthouse

the **Museum of Art** spreads over three floors and features many major American and European names.

From the Art Museum, walk two blocks northeast on Anapamu Street to return to the County Courthouse.

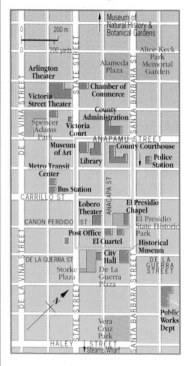

❏ Heritage celebrations make the largest and most enjoyable festivals along the southern section of the Central Coast. The biggest bash is Santa Barbara's weeklong Old Spanish Days held in August; the following month, Solvang remembers its Scandinavian founders with the traditional events of Danish Days. Also in August, the 11-day Ventura County Fair attracts upwards of 270,000 people to events that span cattle shows, flower displays, local arts and crafts exhibits, and (non-alcoholic) drinking contests, in a waterfront setting. ❏

112

▶▶▶ Santa Barbara 103E2

In a wealthy and conservative but appealingly sybaritic community, Santa Barbara's low-lying red roofs poke through thickly wooded green hillsides, the town having rebuilt itself in the image of California's missions after being flattened by an earthquake in 1925.

Ironically, **Mission Santa Barbara**▶▶▶ (2201 Laguna Street; tel: 805/682–4713. *Open* daily 9–5, closed Easter, Thanksgiving, Dec 25. *Admission: inexpensive*) is architecturally far grander than the average mission, with classically influenced twin towers and columns. Restored rooms and a museum record the mission's heyday, and an atmospheric cemetery holds the remains of 4,000 Chumash.

Nearby, displays at the **Museum of Natural History**▶ (2599 Puesta del Sol Road; tel: 805/682–4711) give a thorough background on the Chumash tribe, and five miles of walking trails weave around diverse native Californian vegetation at the **Botanical Gardens**▶▶ (1212 Mission Canyon Road; tel: 805/682–4726).

Except for the mission, Santa Barbara's historical sights are concentrated downtown. The jewel is the 1929 **County Courthouse**▶▶▶ (1100 Anacapa Street; tel: 805/962–6464. *Open* Mon–Fri 8–5, Sat–Sun 9–5, closed Dec 25. *Admission free*), whose architecture embodies the exaggerated mission style that Santa Barbara's architects adopted after the 1925 earthquake.

SOLVANG
Founded by Danes in 1911, Solvang's thatched roofs, wooden storks, and pseudo- windmills are intended to convince tourists that a piece of Denmark has been transported to California. Any Dane visiting today would struggle to hold back the laughter, but the village does make an enjoyable interlude between Santa Barbara and San Luis Obispo, if only to discover that Danish pastries prepared to traditional recipes are much nicer than the sugar-saturated imitations sold elsewhere.

Stearns Wharf, built as the base for Santa Barbara's commercial fishing fleet in 1872

113

Fine Tunisian tilework and outstanding murals are among the courthouse's decorative features; take the elevator to the top of the **El Mirador bell tower**▶▶ for a view over the town. Within a few strides stand a couple of 18th-century adobe buildings and the State Historic Park (123 E. Cañon Perdido Street; tel: 805/965–0093), where several Spanish military buildings are being renovated; the **Historical Museum**▶ (136 E. De La Guerra; tel: 805/966–1601) is another rewarding call.

A mile west of downtown, many people jog and skate beside the broad Santa Barbara beaches, which center on 19th-century Stearns Wharf. Here gift shops and seafood eateries are joined by the Nature Conservancy, with information on the Channel Islands National Park.

SANTA PAULA'S OIL
Twelve miles east of Ventura, Santa Paula's California Oil Museum (1001 E Main Street; tel: 805/933–0076) explains oil production with computer simulations and a working model of an oil rig. There is little, though, to explain why offshore drilling is among the state's most sensitive topics, not least in Santa Barbara, where an offshore spill in 1969 devastated local wildlife.

Drive

The reconstructed version of Mission La Purisima Concepcion

The Santa Ynez Valley

See map on pages 102–103

From Santa Barbara, drive 10 miles north on SR 154, turning right along the twisting Painted Cave Road for the Chumash Painted Cave.
Brilliantly colored abstract designs, dating from AD 1000 and used in rituals by the Chumash people, can be glimpsed through a screen at the **Chumash Painted Cave**▶ ▶ (tel: 805/968–3294).

Return to SR 154 and continue north, crossing the San Marcos Pass and descending into the Santa Ynez Valley; after 26 miles turn left onto SR 246 for Santa Ynez.
In Santa Ynez, the **Valley Historical Society Museum**▶ (tel: 805/688–7889) records the 19th-century settlement of the valley. At the **Gainey Vineyard**▶ (3950 E SR 246, Santa Ynez; tel: 805/688–0558) and the **Santa Ynez Winery**▶ (tel: 805/688–8381) you can sample the wines that have made the valley famous among wine drinkers.

From Santa Ynez, continue for three miles on SR 246 to Solvang.
The Danish features of **Solvang** are described on page 113.

From Solvang, drive 10 miles north on Ballard Canyon Road, passing the hamlet of Ballard, for Los Olivos.

In 1975, the **Firestone Vineyard**▶ (tel: 805/688–3940) in Los Olivos was the first to use local grapes in the wine-making process.

From Los Olivos, drive three miles north on SR 154 and turn south onto Highway 101, continuing for six miles to Buellton.
Buellton is the site of **Pea Soup Andersen's**, a California legend for the pea soup first offered to travelers in the 1920's.

Leave Buellton on SR 246, driving west for 17 miles to Mission La Purisima Concepcion.
Founded in 1787, **Mission La Purisima Concepcion's**▶ ▶ (Mission Gate Road; tel: 805/733–3713) original buildings have long been destroyed, but detailed reconstructions make this the most authentic-looking mission site in the state.

*From the mission, join Highway 1 and drive 26 miles east to the intersection with Highway 101, then take the side road to **Las Cruces Hot Springs.***
At the end of a short foot trail, there are two geothermal springs, Las Cruces Hot Springs▶ (see page 115).

Continue east on Highway 101, passing Refugio and El Capitan state beaches (see page 107) on the 35-mile drive back to Santa Barbara.

▶▶▶ Ventura 103E2

US 101, 28 miles SE of Santa Barbara
(70 miles NW of Los Angeles)

Mainly concerned with farming and industry, and blighted by a large oil refinery, Ventura looks better once you locate the town's two-mile-long beach.

There is more to enjoy on foot in the historic area of Old San Buenaventura, which surrounds the Spanish mission from which the town adapted its name. Founded in 1782 and completed in 1809, the small church of **Mission San Buenaventura**▶▶ (225 E. Main Street; tel: 805/643–4318) is all that survives of the mission's buildings, described in a small museum.

Close to the mission, a productive archeological dig has yielded valuable finds from the time of Spanish settlement, and also unearthed native American relics dated to 1600 BC, some of which are in the **Albinger Archeological Museum**▶ (113 E. Main Street; tel: 805/648–5823). Within a few strides is the **Ortega Adobe**▶, dating from 1857.

Across the street, the **Ventura County Museum of History and Art**▶ (100 E. Main Street; tel: 805/653–0323) documents the diverse nationalities who settled the region in the late 19th century, and charts the discovery of oil deposits.

Elsewhere in Ventura, **Olivas Adobe Historical Park**▶ (4200 Olivas Park Drive; tel: 805/644–4346) is the site of a two-story adobe house. A prime example of the Monterey style prevalent in California during the mid-1800s, it is packed with furnishings typical of the period, while the grandiose columns of the **Ventura County Courthouse**▶ (tel: 805/658–4726) highlight a later obsession with neo-classical architecture.

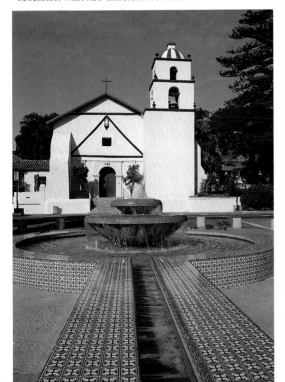

Ventura's Mission San Buenaventura, from which the town took its name, was the last to be founded by Junípero Serra

HOT SPRINGS
Mineral-rich hot springs, some of which have been adopted by commercial spa resorts, crop up fairly often throughout the Central Coast. One place to see springs as nature intended them is at Las Cruces Hot Springs, near the junction of Highway 101 and Highway 1, four miles north of Gaviota. From the parking lot, a trail leads to two pools of water fresh from the bowels of the earth: the first is fairly cool, while the second is warm and ideal for a dip.

115

CHANNEL ISLANDS TOURING
A good reason to be in Ventura is to visit the Channel Islands National Park, 15 miles offshore. The Visitor's Center (1901 Spinnaker Drive; tel: 805/658–5700) provides background on the islands, and Island Packers (1867 Spinnaker Drive; tel: 805/642–1393 or 7688) runs boat trips to them.

Los Angeles

LOS ANGELES CITY

Angeles National Forest

Big Tujunga Res

SAN FERNANDO

Veterans Memorial Park

FOOTHILL FREEWAY

Tujunga

ANGELES CREST HIGHWAY

Switzer Camp

GOLDEN STATE FREEWAY

SAN FERNANDO ROAD

Mission San Fernando Rey

Hansen Lake

MISSION HILLS

LA CRESCENTA

Arroyo Seco

SEPULVEDA BOULEVARD

Verdugo Mountains

Woodbury University

LA CAÑADA FLINTRIDGE

VAN NUYS

Tujunga Wash

Stough Park

Wildwood Canyon Park

MONTROSE

Descanso Gardens

Devil's Gate Res

BURBANK

Brand Park

GLENDALE

Los Angeles

VENTURA FREEWAY

ALAMEDA

San Rafael Hills

Arroyo Seco Park

VENTURA BOULEVARD

134

NBC Studios

Autry Museum of Western Heritage

Rose Bowl

Santa Monica Mountains National Recreation Area

Universal Studios

Griffith Park

Forest Lawn Memorial Park

Norton Simon Museum of Art

134

Zoo

GLENDALE FREEWAY

PASADENA FREEWAY

Stone Canyon Res

Planetarium

Hollywood Bowl

SUNSET

101

Southwest Museum

Arroyo Seco Park

WEST HOLLYWOOD

BOULEVARD

Silver Lake Res

Elysian Park

Lawry's California Center

HUNTINGTON DRIVE

BEVERLY HILLS

Chinese Theatre

SANTA MONICA BOULEVARD

HOLLYWOOD FREEWAY

Dodger Stadium

California State Univ LA

Getty Center

SAN DIEGO FREEWAY

UCLA

LA County Museum of Art

Farmers Market

La Brea Tar Pits

Chinatown

Armand Hammer Museum of Art & Culture Center

WILSHIRE BOULEVARD

SAN BERNARDINO FWY

10

WESTWOOD

George C Page Museum

Music Center

El Pueblo

710

Craft & Folk Art Museum

Century City

Civic Center

Little Tokyo

POMONA FWY

Museum of Tolerance

Ballona Creek

5

WHITTIER BLVD

SANTA

2

SANTA MONICA FREEWAY

72

10

MONICA

LINCOLN BLVD

VENICE BOULEVARD

405

University of S California

10

SANTA ANA FREEWAY

5

Santa Monica Heritage Museum

Venice

CULVER CITY

Natural History Museum

California Science Center

Memorial Coliseum

Maywood

Exposition Park

110

HUNTINGTON PARK

Marina del Rey

Fisherman's Village

MANCHESTER AVENUE

FLORENCE

42

Cudahy

FREEWAY

Santa

The Forum

INGLEWOOD

Watts Towers

SOUTH GATE

Monica

Hollywood Park Race Track

Los Angeles International Airport

CENTURY FREEWAY

105

LYNWOOD

Bay

EL SEGUNDO

107

HAWTHORNE

HARBOR FREEWAY

WILLOW BROOK

105

MANHATTAN BEACH

SEPULVEDA BOULEVARD

Alondra Park

GARDENA

COMPTON

LONG

Los Angeles

LAKEWOOD

ARTESIA

HERMOSA BEACH

ARTESIA BOULEVARD

GARDENA FREEWAY

91

BOULEVARD

REDONDO BEACH

HAWTHORNE BOULEVARD

WESTERN AVE

TORRANCE

California State University Dominguez Hills

710

CARSON

19

Dominguez Channel

110

405

0   2   4   6   8 km

0   2   4 miles

A   1   B   C

EXTREMES The second-largest city in the US, Los Angeles has an identity all its own. Here, the finest of fine art collections are surrounded by garish billboards; image-conscious trendies strike a pose in clubs a short distance away from the homeless; and celebrity-filled movie premieres vie with gang wars and interethnic feuding for attention on national TV.

The entertainment industry has brought parts of L.A. more wealth than it knows what to do with and a population packed with household names, but for every fat cat living it up in the Hollywood Hills, there are thousands enduring grinding poverty in L.A.'s less salubrious areas, and discontent among the city's dispossessed has been known to erupt into violence.

PLEASURES At the same time, 99 percent of visitors to L.A. can enjoy the fabulous beaches, the madcap architecture, and the excellent museums, and generally soak up the L.A. lifestyle without ever exposing themselves to anything more dangerous than exceeding their credit limit in one of the world's greatest consumer paradises.

NEIGHBORHOODS Around the skyscrapers of Downtown, the historic El Pueblo de Los Angeles, Chinatown, and Little Tokyo sit at the core of this enormous city. To the east of Downtown, East L.A. occupies miles of urban sprawl and houses the bulk of L.A.'s vast Latino population.

L.A., as most visitors envisage it, stretches 16 miles west from Downtown, taking in Hollywood, Beverly Hills, and Westwood, reaching the coast at Santa Monica.

South of Santa Monica, Venice Beach, Manhattan Beach, Hermosa Beach, and Redondo Beach occupy the low-lying land that soon rises into the tall bluffs of the Palos Verdes peninsula, L.A.'s southwestern extremity.

East of Palos Verdes, San Pedro and Long Beach sit on the L.A. harbor, south of Downtown and separated from it by the run-down and dangerous South Central L.A. Everything is linked by a network of freeways, clogged during rush hours but essentially the only way to get around this sun-kissed megalopolis.

Los Angeles

117

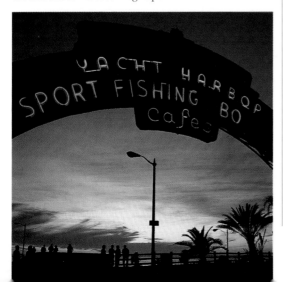

Blazing sunsets are a feature of balmy L.A. evenings

Los Angeles

TOURS
For tours of stars' homes or general sightseeing, contact Oskar J's (tel: 800/458–2388). The Los Angeles Conservancy (tel: 213/623–2489) gives walking tours of historical areas; and Los Angeles Nighthawks (tel: 310/392–1500) has VIP nights on the town, which can be tailored to your particular nocturnal interests.

►► Beverly Hills   116A3

When you see rows of open-topped Rolls Royces waiting at traffic lights and immaculately groomed poodles being exercised along thoroughly scrubbed pavements, then you know you are in Beverly Hills.

From the 1920s, L.A.'s movie idols followed the lead of actors Douglas Fairbanks and Mary Pickford and colonized the hills above Hollywood. Soon Beverly Hills had become a byword for glamor, glitz and mind-boggling wealth.

The stately and secluded hillside homes of the rich and famous still fill Beverly Hills. But it is around the designer-label stores on Rodeo Drive that you are most likely to spot the "big names," even though today's Beverly Hills residents are as likely to be plastic surgeons as film stars.

► Century City   116A3

On the one-time backlot of 20th Century Fox studios, the metal and glass high-rise towers of Century City form L.A.'s most anodyne district. The mood is eased only by the ABC Entertainment Center and the Century City Shopping Center—and the chance to take a peek at the New York street set that starred in the 1960s film *Hello Dolly!*

►► Chinatown   116C3

Pagoda-shaped buildings and dozens of ornamental fire-breathing dragons were among the things L.A.'s sizable Chinese community acquired when it relocated to present-day Chinatown in the 1930s to make way for Union Station. See the live poultry shops, sniff the aromatic herbs, and come back at night when the restaurants are at their liveliest and the neon decorations glow, and you will find one of L.A.'s principal ethnic communities at its least Americanized (see also page 119).

A stronger reason to be in the area is the excellent Museum of Tolerance (see page 137), located on the southern fringe.

Chinatown has retained a distinct identity

A vibrant pot-pourri of races, religions, languages, and cultures, Angelenos are a much more ethnically varied bunch than the stereotype of the well-off Anglo-American would suggest, with immigrant communities dotted around the city.

From Latin America Though visible all over the city, the vast majority of the L.A. area's 4 million Hispanic residents live in East L.A.; the third-largest Mexican community in the world, it is increasingly also home to Guatemalans and other immigrants from elsewhere in Central America. For a taste of local life, stroll among the exotic pet shops and botanicas (supplying the implements of the voodoo-like *Santeria*) of Brooklyn Avenue, and drop into the lively El Mercado indoor market at 3425 E. First Street.

From Asia Many Chinese railroad laborers settled in L.A. around the turn of the century. To make way for Union Station in the 1930s, the original Chinatown was moved a short distance north to the present Chinatown (see page 118) along North Broadway. Crowds spill ceaselessly out of the district's restaurants and shopping plazas, although many Chinese have moved from Chinatown to the suburban San Gabriel Valley.

L.A.'s Japanese community also has a long history, but was devastated in 1942 when almost all its members were forced into internment camps for the duration of the war. Japanese L.A.'s public face is within the traditional-Japanese-meets-modern-American architecture of Little Tokyo, where the Nisei Festival takes place each August and where the Japanese-American National Museum (369 East First Street at Central Avenue; tel: 213/625–0414) displays art and historical items.

Of the city's smaller Asian communities, brightly painted buildings decorate the expanding Koreatown, based on Normandie Avenue, just south of Wilshire Boulevard even though many Korean–Americans left the area during the 1990s and now make up just ten percent of its population; Vietnamese enclaves can be found within Chinatown and in Westchester; and a large Cambodian community is centered on Long Beach's Anaheim Street.

From Europe Armenians, Russians, and Hungarians are evident around the Fairfax section of Wilshire Boulevard, also the heart of the second-largest Jewish community in the U.S., and many Greeks have settled in the area around St. Sophia's Greek Orthodox Church.

From Africa Much of South Central L.A. is home to the bulk of the city's African-American population. A depressed area, it formed a natural starting point for the riots that shook the city in 1992. The violent images of those days, beamed around the world, were seen by some as an expression of the hopelessness many local residents were feeling. However, South Central has many successful community projects and has spawned 50 top rap stars.

CHICANO/LATINO/ HISPANIC
The precise meanings of the terms Chicano, Latino, and Hispanic have become blurred with use (and misuse) and you are likely to hear any one of them used to describe people or a person of Latin American origin or descent. Derived from the Aztec name for Mexico, "Chicano" was first adopted by some U.S. citizens of Mexican origin during a 1970s political movement. Literally, "Hispanic" means "derived from the Spanish," although many so-called Hispanics are actually of Indian blood. A more accurate term is "Latino," which refers to all people of Latin American origin.

119

Hard to believe though it may be, the origins of unrelentingly modern L.A. go back to 1781 and a farming community growing food for California's Spanish missions. The 44 original settlers—Native Americans, blacks, Spanish, mestizos, and mulattos—relocated twice before basing themselves close to what is now El Pueblo State Historic Park, on the northern edge of Downtown.

The Old Plaza Funded in part by donations of cattle and whiskey, the **Plaza Church**▶▶, on North Main Street facing the **Old Plaza**, was commenced in 1818 but was not finished until 40 years later. Greatly modified over the decades, the church has a plain exterior that hides an interior rich with paintings and sacraments of the Catholic faith.

Also by the Old Plaza, the Italianate **Pico House**▶ (424–436 N Main Street) was the finest hotel south of San Francisco when it opened in 1870. It was financed by California's last Mexican governor, Pío Pico, who, so it is said, sat on a bench outside the building and wept after failing to meet the $30,000 mortgage payments.

No trace remains of L.A.'s time as one of the West's most lawless towns—when cockfights were common along its shabby streets, and blood ran as freely as alcohol in its saloons—through the early days of U.S. rule.

Olvera Street Running off the **Old Plaza**▶▶▶, Olvera Street was once the scene of much of the carnage. It has earned an honest living since the 1930s, however, as a would-be Mexican street market, where south-of-the-border arts and crafts are sold, and Mexican food is consumed from hole-in-the-wall cafés.

Once uncharitably described as "the first Disneyland," Olvera Street none-theless makes for enjoyable strolling, and at No. 10 enough remains of the 1818 **Avila Adobe**▶▶ (10 E Olvera Street) to justify its claim as the oldest house in L.A.—inside, recon-structed fittings suggest the local lifestyles as they were in the 1840s.

Film show To learn more about El Pueblo, watch the free film show in the information center on Olvera Street, or join the walking tour from the Visitor Information Center, Sepulveda House, 622 N. Main Street, facing the Old Plaza (tel: 213/628–1274).

A street market in El Pueblo State Historic Park

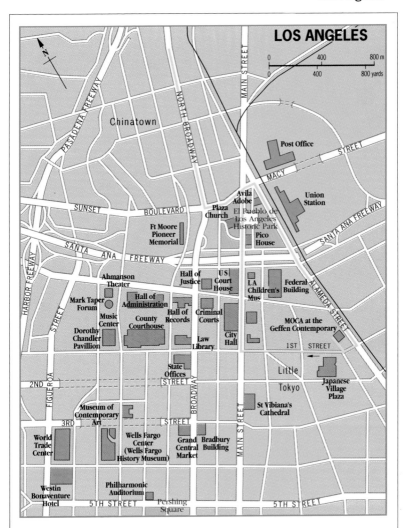

LOS ANGELES

Chinatown

Post Office

Union Station

Avila Adobe

Plaza Church

El Pueblo de Los Angeles Historic Park

Pico House

Ft Moore Pioneer Memorial

Ahmanson Theater

Hall of Justice

US Court House

LA Children's Mus

Federal Building

Mark Taper Forum

Hall of Administration

Music Center

County Courthouse

Hall of Records

Criminal Courts

MOCA at the Geffen Contemporary

Dorothy Chandler Pavillion

Law Library

City Hall

1ST STREET

State Offices

Little Tokyo

Japanese Village Plaza

Museum of Contemporary Art

St Vibiana's Cathedral

World Trade Center

Wells Fargo Center (Wells Fargo History Museum)

Grand Central Market

Bradbury Building

Westin Bonaventure Hotel

Philharmonic Auditorium

5TH STREET

Pershing Square

5TH STREET

121

Walk

Downtown sights of Los Angeles

From the Japanese Village Plaza Mall go west along First Street, turning onto Main Street for City Hall.
The observation deck in the 1928 **City Hall** has great views across L.A.

Go north along Main Street for El Pueblo de Los Angeles (see page 120).

Turn left onto Macy Street then right onto Broadway for Chinatown. From El Pueblo, cross Alameda Street for Union Station.
Union Station has welcomed train passengers to L.A. since 1939.

Walk south along Alameda Street, turn right onto First Street and right again along Central Avenue for the Temporary Contemporary.
MOCA at The Geffen Contemporary is a former police garage filled with oversized modern art works.

Return to First Street and turn right for Japanese Village Plaza Mall.

It may lack the tradition of European cities, but when it comes to architecture L.A. is no slouch. From playful gingerbread homes of the early 1900s to textbook examples of modernism, the city is filled with ingeniously designed buildings that, in some cases, are the finest examples of their kind.

WATTS TOWERS
As famous architects dotted the city with their masterworks and mistakes, one of L.A.'s most enduring structures was being painstakingly assembled by an unknown tilesetter called Simon Rodia. Between 1921 and 1954, Rodia's 100-foot-high Watts Towers (1765 E. 107th Street, Watts; tel: 213/847–4646) evolved from bedsteads, bottletops, and 70,000 shells. Working entirely alone and never giving any explanation for his creation, Rodia was to die in obscurity. Public support has, however, helped the towers survive several demolition threats, and they remain as majestic and as mysterious as ever.

One of the many modernistic sculptures commissioned to decorate the otherwise stern plazas of Downtown's Financial District

Early structures L.A.'s earliest buildings were flat-roofed, single-story adobe (mud-brick) structures. The restored 1818 Avila Adobe in El Pueblo de Los Angeles is one example; a broader sense of the style is given by Rancho Los Cerritos and Rancho Los Alamitos in Long Beach.

Settlers from the eastern United States who arrived in L.A. at the start of the 20th century brought a liking for elaborate ornamentation. The desirable residences of the time were richly decorative wood-built Queen Anne and Eastlake homes; the more turrets and twirls a dwelling had, the more desirable it was. Some handsome survivors can be seen on **Carrol Avenue▶ ▶**, just west of Downtown.

California Bungalows Plainer wooden houses—the city's first low-cost urban housing—sprang up in a medley of styles but, characterized by balconies, porches, and overhanging roofs, they became collectively known as California Bungalows. An expensive adaptation of the California Bungalow appeared in the suburb of Pasadena. Here, the firm of Greene & Greene took its inspiration from England's Arts and Crafts movement and made its definitive statement with the 1908 **Gamble House▶ ▶ ▶** (4 Westmoreland Place, off Orange Grove Boulevard; tel: 626/793–3334. *Open* Thu–Sun 12–3; closed Jan 1, Easter, July 4, Thanksgiving, Dec 25. *Admission: inexpensive.* See page 159), whose highly polished woodwork shows the teak's natural pattern, joints are exposed and exaggerated, and every piece of furniture—from the chairs to the lampshades—originated on the Greene & Greene drawing board.

Plentiful though the California Bungalows were in their various guises, it was the thick walls, open courtyards, arches, and plushly landscaped gardens of the Spanish Colonial Revival that became more strongly associated with L.A., and all of Southern California.

The successes and excesses of the movie industry inspired further large, sometimes ludicrous imitations of European architecture. The symbol of L.A.'s emergence as a modern city, however, was the art-deco explosion of the late 1920s and 1930s, whose aerodynamic contours, porthole windows, and projecting wings were exuberant monuments to the technological age.

L.A.'s outstanding art-deco buildings included the **May Co. Department Store▶ ▶** (6067 Wilshire Boulevard), with an immense finned cylinder joining the two exterior walls, and the **Coca-Cola bottling plant▶ ▶** (1334 S. Central Avenue at 14th Street), thinly disguised as an ocean liner, complete with ship's bridge, hatch covers, and portholes.

As weak art deco and Spanish Colonial Revival swamped the city, influential maverick Frank Lloyd Wright arrived and looked back to pre-Columbian times. In 1917, his **Hollyhock House**▶ ▶ (4800 Hollywood Boulevard; tel: 323/913–4157) was an ambitious fusing of California Bungalow and Aztec temple. Unloved by its owner, the house and its grounds (the present Barnsdall Park) were given to the city. Wright refined his ideas and, in 1924, completed the **Ennis House**▶ ▶ (2607 Glendower Avenue).

Wright's assistant, the Austrian Rudolph Schindler, established his own modernist credentials with his home of concrete slabs and interlocking indoor and outdoor spaces in West Hollywood (835 N. Kings Road; tel: 323/651–1510. *Open* Wed–Sun), complete with open-air sleeping areas.

Encouraged by Schindler, fellow Austrian Richard Neutra arrived from Europe. In 1929, Neutra's **Lovell House**▶ ▶ (4616 Dundee Drive), with suspended balconies projecting from the hillside above Griffith Park, became L.A.'s most acclaimed example of the international style.

More new styles From 1945 to 1964, the Case Study Program of experimental house building solidified L.A.'s reputation as a center of innovative architecture, though, by definition, the city's staggering postwar growth restricted new projects—as have the preservation orders that protect its architectural past.

In the mid-1970s, the glass silos of the **Westin Bonaventure Hotel**▶ ▶ (404 S. Figueroa Street; tel: 213/624–1000 or 800/228–3000) heralded a spate of new Downtown development including Arata Isozaki's red sandstone mating of East and West, housing the **Museum of Contemporary Art**▶ ▶ (250 S. Grand Avenue; tel: 213/626–6222). When the billion-dollar Getty Center (see page 154) opened in 1997, it became L.A.'s latest and perhaps most successful fusing of architecture and landscape.

123

From running stagecoaches across the wild west, Wells Fargo grew into one of the country's major financial institutions

The Autry Museum of Western Heritage

Just one example of the countless statuary filling Malibu's J. Paul Getty Museum

Index of museums in and around L.A.

Armand Hammer Museum of Art and Culture Center
(tel: 310/443–7000) *Open* Tue–Sat 11–7, Thu until 9, Sun 11–5. (See page 136.)
Autry Museum of Western Heritage
(tel: 323/667–2000) *Open* Tue–Sun 10–5. (See page 126.)
Cabrillo Marine Aquarium
(tel: 310/548–7562) *Open* Tue–Fri noon–5, Sat and Sun 10–5. (See page 134.)
California Science Center
(tel: 213/744–7400) *Open* daily 10–5. *Admission free.* (See page 127.)
George C. Page Museum
(tel: 323/934–7243) *Open* Mon–Fri 9:30–5, Sat–Sun 10–5. *Admission: inexpensive.* (See page 138.)
Getty Center
(tel: 310/440–7300) *Open* Tue–Wed 11–7, Thu–Fri 11–9, Sat and Sun 10–6. *Admission free* (fee for parking; reservations required).
Hollywood Entertainment Museum
(tel: 323/465–7900) *Open* Tue–Sun 10–6. (See page 128.)
Hollywood Heritage Museum
(tel: 323/874–2276) *Open* Sat and Sun 11–4. (See page 128.)
Hollywood Wax Museum
(tel: 323/462–8860) *Open* Sun–Thu 10 AM–midnight, Fri–Sat 10 AM–2 AM. (See page 128.)
Huntington Art Collections
(tel: 626/405–2100) *Open* Tue–Sun 10:30–4:30, reduced hours in winter. (See page 155.)
Los Angeles County Museum of Art
(tel: 323/857–6000) *Open* Mon, Tue, and Thu 12–8, Fri 12–9, Sat and Sun 11–8. (See page 138.)
Laguna Beach Museum of Art
(tel: 949/494–6531) *Open* Tue–Sun 11–5. (See page 157.)
Los Angeles Maritime Museum
(tel: 310/548–7618) *Open* Tue–Sun 10–5. *Donation requested.* (See page 134.)
Museum of Contemporary Art (MOCA)
(tel: 213/626–6222) *Open* Tue–Sun 11–5, Thu 11–8. *Free after 5.*
Museum of Tolerance
(tel: 310/553–8403) *Open* Mon–Thu 10–4, Fri 10–1 (Nov–Mar), 10–3 (Apr–Oct), Sun 11–5. (See page 137.)
Natural History Museum
(tel: 213/743–3466) *Open* Tue–Sun 10–5. (See page 127.)
Orange County Museum of Art
(tel: 949/759–1122) *Open* Tue–Sun 11–5. *Entry fee.* (See page 156.)
Norton Simon Museum
(tel: 626/449–6840) *Open* Wed–Sun noon–6, Fri 12–9. (See page 155.)
Pacific Asia Museum
(tel: 626/449–2742) *Open* Wed–Sun 10–5. *Admission: inexpensive.* (See page 159.)
Richard M. Nixon Birthplace and Library
(tel: 714/993–5075) *Open* Mon–Sat 10–5, Sun 11–5. (See page 156.)
Southwest Museum
(tel: 323/221–2164) *Open* Tue–Sun 10–5. (See page 158.)

In the realm of spectator sports, the work-hard, play-hard ethic in L.A. life shows its face as a passion for watching hard, and Angelenos take an avid interest in the exploits of the city's home teams.

National favorites L.A. has five professional teams, two each for baseball and basketball, and one for ice hockey.

The numerous college teams—the major ones being the Trojans (U.S.C.) and the Bruins (U.C.L.A.)—should not be considered second-rate. Many student athletes are on sports scholarships and destined for the professional leagues.

One of the biggest sporting events in L.A., in fact, is the New Year's Day football clash between the student champions of the West and Midwest at Pasadena's 104,000-seat Rose Bowl stadium.

The season's regular events are listed in the phone book. Tickets are generally available; only tickets for major games, and any game by the L.A. Lakers, will prove elusive; use the phone numbers given below for detailed information.

125

Baseball The National League's L.A. Dodgers play at Dodger Stadium, on the edge of Elysian Park, off the Pasadena freeway (tel: 323/224–1400), while their American League counterparts, the California Angels, appear at Orange County's Edison International Field of Anaheim, just off I-5 (tel: 714/634–2000). The season runs from April to October.

Basketball Most tickets to watch the fabled L.A. Lakers, who play downtown at Staples Center, 1111 S Figueroa Street (tel: 310/419–3100), are snapped up before the November-to-April season even starts. The L.A. Clippers appear at the same venue (tel: 213/748–8000).

Football Los Angeles football lovers are still recovering from the loss of both the city's professional teams—the Rams and the Raiders—in the mid-1990s. The search is on for replacements.

Horse racing Major meets are held at Hollywood Park in Inglewood from April to July and during November and December (tel: 310/419–1500); and at Santa Anita Park in Arcadia from July to September and from December to April (tel: 626/574–7223).

Ice hockey The city's professional ice hockey teams are the L.A. Kings, who face off at the Great Western Forum (tel: 310/673–6003), and Orange County's Mighty Ducks of Anaheim, based at Anaheim's Arrowhead Pond (tel: 714/703–2545 for tickets; 714/940–2900 for information). The ice hockey season lasts from October to April.

The strapping football players of U.C.L.A.'s Bruins, who play their home games across the city at Pasadena's Rose Bowl stadium

The map shows Griffith Park area with labels including:

NORTH HOLLYWOOD, Burbank Studios Ranch, NBC Color Television, VENTURA FREEWAY, RIVERSIDE DRIVE, OLIVE AVE, Burbank Studios, RIVERSIDE DRIVE, "Traveltown" Rail Transportation Museum, 134, ZOO DRIVE, GRIFFITH PARK DR, Autry Western Heritage Museum, Universal Studios, FOREST LAWN DRIVE, Forest Lawn Memorial Park, Los Angeles Zoo, Los Angeles R, UNIVERSAL CITY, Cahuenga Peak, Griffith, VENTURA BLVD, HOLLYWOOD FREEWAY, BARHAM BLVD, VISTA DEL VALLE, Los Angeles River, MULHOLLAND DRIVE, Santa Monica Mts, Mount Hollywood, Park, Brush Canyon RD, Bird Sanctuary, Hollywood Lake, Greek Theater, LAUREL CANYON BLVD, WESTERN CANYON RD, Observatory & Planetarium, Ferndell, Pilgrimage Play Theater, Hollywood Bowl, LOS FELIZ BLVD, VERMONT AVE, HILLHURST AVE, HYPERION AVE, Chinese Theatre, HOLLYWOOD BLVD, Hollywood Wax Museum, FRANKLIN AVENUE, SUNSET BLVD, WEST HOLLYWOOD, FAIRFAX AVE, LA BREA AVE, HIGHLAND AVE, CAHUENGA BLVD, VINE ST, CBS Studio, WESTERN AVE, HOLLYWOOD BLVD, Hollyhock House, ABC TV Studio, SANTA MONICA BLVD, Columbia Studio, SUNSET BLVD, SANTA MONICA BLVD, 2 km, 1 mile

126

Drive

A tour around Griffith Park

Enter the park at the Western Canyon Road gate for the Ferndell.
A quiet glade with a natural spring, the **Ferndell▶** is pleasant for picnics.

Drive two miles, then turn right along Observatory Drive for the observatory.

Griffith Park Observatory

Griffith Park Observatory▶ ▶
(2800 East Observatory Road;
tel: 323/664–1191) allows the public access to its telescopes on certain nights; daytime views with the naked eye can also be spectacular.

Descend from the observatory and turn right onto Western Canyon Road, continuing for a mile.
Pass the **Bird Sanctuary▶** (Visitor Center, 4730 Crystal Springs Drive) on the left and Greek Theater on the right.

At Vermont Avenue, turn left onto Commonwealth Canyon Road and then follow Vista Del Valle for 6 miles, turning left onto Griffith Park Drive and then right onto Zoo Drive for the Autry Western Heritage Museum.
The **Autry Museum of Western Heritage▶ ▶ ▶** (see page 124) earns its spurs by cogently portraying the settlement of the western United States. Close by, the **L.A. Zoo▶** (5333 Zoo Drive; tel: 323/644–6400) is another busy attraction.

Drive back along Zoo Drive and head west along Forest Lawn Drive, leaving the park and crossing over the Hollywood Freeway to Mulholland Drive and Laurel Canyon Boulevard (see page 129).

It has been an open-air market and the site of horse- and camel-races. Its majestic L.A. Memorial Coliseum stadium was the site of the Olympic Games in 1932 and 1984. Now Exposition Park is best known for its museums and proximity to the U.S.C. campus.

Visitors to the **California Science Center**►► can examine the wonders of the natural world, and human innovations, as they pass through a series of themed areas, complete with informative displays and simulations. Be it light, gravity, sound or space travel, the fundamentals of science are presented in an easy-to-understand way with an abundance of hands-on exhibits that are great for child-pleasing interactivity. The permanent exhibits are frequently boosted by top quality traveling shows, and special programs. Another treat is the seven-story high, 90-foot-wide IMAX screen, showing ultra-realistic films depicting anything from the lifestyles of microscopic organisms to the climbing of Everest.

The echoing halls and galleries of the Spanish Renaissance-style **Natural History Museum** reveal a substantial collection of pre-Columbian artifacts, a multitude of fossils, and the inevitable reconstructed dinosaur skeletons.

There is no excuse for not using the museum's California history collections to complete your understanding of the state's development. There are detailed rundowns on indigenous Californians, the first European

THE U.S.C. CAMPUS
The University of Southern California (U.S.C.) campus, which borders Exposition Park, will consume any time you have left after visiting the museums. The oldest building here (Widney Hall) dates from the 1880s; do not be misled by the cloistered courtyard and leering gargoyles of the Mudd Hall of Philosophy; they are intended to evoke a sense of medieval European academia.

Note, too, the George Lucas Film School, named for just one of its blockbuster director graduates—Steven Spielberg is another.

127

settlers, and the 1850s Gold Rush. The rapid growth of Los Angeles is chronicled, too, and its place as the first city built for the automobile is acknowledged with an exhibit of unusual old cars.

Finally, take a slow walk through the Hall of Minerals, which features several extremely precious stones, or visit the gardens which have 150 different varieties of roses.

Built in 1921 and hosting the Olympic Games in 1932 and 1984, the L.A. Memorial Coliseum seats 91,000

Greta Garbo is just one of the celebrities remembered by Hollywood's Walk of Fame

DAY OF THE LOCUST
Given the number of accomplished novelists from all over the world who have arrived in Hollywood to try their hand at screenwriting, it is perhaps surprising that few have written about Hollywood itself as well or as caustically as Nathaniel West, whose 1935 *The Day of the Locust* remains the classic satire of Hollywood in the boom years. Interestingly, the run-down rooming house in which West lived at the time of writing still stands, as shabbily as ever in the center of Hollywood, at 1817 N. Ivar Street.

▶▶▶ **Hollywood** 116B3

Centered around Hollywood and Sunset boulevards

L.A. without Hollywood is impossible to imagine. For eight decades it has been the scene of the city's most public triumphs, disasters, scandals, and decadent extravagances.

The beginning Hollywood as the world knows it began in the 1910s when a bunch of hard-up but ambitious film makers came west in search of a warm climate, free natural backdrops, and an escape from the patent laws hindering their activity on the East Coast.

Within a decade, Hollywood seethed with directors, stars, would-be stars, and opportunists, and all of Los Angeles became indelibly marked by the film industry as the unsophisticated early days grew into the prosperous decades of the 1940s and 1950s.

Seedy streets All but one of the major studios have moved out, so to today's Angelenos, Hollywood does not mean movies but seedy, low-rent neighborhoods and streets that are best avoided after dark.

Hollywood's boundaries are hard to define but you will know you have arrived when the **Walk of Fame**▶ appears beneath your feet: nearly 2,000 star-shaped brass plaques are embedded in the Hollywood Boulevard sidewalk, each embossed with the name of an entertainment industry notable who has paid ($15,000) for the privilege.

Opened by Sid Grauman in 1927, **Mann's Chinese Theater**▶▶ (6925 Hollywood Boulevard; tel: 323/464–8111) draws 2 million visitors a year, not for the intricacies of its mock-oriental architecture but for the hand- and footprints of screen idols who literally made their marks here when they were arriving for celebrity-packed movie premieres: look for Betty Grable's leg-print, and the hoof-print of Gene Autry's horse.

Five years earlier, Grauman had celebrated the discovery of King Tut's tomb by erecting the **Egyptian Theater**▶ (6712 Hollywood Boulevard; tel: 323/466–3456), a plaster replica of the Temple of Thebes, which has recently been restored and which was, in its time, among Hollywood's kitschiest excesses.

The **Hollywood Entertainment Museum** (7021 Hollywood Boulevard; see page 124) reveals the flight deck from Star Trek and the bar from Cheers on its behind-the-scenes guided tours, and less impressively demonstrates editing techniques and outlines Hollywood's history.

Famous foundations Max Factor supplied the make-up, but Frederick's of Hollywood (6608 Hollywood Boulevard) supplied the high-fashion bras and corsets that held the famous flesh in place. Celebrities have donated examples,, displayed in the store's Lingerie Museum.

The **Hollywood Wax Museum**▶ (6767 Hollywood Boulevard; see page 124) is popular but predictable; a better place to visit is the **Hollywood Heritage Museum**▶▶ (2100 N. Highland Avenue; see page 124), inside the barn where Cecil B. De Mille directed *The Squaw Man*, Hollywood's first feature film, in 1913.

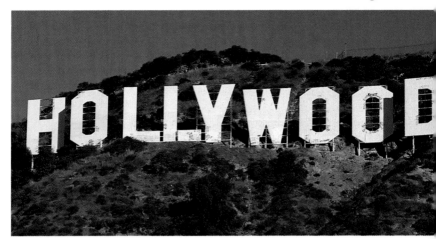

Just across Highland Avenue, the **Hollywood Bowl**, summer base of the L.A. Philharmonic, has staged music under the stars since the 1920s. The Bowl's acoustics were greatly improved by the so-called "Shells," designed by the influential architect Frank Lloyd Wright and completed in 1928.

Cowboy lines From the 1910s, scores of would-be screen cowboys lined up at the junction of Sunset Boulevard and Gower Street for bit parts in B westerns—the modern Gower Gulch shopping plaza, thinly disguised as an Old West frontier town, is their only memorial. The **Hollywood Athletic Club▶** (6525 Sunset Boulevard) now a public bar and grill, served as a watering hole for the likes of John Wayne and Charlie Chaplin.

The end The shady **Hollywood Forever▶▶▶** (6000 Santa Monica Boulevard; tel: 323/469–1181. *Open* daily 8–5. *Admission free.*) provides a final resting place for Tyrone Power, Douglas Fairbanks, and Rudolph Valentino, among many others. Immediately south is Paramount Studios, the last major film company in Hollywood.

As Sunset Boulevard crosses West Hollywood—packed with hip night spots and fashionable restaurants, and the base of L.A.'s gay community—it briefly becomes the Sunset Strip, where enormous "vanity boards" tout new films, new records, and new faces.

Above Hollywood Laurel Canyon Boulevard and Mulholland Drive twist through the canyons of the Hollywood Hills where, over the years, innumerable stars have bought rambling mansions and gazed down on Los Angeles sprawling beneath their balconies.

It is seldom possible to catch more than passing glimpses or distant views of the most interesting homes (by the roadside, vendors sell photocopied and often out-of-date locator maps for the stars' homes), but among the highlights are Rudolph Valentino's "Falcon Lair" (1436 Bella Drive), Harold Lloyd's "Greenacres" (1740 Green Acres Place), and Errol Flynn's "Mulholland House" (3100 Torreyson Place).

With $27,000 donated by local residents, the much decayed Hollywood sign was restored to its former glory in 1978

HOLLYWOOD SIGN
Erected in 1923 and illuminated with thousands of flashing light bulbs to advertise land sales in Beachwood Canyon (in the Hollywood Hills), the 50-foot-high Hollywood sign became famous throughout the world as the movie-making area's most enduring marker. Unhappy actress Peg Entwhistle committed suicide by jumping off it in 1932, but the closest anyone can legally get to the sign today is Beachwood Drive, which ends about 100 yards from its base.

Long Beach walk

Begin on the Promenade, beside the Long Beach Mural.
Long Beach grew rapidly in the 19th century. Boat cruises to Catalina Island depart from the end of Golden Shore Boulevard and from Pier J (see later in this walk).

Funded by the Depression-era Federal Arts Project, the **Long Beach Mural**▶ depicts 1930s Long Beach.

Walk south to Shoreline Park and turn left for Shoreline Village (on Shoreline Village Drive).
With souvenir shops, specialty stores, and lively restaurants, **Shoreline Village**▶ (tel: 562/435–2668) stretches along the waterfront. There is a restored carousel and regular live entertainment on the boardwalk.

But the major attraction is **Long Beach Aquarium of the Pacific**▶▶ (100 Aquarium Way; tel: 562/590-3100; www.aquariumofpacific.org) with replicas of habitats and an abundance of ocean-dwelling creatures from sea lions to spider crabs.

Take the water-taxi across Queensway Bay for the *Queen Mary*.

The *Queen Mary*▶▶ (1126 Queens Highway; tel: 562/435–3511) was the last word in oceangoing luxury in the 1930s. For a fee, the stately old liner can be boarded.

Return to the Promenade.

▶▶▶ Santa Monica 116A3

Groomed as a beachside resort beginning in 1875, Santa Monica enjoys cleaner air and cooler temperatures than the rest of L.A. and is the stamping ground of unconventional writers, artists, and left-wing politicians. Santa Monica's pride and joy, however, despite pollution problems, is a white-sand beach wide enough to accommodate thousands of cyclists, joggers, sunbathers, and swimmers. The wooden **Santa Monica Pier▶▶** (Ocean Avenue) has been around almost as long as the town, and displays a collection of fading monochrome snapshots from its youth. Along the pier are snack stands and a 70-year-old carousel.

Away from the beach, the **Third Street Promenade ▶▶▶** (Third Street between Broadway and Wilshire Boulevard) attracts a daily procession of street musicians and artists, and has trendy sidewalk cafés. At the southern end of the promenade, **Santa Monica Place** is among the best shopping malls in L.A. for people-watching, and was designed by architect Frank Gehry, whose own former home stands at 1002 22nd Street.

Santa Monica's social profile rose greatly through the 1990s, when several luxury hotels were built beside the beach and their restaurants and public areas quickly drew the attention of L.A. and international celebrities. Another impressive development was the trans-formation of industrial warehouses into the collection of art galleries that make up **Bergamot Station**, 2525 Michigan Avenue, also the site of the **Santa Monica Museum of Art** (tel: 310/586–6488), with exhibitions focusing on modern and contemporary work from around the world.

Elsewhere, the **California Heritage Museum** (2612 Main Street; tel: 310/392–8537) fills an 1894 Queen Anne house with period-furnished rooms, while the **Museum of Flying**, (2772 Donald Douglas Loop N; tel: 310/392–8822) explores aviation past and present with interactive displays.

MURALS

Murals are a distinctive feature of the cityscape in Santa Monica and Venice. Along Ocean Park Boulevard in Santa Monica are the *Whale Mural* and the 600-foot-long *Unbridled*, depicting horses escaping from the carousel. In Venice, look along Windward Avenue: inside the post office there is a large trompe l'oeil and, on the corner of Ocean Walk, the *Rebirth of Venus*, a witty parody of Botticelli.

VENICE

The name is all that remains from a doomed turn-of-the-century attempt to reclaim marshland and re-create the canals of the Italian city. These canals were soon turned into streets. The beachside boardwalk is now a menagerie of fire-eaters, tap-dancers, fortune-tellers, skateboarders and rollerbladers while musclemen pump iron in the open-air gym on Muscle Beach.

131

Santa Monica at night

These days it is not would-be film idols who walk the streets of Hollywood but would-be musicians, singers and song writers, all clutching demo tapes and hoping for at least a few minutes of fame.

LICENSE TO SERENADE
In 1838 a law was passed in Los Angeles banning the serenading of women without a license.

132

Mike Love of the Beach Boys, whose music epitomized for many people around the world the California of sun, sea, and surf

Home of La Bamba The base of several major record companies, L.A. is a magnet for aspiring rock musicians from all over the United States. Every night, hundreds of venues pulsate to the latest bands, and the city's place in rock history is only slightly less formidable than its role in the rise of the movies.

The first native Angeleno to make it big was Richie Valens (Richard Valenzuela), a 17-year-old Hispanic boy from East L.A. whose "La Bamba" topped the charts in 1958 (and who, tragically, died a year later in a plane crash).

Surfin' Safari Predictably, it was not Valens's impoverished East L.A. but the coastal communities' idyllic surfing and hot-rodding lifestyles eulogized beginning in the early 1960s by The Beach Boys, Jan & Dean, and their imitators, that gave the record-buying public a lingering image of L.A.

Love and peace in the hills Later, while San Francisco was the undisputed world capital of flower-power, many of the psychedelic era's most influential bands were based in L.A.

One was Buffalo Springfield (whose artists included future solo stars Neil Young and Stephen Stills); its 1967 debut single "For What It's Worth" was a response to the "Sunset Strip riot," when baton-wielding police attempted to move the hippies—hundreds of whom were arriving in the city—intent on taking over the Sunset Strip, then a collection of upscale supper clubs.

Other seminal L.A. groups included Iron Butterfly and Love, but it was The Doors who garnered the most vociferous response, thanks in no small part to their iconoclastic lead singer, Jim Morrison, whose lyrics were considered poetry and whose drinking exploits around the L.A. bars became legendary.

As the hippies flooded Sunset Strip, the musicians retreated to Topanga Canyon, a patch of wild country in the hills just a few minutes' drive from the city's clubs and studios. The canyon saw many night-long parties and star-studded jam sessions, and one resident band, The Byrds, used the stables at the head of the canyon's horse trails on the cover of their "Notorious Byrd Brothers" album.

L.A. lays back By the early 1970s, the idealism had waned and the profit-motivated music industry had, after earlier doubts, decided there was a fortune to be made from the embryonic rock culture.

The showcase clubs of the city became dominated by record-company-approved acts, and the easy-listening rock of commercially mega-successful bands such as The Eagles and Fleetwood Mac, and singer-songwriters such as Jackson Browne, became the standard bearers of a cozy and complacent L.A. rock scene.

A new order With many of the most creative names of the 1960s gaining weight and drug habits in the Hollywood Hills, and music business executives too worried about losing their privileged positions to take risks, an artistic void had opened up by the mid-1970s, into which stepped the first L.A. punk bands—among them The Zeroes, The Plugz, The Dils, and X. In a city where façade usually counted for more than content, it was little surprise that the 1980s were dominated by the rise of glam-metal and the emergence of make-up wearing ear-crunchers such as Poison and Mötley Crüe.

A bit of everything The biggest 1980s success story, however, was the hard-rocking Guns 'n' Roses, carrying the rock-star-as-outlaw myth as far as it would go and becoming the role model for thousands of bandana-wearing hopefuls. Meanwhile, Los Lobos grew out of the bars of East L.A. and found an international audience appreciative of their mixing of corridos (Mexican folk songs) and rock-and-roll. As of the late 1990s the strongest sounds have been emerging from the ghettos of South Central L.A., which have spawned globally acclaimed rap acts such as Ice-T and NWA. At the same time, L.A. has reflected the globalization of music and its mixing of past and present with a scene diverse enough to include singer-songwriter Sheryl Crow and swing band revivals.

The Doors' singer Jim Morrison and keyboardist Ray Manzarek peer from the Downtown hotel, which gave the band's fifth album its title

L.A. JAZZ
Through the 1930s and 1940s, the predominantly African-American area of South Central L.A. was among the country's hottest jazz spots, with the likes of Dexter Gordon, Eric Dolphy, and Charles Mingus regularly appearing in various groups. Meanwhile, band leaders Stan Kenton and Gerry Mulligan, and trumpeter Chet Baker, were among the L.A. jazzsters credited with pioneering the laid-back style dubbed "California cool."

Coastal route from Marina del Rey to San Pedro

See map on page 135.

Begin at Fisherman's Village in Marina del Rey.
Owners and crews of the private yachts berthed in **Marina del Rey▶** fill the pricey seafood restaurants of **Fisherman's Village▶**, facing the world's largest artificial harbor.

Drive the quarter-mile from Fisherman's Village to Vista del Mar and turn left, continuing south to Manhattan Beach.
Nets on the sands signify **Manhattan Beach's▶▶** place as the home of beach volleyball, whose professional participants can often be seen here.

Drive south along Highland Avenue to Hermosa Beach, turn left onto Pier Avenue.
The quintessential, quiet L.A. coastal community of **Hermosa Beach▶** honored a local surfer of the 1960s with a statue at the end of Pier Avenue.

Continue south along Highland Avenue to Redondo Beach.
Redondo Beach, Fisherman's Wharf▶ has stalls selling fresh seafood. Adjacent, the white-sand **Redondo State Beach▶** is popular with surfers.

Continue south, turn right along Palos Verdes Drive West, rounding the Palos Verdes peninsula.
The tree-covered **Palos Verdes peninsula▶▶** has many beaches, often reached by steep footpaths.

Continue on Palos Verdes Drive South.
On the left, Frank Lloyd Wright's 1946 **Wayfarer's Chapel▶▶▶** (5755 Palos Verdes Drive South; tel: 310/377–1650. *Open* daily 7–5. *Admission free*) is a monument to

18th-century Swedish mystic Emanuel Swedenborg, its glass walls allowing it to merge into a redwood grove on the hillside.

Continue to the end of Palos Verdes Drive South, turn right onto Paseo Del Mar for Point Fermin Park.
A launch point for hang gliders, **Point Fermin Park▶** also has an interesting example of a 19th-century lighthouse.

Drive to the end of Paseo Del Mar and turn right along Stephen Wright Drive for the Cabrillo Marine Museum.
Well-stocked aquariums, large collections of shells, and informative displays on marine ecology fill the **Cabrillo Marine Museum▶▶** (*Open* Tue–Fri noon–5, Sat–Sun 10–5. See page 124).

❑ Santa Monica's pier is easily the best of the bunch that exist along this section of L.A.'s coast, a classic seaside addition dating from 1909. Farther south, Manhattan Beach's barren strip of concrete deserves an award for dullness; Hermosa Beach's pier draws the thickest concentration of patient anglers; while the Redondo Sportfishing pier is the departure point for fishermen with a more substantial catch in mind. The quaintest pier in the L.A. area, however, belongs to Avalon on Santa Catalina Island. ❑

Turn left onto Pacific Avenue and enter San Pedro.
Originally a small fishing community, San Pedro quickly grew as the Port of Los Angeles developed. Much of the seafaring flavor of bygone times remains strong around the short streets of **Old San Pedro▶**, and the **Los Angeles Maritime Museum▶** (see page 124) documents the growth of the town and the port. Close by, overrated **Ports O'Call Village▶** has souvenir shops and restaurants.

SANTA MONICA
VENICE

MARINA DEL REY

PLAYA DEL REY

CULVER CITY

WINDSOR HILLS

CENTINELA AVE

LA BREA AVE

LOS ANGELES

LINCOLN BOULEVARD

Ballona Creek

Fisherman's Village

Loyola Marymount University

Northrop University

42

1

Los Angeles International Airport

VISTA DEL MAR

Dockweiler State Beach

Manhattan State Beach

MANHATTAN BEACH

405

The Forum

MANCHESTER AVENUE

107

INGLEWOOD

Hollywood Park Race Track

Wineries

LENNOX

CENTURY FREEWAY

105

SEPULVEDA

SAN DIEGO FREEWAY

EL SEGUNDO

EL PORTO BEACH

LAWNDALE

HIGHLAND AVENUE

BOULEVARD

91

ARTESIA

Hawthorne Municipal Airport

HAWTHORNE

HAWTHORNE

Alondra Park

EL NIDO

GARDENA

Dominguez Channel

BOULEVARD

ATHENS

Chester Washington Golf Course

91

135

Santa Monica Bay

HERMOSA BEACH

King Harbor

REDONDO BEACH

Redondo State Beach

1

CLIFTON

Malaga Cove

Flat Rock Point

Bluff Cove

Palos Verdes Point

Lunada Bay

Resort Point

Los Verdes Golf and Country Club

Point Vicente

Marineland Long Point

Abalone Cove

EL NIDO

405

TORRANCE

BOULEVARD

213

Palos Verdes Golf Club

PALOS VERDES DRIVE WEST

107

PACIFIC COAST

PALOS VERDES ESTATES

ROLLING HILLS ESTATES

Palos Verdes Hills

RANCHO PALOS VERDES

Wayfarer's Chapel

PALOS VERDES DRIVE SOUTH

Portuguese Point

Royal Palms State Beach

Whites Point

LOMITA

Torrance Municipal Airport

WALTERIA

South Coast Botanic Gardens

ROLLING HILLS

CARSON

Los Angeles Harbor General Hospital

Lomita Railroad Museum

HARBOR CITY

Rolling Hills Country Club

213

MIRALESTE

PORTUGUESE BEND

Friendship Regional Park

SAN PEDRO

Point Fermin

HARBOR FREEWAY

Harbor Park

US Naval Re

110

Peck Park

WESTERN AVENUE

Los Angeles Maritime Museum

Ports O' Call Village

PASEO DEL MAR

PACIFIC AVE

Point Fermin Park & Lighthouse

Cabrillo Marine Museum

0	2	4	6 km

0	1	2	3 miles

Los Angeles

SNEAK PREVIEWS
Outside movie theaters in Westwood, and to a lesser extent in other parts of L.A., you may be offered free tickets to a sneak preview of a new movie or unfinished film, screened to gauge audience reactions before final cuts are made. These are offered only to people who appear to be members of the social group expected to be interested in the film. After viewing, you will be given a questionnaire to fill out, which is used to help plan the marketing of the movie.

Some of the many movie theaters in Westwood

▶▶ Westwood
116A3

Planned as a Mediterranean-style shopping village in the 1920s, Westwood is a network of narrow streets laden with book, T-shirt, and souvenir stores, and a variety of informal restaurants catering to the crowds who flock to the neighborhood's first-run movie theaters, eager to see films still fresh from the studios' editing suites (see panel, left). Marilyn Monroe is buried in Westwood Memorial Park.

Westwood is one of the few places in L.A. intended for walking, although it is also favored by adolescents (many from the adjoining UCLA campus) for bumper-to-bumper car cruising; the evening traffic can be intense, although a free minibus eases some of the strain.

A recent addition to Westwood is the **Armand Hammer Museum of Art and Culture Center**▶▶▶ (see page 124) displaying the ample fruits of 50 years of collecting by the extremely rich oil magnate. The main gallery reads like a Who's Who of European fine art—and includes an outstanding set of lithographs by 19th-century caricaturist Honoré Daumier, while a separate gallery is devoted entirely to the Codex Hammer, pages from the notebooks of 15th-century genius Leonardo da Vinci. In keeping with the history of the Codex's ownership, Hammer renamed it after himself.

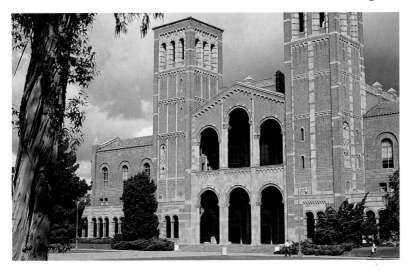

▶▶ UCLA 116A3

405 Hilgard Avenue

The Romanesque brick buildings around the central quadrangle of the University of California at Los Angeles (UCLA) form the heart of the oldest and most respected of L.A.'s academic institutions, founded in 1929. The buildings are full of character and, together with their carefully tended gardens, they provide a break from the corporate towers that fill much of the surrounding area.

There is plenty to see on the campus, but to find your way around, pick up a free map at one of the entrances. Stop first at the **Powell Library▶▶**, for its grand staircase and imposing rotunda, and then enjoy the diverse folk art inside the neighboring **Fowler Museum of Cultural History▶** (tel: 310/825–4361). Cutting-edge American art is usually on show at the Wright Art Gallery, outside which the five-acre jacaranda-shaded **Franklin D. Murphy Sculpture Garden▶** provides surprises of all shapes and sizes—not least works by Rodin and Matisse.

Nonacademic Angelenos appreciate UCLA most of all for the Bruins, the university's sports teams whose success is recalled by wall-to-wall trophies glinting inside the **Athletic Hall of Fame▶** (open from January 2001).

Take a look, too, at the Inverted Fountain, where 10,000 unseen gallons of recycled water re-create the sounds of a mountain stream.

▶ Wilshire Boulevard 116B3

Bearing the name of H. Gaylord Wilshire, the socialist entrepreneur who, in the 1880s, purchased a row of bean fields and marked out its route, Wilshire Boulevard crosses between Downtown and the coast through 16 miles of ethnic diversity and landmark architecture, and passes by the city's major art collection.

At the turn of the century, the shovel of one-time gold prospector and future multimillionaire, Edward L. Doheny, struck oil and much of Wilshire Boulevard disappeared beneath a forest of oil derricks.

Royce Hall, on the UCLA campus

MUSEUM OF TOLERANCE
Just south of Wilshire Boulevard, the Museum of Tolerance (9786 Pico Boulevard; see page 124) uses the latest multimedia and interactive technologies to present a thought-provoking and often harrowing examination of bigotry and racism, past and present. The $50 million museum is closely linked to the Simon Wiesenthal Center, known internationally for its human rights work. Its two main exhibits focus on the Holocaust and on prejudice in the U.S., including an explo-ration of the events surrounding the 1992 L.A. riots.

Miracle Mile As it turned out, the oil reserves were soon exhausted and a longer-lasting boom came in the 1920s and 1930s when Wilshire Boulevard acquired the fabulous art-deco department stores of the Miracle Mile—the first department stores in what were then the L.A. suburbs, and the first step on the way toward the city's decentralization and dependence on the automobile; uniquely for the period, the stores were designed with their own parking lots.

Officially, the Miracle Mile extends between La Brea and Fairfax avenues, but the finest example of the art deco that dominates it is just east, with the (now closed) **Bullocks Wilshire Building**▶▶ (No. 3050). Many of the other structures have aged less gracefully and are now surrounded by busy food shops serving one of the most varied quarters of the city: a melting pot of predominantly Mexican, Filipino, and Korean settlers.

A forerunner of the Miracle Mile, the **Ambassador Hotel**▶ (No. 3400) cost $5 million and occupied 23 acres when it opened in 1921. The Ambassador's place in L.A. history is assured: besides the tales of Hollywood celebrities making fools of themselves in its Cocoanut Grove nightclub, it was here in 1968 that Senator Robert Kennedy was assassinated.

The buildings of the Miracle Mile could hardly have a less architecturally inspiring neighbor than the **Los Angeles County Museum of Art**▶▶▶ (No. 5905). Within the vast museum's stern 1960s exterior, however, centuries' worth of European painting and sculpture, influential contemporary American works, and countless treasures among the Asiatic collections provide several hours of enjoyable viewing.

Be certain to tour the museum's newest addition, the Japanese Pavilion, whose beautiful Edo-period paintings are greatly enhanced by the luminous qualities of the purpose-built pavilion.

Next door to the Museum of Art, several fiberglass mastodons partially sunk in tar frame the grounds of the **George C. Page Museum**▶▶ (No. 5801 Hancock Park; tel: 323/934–7243, see page 124), which informatively annotates the fossils and reconstructs the skeletons of many of the creatures that came, literally, to a sticky end 2 million years ago in the **La Brea Tar Pits**▶. The tar, once used by Native Americans to waterproof their homes, still seeps to the surface of streets in the area.

The **Craft and Folk Art Museum**▶ (No. 5814; tel: 323/937–4230) has entertaining small temporary exhibitions of old and new folk art, and in a rough neighborhood just south of Wilshire Boulevard, the **St. Elmo's Village Art Center**▶ (4830 St. Elmo Drive; tel: 323/931–3409) is an off-the-beaten-track art discovery: the community's success in creating and maintaining the mural-enshrouded art center is celebrated in May with the Festival of the Art of Survival.

Community area The Fairfax Avenue section of Wilshire Boulevard passes through one of the United States' largest Jewish communities. Inside the Jewish Community Building (No. 6006), the **L.A. Museum of Holocaust**▶ (tel: 323/761–8170) has stark reminders of the horrors of Hitler's concentration camps, and emotive paintings by

GARDENS IN THE CITY
Flowers, shrubs, and trees fare surprisingly well in this city of freeways and smog in several caringly nurtured gardens. To escape the metropolis, take a picnic lunch to one of the following: the Rose Garden in Exposition Park; the grounds of Greystone Park (905 Loma Vista Drive, Beverly Hills); the gardens of UCLA; the South Coast Botanical Gardens (26300 Crenshaw Boulevard in Rancho Palos Verdes); the Fern Dell section of Griffith Park; or the Japanese Garden of the CSULB campus in Long Beach.

MACARTHUR PARK
Because singer Richard Harris had a hit in 1968 with a song named after it, MacArthur Park, bisected by Wilshire Boulevard west of Alvarado Street, enjoys a certain fame. However, few people realize this 32-acre green slab was the city's first public park, created in 1890. Enjoyed mostly by Latino mothers with toddlers by day, the park becomes a domain of drug dealers by night.

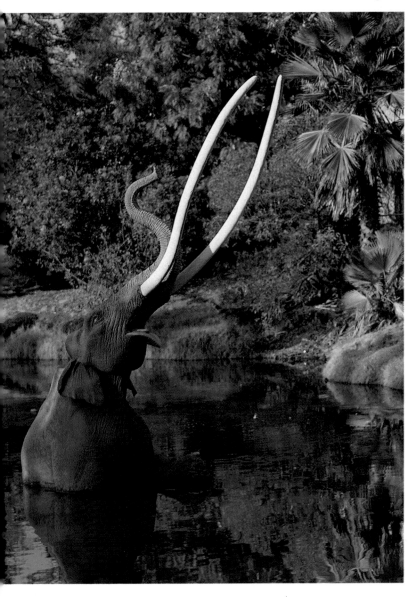

some of those interned in them. Just south of Wilshire Boulevard, the **Farmers' Market▶** (6333 West 3rd Avenue, at Fairfax Avenue; tel: 323/933–9211) began when a small group of farmers, poverty-stricken by the Depression, were allowed to sell their produce for free from a patch of open ground. Nowadays, it has grown into a curious mix of groaning fruit and vegetable stalls, tacky souvenir shops, and food stands offering plenty of cheap, tasty snacks. Around 40,000 people visit Farmers' Market daily, many of them Angelenos enjoying the experience of shopping somewhere other than an air-conditioned mall.

Many prehistoric creatures, such as this mastodon re-created at the George C. Page Museum, became trapped in the local tar pits, their remains first discovered in 1906

Bizarre merchandise is the stock-in-trade of shops on the West Hollywood section of Melrose Avenue

MARKETS
Some 30,000 people a day weave around the food stalls of the indoor Grand Central Market (317 S. Broadway), where the noise level is not for the nervous. Sweet smells and bright colors abound at the Flower Market, between Seventh and Eighth streets (9 AM–6 PM).

PRODUCE MARKET
Mountainous piles of fruit and vegetables from the state's farms are unloaded at the Produce Market (on Eighth and Ninth streets near Central Avenue).

Shopping

Consuming passions run high in L.A., and shopping is one of the city's favorite pastimes. Several areas, such as Farmers' Market, Fisherman's Wharf, and Ports O'Call Village are noted for their tourist appeal but there are many better and more interesting places—from luxury malls to thrift stores—to pursue the art of acquiring.

Something for everyone Few cities can equal L.A.'s state-of-the-art shopping malls, gigantic air-conditioned shrines to consumerism. Two of the flashiest are The Beverly Center (bordered by Beverly and La Cienega boulevards), packed with stylish, refined shops that attract the affluent of West L.A., and the Century City Shopping Center (10250 Santa Monica Boulevard). But the most architectually imaginative place to shop is the Santa Monica Place (Fourth Street and Broadway) with all the usual retail outlets plus two department stores.

Elsewhere, two smaller malls reflect contrasting ethnic groups. Little Tokyo's Japanese Village Plaza Mall (Central Avenue between First and Second streets) has numerous outlets for Japanese goods, food, and clothes. Meanwhile, Latino East L.A. does its shopping at the lively El Mercado market (3425 E. First Street).

Upscale department stores All over the city, there are branches of fine stores such as Nordstrom, Neiman-Marcus, and Saks Fifth Avenue. Beverly Hills' Rodeo Drive and the Rodeo Center (see page 118) are the domain of the ultra-expensive.

Cheap clothing Substantially less expensive good-quality clothing can be found in Downtown's Garment District (centered on Los Angeles Street, between Seventh Street and Washington Boulevard), where a rake through the immense stocks of the Cooper Building (860 Los Angeles Street) will uncover many bargains. **CaliforniaMart**, on the edge of Downtown, 110 E Ninth Street, is among the largest clothing centers in the U.S. But the general public is not allowed to buy anything here except during the widely-advertized, five-times-a-year Super Sale Saturdays, when designer items are offered at give-away prices. A few miles south, another outlet for top-name togs at wholesale prices is the Citadel (5675 E. Telegraph Road; tel: 323/898-1220).

American Rag, Cie (150 S. La Brea Avenue) stocks classic lines in casualwear from the 1930s to the 1990s.

Accessories If money is no object, muster your credit and cruise the well-filled shelves of Hermès (343 N. Rodeo Drive) or Louis Vuitton (307 N. Rodeo Drive). At the other extreme, NaNa (1245 Third Street, Santa Monica) is stuffed with daring hats, bizarre gloves, and other eccentric items.

The remnants of Downtown's once-thriving jewelry district are the best places to seek out wearable gems at the right price: try the St. Vincent Jewelry Center (650 S. Hill Street) or the International Jewelry Center. Alternatively, head to Santa Monica and investigate the wares of Indian Arts (1244 Third Street), featuring jewelry and more from South America.

For the antique collector Searching for antiques and collectibles in this futuristic city may seem perverse, but the Santa Monica Antiques Market (1607 Lincoln Boulevard) makes for entertaining browsing with over 200 dealers sharing the space. Kitsch Americana fills Off the Wall (7325 Melrose Avenue), while devotees of Hollywood movie nostalgia should find something to tempt them at Chick-a-Boom (6817 Melrose Avenue).

For book lovers Impressively well-filled bookstores are found throughout L.A. The long-established Larry Edmunds Cinema Bookshop (6644 Hollywood Boulevard) leads the field in movie and theater books and posters, although the Hollywood Book and Poster Company (6349 Hollywood Boulevard) is fast catching up.

For fiction, and everything else, allocate a day for scrutinizing the endless shelves of Acres of Books (240 Long Beach Boulevard). Book Soup (8818 Sunset Boulevard) not only has the latest alternative, mainstream, and classical fiction, but also attracts prestigious names to its regular author signings and readings, and has a knowledgeable crowd browsing its shelves nightly until midnight.

Author readings are also a feature of the left-leaning political bookstore Midnight Special (1350 Third Street, Santa Monica), and the gay and lesbian orientated A Different Light (8853 Santa Monica Boulevard). Hard-to-find art and architecture volumes turn up in Arcana Books on the Arts (1229 Third Street Promenade, Santa Monica).

To turn browsing into meditation, visit the Bodhi Tree Bookstore (8585 Melrose Avenue), packed with New Age, healing, psychology, religious and philosophical titles.

A few of the basic essentials of life that are on hand for Beverly Hills shoppers

MEAL COSTS

On average, you should budget for about $6 to $8 for breakfast in Los Angeles; $8 to $12 for lunch; and around $15 to $25 for dinner. Some establishments serve enormous helpings at mealtimes.

THEY MADE IT HERE FIRST

At least two popular cocktails were dreamed up in the Bay Area. The late newspaper columnist Stanton Delaplane is credited with creating the first Irish coffee at the Buena Vista Café in Fisherman's Wharf. The invention of the martini, that lethal combination of gin and a certain amount of vermouth, is credited to a nameless bar in the East Bay riverfront town of Martinez.

Food and drink

International flavor Gastronomically speaking, L.A. is at the crossroads of the world. Coffee shops, delis, and burger joints are as common here as anywhere else in the country (if often in unusual forms, such as fancy hot dog stands and 1950s-themed diners), but overall American food is less prevalent than the scores of ethnic cuisines offered at anything from roadside stalls to reservation-only restaurants.

Angelenos and visitors alike enjoy a culinary choice that few cities can beat. What is more, you do not need to be rich to indulge.

Even the famously bizarre concoctions of L.A.'s world-class chefs soon filter down from the temples of fine dining to affordable street-level outlets. Designer pizza, for example, with its exotic toppings, was born in the exclusive Spago's, but is now plied to the masses through the branches of California Pizza Kitchen.

The freshness of the fruit and vegetables raised on the state's farms heightens the flavors of many dishes, and salads are often full meals in themselves, with strawberries, orange sections, and grapes alongside the more usual ingredients.

Having the Pacific Ocean for a neighbor keeps the quality high in L.A.'s seafood restaurants which offer abalone, tuna, swordfish, and fist-size shrimps. Innumerable cafés along the coast offer tasty fish snacks as refreshments to accompany a day's tanning.

California cuisine Born from the free-wheeling spirit that characterizes the Sunshine State, contemporary California cuisine combines fresh ingredients, bold flavors and culinary creativity to produce an exciting, vibrant style of cooking. Ask your waiter to describe the items on the menu, because, chances are, they will offer a few delicious suprises.

Mexican Most Mexican dishes served in the U.S. are based on variations of the tortilla, a doughy pancake made from cornmeal or wheat, which can be baked or fried and then rolled or folded around food, or laid flat beneath it. Mashed or refried beans, rice, chilis, beef, and cheese are the other staple ingredients. Fish tacos, and the melted-cheese-filled tortilla called a *quesadilla*, are a couple of the meat-free alternatives.

Bowls of tortilla chips and spicy salsa are laid out as free hors d'oeuvres in Mexican restaurants; tortilla chips with melted cheese, known as nachos, make a good snack.

L.A.'s Mexican menus also include the burrito—a large flour tortilla filled with beef, cheese, chilis, and beans—which you will not find at all in Mexico.

Asian Not as cheap as Mexican, but enticingly priced restaurants are all over the place; the most interesting are in Little Tokyo, where curry dishes are popular, and steaming sake is always on hand to help down the food.

Chinese food in its various forms comes best, not surprisingly, in the hundreds of restaurants filling Chinatown, and Korean cuisine is making steady headway from its Koreatown base.

Italian food is not hard to come by in L.A.

European and North African The many sailors who have settled in San Pedro give rise to a globe-spanning group of eateries, including Greek, Moroccan, and Eastern European, all of which can be found in the small harborside town. Taken together, they're an easy way to learn about Mediterranean cuisine.

Italian Italian cooking is hard to miss. Pasta and pizza stops are everywhere, and in the classier places, top Italian chefs are inspired by the similarities in climate and natural produce between their homeland and southern California.

Drinks These are dispensed as eagerly as food. You may need to request a glass of ice water in these conservation-minded times, but rare is the coffee shop or diner that does not keep your coffee cup—choose between regular and decaf—filled to the brim. Ice tea is common and is the ideal coolant on a hot day; refills are usually free.

Most restaurants are fully licensed and some are regarded as places to drink as much as places to eat. Several Mexican eateries are better known for the strength of their margaritas—often available in fruit-flavored forms besides the "original" mix of tequila, Triple Sec, and lime juice, with optional salt around the glass—than for the quality of their food.

Listings of recommended L.A. restaurants begin on page 272 of the Hotels and Restaurants section.

CHEESEBURGERS IN PARADISE
Southern California's automobile-based culture was the natural spawning ground for the first McDonald's (in Downey, circa 1937), Carl's Jr., Denny's, and Wenchell's. The world's first double-decker hamburger was served at Bob's Big Boy in Burbank. (By the way, the first McDonald's sold only hot dogs, as did Carl's Jr., which began as a hot dog stand at Florence and Central Avenue in 1941.)

VEGETARIAN FOOD
A city where eating and health are both taken very seriously, it should be no surprise that L.A. has a generous number of vegetarian and wholefood eateries offering dishes free not only of meat but of almost anything remotely bad for you.

L.A.'s Hard Rock Café, the first in what is now a worldwide chain, had to pay a Downtown diner with the same name for the right to use the title

144

NIGHTLIFE ON THE NET
A growing number of web sites enable users to keep their fingers on the pulse of Los Angeles nightlife from anywhere in the world, as well as being general sources of city information: www.calendar.live.com is the entertainment section of the *Los Angeles Times*; www.laweekly.com belongs to the city's leading alternative newspaper, *L.A. Weekly*; www.newtimesla.com is operated by its main rival, *New Times*. Another useful L.A. site is www.losangeles.com, part of the Boulevard network of alternative urban information sources.

Nightlife

You could spend months exploring nocturnal L.A. and still only scratch the surface. For the latest on what's happening where, the best option is to read the listings in the *L.A. Weekly* newspaper.

Jazz, rock, and R&B These are the main fare of the city's innumerable live music venues.

The Troubador, 9081 Santa Monica Boulevard (tel: 310/276–6168), made its name as a folk venue and now features rock acts; the Roxy, 9009 Sunset Boulevard (tel: 310/276–2222), has hopeful new bands; and Whisky A Go Go, 8901 Sunset Boulevard (tel: 310/652–4202), is the archetypal long-running L.A. rock club. More recent, and since the death there of River Phoenix, more notorious, is the Viper Room, 8852 Sunset Boulevard (tel: 310/358–1880), usually with counterculture celebrities in the audience as well as on stage.

Harvelle's Blues Club, 1432 Fourth Street, Santa Monica (tel: 310/395–1675), presents top-rated blues and R&B artists in a replica of a Chicago blues bar; for similar music from local and national names in a mock Deep South setting, pay a visit to B.B. King's Blues Club, 1000 Universal Center Drive (tel: 818/6–BBKING), which really is owned by the legendary blues guitarist, or the House of Blues, 8430 Sunset Boulevard (tel: 323/848–5100).

Noted for their knowledgeable audiences and constantly good shows, the pick of the jazz clubs include: The Baked Potato, 3787 Cahuenga Boulevard (tel: 818/980–1615) and Catalina Bar & Grill, 1640 N. Cahuenga Boulevard (tel: 323/466–2210).

Cabaret, comedy and magic These are all in plentiful supply in L.A. The Comedy Store, 8433 Sunset Boulevard (tel: 323/656–6225), is the main stage for proven comics; the Improvisation, 8162 Melrose Avenue (tel: 323/651–2583), features acts on the rise; the Groundlings Theater, 7307 Melrose Avenue (tel: 323/934–9700), has a well-deserved reputation for the very best improvised sketches. Luna Park, 665 N Robertson Boulevard (tel: 310/652–0611) is a multi-leveled venue often with established comedy acts.

Conjuring connoisseurs will love the Magic Castle, 7001 Franklin Avenue (tel: 323/851–3314), a building devoted to trickery where the strange happenings are not limited to the stage. The Castle is for members only, but your hotel receptionist should be able to arrange entry.

Theater, dancing, and music If you simply want to dance, go to the Crush Bar, 1743 N. Cahuenga Boulevard (tel: 323/463–7685), and join the not-quite-fashionable crowd gyrating 60s-style across two spacious floors; The World, 7070 Hollywood Boulevard (tel: 323/467–7070), has a different musical theme nightly. If you want to be seen with the L.A. jet-set, try to look fashionable and show up at the Viper Room, 8852 Sunset Boulevard (tel: 310/358–1880), owned by actor Johnny Depp.

Classical music centers on the Music Center, located on 135 N. Grand Avenue, whose Dorothy Chandler Pavilion is the venue for the Los Angeles Master Chorale (tel: 213/626–0624), Los Angeles Opera (tel: 213/972–7219), and Los Angeles Philharmonic (tel: 323/850–2000), which also plays a summer season at the Hollywood Bowl, 2301 N. Highland Avenue. Also at the Music Center, the Mark Taper Forum (tel: (213/972–0700) runs contemporary plays, and the Ahmanson Theater (tel: (213/628–2772) hosts Broadway blockbusters. The Shubert Theater, 2020 Avenue of the Stars (tel: 310/201–1500), also mounts touring productions of New York shows.

Scores of smaller theaters are found all over L.A. and often feature plays written and acted to exceptionally high levels. Locations and productions change frequently; check the papers for listings and reviews.

Bars There are few of the smoky bars that predominate in many U.S. cities; if you're seeking local color, try Barney's Beanery, 8447 Santa Monica Boulevard (tel: 323/654–2287), with its pool tables and dozens of imported brews, or Al's Bar, 305 S. Hewitt Street (tel: 213/625–9703), supplying beer and arty music to a bohemian crowd.

Hotel choice Among the distinctive hotel bars are the Biltmore Hotel's Gallery Bar, 506 S. Grand Avenue (tel: 213/624–1011), with its marble columns and Mies van der Rohe chairs, the revolving Bonavista Lounge of the Westin Bonaventure, 404 S. Figueroa Street (tel: 213/624–1000), and the most famous place in Los Angeles for an overpriced tipple, the Polo Lounge of the Beverly Hills Hotel, 9641 Sunset Boulevard (tel: 310/276–2251).

COFFEE BARS
The last ten years have seen L.A.'s nightlife enriched by an influx of coffee bars. As their name suggests, such places serve coffee (usually a wide variety, all available with or without caffeine) rather than alcohol, and include haunts such as Highland Grounds, 742 N. Highland Boulevard, West Hollywood (tel: 323/466–1507), or wackily decorated hangouts of would-be avant-garde writers and poets such as the sleekly appointed **City Bean**, 8457 Santa Monica Boulevard (tel: 323/848–8500), which has inviting sidewalk tables. Another of these is **Bourgeois Pig**, 5931 Franklin Avenue (tel: 323/962–6366), decorated with chandeliers and gold-framed mirrors.

145

Named for the 'strip' of glamorous nightclubs that lined this mile-long section of Sunset Boulevard from the 1940s, Sunset Strip is still a major nightlife area as well as a prime site for large and colorful billboards, usually advertising new films or record releases

Los Angeles

146

HOLLYWOODS'S LURE
Anyone drawn to Los Angeles by Hollywood and silver screen nostalgia should be advised that while good rooms can be found, they will be costly and you should, as ever, reserve as early as possible. Unfortunately, many accommodations on the central and eastern sections of Hollywood Boulevard and Sunset Boulevard are rundown and seedy, their rooms more often rented by the hour than by the night.

Accommodations

From whirlpool-equipped luxury suites to dependable no-frills motel rooms and budget-priced beds in youth hostel dormitories, there is no shortage of places to stay in L.A.

Book in advance Wherever you plan to stay and however much you plan to spend, it is wise to book as far in advance as possible. Many hotels have toll-free 800 phone numbers enabling you to call them free of charge from anywhere within the United States.

If you do not have a reservation, any of the visitor information offices listed on page 149 can help find a place to stay; each has shelves laden with hotel, motel, and hostel brochures, which sometimes offer a few dollars' discount on the regular price.

Getting around L.A. is nearly impossible without a car, which means location is of less importance when seeking accommodations than ease of access to the city's freeways. If you are not using a car, spread your stay across several areas to avoid long hours riding the L.A. buses. Location does make a difference to the cost, however, and you should also note that very few parts of L.A. are safe to walk around in after dark.

The five mirrored cylinders of L.A.'s Bonaventure Hotel became a futuristic addition to the Downtown landscape in 1978

At a price to suit every pocket, Downtown accommodations span everything from low-rent flophouses to architecturally inventive hotels for business travelers. Between these extremes, a growing number of hotels ($70 to $90) offer solid value and make a good base for exploring the area—a rare instance of an L.A. district geared, in daylight, to walking.

Promising Old World elegance in the heart of Beverly Hills, the Beverly Wilshire Hotel has hosted the rich and famous since 1928

147

Moving west, central Hollywood, holding the main remnants from the movie industry's golden years, has a dozen or so comfortable hotels ($85 to $105) close to Hollywood Boulevard; just south, numerous motels ($70 to $100) of varying quality can be found along Sunset Boulevard.

Standards and prices rise in unison as you continue west into West Hollywood, Beverly Hills, and Westwood. It is here that you will find plush hotels with fitness facilities and rooftop tennis courts intended to help visiting entertainment industry moguls unwind. Prices begin at around $150 and increase swiftly; this is a very refined area in which to stay, and several sections are safe for evening strolling.

At the coast The building of new ocean-view hotels and renovations of older accommodations has made Santa Monica one of L.A.'s best areas for quality accommodation. There are still a few shabby but serviceable motels (upwards of $60) on the periphery, but the town itself boasts stylish mid-range options (around $110) and several full-service resorts (upwards of $150). To the south, through rowdy Venice Beach and on to the quieter communities of Manhattan Beach, Hermosa Beach, and Redondo Beach, there is a wide choice of medium-priced hotels and motels ($60 to $90). A good way to save money is to seek out accommodations a few blocks inland where you will often pay $10 or $20 less than at a hotel facing the beach.

Around the Palos Verdes peninsula San Pedro has a good mix of modern chain hotels and trusty motels (from $80 and $50 respectively), as does, to a lesser extent, nearby Long Beach.

Flying in very late or flying out very early are the only reasons to opt for one of the pricey hotels surrounding the airport. Many hotels in other areas provide free airport transportation; even if they do not, airport shuttle buses are plentiful.

Listings of recommended L.A. accommodations begin on page 271.

Los Angeles

What might look like a futuristic air traffic control center is actually the Theme Building at LAX, Los Angeles International Airport, mostly visited for its restaurant

Practical points

Arriving by plane All international flights and most domestic flights land at Los Angeles International Airport (LAX, tel: 310/646–5252), 18 miles southwest of Downtown and a mile east of the coast. Some domestic airlines also land at Burbank (tel: 818/840–8847) and Orange County (tel: 949/252–5252) airports: these can be much more convenient than LAX, especially for Disneyland or Burbank.

To get from the airport to other parts of the city, use one of the shuttle buses (there are dozens, run by private firms) that pick up passengers from the airport concourse and deliver them to almost any address in L.A. The shuttle buses charge according to how far you are going: most fares are between $12 and $20. Local buses (see below) are cheaper, but L.A.'s bus network can be bewildering for first-time arrivals. Taking a taxi from the airport is likely to cost in excess of $30.

Airlines All the major airlines have several offices around L.A. Their main phone numbers are: American Airlines (tel: 800/433–7300); British Airways (tel: 800/247–9297); Continental (tel: 800/525–1700); Delta (tel: 213/221–1212); Northwest (tel: 800/225–2525); United (tel: 800/241–6522); Virgin (tel: 800/862–8621).

Arriving by bus or train All long-distance buses into L.A. stop in Downtown at 1716 E. Seventh Street (tel: 213/629–8400); some services also run to Hollywood, 1409 Vine Street (tel: 213/466–6382), and Santa Monica, 1433 Fifth Street (tel: 310/394–5433).

L.A.'s railroad station is Union Station, 800 N. Alameda Street in Downtown (tel: 800/872–7245).

Getting around As mentioned earlier, it is easiest to get around L.A. by car. The bus system, however, is comprehensive, and there are taxi services.

Car rental—If you have arranged car rental ahead of arrival, your car can be picked up at the airport; just look for the appropriate car rental desk. You can also rent on arrival at the airport, or elsewhere in L.A., by phoning one of the numerous car-rental firms (whose offices are all over the city) at one of the following numbers:

SAFETY
Despite the globally publicized riots of 1992 L.A. is no more dangerous than any other major U.S. city. As elsewhere, it is sufficient to take simple precautions: keep your bags close at hand and difficult to snatch, avoid run-down areas (following advice from your hotel), and keep car doors locked.

Alamo (tel: 800/327–9633); Avis (tel: 800/331–1212); Budget (tel: 800/221–1203); or Hertz (tel: 800/654–3131).

Local buses—L.A. has the largest bus service in the country, but traveling by bus can be time-consuming.

Most services are run by the MTA (for information, tel: 800/266–6883 COMMUTE) and have a flat single-journey fare, payable with exact change when boarding.

Buses run every ten minutes (less frequently at night) along the main streets linking Downtown and the coast, passing through Hollywood and Beverly Hills before reaching Santa Monica or Venice. Useful routes are 1 (along Hollywood Boulevard); 2 (along Sunset Boulevard); 4 (along Santa Monica Boulevard); 11 (along Melrose Avenue); and 20, 21, and 22 (along Wilshire Boulevard).

Taxis—L.A.'s taxis charge a fee at the flag (that is, when your trip commences) and then a further fixed charge per mile. They need to be phoned for rather than hailed from the curb: Checker Cab (tel: 800/300–5007) and L.A. Taxi (tel: 310/715–1968) are two major firms; others are listed in the phone book.

Useful phone numbers
Dentist referral service (tel: 800/422–8338)
Emergency services 911
Time (tel: 213/853–1212)
Traveler's Info Line (tel: 323/686–0950)
Weather (tel: 213/554–1212).

Visitor information The biggest source of tourist information in the city is the Visitor Information Center, 685 S. Figueroa Street, Downtown (tel: 213/689–8822 or 800/228–2452; www.lacvb.com).

Smaller but equally useful offices in other areas include Beverly Hills Visitors Bureau, 239 S. Beverly Drive, Beverly Hills (tel: 310/248–1015); the Janes House, 6541 Hollywood Boulevard, Hollywood (tel: 213/689–8822); Santa Monica Convention & Visitors Bureau, 520 Broadway, Santa Monica (tel: 310/319–6263); Long Beach Visitor and Convention Council, 1 World Trade Center, Suite 300, Long Beach (tel: 562/436–3645); and San Pedro Peninsula Chamber of Commerce, 390 W. Seventh Street, San Pedro (tel: 310/832–7272). For information on-line, the *L.A. Times* website, www.latimes.com, has news, views and copious listings.

THE L.A. SUBWAY
After years of planning and the spending of many millions of dollars, Los Angeles set about reducing its dependency on the car by opening the first section of the Metro Rail subway system in 1990. The still-growing network of color-coded lines link Downtown and Longbeach (Blue Line), Downtown and Redondo Beach via LAX (Green Line), while work continues on the Red Line, which will eventually connect Downtown, Hollywood, and the San Fernando Valley.

149

Among many taxi companies, L.A. has its share of Yellow Cabs. Their color was chosen after a report suggested that yellow was the color most easily spotted on the street

AROUND LOS ANGELES

FRANTIC GROWTH During the last fifty years of it Los Angeles has spread across hills, through valleys, and along the coast, absorbing entire communities and turning former farmland into a uniform suburbia stretching as far as the eye can see.

But there are a few stops of note for visitors. Several older towns have retained their character in this commuter-dominated territory, and it is also around L.A. that some of the state's very best art collections are stashed. Here, too, Disneyland blazed a trail for theme parks throughout the world, and the coastline spans everything from broad sandy beaches to towering rocky bluffs.

Beside the ocean just north of L.A., Malibu draws visitors in search of California's rich and beautiful people. Much more apparent, however, are the surfer-dominated sands and, just inland, rugged canyons that

The beauty of Malibu: a beach nearby, on the Pacific Coast Highway

shelter secluded hamlets and provide boundless scope for wilderness hiking.

To the south, the Orange County shoreline is sculpted into numerous coves and inlets, along which several distinctive and personable communities stand in marked contrast to inland Orange County. This is a network of middle-class suburbs (among the most affluent and conservative places to live in the U.S.) pockmarked by theme parks—most famously Disneyland—the only reason for most people to penetrate the area's blandness.

Beyond the hills on L.A.'s northern edge, an immense population fills the flat floors of the San Gabriel and San Fernando valleys. The luckiest of the valley dwellers are those who live in long-established settlements such as Pasadena—with a clutch of museums and a pleasingly restored downtown area—the only valley town worth spending time in, and a useful base for exploring several historic sites scattered through the valleys.

Around Los Angeles

Around Los Angeles

The seemingly ramshackle nature of these beachside homes in Malibu belies the fact that some of their owners are extremely wealthy and some are household names. With hills so close to the beach, many Malibu homes are damaged each year by the landslides that follow heavy rains, a feature of the L.A. winter

▶▶▶ Malibu   150A3

Many of L.A.'s—and the world's—richest and most glamorous people own million-dollar homes in Malibu, immediately north of Santa Monica. However, it is the dramatic Malibu hills, twisting canyons, and inviting beaches that impress.

A century ago, a well-off settler called Frederick H. Rindge bought the Mexican rancho which, at that time, covered Malibu. As L.A. expanded, Rindge (and later, after his death, his widow, Mary) fought tooth and nail against state plans to put a road through their land, only to be defeated in the Supreme Court and subsequently to lose their fortune in the Wall Street Crash.

The Malibu Beach Colony From the 1920s, a secluded beachside enclave of Hollywood notables, which included Clara Bow, Barbara Stanwyck, and Gloria Swanson, began turning Malibu into a desirable address. Even today, Malibu's rock stars, TV personalities, and sports stars carefully (if illegally) prevent public access to the beaches close to their homes.

Approaching Malibu from the south brings you first through Pacific Palisades, where the **Will Rogers State Park**▶▶ (1501 Will Rogers State Park Road; tel: 310/454–8212) holds the former home of the "Cowboy Philosopher," whose homespun wisdom and one-line witticisms kept Americans amused through the 1920s and 1930s. Old-West artifacts are piled high inside the humorist's former home, and the 187-acre grounds include numerous picnic spots, walking and hiking trails, and as a polo field.

A mile to the north, the **Self-Realization Fellowship**▶, (17190 Sunset Boulevard; tel: 310/454–4114) founded in 1950, seeks to express the universality of the world's major religions. Arranged around a swan-filled lake, the fellowship evokes a suitable mood of serenity and contemplation.

Health and nature In the psychedelic 1960s, a hippie colony arrived in **Topanga Canyon** and established a base for alternative lifestyles and exploring the inner self. By the 1990s, people were more interested in the untamed natural beauty, but there is still a strong sense

THE GRUNION RUN
Between March and August on nights following high tides, small fish called grunion come ashore for a frantic three-hour bout of spawning and egg-burying known as the Grunion Run. Seeing the beach crawling with thousands of these squirming fish, the only kind to lay their eggs on land, is an amazing sight that pulls big crowds. Any beach in the L.A. area is a likely vantage point for this only-in-California phenomenon.

of the 1960s and the 1980s New Age movement, most evident in the health food restaurants, handicraft shops, and bookstores.

A network of hiking trails weaves across the chaparral-covered slopes of the 10,000-acre **Topanga State Park▶▶** (tel: 310/455–2465), emerging to breathtaking views of ocean, mountains, and sprawling L.A.

Similar terrain fills **Malibu Creek State Park▶** (tel: 818/880–0367), once used by 20th-Century Fox as the setting of *M*A*S*H*, among many other film and TV productions, and where wildflowers brighten the spring meadows.

The town of Malibu is surprisingly nondescript, and it has been the local beaches that have pulled the crowds since Surfrider Beach provided the setting for the low-budget beach party movies of the late 1950s.

Surfrider Beach, now renamed Malibu Lagoon State Beach, has been overlooked for almost a century by the 700-foot **Malibu Pier▶**. Besides making a prime vantage point for watching the surfers, the pier (built by Frederick Rindge to unload supply ships) also marks the site of the **Adamson House▶▶** (23200 Pacific Coast Highway; tel: 310/456-8452) built in 1929 and inhabited by a member of the Rindge family until 1964. Inside the house the Spanish colonial design is enhanced by the colorful ceramics known as "Malibu tiles," and a fine assortment of decorative ironwork and murals. The adjoining museum peeps into Malibu's past.

Las Tunas and Corral beaches are noted for their scuba diving, Paradise Cove is ideal for beachcombing, the picnic tables and snack stands of Zuma Beach attract thousands of San Fernando Valley dwellers every weekend, and **Leo Carrillo State Beach▶** (which takes its name from the actor who played Pancho in the *Cisco Kid* TV series) is split in two by Sequit Point, a bluff through which wave action has gouged a large tunnel.

UNDERWATER ADVENTURE

Surfing, swimming, and sunbathing are not the only activities enjoyed along the L.A. area's coastline. From Malibu in the north to San Clemente in the south, there are ample opportunities for snorkeling and scuba diving. Explorable underwater caves are plentiful, rich kelp beds attract shoals of brightly colored fish, and the deep water on the ocean side of Santa Catalina (see page 162) has several submerged wrecks. Equipment rental outlets are easy to find anywhere where conditions are suitable.

153

Many beaches around L.A. have ideal surfing conditions

Three exceptional but very different art museums lie within the Los Angeles area. One of them, the Getty Center, should be seen for its setting alone: high above West L.A., occupying what is said to be the most expensive building ever built in the United States. The Norton Simon and the Huntingdon also hold important collections.

154

The impressive purpose-built Getty Center houses an incredible display of art and antiquities from all round the world

Building for beauty Designed by architect Richard Meier at a cost of a billion dollars, the Getty Center sits with considerable aplomb in a magnificent hillside site. Opened in December 1997, the center is the latest and grandest addition to the Getty holdings. These began with the Greek and Roman antiquities, French furnishings, and European paintings collected by the immensely rich oil tycoon John Paul Getty. They were first publicly displayed in 1974 in a re-creation of a Pompeiian villa (see panel), and continued after the man's death with a $700 million endowment that made this art museum the richest in the world.

Only a part of the Getty Center is a museum: sharing the site are the offices of the Getty research, conservation, and education institutes, all as well financed as the museum itself.

Almost inevitably, the building—arranged in a series of pavilions linked by plazas and terraces that provide stunning panoramas across L.A.—completely steals attention from the art exhibited inside.

THE GETTY VILLA
In a hilltop location in Malibu overlooking the ocean, the Getty Villa, formerly the site of the Getty collections, is a replica of the Villa del Papiri, an Italian villa destroyed by the eruption of Vesuvius in AD 79. Currently being remodeled, the villa will reopen in 2001 as the home of Getty's Greek and Roman antiquities and as a research center for studies in comparative cultures and archeology.

The exhibits Appreciating the collections, chiefly European art from the Renaissance to the Post-impressionists, is aided by the excellent Art Information Rooms, with books and interactive multimedia screens enabling visitors to discover more about the art and artists whose work is displayed. Temporary exhibitions are of exceptional standard, and among the highlights of the permanent display are paintings such as Van Gogh's *Irises* and Monet's haystack series, the Drawings Collection with works from 1400 onward, and the many masterpieces of medieval artwork in the Illuminated Manuscripts Collection.

The Norton Simon Museum It may be less famous and much less rich, but the quality of the paintings within the Norton Simon Museum in Pasadena surpasses those of the Getty. Here, Rubens, Rembrandt, Raphael, and Brueghel delight among the Old Masters; Cézanne, Renoir, and Van Gogh shine out in well-filled Impressionist and Postimpressionist galleries; a Degas collection includes a set of small, sculpted dancers; and the 20th-century collection features works by Picasso, Matisse, and the German Expressionists.

The European displays are matched by the museum's stunning Asian collections, spanning 2,000 years of North Indian Buddhist art and Hindu sculpture, and South Indian, Himalayan, and Southeast Asian art.

The Huntington Art Collections Just a few miles east of the Norton, the Huntington Art Collections house an extraordinary stock of English 18th-century portraiture and 19th-century landscapes.

In the former home of railroad tycoon Henry E. Huntington, who instigated L.A.'s first (and last) efficient mass transit system during the early 1900s, the ornately furnished gallery rooms hold works by Hogarth, Turner, and Constable, and lead to the prized exhibits: Gainsborough's *The Blue Boy*, Sir Thomas Lawrence's *Pinkie*, and Reynolds' *Mrs. Siddons as the Tragic Muse*.

Other sections of the house contain Renaissance paintings and 18th-century French sculpture, and the adjoining Virginia Steele Scott Gallery shows American art from colonial times to the present, and includes a section on the architectural firm of Greene & Greene.

Rare books and manuscripts Elsewhere on the Huntington estate, 2 million manuscripts and 600,000 rare books are housed in the **Huntington Library**— among them the *Ellesmere Chaucer*, believed to be the most complete and reliable manuscript of The *Canterbury Tales*, and dated to 1410. Other highlights include a *Gutenberg Bible*, one of 12 surviving copies printed on vellum, and Shakespeare's **First Folio**, the first edition of the bard's plays, printed in 1623.

NORTON SIMON
Compared to the flamboyant and controversial J. Paul Getty, Norton Simon is a relatively unsung patron of the arts whose personal collection— forming the Norton Simon Museum—was financed by the vast wealth accruing from his large and diverse business empire. Already a long-established collector of European Old Masters, Simon allegedly acquired his taste for art from the subcontinent during a visit to India's National Museum in 1971.

155

An exhibit at the J. Paul Getty Museum

THE HUNTINGTON GARDENS
After filling your head with the Huntington Collection's art and books, unwind with a lengthy stroll through the immaculately groomed Huntington Botanical Gardens.

The northern section of 3-mile-long Balboa Beach, overlooked by luxurious ocean-view homes

Orange County

Aside from cutting inland to visit Disneyland and a few other theme parks, the best way to take in Orange County—characterized by plain shopping malls, identical houses, and freeway interchanges—is by sticking to its coast.

One place warranting a detour deep in suburbia, however, is the **Richard M. Nixon Birthplace and Library▶▶** (see page 124) at Yorba Linda, which records in a lavish (and entirely uncritical) manner the extraordinary career of the nation's 37th president (who is also buried here).

The first of the coastal towns, **Huntington Beach▶** has been a surfing hot spot since the 1920s when California's earliest surfing contests were held beside its pier. In the evening, the action moves ashore with dozens of impromptu barbecues held around the beach's firerings. By contrast, well-heeled yacht owners help make neighboring **Newport Beach▶** a shrine to moneyed living, with only the three-mile-long **Balboa Peninsula▶▶** offering any inducement to visitors.

A fine-sand beach lines the peninsula, whose southern end holds the wooden Balboa Pavilion, a ritzy dance hall from 1905 that is now filled with souvenir shops and amusement arcades. Pleasure craft cruise the harbor from the nearby marina, and another short boat trip is the 35¢ ride offered by the Balboa ferry, which has plied the almost jumpable gap between the peninsula and Balboa Isle—an artificial island packed with expensive homes—since 1909.

Away from the beach, local life revolves around the high-fashion clothing stores of the primly landscaped Fashion Island shopping center, and the **Orange County Museum of Art▶▶** (see page 124), justly acclaimed for its displays of contemporary southern Californian art.

South of Newport Beach, **Crystal Cove State Park▶** (tel: 949/494–3539) has a refreshingly unkempt and under-used beach, while hiking trails through the inland section of the park lead into the San Joaquin Hills, once a grazing place for the cattle of Mission San Juan Capistrano.

THE CRYSTAL CATHEDRAL
Made entirely of glass, save for its white steel trusses and wooden fittings, the multimillion-dollar Crystal Cathedral (12141 Lewis Street, Garden Grove; tel: 714/971–4013) was built in 1980 at the behest of TV evangelist Robert Schuller. In 1955, Schuller's preaching career began in an abandoned drive-in movie theater, later moved to the world's first drive-in church, and now centers on showbiz-style sermons, delivered from the Crystal Cathedral's pulpit, which are broadcast live on cable TV.

Powdery-sand beaches, rocky outcrops, and secluded inlets make the **Laguna Beach►►** shoreline the most attractive in Orange County.

Art galleries and handicraft stalls line Laguna's short streets. Dropping into the **Laguna Art Museum►** (307 Cliff Drive; tel: 949/494–6531) reveals the best works of the local artists, and during July and August, thousands flock to the Pageant of the Masters arts festival (see page 158). South of Laguna Beach, the dramatic headland of **Dana Point►** rises high above the ocean. It was named after Richard Henry Dana, who described how cowhides were flung over the cliffs to be loaded onto boats below in his classic *Two Years Before the Mast*, of 1840.

At the southern tip of Orange County, **San Clemente►** is a likable if unexciting resort town, with a cliff-walled beach. To Californians, the town is best known as the location of Richard Nixon's "Western White House," where the ex-president sat out his post-resignation years.

Mission San Juan Capistrano►►► (Ortega Highway; tel: 949/248–2049. *Open* daily 8:30–5. Closed Jan 1, Good Friday PM, Thanksgiving, Dec 25. *Admission: inexpensive*) was completed in 1806; its **Serra Chapel** is believed to be the state's oldest building. A replica of the Great Stone Church, an immense structure with seven domes and a 120-foot high bell tower that stood in the mission until destroyed by an earthquake in 1812, stands to the north along El Camino Real and serves the local Catholic community. Follow El Camino Real south downhill and turn right onto Verdugo Street to see the **Capistrano Depot►**, still the railway terminal, with Spanish arches and decorative tiles. Nearby, on Los Rios Street, is the **O'Neill Museum►** (tel: 949/493–8444), which shows the locations of 19th-century adobe homes in the adjacent **Los Rios Historic District►**.

SWALLOW SONG
Since Spanish times, swallows have nested at Mission San Juan Capistrano. Legend has it that they return from their winter migration each March 19, St. Joseph's Day. In fact, the swallows return throughout the spring. Nonetheless, crowds of visitors arrive on March 19 for the Fiestas de la Golondrinia, a welcome-home carnival that takes place with or without the swallows, and for October's Adios de las Golondrinias, a smaller event marking the swallows' winter departure.

157

Mission San Juan Capistrano. Around the courtyard are a small museum and re-created workshops in the style of the Spanish era

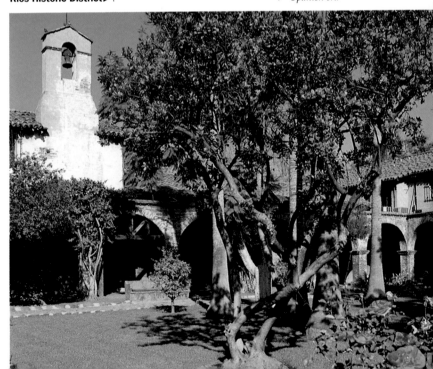

Around Los Angeles

*In the distance, the
slopes of the San Gabriel
Mountains rise sharply
above the tree-lined
streets of Pasadena*

San Gabriel Valley

In the 1920s, the San Gabriel Valley was a verdant
landscape of walnut, orange, and lemon groves, dotted
with small settlements to which Angelenos repaired to
improve their health. Today, the valley communities
have blurred into an almighty slab of suburbia and suffer
in the summer months from the infamous L.A. smog,
often thick enough to obscure the nearby mountains, and
noxious enough to warrant health warnings.

Conditions permitting, the best base for seeing the
valley is **Pasadena▶▶▶** (Northeast of downtown LA,
off Highway 101) within easy reach of the Gamble
House (see page 159), the Norton Simon Museum, and
the Huntington Art Collections (see page 155), and a
section of Colorado Boulevard that has been
transformed into a very attractive "Old Town."

A few miles south, the first fixed settlement in the
valley grew up around **Mission San Gabriel Arcangel▶**
(537 West Mission Drive, San Gabriel; tel: 626/457–
3048), founded in 1771.

Within the five-foot-thick buttressed walls, the
mission's original altar remains, and many smaller
original items, including some of California's earliest
winemaking equipment, are gathered in the museum.

Reminders of the valley's green past are provided by
the **L.A. Arboretum▶** (301 N. Baldwin Avenue, Arcadia;
tel: 626/821–3222), filling 127 acres of a former Mexican
rancho with an exotic array of over 30,000 plants
collected from every continent, and by **Descanso
Gardens▶** (1481 Descanso Drive, La Canada; tel:
818/952–4400), with more flowers, which also boasts an
oriental teahouse dispensing refreshments.

Don't miss the **Southwest Museum▶▶** (just off the
Pasadena Freeway at 234 Museum Drive, Highland
Park; tel: 323/221–2164), the brainchild of Charles
Lummis, an early protector of L.A.'s architectural
heritage (see pages 122–123). Together with a
reconstruction of an 1850s adobe building, typical of
Mexican California, it offers a record of American
cultures. It is the oldest museum in L.A., opened in 1907.

Drive

The San Gabriel Valley

Begin at the Southwest Museum in Highland Park. Drive north on the Pasadena Freeway, exiting onto Arroyo Boulevard and continuing north to the Rose Bowl Stadium.
The **Rose Bowl Stadium▶** has staged the New Year's Day Rose Bowl since 1923.

Go along Rosemont Boulevard and follow signs for the Gamble House.

The **Gamble House▶▶▶** (see page 122) is a fine example of the California Arts & Crafts architectural movement.

Drive half a mile south on Prospect Street before turning left onto Colorado Boulevard, continuing for six miles to Santa Anita Racetrack.
Birthplace of the photo-finish, the **Santa Anita Racetrack▶** (see page 125) is a famous horse-racing venue.

Backtrack briefly and turn south onto Rosemead Boulevard. After three miles exit west onto Las Tunas Drive, following signs for Mission San Gabriel Arcangel.
Once the only permanent settlement in the valley, the heavily restored **Mission San Gabriel Arcangel▶** is now engulfed by suburbia.

Walk

Pasadena

Begin at the public library, 285 E. Walnut Street.
The Renaissance-style **public library** was completed in 1927.

Walk south along Garfield Avenue for Pasadena **City Hall**.
The courtyard of the Spanish baroque-style City Hall surrounds a fountained garden, and a staircase provides access to the dome.

Continue along Garfield Avenue, shortly turning right along Colorado Boulevard and crossing Raymond Avenue for the "Old Town."
Pasadena's "**Old Town**" has numerous restored shop façades from the 1910s and 1920s.

Continue along Colorado Boulevard for the Norton Simon Museum (see page 155). Backtrack along Colorado Boulevard to Los Robles Avenue, turning left for the Pacific Asia Museum.
Housed in a 1924 re-creation of a Chinese palace, the **Pacific Asia Museum** (see page 124) exhibits the arts of the Far East and Pacific Rim.

Continue along Los Robles Avenue to Walnut Street, turning left to the library.

In a perfect example of L.A.'s contrasts and extremes, the city's environs contain not only three world-class art collections (see pages 154–155) but also three enormously popular theme parks, including Disneyland, the world's very first theme park.

Kids love California's theme and amusement parks, even though the state has been overtaken by Florida as the provider of the world's most innovative entertainment parks

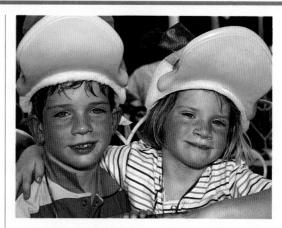

MEDIEVAL TIMES
A four-course banquet inside a mock 11th-century castle, complete with javelin-throwing contests, sword fights, and jousting knights on horseback, is just the ticket after a day spent wandering through a theme park. And that is precisely what is offered at Medieval Times (7662 Beach Boulevard, Buena Park). Reservations are a good idea (tel: 800/899–6600).

Disneyland▶ ▶ ▶ More than 300 million people have visited Disneyland (1313 South Harbor Boulevard, Anaheim, off Interstate 5; tel: 714/781–4565; www.disney.com. *Open* 8–10 AM to 6PM–3 AM, depending on date. *Admission: expensive*) since it opened in 1955, and very few of them have left disappointed. Whether you're shaking hands with Mickey Mouse or flying through outer space, Disneyland offers escapism at its most innovative in a multitude of constantly updated rides and shows.

Extraordinary though it may seem now, visionary animator Walt Disney had to struggle to convince his business partners of the viability of Disneyland, which he described as "a place for people to find happiness and knowledge." Disney had the last laugh when a million visitors arrived in the first seven weeks and the park paid off its $9 million debt within a year.

The jungle of tourist hotels and restaurants that surround it are proof that Disneyland is never deserted, but being selective about when you come may well save hours of standing in line for the most popular attractions: if possible, come midweek between mid-September and mid-June.

In the park, head first for **Tomorrowland**, which holds the most imaginative and popular rides. Here you can fasten your seatbelt for Star Tours (a space trip based on the *Star Wars* film), enjoy a nerve-jangling "flight" through Space Mountain, a darkened indoor roller coaster (each seat has its own computerised sound system) or become a test pilot on Rocket Rods. In nearby **Adventureland** you can explore an ancient temple in the company of Indiana Jones.

Many early Disney characters appear in the less hair-raising rides of **Fantasyland**, among them Snow White's Scary Adventures, Peter Pan's Flight, Mr. Toad's Wild

Ride, and Pinocchio's Daring Journey. Pioneer-period **Frontierland** puts you aboard a runaway train, the Big Thunder Mountain Railroad, and next door, beneath the iron balconies of New Orleans Square, you can cast off with the Pirates of the Caribbean or count the ghosts in the Haunted Mansion.

When you tire, take a ride on the **Disney monorail**, looping from the entrance to Tomorrowland and back, or on the Santa Fe & Disneyland Railroad, which circles the park, negotiating the Grand Canyon on the way.

Knotts Berry Farm▶ Smaller and far less slick than Disneyland, Knotts Berry Farm (8039 Beach Boulevard, Buena Park; tel: 714/220–5200) grew from an 1848 gold-rush town re-created during the Depression by farmer John Knott to entertain customers arriving for his wife's 65¢ dinners.

The ghost town section still remains, although millions of dollars have been pumped into the park since Knott's time. Today's thrills include the Windjammer and Hammerhead roller coasters, themed on Southern California beach culture, and the thrills-a-minute boat trip through Big Foot Rapids. Elsewhere, **Camp Snoopy** entertains youngsters with characters from the *Peanuts* cartoon strip, and Fiesta Village sentimentally showcases south-of-the-border life.

Six Flags Magic Mountain▶▶ (26101 Magic Mountain Parkway, Valencia; tel: 818/367–5965) has 200 acres that are almost entirely devoted to scaring people witless on roller coasters and other attractions.

161

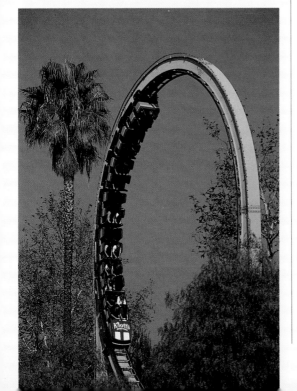

This roller coaster thrills riders at Knotts Berry Farm

A MOUSE IN HOLLYWOOD

Wearing a bright red bow tie and with $40 in his pocket, the 22-year-old Walter Elias Disney arrived in Hollywood in 1923, soon opening his own studio to develop his groundbreaking animation ideas. The advent of talkies paved the way not only for speaking actors but also for cartoon characters with a voice. In 1928, Walt premiered his masterpiece, a talking mouse originally called Mortimer but quickly renamed Mickey by Walt's wife.

CATALINA CREATURES

Separation from the mainland has enabled Catalina to support a variety of unique flora and fauna. Among the latter is the Catalina shrew, so rare it has only been officially sighted twice, and the more commonly seen Catalina mouse, a species larger and happier than its mainland cousins due to the extinction of its natural enemies and an abundance of food amid Catalina's vegetation. This includes coreopsis, blue-eyed grass, western thistle, cholla cactus, snake cactus, and trees such as island cherry, island oak, and ironwood.

Looking north over the colorful rooftops of Avalon which, with 3,200 inhabitants, is Santa Catalina's main town. The art-deco Avalon Ballroom is easy to spot at the edge of the bay

Santa Catalina

The best day-trip in the L.A. area starts with an hour-long ferry crossing to Santa Catalina, an island 26 miles off the Orange County coast. An enticing mix of romantic vacation hideaway and wild backcountry, Catalina also holds the only city in California (Avalon, population 3,200) where nobody travels by car.

Practicalities Several sailings to Santa Catalina depart daily from San Pedro, Long Beach, and (in summer) Newport Beach. Operators are Catalina Cruises (tel: 800/228–2546), Catalina Express (tel: 800/805–9201 and 310/519–1212), and Catalina Passenger Service (tel: 949/673–5245). Once ashore, visitors can see the sights of Avalon by bicycle or electric cart, both available from stands on Crescent Avenue. Trekking into the interior requires a permit from the Visitor Information Center, which faces the pier.

History A 4,000-year occupancy of the island by the Gabrieleño was ended in the early 1800s when white fur-trappers arrived and the tribe was forcibly resettled on the mainland. Catalina became a haunt of smugglers and pirates until William Wrigley, Jr. (of the Wrigley chewing-gum dynasty), bought it in 1911, discovered a loophole in the state's antigambling laws, and opened the Avalon Casino to entice moneyed mainlanders.

With its art-deco features restored to their original glory, the casino is now known as the **Avalon Ballroom▶▶** and demands to be toured (tel: 310/510–2500). More about the island's unusual history can be gleaned inside the adjacent **Catalina Museum▶** (tel: 310/510–2414).

Avalon also has an enjoyable pier, glass-bottomed and "semi-submersible" submarine-like boat trips, a small sandy beach, whimsical residential architecture galore, and the curious sight of islanders weaving around on electrically powered carts (to prevent pollution; cars are as good as banned).

Outside Avalon To see the rest of Catalina, you need to venture into the pristine interior. The only road, actually a narrow track, runs to the island's airport, passing the flat-topped **Mt. Orizaba**, Catalina's highest point.

162

William Wrigley, Jr., plowed some of the casino's profits into the Santa Catalina Conservancy, which has restricted commercial development and protected much of the island's unique flora and fauna—including an extraordinary variety of wildflowers—easily appreciated at the **Wrigley Memorial Gardens▶** (1400 Avalon Canyon Road; tel: 310/510–2288).

The former Wrigley mansion (398 Wrigley Road; known as The Inn on Mt Ada), a summer home of the family, is now a guest house, as is the pueblo-style former dwelling of Western author Zane Grey (The **Zane Grey Hotel▶▶**, 199 Chimes Tower Road; tel: 310/510–0966), who arrived in Catalina for the filming of his book, *The Vanishing American*, and liked it here so much he never left. It is possible to tour both ex-homes.

San Fernando Valley

The ultimate dormitory community for the ultimate metropolis: 1.4 million people fill the 222 square miles of the San Fernando Valley, occupying a vast expanse of identical stuccoed bungalows and doing their shopping in malls haunted by the legendary Valley Girls, who added tidbits such as "gag me with a spoon," to America's vernacular.

Like the San Gabriel Valley to the east, white settlement in the San Fernando Valley began with a Spanish mission and later, through the Mexican period, was divided into gigantic landholdings roamed by herds of cattle.

Expansion Not until water began pouring along the Owens Valley Aqueduct in 1913 and the San Fernando Valley joined itself administratively to L.A., did growth truly begin. Film companies arrived to escape the high rents and confined spaces of Hollywood, heavy industries followed, and the advent of freeways made the valley a viable L.A. commuter base.

The sights All that most tourists see of the valley are the film and TV-studio tours in North Hollywood and Burbank (see panel), the roller coasters of the Six Flags Magic Mountain theme park (see page 161), and Glendale's Forest Lawn Cemetery (see page 165). Yet while first appearances may suggest otherwise, the San Fernando Valley does a pretty good job of preserving its past.

Now unceremoniously skirted by freeways, the focal point of valley life at the turn of the 19th century was **Mission San Fernando Rey▶** (15151 San Fernando Mission Boulevard; tel: 818/361–0186), whose church, bell tower, and monastery have been completely rebuilt and many of the original workshops and storerooms re-created to give visitors a sound grounding in the fundamentals of mission life.

In Brand Park, facing the mission, a selection of various plants and shrubs from California's other missions are grown and, a few streets away, the San Fernando Historical Society mounts temporary exhibitions inside the Indian-built **Andres Pico Adobe▶** (10940 Sepulveda Boulevard; tel: 818/365–7810), L.A.'s second-oldest home, dating from 1834.

see page 161
see page 165

STUDIO TOURS
The stunt-filled Universal Studios Tour (tel: 818/622–3801), which puts on a saloon bar shoot-out, a meeting with Jaws, and the parting of the Red Sea for its visitors, is the most spectacular of the film and TV studio tours available in the San Fernando Valley. To learn about actual production techniques, reserve a place on the Warner Brothers Studios VIP tour (tel: 818/972–8687), which includes visiting in-use sound stages and editing suites.

163

WATER WARS
When water arrived in the San Fernando Aqueduct, a feat of engineering that took six years and cost $25 million, it controversially robbed the people of Owens Valley of their own water supply. Controversy was followed by disaster in 1928, when the aqueduct's St. Francis Dam collapsed, killing 400 people.

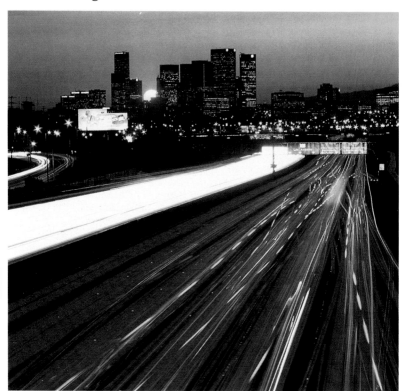

The 8 million vehicles driven by the 8.6 million residents of metropolitan L.A. keep roads busy night and day

TUJUNGA WASH
Half a mile long and still growing, the *Tujunga Wash* mural is the longest such artwork in the world, and the account of California history it depicts does not spare the murkier episodes staining the state's back pages. You will find the mural, a collaborative project overseen by the Social and Public Art Resource Center (SPARC), on Coldwater Canyon Boulevard, between Burbank Boulevard and Oxnard Street.

Encino▶ Several further points of historical appeal lie in Encino, a leafy well-to-do district on the western side of the valley. Here, the nine-acre **Los Encinos State Historic Park▶** (tel: 818/784–4849) is filled with eucalyptus trees and contains a natural spring that quenched the thirst of a Spanish discovery party in 1769. It also contains the nine-room Osa Adobe built in 1849. A less expected sight in the park is a limestone French-style house, the work of two Basque brothers in 1872.

Calabasas▶ The cobwebs are kept off two more aging homes in Calabasas, an Old West–flavored town making much of its past as a stagecoach stop. The **Leonis Adobe▶** (23537 Calabasas Road; tel: 818/222–6511) had its second story added by Miguel Leonis, a smuggler turned sheep farmer, in imitation of the Monterey style in vogue during the 1840s. The **Plummer House▶**, dating from 1879, now forms the entrance to the Leonis Adobe and has displays on the valley's rancho period.

At the northern end of the valley, the mansion and grounds of the hilltop **William S. Hart County Park▶▶** (24151 San Fernando Road; tel: 661/254–4584) belonged to a silent-era movie cowboy, who became the role model for all subsequent celluloid western heroes. Packed with Old West furnishings and ornaments, and intriguing bits and pieces from Hart's acting career, the home is set at the heart of a 260-acre park, and watched over by the grazing bison.

Forest Lawn cemetery has several branches around L.A., but the most famous of them—and the one that inspired Evelyn Waugh's satirical novel The Loved One—*fills a 300-acre site on the edge of the San Fernando Valley (1712 S. Glendale Avenue, Glendale; tel: 323/254–3131).*

A unique concept Founded in 1917, Forest Lawn was designed to create a fusion of art and landscaping to uplift the living as much as to remember the dead. To this end, the cemetery boasts almost 1,000 pieces of classical statuary, including replicas of all of Michelangelo's most noted works, a huge stained-glass replica of da Vinci's *The Last Supper,* and a 500-square-foot mosaic based on the *Signing of the Declaration of Independence.*

Forest Lawn's small amount of original art is no less grandiose. In the **Hall of the Crucifixion-Resurrection**▶ ▶, Jan Styka's 195-foot-by-45-foot *Crucifixion* is claimed to be the world's largest religious work on canvas, and it partners Robert Clark's only slightly smaller *The Resurrection.* Meanwhile, funeral services (and, surprisingly perhaps, a large number of weddings) take place in the cemetery's churches: pains-

Forest Lawn statuary

taking re-creations of 10th- and 14th-century English and Scottish buildings.

Last stop for the rich and famous
The fame of the cemetery itself tends to eclipse the stature of the many movie idols spending eternity within its grounds. The tombs of Clark Gable, Carole Lombard, Jean Harlow, and W. C. Fields are inside the **Great Mausoleum**▶ ▶, while Clara Bow, Chico Marx, Alan Ladd, and Nat King Cole are among those interred in the **Freedom Mausoleum**▶, just outside of which lies Errol Flynn—allegedly sharing his coffin with six bottles of whiskey.

The other main branch of Forest Lawn is in the Hollywood Hills on the edge of Griffith Park (6300 Forest Lawn Drive; tel: 800/204–3131) where, besides another batch of imitation European sculpture, the roll call of the deceased includes greats such as Buster Keaton, Stan Laurel, George Raft, and Liberace.

165

see Drive
page 177

Map labels: Temecula, Radec, Aguanga, Iron Springs Mt 5755ft, Camp Pendelton Marine Base, Santa Margarita, Rainbow, Cleveland, Oak Grove, Margarita Mts, Fallbrook, Pala, Pala Mission, Palomar Mountain, Palomar Observatory, National, Birch Hill, Hot Springs Mt 6532ft, Pala Mesa, Pala Indian Res, San Diego Aqueduct, San Luis Rey, Rincon, Forest, Lake Henshaw, Warner Springs, Guajome Regional Park, Mission San Luis Rey de Francia, San Luis Rey, Pine Mt 4222ft, Volcan Mts, Oceanside, Vista, San Marcos, Valley Center, Mesa Grande, Carlsbad, Lake San Marcos, Escondido, San Diego Wild Animal Park, Santa Ysabel Cr, Sutherland Lake, Santa Ysabel, Whispering Pines, Julian, Leucadia, Moonlight State Beach, Encinitas, Escondido, Rancho Santa Fe, Lake Hodges, San Pasqual Battlefield St Hist Park, Ramona, Julian Pioneer Museum, Cuyamaca Res, San Onofre State Beach, Cardiff-by-the-Sea, Solana Beach, San Dieguito, Rancho Bernardo, Fernbrook, Cleveland, Cuyamaca Mts, Cuyamaca Peak 6194ft, Rancho S P, Del Mar, Los Peñasquitos Canyon, Poway, San Vicente Res, Barona, El Capitan Res, Green Valley Falls, Miramar, Lakeside, National, Birch Aquarium at Scripps, Museum of Contemporary Art, Ellen Scripps Browning Park, La Jolla, San Diego R, Santee, Alpine, Pine Valley, Pacific Beach, Clairemont, Mission San Diego de Alcala, Flinn Springs, Suncrest, Pine Valley Cr, Mission Beach, Mission Bay, Old Town, El Cajon, Loveland Res, Forest, SeaWorld, Ocean Beach, SAN DIEGO, Zoo, Balboa Park, La Mesa, Spring Valley, Sweetwater, Barrett Lake, Point Loma, Downtown, La Presa, Lemon Grove, Villa Montezuma, Jamul, Sweetwater Res, Cabrillo Nat Monument, Coronado, San Diego Bay, National City, Chula Vista, Morena Village, SAN DIEGO, Silver Strand St Beach, Imperial Beach, Lower Otay Res, Cottonwood Cr, Campo, San Ysidro, Otay, Tecate, MEX

0 10 20 km
0 10 miles

166

A   B   C

JUAN CABRILLO
A Portuguese soldier who rose to the command of a Spanish ship and was charged with exploring the California coastline, Juan Cabrillo and his crew sheltered from a storm in what became San Diego Bay on September 1542, making the first European sighting of the California mainland. Cabrillo died later in the voyage and the expedition was regarded as a failure, despite its lasting place in California's history.

DAILY SUNSHINE Affluent and comfortable, San Diego is as close to the ideal vacation destination as it is possible to get. While lacking the romance of San Francisco and the glamor of Los Angeles, San Diego is free of smog and inner-city social problems, and nobody who lives there—whether they are basking on the best beaches in California or making their fortune in the city's international banking market—would trade California's second-biggest city for any other.

Sheltering from a storm in 1542, Juan Cabrillo and crew dropped anchor in what is now San Diego Bay. Yet it was not until the building of California's first mission in 1769 that San Diego's settlement began, in what is now the Old Town, six miles northwest of today's Downtown.

DOWNTOWN itself came into being only a few decades after U.S. rule was established, the center of a classic rough-and-ready frontier town. San Diego did itself a power of good by staging the 1915 Panama–California Exposition. This brought international prestige, and turned Balboa Park—a mile north of Downtown—into a nationally known showcase of Spanish-style architecture and landscape gardening.

Another economic boost came in the 1940s when San Diego became the base of the U.S. Navy's Pacific fleet. Aircraft carriers and frigates became a common sight, and the military presence fueled the city's reputation for conservatism.

Today's San Diego knows how to look after itself. Restoration programs have kept many of the historic areas intact and accessible, numerous parks and waterways are set aside for recreational use, and the investment of $165 million in a sparkling Convention Center, booked solidly for many years ahead, proved the city's intention to be among the nation's most up-to-date and user-friendly cities.

AROUND SAN DIEGO There is a sharp distinction between the heavily populated suburban communities lining the coast and the sleepy rural towns dotting a sparse inland area, which is flanked by pine-coated hills.

San Diego is also on Mexico's doorstep: the city's public transportation runs to the border, and Tijuana, just over it, can easily be toured as a half-day excursion. It is also enjoying an economic boom thanks to 1994's North American Free Trade Agreement, increasing the level of commerce with nearby Mexico.

▶▶▶ REGION HIGHLIGHTS

A San Diego street

San Diego

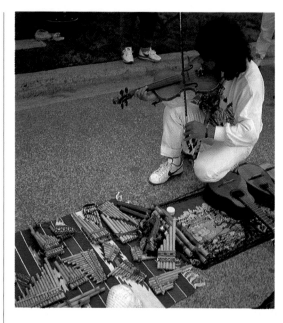

MUSEUM COSTS
Entry to almost all the Balboa Park museums is free on the first Tuesday of every month, otherwise admission ranges from inexpensive to expensive. Buying a $21 Balboa Passport allows you into a dozen museums during any week. Most of the museums are closed on Mondays and/or Tuesdays.

Saturdays on El Prado in Balboa Park find street performers, often of Central or South American origin, entertaining the crowds

THE OLD GLOBE THEATER
The 500-seat Old Globe Theater (in Balboa Park), an approximate replica of London's 15th-century original, is one of three theaters forming the Simon Edison Complex for the Performing Arts. To find out what is playing, tel: 619/239-2255.

▶▶▶ **Balboa Park**   *166B1*

Balboa Park Visitors Center, House of Hospitality, 1549 El Prado (tel: 619/239–0512). Open: daily 9–4. Admission free, but museum charges vary.

Leasing a section of the rattlesnake-infested scrubland on the northern outskirts of late-1800s San Diego paid off for the local authorities. Planting trees in lieu of houses, a local botanist started what officially became Balboa Park in 1911—1,000 green acres of lush, tropical landscaping only a mile from Downtown. The park is sprinkled with Spanish baroque-style buildings, erected for the Panama–California Exposition of 1915 and the California–Pacific International Exposition of 1935; it is one of the largest groupings of museums in the country.

In the northern half of the park, the **San Diego Museum of Art**▶▶ (1450 El Prado; tel: 619/232–7931) has an ample collection of European Old Masters, squatting Buddhas, gleaming jewels from the East, and vigorous American pop art.

The smaller **Timkin Museum of Art**▶▶▶ (1500 El Prado; tel: 619/239–5548. *Open* Tue–Sat 10–4:30, Sun 1:30–4:30) is more selective, with outstanding Russian icons, Old Masters, and quality 19th-century American paintings. Nearby, the **Mengei International Museum** has excellent folk art exhibits, and the temporary exhibitions at the **Museum of Photographic Arts**▶ (1649 El Prado in Casa de Balboa) are rarely dull.

Away from art, there are hands-on exhibits in the **Museum of Natural History**▶ (tel: 619/232–3821), and at the **Reuben H. Fleet Space Theater and Science Center**▶▶ (tel: 619/238–1233), IMAX films are projected onto a gigantic screen; the shows—ranging from space trips to mountain ascents—are breathtakingly realistic.

The **Museum of Man**▶ (tel: 619/239–2001) reveals something of the Native American cultures of the southwest and the efforts of anthropologists to examine them, though the overall effect is slightly shallow. The **Museum of San Diego History**▶ (tel: 619/232–6203) is more enjoyable, recording the rise of the city. In the center of Balboa Park, the open-air Spreckels Organ Pavilion houses the world's largest pipe organ (there is a free recital each Sunday afternoon), and each of the cottages of the House of Pacific Relations has a few cultural knickknacks from foreign countries. Green-thumbed visitors are better advised to spend time amid the ferns, orchids, and begonias in the **Botanical Building**▶▶ (tel: 619/235–1100).

At the southern section of the park (reached on foot or aboard a free trolley), the **Aerospace Museum**▶▶▶ (2001 Pan American Plaza; tel: 619/234–8291. *Open* daily 10–4:30) showcases entertaining collections related to flight and fliers from the beginnings of manned flight to the conquest of space. Next door, the **Automotive Museum**▶ (tel: 619/231–2886) does a less thorough job for land-based transportation, via rows of the streamlined 1940s and 1950s cars.

▶▶ Coronado   166A1

Across the curling Coronado Bridge from Downtown, and also accessible by the ferry from San Diego Harbor, the tidy community of Coronado grew up around the **Hotel Del Coronado,** a whimsical Victorian pile of wooden turrets and towers built to lure wealthy, ailing Easterners to the balmy southern climate.

The hotel has been spoiling its guests since the 1880s, the most notable of whom—including the future Edward VIII and Mrs. Simpson, who allegedly met here in 1920—are remembered in the hotel's small museum. You will also spot memorabilia from the 1950s movie *Some Like It Hot*, which found Marilyn Monroe, Jack Lemmon, and Tony Curtis cavorting in the hotel grounds.

FESTIVALS
Festivals are a dime a dozen in San Diego, but the following are the most enjoyable: the Mexican Cinco de Mayo (May 5) celebration in the Old Town; the Cabrillo Festival, centered on Point Loma, a reenactment of the first European landing in California (late September, early October); the San Diego Street Scene, open-air rock music in Downtown's Gaslamp Quarter (September); and the Over-the-Line softball tournament contested by 1,000 teams on the city's beaches every July. Around San Diego, the major event is the Del Mar Fair, a three-week-long re-creation of an old-time state fair, running from mid-June.

When it opened in 1888, the Hotel Del Coronado had more indoor toilets, 75 for its 399 guest rooms, than any other building in the U.S.

Few California cities have been as careful or as successful as San Diego in protecting and restoring their architectural heritage. From the squat adobe homes of pioneer settlers to the streamlined office blocks of contemporary San Diego, the city's buildings are seldom individually striking, but collectively they provide a lucid insight into the community's development.

170

Old Town Many cramped but comfortable adobe homes were built in what is now the Old Town, with thick mud-brick walls to keep the rooms cool in summer while improvised carpets of straw softened the rough floors. Several good examples remain, their survival largely due to the relocation of the city to the present Downtown during the late 1800s.

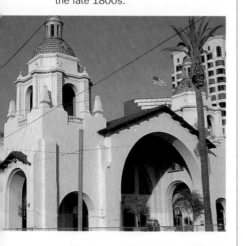

Santa Fe Railroad Depot, a fine example of Spanish-Moorish style

The Gaslamp Quarter Downtown, the boom years are remembered by the tidied, turn-of-the-century commercial brick buildings of the Gaslamp Quarter, whose owners grew rich and secreted themselves in picturesque Queen Anne homes, many of which still stand a few miles north in the Hillcrest area. The liveliest streets are 4th and 5th avenues.

❑ Tijuana is only 23 miles from San Diego and a visit does give a taste of south-of-the-border life. There are no customs or immigration formalities but, to reenter the U.S., passport holders who are not U.S. citizens and who require a visa for entry into the U.S. will need to meet the usual requirements. ❑

Expo Although San Diego originally grew around a Spanish mission, it was not until 1915 that the city made a fuss about its roots, erecting half a dozen Spanish baroque-style buildings in Balboa Park for the Panama–California Exposition.

Few of these buildings were intended to last, but the success of the Exposition in putting San Diego on the map, and the popularity of the buildings—with their elaborate facades and sculpture-filled courtyards—among local people was impossible to ignore.

Strengthening and rebuilding took place, and a second Exposition was held in 1935, this time signaling the city's emergence from the Depression. The spacious Spanish-Moorish Santa Fe Railroad Depot, on Broadway in Downtown, was also designed for the 1915 Expo and continues to be a pleasing sight for train travelers.

Now the station is overshadowed by the black, bronze, and silver exteriors of American Plaza, a complex of stores and offices rising up to proclaim the city's present-day role as a center of U.S.–Far East high finance.

▶▶▶ Downtown 166A1

A frantic swirl of bankers, beggars, locals, and tourists, Downtown San Diego's easily walked **Gaslamp Quarter▶▶▶** should not be missed. It comprises 16 short blocks lined by restored buildings just south of Broadway between 4th and 6th avenues.

Patterned red-brickwork and other Romanesque revival trimmings decorate many of the district's structures, erected between the 1860s and 1920s, though the best place to begin is at the 1850 **William Heath Davis House▶** (410 Island Avenue; tel: 619/233–4692; also the departure point for Saturday walking tours), a simple wooden dwelling.

▶▶ Mission Bay 166A1

The marshland that once filled the gap between Downtown and Mission Beach has been transformed into the sculptured lagoons and beaches of Mission Bay Park. Mission Bay is also the home of **SeaWorld▶▶▶** (SeaWorld Adventure Park, Sea World Drive, off I 5; tel: 619/226–3901. *Open* 10–dusk; late hours in summer. *Admission: expensive*), whose theatrical shows by killer whales and dolphins draw thousands of people; the penguin and shark exhibits are among the best of their kind. Equally good is **Wild Arctic,** a simulated journey to an abandoned polar research station that begins with a helicopter flight though a blizzard and concludes at a series of replicated habitats.

▶ Mission Valley 166B2

From 1769, California's first Spanish mission sat on the hilltop overlooking what is now the Old Town, where San Diego began. Half a decade on, the mission was moved six miles north, and the Old Town almost disappeared when the new San Diego (the present Downtown) was founded.

The restored buildings of the Old Town merit a stroll, though for atmosphere, few match the reconstructed **San Diego Mission▶▶** (10818 San Diego Mission Road; tel: 619/281–8449), still serving a spiritual function but now in the urban sprawl of Mission Valley.

The social scene at Mission Beach, a San Diego community almost entirely devoted to sun, sand, and surf

VILLA MONTEZUMA
San Diego in the late 19th century was better known for its saloons and brothels than its culture. Endeavoring to change things, a band of wealthy settlers banded together and built an irresistible mansion—the Villa Montezuma (1925 K Street at 20th Avenue; tel: 619/239–2211)—to lure a renowned English-born esthete and entertainer, Jesse Shepard, to the fledgling city. Shepard's effect on the community, and his penchant for stained glass and spiritualism, can be assessed on guided tours of the lovingly restored abode.

San Diego

Shielded from the southern California sun, diners sample Mexican fare offered at Bazaar del Mundo, adjacent to Old Town State Historic Park

▶ ▶ ▶ Old Town   166A1

Bordered by Taylor, Juan, Twiggs and Congress streets;
Open: daily 10–5. Admission free

San Diego's first permanent settlement mostly comprised presidio (the military fort protecting the mission) personnel and their families living at the foot of the hill beneath the mission. Within the Old Town State Historic Park (tel: 619/220–5422) several of San Diego's earliest buildings have been restored, and many more are devoted to preserving the memory of bygone times.

The adobe structures of the early 1800s are by far the most interesting buildings. The largest of them, the **Casa de Estudillo**▶ ▶ (4001 Mason Street) belonged to José Estudillo, the first commander of the presidio.

José Estudillo's son-in-law, Juan Bandini, was another significant figure in early San Diego, who turned his home—Casa de Bandini—into a noted social gathering place. When Bandini fell on hard times, the house became a hotel; it is now an enjoyable Mexican restaurant.

San Diego came under U.S. rule in 1846, an era evoked by several things: the single-classroom **Mason Street School**▶ ▶ (Mason and Congress streets); the Western memorabilia inside the Seeley Stables; the **San Diego Union Building**▶ (2602 San Diego Avenue) where the first edition of what is still the city's main newspaper was assembled in 1868; and the **Whaley House Museum**▶ (just outside the park at 2482 San Diego Avenue; tel: 619/298–2482), San Diego's first brick-built house, stuffed with the fixtures and fittings typical of a well-to-do settler of the 1850s. The Whaley House, incidentally, is one of only two in California officially recognized by the state government as being haunted: the spirits are thought to be former residents Thomas and Anna Whaley.

One edge of the park is consumed by **Bazaar del Mundo**, an entertaining imitation of a Mexican street bazaar, with restaurants and crafts shops.

►►► Point Loma   166A1
Cabrillo Memorial Drive
Wealthy residential areas, naval bases, thick woodlands, and coastal bluffs reminiscent of the state's Central Coast characterize the 10-mile-long Point Loma peninsula that divides San Diego Bay from the Pacific.

At Point Loma's southernmost point, the unspectacular **Cabrillo National Monument►** (tel: 619/557–5450) marks the landing of Juan Cabrillo, a Portuguese adventurer, in September 1542. The view over the bay to the San Diego skyline is sufficient reason to come here, however, and there is also a 19th-century lighthouse to explore, and footpaths leading to the tidal pools beneath the bluffs.

► Presidio Park   166A1
In a faithful reconstruction of the original mission, and close to its original site at the crown of Presidio Park, the Junípero Serra Museum (2727 Presidio Drive; tel: 619/297–3258) provides a modest insight into Spanish mission life in California. The contrast of early photos and the current view through the windows makes plain the incredible recent growth of the city.

► San Diego Harbor   166A1
The departure point for numerous sailings and the site of a sea-oriented museum, San Diego Harbor is where the city displays its nautical connections. The pick of three vintage vessels moored in the **Maritime Museum►** (tel: 619/234–9153) is the *Star of India*, a fully equipped three-mast sailing ship that plied the seas from 1863.

The nearby piers are the embarkation points for harbor cruises, whale-watching trips, and the ferry to Coronado (see page 169). If dry land holds more appeal than water, however, follow the **Embarcadero►►**. On this pleasant walkway you will pass kite-flyers, joggers, and roller-skaters before reaching the shops of **Seaport Village►** (Harbor Drive from Pacific Highway to Market Place; tel: 619/235–4014). The Embarcadero continues past the Convention Center to the edge of the Gaslamp District.

►►► San Diego Zoo   166B1
Off Park Boulevard, Balboa Park (tel: 619/234–3153)
Open: late Jun–early Sep 7:30–9 (grounds close at 10); early Sep–late Jun 9–4 (grounds close 5 or 6). Admission: expensive
To the north of Balboa Park, San Diego Zoo got started with animals left over from the 1915 Panama–California Exposition. It has since grown into one of the world's leading zoos, re-creating a range of habitats—from deep canyons to equatorial rain forests. Wherever possible, moats and other natural obstacles are used instead of cages.

Among nearly 4,000 inhabitants on the 128 acres of lushly vegetated grounds is the nation's largest gathering of koalas, some flourishing Galapagos turtles (like koalas, an endangered species), and an excellent collection of primates. Many other smaller, strokable creatures reside in the **Children's Zoo►**.

These inhabitants of the Flamingo Lagoon are among the 800 animal species resident at San Diego Zoo

173

ON THE BAY
Whenever schedules permit, the U.S. Navy berths one or more of its vessels at the end of Broadway Pier for free public viewing. Nearby are the departure points for civilian ferries and pleasure boats, such as the San Diego Bay Ferry (also called the Coronado Ferry) to Coronado, and numerous sightseeing trips around the bay.

San Diego is great news for sea and sand addicts. Whether you want to surf, swim, sunbathe, or snorkel, you will find the perfect spot somewhere along the 70 miles of coastline in and around the city.

WATER SPORTS

In a city almost surrounded by water, it should be no surprise that water sports are big news in San Diego. Yachting is favored by the jet set, but it is surfing that captures the imagination and there is no better place in the state to try your luck. Boards can be rented for around $18 a day from any of the numerous shops around Ocean Beach and Mission Beach. If you prefer, sit back and watch accomplished exponents of the art in action at Tourmaline Surfing Park and Windansea Beach in La Jolla.

174

Imperial Beach▶ Quiet and secluded (not least because of fears of sewage spills from Mexico), Imperial Beach is an inauspicious beginning at San Diego's southern extremity, but its northern edge meets the more promising Silver Strand State Beach, a 15-mile-long sliver of sand dividing San Diego Bay from the Pacific Ocean.

Silver Strand State Beach▶▶ Some parts of Silver Strand are high-grade beachcombing territory (indeed, its name is derived from the millions of tiny silver seashells that are washed up on it). Other sections of the beach are equipped with picnic tables and fire rings that attract families on weekends. Silver Strand also provides the sole link between the mainland and Coronado, where a lack of strong currents makes Coronado Shores Beach an ideal base for a swim.

Ocean Beach▶▶ Across the bay, sheer-sided cliffs are typical of the Point Loma shoreline. A notable exception, though, is Ocean Beach, a haunt of surfers and beach revelers, if much less the all-out party venue today than it was a few years ago. At the nearby northern end, in a very California gesture, Dog Beach is reserved for untethered canines and their owners.

Mission Beach▶▶▶ You should not miss Mission Beach. Seething with surfers and barely covered tanning flesh, and buzzing with impromptu games of beach volleyball, Mission Beach is a perfect example of the southern California beach strip. Beside the beach a restored vintage carousel began turning once again in 1991, and the chic stores and fitness center of Belmont Park replaced what used to be a crumbling roadway. All of these things have encouraged more families to visit Mission Beach but have done little to dent the pervading sense of youthful hedonism.

Pacific Beach▶▶ Directly north of Mission Beach, Pacific Beach is calmer and more refined. Nevertheless,

Residents and locals enjoy a section of the 3-mile-long beachside boardwalk running between Mission and Pacific Beach

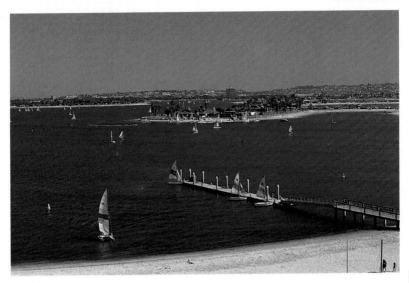

it's here you'll find most of the bars and clubs favored by Mission Beach revelers after dark. It also eases the transition from San Diego into La Jolla, where **Tourmaline Surfing Park**▶▶ and **Windansea Beach**▶▶ are legendary among skilled surfers (novices are welcome only as spectators). Also in La Jolla, the crystal-clear waters of **La Jolla Cove**▶▶▶ cover a marine park and a series of caves, which are enjoyable to explore with the aid of a snorkel, and **La Jolla Shores**▶▶ is an inviting swath of sand where well-heeled locals parade their designer swimwear.

Until mid-1999, the soft sands of **Black's Beach** were the place to get that all-over tan, as the authorities turned a blind-eye to a 1971 law forbidding nudity (perhaps because the beach is obscured by 100-foot-high sandstone cliff and can only be reached by a treacherous pathway). Since then the ban has been strictly enforced and the nude volleyball matches are no more!

Star-spotting This plays a key part of the activity on **Del Mar Beach**▶, though often the film, TV, and sports celebrities who live in the town take the rays from the privacy of their poolside. A few miles north, **Solana Beach**▶ has a more egalitarian mood, as does **Moonlight State Beach**▶▶, between Leucadia and Encinitas, the start of a surfer-dominated strand stretching for 10 miles to **Carlsbad**▶. There the classic Beach Boys' songs still ring true and board-clutching blonds appear whenever the surf's up. The bars and diners here also retain a laid-back ambience.

Camp Pendleton Marine Base Here, except for a nuclear power station, no buildings blot the landscape and **San Onofre State Beach**▶▶ offers what is generally acknowledged as the best surfing in the United States; check first because the beach is only open to the public on a few specific days.

The placid lagoon of Mission Bay enables San Diegans to enjoy water sports safely; on its edge are man-made beaches and moorings for 2,500 boats

SEEING GRAY WHALES
The much-loved California gray whales head south from the Arctic Ocean to the warm waters off Baja California from mid-December to March. With luck, you will catch sight of them from the viewing platforms close to the Cabrillo National Monument on Point Loma, or from Whale Point in La Jolla. For a closer look, numerous companies run boat tours, advertised along San Diego Harbor.

TORREY PINES STATE PRESERVE

(North Torrey Pines Road south of Carmel Valley Road; tel: 858/755–2063) The tall bluffs that divide La Jolla from Del Mar are covered by the 1,000-acre Torrey Pines State Preserve, holding one of the world's two surviving stands of the Torrey pine tree. Because of salty soil, the pines here grow as little as 10 feet in 100 years, while ocean winds force them into strange, stumpy shapes that make any of the short walking trails a memorable experience.

The Indian Museum at Cuyamaca Rancho State Park. The word Cuyamaca, meaning "rainy region," comes from Diegueño native dialect

Around San Diego

▶ Carlsbad
166A3

Among the more distinctive of the coastal communities in the San Diego hinterland, Carlsbad is also one of the nicest for strolling, with several tourist-friendly shops in the downtown area. Carlsbad prospered from the late 1800s with a natural well, the waters of which became famous for their healthful qualities. Currently, Carlsbad is best-known for **Legoland California**, a 128-acre area of family-aimed attractions based on the children's building bricks.

▶ Chula Vista
166B1

Striving to forge an identity of its own within the metropolitan San Diego area, Chula Vista benefits from a bayside location: its enjoyable harborside walk meanders beside a multitude of yachts and fishing boats, and the **Chula Vista Nature Center▶▶** (1000 Gunpowder Point Drive; tel: 619/422–2481) provides a solid introduction to the diverse and interesting ecological zones of California's wetlands; some of the 130 species of bird that inhabit them can be spied from the observation tower and foot trails.

▶ Cuyamaca
166C2

Often neglected by visitors making for the neighboring Anza-Borrego Desert, Cuyamaca and its enormous **Cuyamaca Rancho State Park▶▶** (State Road 79; tel: 760/765–0755) offer landscapes ranging from forests of oak and pine to upland meadows riven by mountain streams. It is a place best appreciated by hiking and camping: this is easily done, as hundreds of miles of trails cross the park's 26,000 acres, and campsites are plentiful.

Near the information center there is also a small museum recording the resistance of the local Native American tribes to 19th-century white settlers' attempts to plunder the region of its native oak and pine tree stocks.

▶ Del Mar
166A2

Actor Bing Crosby and singer Pat O'Brien took a shine to the seaside resort of Del Mar during the 1930s and pumped money into the local racetrack, which soon became a palm-bordered architectural masterpiece and helped solidify the town's reputation as a playground for Hollywood's rich and famous. Many names still have vacation homes here, though the real draws are the beach and the shops and restaurants along 15th Street.

Drive

Highway 76 and Highway 78

(See map on page 166.)

Leave Oceanside on Highway 76; drive for five miles to San Luis Rey.
On the left, **Mission San Luis Rey de Francia**▶▶ dates from 1798, and is the largest of the California missions (see page 181). The ruins of the guards' barracks are on the right.

Continue for three miles.
On the right, the **Guajome Adobe**▶ was at the center of Rancho Guajome (see panel, this page), a major landholding during Mexican rule in the 19th century; it now sits at the heart of the 500-acre **Guajome Regional Park**▶.

Continue on Highway 76, entering the Pala Indian Reservation.
On the left, the small **Pala Mission**▶▶ was founded in 1816 and serves the spiritual and educational needs of reservation dwellers. The **chapel** is decorated by Pala murals (see page 180).

Continue for 24 miles and turn left along Road S6 for the Palomar Observatory.
Since the 1940s, the 200-inch telescope in the **Palomar Observatory**▶▶ (tel: 760/742–2119) has tracked and photographed galaxies at the edge of the known universe. The museum has photos and explanatory displays, and the mighty telescope can be viewed from the visitors' gallery.

Return to Highway 76 and continue for 30 miles to the intersection with Highway 78 at Santa Ysabel.
Just before the intersection, the tiny **Mission Santa Ysabel**▶▶ stands on the left, with a one-room museum and a large Native American cemetery.

Drive west for 32 miles on Highway 78, passing Ramona and San Diego

❏ Following Mexican independence from Spain, large chunks of mission-owned land were granted to Spanish-Mexican settlers, the so-called Californios, for farming. One of these major farms became Rancho Guajome, at the center of which was the 20-room Guajome Adobe, now rated as one of the finest examples of the period's domestic architecture. Eight miles from Oceanside on Highway 76, the adobe is best appreciated by joining the guided tour (for further details, tel: 760/724–4082). ❏

Wild Animal Park, to Escondido.
Escondido▶ is best known as the former home of Lawrence Welk, whose museum, recording the growth of his "champagne music," with the golf course consumes the northern edge of town.

Continue for 24 miles on Highway 78, to Carlsbad.
The surfer-packed beach at **Carlsbad**▶ is typical of San Diego's coastal towns, but its past glory as a spa resort makes it one of the more historically distinguished (see page 176).

The Palomar Observatory

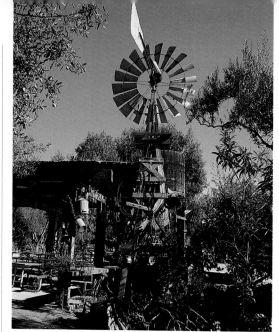

The grounds of Bernardo Winery, near Escondido, one of the oldest of several noted San Diego area wineries

► Escondido 166B3

A quiet residential community, Escondido is also the former home of entertainer Lawrence Welk, whose **Welk Resort Theater►** (tel: 760/749–3448) containing a dinner theater and a museum devoted to his career, sits on the edge of town. Welk's lightweight accordion-based music underpinned his TV variety show, which ran for 27 years and made him a household name.

· Close by are a couple of commendable wineries—Bernardo and Orfila—both of which offer free tastings and tours. A bigger attraction is the expansive **San Diego Wild Animal Park►►** (1550 San Pasqual Valley Road; tel: 760/747–8702) six miles east, which re-creates African and Asian terrains, including animals.

►►► Julian 166C2

First settled by gold miners in the 1860s, Julian's present population is just 1,300, with locals outnumbered on weekends by visitors enjoying the town's setting in thickly forested mountain foothills. The **Pioneer Museum►►** (2811 Washington Street; tel: 760/765–0227) records the town's rough-and-ready early days.

Inside the **Julian Cider Mill►** (2103 Main Street; tel: 760/765–1430) a right turn off Main Street, you can inspect the process of turning apples into cider, see peanut butter being made, and sample honey produced by the mill's own beehive. Across Main Street and B Street, the **Julian Hotel►** (tel: 760/765–0201) founded by freed slaves, has been offering accommodations since 1899, but keeps its quaintly furnished interior for viewing by guests only. Back along Main Street and to the right along C Street are signs showing the way to the **Eagle and High Peaks Mine Museum►►** (End of C Street; tel: 760/765–0036) which stores the last vestiges of Julian's gold-mining industry and has a former mineshaft open for public scrutiny.

A BOUNTIFUL HARVEST
The comparatively cool climate and fertile soils found in the foothills of the mountains dividing San Diego County from the inland deserts allow the cultivation of apples, peaches, pears, and other fruit that are otherwise in short supply. Drive anywhere close to Julian and you will find roadside stalls offering locally grown fruit and jam, and each October the town lets its hair down for the month-long Apple Harvest Season.

San Diego's priciest homes, most expensive stores and smartest restaurants are along the hibiscus-lined lanes of La Jolla (pronounced "La Hoya"), a hillside community rising high above the Pacific directly north of the city.

Chic and nonconformist Its showpiece Prospect Street and Girard Avenue filled with trendy art galleries, expensive boutiques, members-only fitness centers, and chic top-notch eateries, La Jolla is a place with pretensions. However, it also has a streak of non-conformity, stemming from its many resident artists and writers and its proximity to the sprawling campus of the University of California.

The town, whose name either means "the jewel" (from the Spanish) or "cave" (from Native American legend) depending on who tells the tale, also boasts a picturesque coastline, a fine modern art museum, and fancy wrought-iron benches that are a welcome sight when you're in need of a breather.

Modern art After admiring the contours of the coast from **Ellen Scripps Browning Park**▶▶, a small and tidy green patch flanked by palm trees above La Jolla Cove, look into the **Museum of Contemporary Art**▶▶ (700 Prospect Street; tel: 858/454–3541) which specializes in modern works from the California minimalist and pop art genres (the museum also stages impressive temporary exhibitions in its Downtown San Diego space, junction of Kettner Boulevard and Broadway; tel: 619/234–1001). Most of the museum itself is a modern work, too, designed by renowned San Diego architect Irving Gill. Its origins go back to 1915 and an oceanside villa belonging to Ellen Browning Scripps, wealthy sister of a publishing magnate, who poured money into La Jolla throughout her life.

Marine research Scripps is to be thanked for keeping much of La Jolla free from developer-led devastation,

most spectacularly the Torrey Pines State Preserve (see page 176). Her money financed the **Scripps Oceanographic Institute** and the **Birch Aquarium at Scripps**▶▶ (2300 Expedition Way; tel: 858/534–3474) in which stunning re-creations of marine habitats illuminate the mysteries of the deep. Perched above the ocean, the **Salk Institute** is an extremely well-equipped biological research center occupying an imposing concrete structure. The institute is named after its founder, Jonas Salk, the epidemiologist who developed the first polio vaccine.

179

A university campus sculpture

RANCHO SANTA FE

One of southern California's most exclusive communities lies five miles inland from Solana Beach on Road S8. Here, in the 1920s, Hollywood's favorite couple, Douglas Fairbanks and Mary Pickford, bought a ranch and soon turned the area into a millionaires' playground known as Rancho Santa Fe. Many fabulous hillside mansions are obscured from public view by trees, though anyone can walk around the town's ultra chic Rancho Santa Fe Inn in the hope that some of the glamour may rub off on them.

The Pala-Indian Culture Center. The Pala Indian reservation is one of three in California predating U.S. rule

▶ Oceanside   *166A3*

The town has a decent beach, but most of Oceanside is dominated by the Marines from the neighboring Camp Pendleton base, the U.S. military's main center for amphibious landing training, and the reason why 125,000 acres along the coast north from Oceanside are totally free of development. There is a Landing Vehicle Track Museum inside the base where you can learn about the tricks of the amphibious landing trade. Back in town, the pier's **Surf Museum** (223 N Coast Highway; tel: 760/725–2468) displays vintage boards and other memorabilia of surfing.

▶ Pala   *166B4*

The tiny community of Pala sits just inside the Pala reservation and is the site of the only mission in California still serving Native Americans as a place of worship and education.

Built in 1816 as a branch of Mission San Luis Rey, the **Pala Mission▶▶** (known formally as Mission Assistencia de San Antonio de Pala; Pala Mission Road; tel: 760/742–3317) had suffered considerable deterioration by the time the Cupeño tribe was forcibly moved to the area in 1903. Some parts of the mission have been finely restored and the interior walls of the chapel are covered with intriguing frescoes, but the bumpy brick floors and the splintered beams give the whole place a rustic appearance, something which is matched by the handmade wooden crosses marking the tombs of the Native American cemetery, just outside.

▶▶ San Luis Rey   *166A3*

Once described as "the most beautiful, most symmetrical, and the most substantial mission in California," the **Mission San Luis Rey de Francia**▶▶ (4050 Mission Avenue; tel: 760/757–3651) had 3,000 Native Americans (more than any other California Mission) under its jurisdiction during the early 1800s, and even today is an impressive sight as it emerges from the anonymous suburbia that fills the five miles between it and uninteresting, military-dominated Oceanside.

While only the 1807 church is original, the mission has been kept in good repair by the order of Franciscan monks who have occupied it since 1893. The museum gives an instructive account of mission-era life, and there are numerous pieces from the time of the mission's founder, Padre Fermin de Lasuén.

In mid-July, a fiesta based around the traditional Blessing of the Animals ceremony takes place in the mission's grounds.

▶ Santa Ysabel   *166C3*

Most people visit Santa Ysabel, a community of a few hundred people around the intersection of Highway 78 and Highway 79, only long enough to buy bread from **Dudley's Bakery**▶, where the choice of still-warm loaves spans jalapeño, onion, potato, and pumpernickel.

A short way along Highway 79, the minuscule **Mission Santa Ysabel**▶▶ (23013 Highway 79; tel: 760/765–0810) is of historical significance and interest, founded in 1818 as a branch of the San Diego Mission. The small church that stands here now dates from 1924, and is not as interesting as the mission's one-room museum, which is packed with historic photos and objects, and carries a text describing the mystery of the mission's missing bells. There is a box inside the museum for your dollar donation, and a sign reminding you to switch off the light when you leave.

If you visit in November, you will see the mission's Native American cemetery bathed in candle-light; traditionally at this time, a candle is placed on every grave.

Mission San Luis Rey de Francia, the eighteenth of California's missions, was also the largest, originally covering 6 acres with space for 1,000 worshippers inside its church

181

FLOWER POWER
From May to September, the hillsides of Encinitas, halfway between Del Mar and Carlsbad, are covered with a colorful carpet of blooming flowers—an indication of the town's place as a major flower-producing center. To revel in the sights and fragrances, stop at the Quail Botanical Gardens (230 Quail Gardens Drive; tel: 760/436–3036) and follow the self-guided walking tour.

THE DESERTS

0   40   80 km

0   20   40 miles

STUNNING VISTAS Far from being the barren wastelands many people expect, the three deserts that occupy the southern and eastern parts of the state provide some of the most striking panoramas in all of California.

FLORA AND FAUNA These climatically extreme but ecologically delicate regions teem with exotic plant and animal life, and contain often monotonous—but sometimes spectacular—landscapes of rippled sand dunes, weather-sculpted rocks, and eerily shaped trees, interspersed with palm-filled oases and bordered by snow-capped mountain ranges.

The high elevation of the northernmost desert, the Great Basin, pushing into the Owens Valley from Nevada, limits its vegetation to the bush shrub—making for the least interesting of the three deserts. Immediately south is the Mojave Desert, the site of Death Valley, one of the natural world's most remarkable places, and the more subdued but equally haunting Joshua Tree National Monument.

South of the San Jacinto Mountains, the mild winters of the Colorado Desert support a multitude of desert vegetation, best examined in the Anza-Borrego Desert, an area steeped in pioneer-period history, whose higher points give views to the Salton Sea, a vast inland lake created, bizarrely, by human error.

GHOST TOWNS AND RUINED GOLD MINES Particularly plentiful in the Mojave, these are testament to the fact that desert life has never been easy (even today; see the tips on pages 194–195), although Native American habitation of these fierce regions goes back thousands of years, and there are many markers to aboriginal culture—most impressively the ancient rock drawings called petroglyphs.

While large towns such as Riverside occupy the fertile lands on the extreme western edge of the deserts, other substantial communities have grown up as health resorts at the numerous natural hot springs. And in the oases towns of the Coachella Valley, most famously Palm Springs, desert living means luxury living for the nation's highest rollers. Also rife are reminders of the 19th-century travelers who sought a route through the deserts to the ocean as the U.S. embraced westward expansion. Their failure became the stuff of legend and gave Death Valley its name.

▶▶▶ REGION HIGHLIGHTS

Anza-Borrego Desert
page 184
Death Valley page 187
Joshua Tree National Monument page 188
Palm Springs
pages 189–190
Palm Springs Aerial Tramway page 190
Rainbow Basin
page 192
Riverside page 193
Salton Sea page 193

183

Desert vegetation silhouetted against the twilight sky in Anza-Borrego State Park

Color in the wilderness: Anza-Borrego Desert

PEGLEG SMITH
One-legged Thomas Long "Pegleg" Smith was journeying across the Anza-Borrego Desert in the mid-1800s when he picked up several black stones, which turned out to be almost pure gold. Pegleg gradually embellished the story of his discovery until, by the time he died in 1866, he was claiming ownership of an entire gold mine. Every April, Pegleg's tall tales—and their place in desert folklore—are remembered by the Pegleg Liars Competition, held at the pile of stones beside Road 22 known as Pegleg's Monument.

▶▶ **Anza-Borrego Desert**   *182B1*

Eastern side of San Diego County (tel: 760/767–5311)
Named after Juan Bautista de Anza, a Spaniard who made the first recorded crossing of it in 1774, and for the bighorn sheep (or borrego) who once roamed it in force, the 600,000-acre Anza-Borrego Desert is a mixture of sun-scorched lowlands and narrow, twisting canyons, and forms the largest state park in the United States.

Holding the only accommodations (other than basic hikers' campsites), the mountain-ringed oasis town of **Borrego Springs** is an obvious base for touring Anza-Borrego—though even here, summer temperatures frequently rise above 100° F (38° C).

The park's visitor center, set into the mountainside two miles west of Borrego Springs at **Palm Canyon**▶▶ (200 Palm Canyon Drive off County Road S22; tel: 760/767–4205) carries essential maps and information, and mounts displays on desert history, geology, and climate. Outside, a cactus garden and a simple nature trail will whet your appetite for what lies beyond.

Sandstone formations warped by millions of years of erosion are a common and evocative sight throughout the park, but the most striking views come at **Font's Point**▶▶, off Road S22, which overlooks the bone-dry creek beds and steep-sided ravines of the Borrego Badlands, a vegetation-free mass inhabited only by lizards and snakes.

Through the southerly sections of the park, 1840s gold prospectors hacked out the only snow-free route into California, a Native American trail discovered by Pedro Fages in 1782, and used as the Mexican mail route from 1826. The trail was also followed by General Kearny and the Army of the West just before the 1846 battle at San Pasqual, the deadliest battle of the Mexican War in California, and by the Butterfield Overland Mail company, whose stagecoaches carried passengers and post to the infant communities of Los Angeles and San Diego. From **Box Canyon Monument**▶ on Road S2, a path leads to a lookout point above the old trail.

The barren vistas may suggest otherwise, but desert ecology is a fragile affair, and its subtleties are highlighted from March to May as wildflowers bloom across the Anza-Borrego hillsides, bringing tens of thousands of Californians to enjoy the colors and sweet smells.

By contrast, frustrated rally drivers power off-road vehicles over the dunes of the **Ocotillo Wells Recreational Area**, on the park's eastern edge.

▶ **Barstow**   *182A3*

Most visitors to Barstow are bus passengers on their way to or from Las Vegas, or shoppers from L.A. driving out for the discounted designer-label clothes and the goods sold at the town's **Factory Merchants' Outlet Plaza**▶.

More edifying matter fills the **California Desert Information Center**▶▶ (2796 Tanger Way, Suite 106; tel: 760/253–4782), packed with exhibits on desert ecology and practical information about the area.

▶ **Big Bear Lake**   *182A2*

High in the San Bernardino Mountains, the seven-mile-long Big Bear Lake, formed by a dam in 1883, is a center for water sports and horseback riding in summer, for skiing in winter. You can tour the lake on a paddle wheeler, Big Bear Queen, between May and October.

▶ Blythe   *182C2*

A blink-and-you-miss-it town on the Arizona border, Blythe is slowly transforming itself into a desert health resort, although as yet local interest begins and ends with the giant-sized **rock drawings** on the Colorado River Indian Reservation, immediately to the northeast of the town.

▶ Calico   *182B3*

Since 1968, archeological excavations close to Calico have revealed more and more of a "tool factory" claimed to be 200,000 years old. If such advanced age can be proven, this is both the oldest known site of human habitation in the United States and one that overturns all the established theories concerning the earliest Americans. The dig site can be viewed, although the visitor's center is more informative.

The town of Calico flourished a century ago because of silver and borax mines that yielded millions of dollars' worth of the metals. Like other Califonia mining towns, the community declined when the mines were exhausted—unlike other abandoned mining settlements, Calico was reactivated in the 1950s as a tourist attraction: **Calico Ghost Town** (11 miles NE of Barstow; tel: 760/254–2122). The walk-through mine,

185

A vision of the past: Calico rebuilt

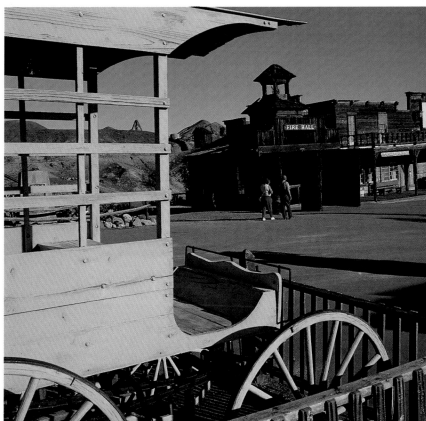

The Deserts

OPERA IN THE DESERT
A one-time New York ballerina, Marta Beckett stages solo dance and mime performances every Saturday and Monday evening throughout the winter at the tiny Amargosa Opera House in Death Valley Junction near the intersections of Road 127 and Road 190 (for more details, tel: 760/852–4441).

steam railway and wooden buildings, now mostly holding stores—linked by raised wooden sidewalks—are the main attractions, along with pseudo-miners who merrily strum banjos.

▶ Cherry Valley   182A2
An unlikely find in apple-filled Cherry Valley, near San Bernardino, is a gathering of furniture and 17th- to 19th-century European and Asian art at the **Edward-Dean Museum of Decorative Arts▶** (9401 Oak Glen Road; tel: 909/845–2626).

▶ Daggett   182A3
If you find yourself in this town, the **Stone Hotel▶** has provided shelter for desert travelers since 1875.

▶ Darwin   182A4
Darwin is one of several short-lived silver prospectors' communities that now stand in ruins near the junction of Highway 395 and Highway 190 on the approach to Death Valley. A dirt track to the south leads to the secluded Darwin Falls, a waterfall fed by a natural spring.

Drive

"The Rim of the World"

Drive north from San Bernardino on Road 18 to Crestline, then join Road 138 for 10 miles to the Silverwood Lake State Recreation Area.
Picnicking, hiking, swimming, and varied birdlife are the primary attractions here.

Return to Road 18 and drive east for 15 miles to Lake Arrowhead.
L.A.'s wealthy socialites pass leisurely weekends in luxury homes secreted in the wooded hillsides surrounding **Lake Arrowhead▶▶**. The 195 foot-high tower in the center of the lake conceals the pipework diverting water to the nearby desert communities.

Continue for 33 miles on Road 18 for Big Bear Lake.
L.A. residents who cannot afford to weekend at Lake Arrowhead make the most of **Big Bear Lake▶** (see page 184).

Continue east on Road 18 for 12 miles, joining Road 38 at Big Bear City. From here, make a 50-mile winding descent to Redlands (see pages 192–193).

Filled by a larger-than-life landscape of sand dunes, volcanic craters, salt flats, and multi-colored mountain walls, Death Valley is one of the hottest and driest places in the world—yet also one of the most misleadingly named.

Life in Death Valley Death Valley's seemingly inhospitable environs actually support a rich diversity of life. A unique species of tiny fish lives in its ponds, wild asses and bighorn sheep roam the hillsides, and mesquite and bristlecone pines are among the 900 varieties of plant life here.

Signs of human habitation have been dated to 5000 BC, when much of the valley was filled by a lake. The most recent permanent inhabitants were the Shoshone, here during the 1880s when the first white men arrived to mine a rich strain of borax.

A few hours of carefully planned driving will reveal stunning sights, but seeing all of Death Valley on anything less than a lengthy hiking expedition is impossible—and even short hikes should be undertaken with care (see pages 194–195).

Points of interest Signposted viewing points on the 9-mile **Artists Drive**▶▶▶ reveal the varying colors of the valley's rock walls, caused by the presence in the rock of oxides, copper, and mica. To the north, a turnoff leads to **Golden Canyon**▶▶, whose metallic tints make

Barren beauty in Death Valley

❑ Chicago millionaire Albert Johnson lived in an unfinished Spanish-Moorish mansion at the northern edge of Death Valley with a con man called Scot. Johnson died in 1948, and Scot followed him in 1954. Scotties Castle, as it's known, is now a regular part of Death Valley tours (tel: 760/786–2395. ❑

187

it live up to its name at sunrise and sunset. On the northern side of Road 198, east of **Stovepipe Wells**▶▶▶, sand dunes form a 14-square-mile rippled yellow carpet.

Deposited between 2 million and 12 million years ago, the mud flats of **Zabriskie Point**▶▶▶ (off Road 190) are legendary for the almost hypnotic effect they have on visitors.

Dante's View▶▶▶ (off Road 190) overlooks the entire valley and makes visible two of the highest and lowest points in the United States: Badwater, 282 feet below sea level and, 60 miles distant, 14,495-foot-high Mount Whitney.

Death Valley Visitor Center is at Highway 190, Furnace Creek; tel: 760/786-2331.

The Deserts

182B2

LOST HORSE MINE

The Joshua Tree National Monument area has been prized not only for its trees but also for its deposits of gold. Between 1896 and 1899, the Lost Horse Mine produced gold worth around $3,000 a day. Marked on maps distributed at the visitor center, the mine is easily accessible and is only a short walk from the road. The old stamp mill and other mining implements can be seen.

▶ Desert Hot Springs

In Desert Hot Springs, a health resort community close to Palm Springs, **Cabot's Old Indian Pueblo Museum** has an intriguing collection of pioneer-era desert relics and Native American artifacts These include a 20-ton monument carved from a sequoia tree that fills the spacious four-story former home of one of the area's first settlers. Check that the museum has re-opened after its renovation (tel: 760/329–6411 ext. 503).

▶ Indio 182B2

The National Date Festival has been held each February in Indio since 1921, and the celebrations of the town's best-known product include ostrich and camel races. Meanwhile, the **Coachella Valley Museum and Cultural Center** (82616 Miles Avenue; tel: 760/342–6651) fills a building only slightly younger than the Date Festival with memorabilia spanning 70 years of local life.

▶▶ Joshua Tree National Monument 182B2

Main entrance: Utah Trail off Highway 62,
Twentynine Palms (tel: 760/367–5500)

High and low desert meet in the 850 square miles of the Joshua Tree National Monument, whose name comes from the trees, a species of yucca growing up to 50 feet tall that were christened by west-bound Mormon travelers who saw their upraised branches as the arms of the prophet Joshua, pointing the route west.

The weird look of the trees and the huge quartz boulders nearby endow the western section of the monument with an eerie quality, particularly when bathed in the red glow of sunrise or sunset. (The eastern half is best left to seasoned desert adventurers.)

More prosaically, the irregular formations of the granite slopes are prized by climbers. Many hiking trails crisscross the wild landscapes, and there is plenty to be appreciated by car—but do not undertake any kind of visit without first stopping to pick up maps and advice from the visitor center at Oasis, just south of Twentynine Palms (or at Cottonwood and Blackrock Canyon).

Within the monument, **Key's View▶▶** is an essential stop: a high vantage point with panoramic views over the Joshua Tree area and, on a clear day, to Palm Springs and the Salton Sea, 40 miles away.

A signposted side road, nine miles south of the Oasis visitor center, leads to the **Cholla Cactus Garden▶**, where a foot trail passes a variety of plants—and also quite a few creatures—which have adapted themselves for desert survival.

The Geology Tour Road▶▶▶ runs through 18 miles of strange terrain, and a free brochure from the visitor center aids understanding of the subterranean upheaval that gave rise to these spectacular scenes.

Gold mining flourished here from the 1880s and continued into the 1940s. Of the disused mines strewn across the area, the Lost Horse Mine, said to have produced $3,000 worth of gold a day (see panel), repays a 1½-mile hike, while another, the Desert Queen Ranch, can be reached only with a ranger-led tour, usually weekends only, more frequent tours in summer.

Growing up to 50 feet tall, Joshua trees are found in California's desert regions at altitudes of 3,000–5,000 feet

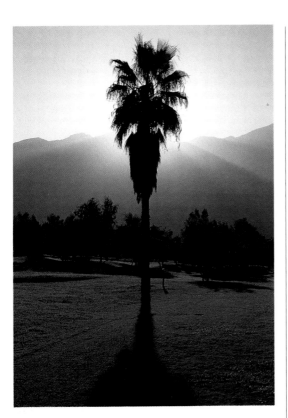

A Palm Springs palm tree. Close to the town, the canyons of the San Jacinto mountains hold the world's largest gathering of Washington palms, the only palm type native to California

▶▶ Palm Springs   *182B2*

The best-known and by far the nicest of half a dozen shoulder-to-shoulder towns (collectively known as the "desert communities") lining Highway 111, which loops off Interstate 10 in the Coachella Valley, Palm Springs attracts 2 million visitors a year, many of them drawn by the glamorous reputation of the country's most famous resort.

The healthful qualities of the local mineral springs encouraged efforts to market Palm Springs as a spa town as early as the 1890s, but it was not until actors Charlie Farrel and Ralph Bellamy founded the Palm Springs Racket Club in 1931 that Palm Springs really took off. They lured their Hollywood celebrity chums—Humphrey Bogart, Clark Gable, and Marlene Dietrich among many—with the promise of inexpensive luxury homes, a balmy winter climate, and relaxation far from the madding crowds.

Comedian Jack Benny's broadcasts from the town's Plaza Theater and the arrival of many more show-biz names (and later, political ones, including former president Gerald Ford and his wife, Betty, who put her name to the nation's best-known detoxification clinic) helped cement the town's links with affluent and influential high society.

Surprisingly perhaps, for all its upscale trappings, Palm Springs is small (with only 40,200 residents) and very affable and street crime is virtually unknown.

THE EASTERN MOJAVE
Known to locals as the "lonesome triangle," the eastern Mojave desert lies mostly between Interstate 15, Interstate 40, and the Colorado River. One of the rewards for braving its 1.5 million acres of arid and unyielding terrain is the Mitchell Caverns in the Providence Mountains State Recreation Area, about 80 miles east of Barstow. They are filled with strange limestone formations and their smoke-blackened walls indicate 500 years of Native American use.

The Deserts

INDIAN CANYONS

Drive five miles from the center of Palm Springs along South Palm Canyon Drive and you reach a toll road leading into the Indian Canyons, once the domain of a large group of Cahuillas. The easiest to explore is Palm Canyon, lined for its first seven miles by native Californian palms, their greenery providing a vivid counterpoint to the stark canyon walls. Beyond its parking lot, Palm Canyon—like the other canyons—can be investigated further on foot or horseback (tel: 760/325–5673 for guided tour times).

Strange territory Palm Springs has many curious features. Its dozens of golf courses are sprayed with a million gallons of recycled water per week; palm trees cover the tops of street lights to prevent their glare from diminishing the clarity of the star-filled night sky; and the town's major landowners are the Agua Caliente, from whom businesses rent land on 99-year leases.

Favorite Palm Springs pastimes are poolside tanning, shopping in the air-conditioned malls, and eating in the restaurants along Palm Canyon Drive, where fine clouds of water are sprayed by micromist systems to cool patio diners.

Other activities include exploring **Moorten's Botanical Garden►►** (1701 S. Palm Canyon Drive; tel: 760/327–6555), a jungle-like collection of cacti and other imposing desert vegetation. Equally recommended is the **Desert Museum►►** (101 Museum Drive; tel: 760/325–0189), with imaginative indoor exhibitions of desert-related art, natural history and anthropology, and fielding a strong winter program of performing arts in the adjoining Annenberg Theater.

Vestiges of Palm Springs' earlier times are maintained at the **Village Green Heritage Center►** (221 S. Palm Canyon Drive), with the 1884 McCallum Adobe, the 1893 Cornelia White's House and the re-created 1930s Ruddy's General Store.

You can reach the Jacinto State Park on the **Aerial Tramway►►►** (Tramway Road, off North Palm Canyon Drive (at San Rafael Road); tel: 760/325–1391 or 888/515–8726. *Admission: expensive*). The views alone make the ascent worthwhile, even if you do not plan to use the park's 50 miles of hiking and horseback riding trails, which become cross-country ski trails in winter.

Climbing 6,000 feet in 14 minutes, this cable car on the Park Springs Aerial Tramway gives its passengers views of the broad and flat Coachella Valley and the distant Indio Hills as it ascends into the San Jacinto Mountains

Drive

Around Palm Springs

Drive south from Palm Springs on Road 111 to Rancho Mirage.
Many of the wealthy who supposedly live in Palm Springs actually live among the golf courses and country clubs of **Rancho Mirage►►**.

Continue to Palm Desert.
The ultrarich of the desert communities do their shopping along the pricey **El Paseo►►** in Palm Desert. A less costly stop is the 900-acre **Living Desert Reserve►►** (47-900 Portola Avenue (north of Highway 111; tel: 760/346–5694), revealing much about desert ecology.

From Palm Desert, take Road 74 and climb for 54 miles into the San Jacinto Mountains; at the junction with Road 243, turn right onto Road 243 for Idyllwild.
A mile high and surrounded by tall pines, **Idyllwild►** is a mountain resort that is also noted for its School of Music and Arts.

Continue on Road 234 for 21 miles to Interstate 10; drive east on Interstate 10 for 12 miles before exiting onto Road 111 and returning to Palm Springs.

❏ The first date-palm seeds in North America arrived with the Spanish in the late 1700s, but only this century did the U.S. Department of Agriculture develop a strain suited to life in the California desert, the only place in the United States where climate and soil are right. The most productive area is around Indio, where 4,000 acres of date palms annually produce $30 million worth of the fruit. ❏

▶▶ **Rainbow Basin**   *182A3*

Fossil Bed Road (tel: 760/252–6060)

At the heart of the Rainbow Basin, 15 miles west of Barstow, you will find a steep gorge with colorful, striped sides—caused by different layers of sediment. The rock walls hold the fossils of three-toed horses, dog-bears, mastodons, and other prehistoric creatures that inhabited this once lake-filled area.

▶ **Randsburg**   *182A3*

Many buildings dating to the 1890s—when the discovery of gold brought the town a 3,000-strong population and made it a stop on the Santa Fe Railroad—have been carefully preserved in Randsburg, and the Desert Museum (161 Butte Avenue) is filled to its rafters with unusual remnants from mining days.

Although it might look an inviting place for a dip, the Salton Sea developed from a salt marsh and its heavily saline waters make swimming uncomfortable; it also holds high levels of selenium

THE INTEGRATON
The mysterious Integraton, a large domelike structure, was built at Giant Rock Airport (an extremely remote spot about 12 miles north of Yucca Valley) by 1950s UFOlogist George van Tassel. Van Tassel, and followers of his alien-contactee cult known as the Ministry of Universal Wisdom, claimed the Integraton could revitalize aging body cells, reverse gravity, and allow time travel.

▶ **Redlands**   *182A2*

Redlands flourished as a citrus farming center thanks to the diverting of water from Big Bear Lake in the 1880s. At the same time, the town found favor with wealthy wintering Easterners, whose money financed the ornately gabled and turreted wooden homes still standing along Olive Street, although these are outdone in grandeur by the chateau-style **Kimberly Crest** (1325 Prospect Drive; tel: 909/792–2111), which is sometimes open for tours.

In Smiley Park in the town center, the Redlands Bowl auditorium is known throughout the state for its summer ballet and opera programs, and, nearby, the **Lincoln Memorial Shrine**▶ (125 W Vine Street) ranks among California's most obsessive historical collections, completely devoted to President Abraham Lincoln.

On the fringes of Redlands, the wide-ranging displays of the **San Bernardino County Museum**▶▶ (2024 Orange Tree Lane; tel: 909/307–2669) are worth a visit, though more evocative of life in the early 1800s is the two-room museum at the restored **San Bernardino Asistencia** (26930 Barton Road; tel: 909/793–5402), a branch of Mission San Gabriel Arcangel.

Ridgecrest   182A3

The sole redeeming feature of Ridgecrest, mostly housing military personnel from the China Lake Naval Weapons Center, is the **Mutarango Museum**▶▶ (100 E Las Flores Avenue; tel: 760/375–6900), with a small but engaging collection of the native art and culture of the eastern Mojave, and a special display on the rock inscriptions found in the China Lake area.

▶▶ Riverside   182A2

The California orange—the navel—was born in Riverside in the 1870s, and the town's resultant affluence saw the building of the **Mission Inn** (tel: 909/784–0300), a Spanish-style exercise in luxury whose bedrooms, music rooms, terraces, and patios were decorated by $1 million worth of antiques. Guided tours of the inn, now restored, are occasionally offered.

A busy industrial center as well as an agricultural base, Riverside also has the **Municipal Museum**▶ (tel: 909/782–5273), which preserves the city's past.

Just east of the town, the local branch of the University of California looks after the 39-acre **Botanical Gardens**▶, which specialize in winter-blooming, dry-climate plants and feature formidable cacti. To the west, the **March Field Museum**▶▶ (16222 1–215; tel: 909/697–6600) displays mostly military aircraft from 1918 onward.

Wild cacti cover much of **Mount Rubidoux**, to the west of Riverside, the 1,300-foot summit of which can be reached by a twisting lane. At the top, there are impressive views and the Serra Cross, the venue for Easter sunrise services since 1909.

▶ Salton Sea   182B1

One of the largest inland seas in the world, the Salton Sea was created in 1905 by an engineering blunder and a severe winter, which caused the Colorado River to breach the canals directing it to the Imperial Valley, and to flood a dried-up lake bed just east of the Anza-Borrego Desert.

Enormous but very shallow, the Salton Sea was stocked with ocean fish when its water turned saline, and anglers were quick to take advantage of the marinas and campgrounds of the Salton Sea Recreation Area created on its eastern bank. Nowadays you'll also find watersports fans.

Meanwhile, bird-watchers arrive in search of herons and egrets, among a host of much rarer winged creatures who are regular visitors to the Salton Sea Wildlife Refuge, on the sea's southern edge.

▶ Twentynine Palms   182B2

Ignored by many travelers speeding through on their way to the nearby Joshua Tree National Monument (see page 188), Twentynine Palms is worth a stop for the **Historical Society Museum**▶ (6136 Adobe Road; tel: 760/367–3926), charting the origins and growth of this little desert settlement.

GOLF AND PALM SPRINGS
Seventy courses have earned Palm Springs and the desert communities the title of "Golf Capital of America." Many top tournaments are held here and famous names—be they golfers, entertainers, or ex-presidents—are familiar figures on the fairways. Many courses are members-only or very expensive, although local municipal courses (listed in the phone book) are always cheap and open to all. Interestingly, to conserve water, new courses have to be laid on a bed of tile; this enables precious water to be collected after irrigating the greens, and then recycled.

193

DESERT HOT SPRINGS
California's desert regions are sprinkled with hot springs, whose thermally heated, mineral-rich water bubbles up through the earth's crust. Opportunities to sample the waters, and put their alleged health-improving qualities to the test, are numerous and range from whirlpool- and sauna-equipped spa resorts to the free mineral baths at Tecopa Hot Springs County Park (tel: 760/852–4264), close to Road 127, just east of Death Valley.

By world standards, California's three deserts are lush and young, formed 1 million to 5 million years ago, primarily because rainbearing clouds could not cross the Sierra Nevada mountains. Their landscapes are extremely varied, as are their flora and fauna, some of which are unique and all of which have been able to adapt to desert conditions in a variety of inventive ways.

Desert flora The cactus is the most obvious example of the succulent desert plant, one that stores water whenever it is available, using a shallow but extensive root system.

Some nonsucculent plants can become dormant in the absence of water, while others—such as the brittle bush and creosote bush—can reduce the size and density of their leaves to reduce water loss, and, when necessary, shed all their leaves and branches to protect their root system.

Other than the Joshua trees of the Joshua Tree National Monument, the plants that bring most people to the deserts are the springtime wildflowers. These grow from seeds that germinate only in response to a precise amount of rainfall, which ensures the survival of the plant.

Desert fauna Desert animals are no less inventive. The kangaroo rat never drinks but creates water inside its body after eating dry seeds and is able to condense moisture while exhaling air; the red-spotted toad can absorb its own urine; and desert insects respond to unfavorable conditions by entering a form of suspended animation called estivation.

Aside from cold-blooded reptiles such as lizards, which scamper from sunlight to shade to regulate their body temperature, and a multitude of birds ranging from turkey vultures to scrub jays, most desert creatures are nocturnal and spend time in the heat of the day sleeping behind rocks or plants.

Desert animals that you are most likely to encounter are the chipmunklike antelope ground squirrel and the large desert tortoises, most commonly found chewing on grasses and wildflowers in spring. With luck, training your binoculars on distant slopes will bring a glimpse of the rarely sighted bighorn sheep.

Desert travel tips Careful preparation will help you to experience the desert comfortably and safely—and may even save your life.

The only sensible time for desert travel is between November and April, when daytime temperatures are warm but bearable (though the nights can be freezing), and well short of the roasting heat of the summer, when tourist services such as visitor centers are likely to be closed.

FLOWERS OF ANTELOPE VALLEY
You will not see any antelopes in Antelope Valley, but arrive between March and May and you will see millions of orange and purple wildflowers brightening the hillsides that rim the western edge of the Mojave Desert. And at the Antelope Valley California Poppy Reserve, 2,000 acres are set aside for the careful nurturing of California's state flower—the subtleties of which are explained inside a specially built, energy-conserving visitor center (Lancaster Road; tel: 661/724–1180).

Desert driving Before setting out, ensure that your vehicle is in perfect condition, and stock up with ample food and—most crucially of all—at least a gallon of drinking water per person per day.

You should also take around five gallons of spare fuel—desert driving means fewer miles per gallon than on regular roads—and a similar amount of spare water for the radiator.

In the desert, never drive off the marked roads—doing so causes environmental damage. If you intend to travel on one of the isolated side roads, inform a park ranger, or other relevant authority of your plans.

If your car breaks down, do not leave it. Wait until another car passes and signal for assistance. This may involve a long wait.

Other useful tools include a first-aid kit, a flashlight, and waterproof matches.

Desert hiking and walking Many trails can be easily hiked in a few hours, but do not embark on one without a detailed map and some water.

Even on a short walk, be sure to drink water regularly even if you do not feel thirsty. Keep in the shade whenever possible, and stop for a rest at the first sign of dizziness.

Wear loose, light-colored clothing, dark glasses of good quality, and a wide-brimmed hat, and apply sunscreen liberally. At night the desert is a cold place, so plan accordingly. On your feet, wear sneakers or hiking boots with socks—do not wear sandals.

Be careful where you put your hands and feet, and be wary when turning over rocks. These precautions will help avoid potentially fatal contact with black widow spiders, scorpions, and rattlesnakes, and the less harmful tarantulas and centipedes.

Know what to do if you are bitten by a desert creature—details are available from any desert visitor center or rangers' office.

BORAX MINING
In the California of the late 1800s, gold mining was more glamorous but less lucrative than borax mining. Rich deposits of borax—used in the manufacture of glass and in glazes for ceramics—were discovered in Death Valley (see page 187). Getting the mineral out of the ground proved a lot easier than getting it out of Death Valley, however, and it took 20-strong mule teams ten days to haul their loads to the nearest train station. Nowadays, most of the world's borax comes from the Boron area, about 80 miles west of Death Valley.

195

Cholla cacti, distinguished by its cylindrical stems and found in nine varieties in California's deserts, in Joshua Tree National Monument

Sierra Nevada

SIERRA NEVADA

0   20   40   60 km
0   10   20   30   40 miles

NEVADA

Taboe Donner
Truckee
Donner Memorial SP
Kings Beach St Rec Area
Tahoe City
Lake Tahoe
DLBliss SP
Eldorado National Forest
South Lake Tahoe
9859ft
Kirkwood Ski Resort
Grover Hot Springs SP
Mokelumne
Mt Reba Bear Valley Ski Area
Stanislaus
Dardanelle
Toiyabe National Forest
Calaveras Big Trees SP
National Forest
Bodie SHP
Columbia SHP
Dodge Ridge Ski Area
Bridgeport
Sonora
1078ft
Yosemite
Mono Lakes
Mono Lake
Buck Meadows
El Capitan
7569ft
National
Tuolumne Meadows
Mono Basin Scenic Area Visitor Center
Coulterville
Park
June Mtn Ski Area
Inyo National Forest
Benton
Merced
Yosemite Valley Badger Pass Ski Area
Lake McClure
Devils Postpile Nat Mon
Mammoth Lakes
Lake Crowley
Wawona
Mariposa
Wassama Round House SHP
John Muir Wilderness 13747ft
Owens
Laws
Railroad Mus and Hist Site
Oakhurst
Bass Lake
Bishop
Chowchilla
Sierra National Forest
Mono Hot Springs
Sierra Summit Ski Area
Schulman Grove
Bass Lake
Inyo
Millerton Lake St Rec Area
Big Pine
National
Fresno
Millerton Lake
California State Univ Fresno
Pine Flat Lake
Kings
N Palisade 14242ft
Forest
Scotty's Castle
Madera
San Joaquin
Clovis
Kings
Canyon
Boyden Cave
Cedar Grove
Independence
Death Valley National Monument
Fresno
Wilsonia
National
Wolverton Ski Area
Selma
Dinuba
Muir Grove Big Trees
Giant Forest
Park
Mt Whitney 14495ft
(Highest Point in California)
Owens Lake
Hanford
Visalia
Sequoia National Park
Mineral King
Tulare
Lake Kaweah
Garfield Grove Big Trees
12123ft
Olancha
Darwin
Coalinga
Lakeland Canal
Lake Success
Haiwee Res
Kettleman City
Tulare Lake
Porterville
Sequoia
Cholame
Tule River Ind Res
National
Kern
S Fork Kern
Little Lake
Colonel Allensworth St His Park
9977ft
Forest
China Lake (Dry)
Delano
Los Angeles Aqueduct
Ridgecrest
Wasco
Lake Isabella
Shirley Meadows Ski Area
Weldon
5
Bakersfield
Hillcrest Center
Koehn Lake (Dry)
Randsburg
California State Univ Bakersfield
Red Rock Canyon

San Joaquin Valley

Owens Valley
White Mtns
Inyo Mtns

A   B   C

A GREAT DIVIDE You might be a geological ignoramus when you arrive in the Sierra Nevada region, but you will leave with a much surer knowledge of earthly forces and how they have shaped—and continue to shape—California. An expanse of granite domes, pinnacles, and ridges some 450 miles long and up to 80 miles wide, the Sierra Nevada mountains give the region its name and divide the state's fertile Central Valley from the arid eastern deserts.

HOT STUFF Despite the feelings of permanence evoked by the colossal peaks, the Sierra Nevada is one of North America's most geologically volatile regions; the hot springs that litter the area are merely the most benign manifestation of the tensions lying deep underground.

Historically, the Sierra Nevada provided one of the major obstacles for would-be settlers approaching by land. Now, travelers still have to plan carefully how—and when—they tour the area.

Approaching from the west, it is tempting to make a beeline for the national parks at the heart of the region—world-famous Yosemite, and less visited but equally worthwhile Sequoia and Kings Canyon—and not worry too much about pressing farther east.

EASTERN PLEASURES It is in the east, however, that the sheer-sided Owens Valley forms a slender and visually spectacular corridor, linking the Sierra Nevada's wealth of strange geological phenomena—such as the eerie tufa formations around Mono Lake, a heavily saline body of water at the heart of a long-running ecological dispute, and the geometrically precise basalt colums of the Devil's Postpile Monument—while giving access to scores of sparkling alpine lakes, including stunning Lake Tahoe, on the region's northern edge.

Unfailingly, the Sierra Nevada's natural sights exert greater appeal than its towns. A few bear witness to the region's pioneer days (and one, Bodie, is a genuine Gold-Rush ghost town) but most of the modestly sized settlements are geared to serving the hikers and climbers who are the lifeblood of local economies.

In winter, mountain roads are closed and hiking routes inaccessible, rendering the most pristine sections of the Sierra Nevada's magical icy landscapes off-limits. The bulk of the region's visitors at this time of the year are skiers—and snowboarders—who turn Lake Tahoe and Mammoth Lakes into the country's busiest winter sports centers.

Sierra Nevada

197

▶▶▶ REGION HIGHLIGHTS

Ancient Bristlecone Pine Forest *page 198*

Devil's Postpile Monument *page 203*

Eastern California Museum *page 200*

Lake Tahoe *page 205*

Mammoth Lakes *page 199*

Mono Lake *page 204*

Sequoia & Kings Canyon National Parks *page 201*

Vikingsholm *page 205*

Yosemite National Park *pages 208–209*

Winter transportation in Mammoth Lakes

OLDEST LIVING THING
Research during the 1950s by Professor Edmund Shulman of the University of Arizona dated the oldest of the bristlecone pines at 4,600 years, the prelude to much hullabaloo over the discovery of the world's oldest living things. In 1980, however, the bristlecones were made to look like mere infants by a desert shrub, the creosote bush, one of which was found by a botanist to have lived to the ripe old age of 11,500 years.

▶ **Bass Lake**   196A3

A large reservoir in the pine-covered foothills on the southern approach to Yosemite National Park (see pages 208–209), Bass Lake (tel: 559/658–7588) is one of the state's busiest recreational areas. Speedboats and water-skiers skim across the surface, anglers are tempted by the spiny-finned fish that give the lake its name, and a series of trails pick through the surrounding country-side, offering some respite from the crowds that pack the lakeside cottages and campsites throughout the summer.

▶ **Big Pine**   196C3

Like most Owens Valley towns, Big Pine offers little other than food, lodging, and access to spectacular natural areas. Above the town, the Palisades Glacier—North America's most southerly ice sheet—draws expert ice climbers to its tricky slopes. The world's oldest living trees are at the **Ancient Bristlecone Pine Forest**▶▶ (tel: 760/873–2500) 12 miles east and reached by State Road 168.

The **Visitor Center at Schulman Grove**▶▶▶ (*Open daily mid-Jun–early Sep*) provides an introduction to the strange, warped forms of the 4,000-year-old bristlecone pines, which dominate this extraordinary landscape, each one growing barely an inch per year and looking more dead than alive. The pines survive due to a widely spread root system, which enables them to draw in whatever moisture is available; the distance between the

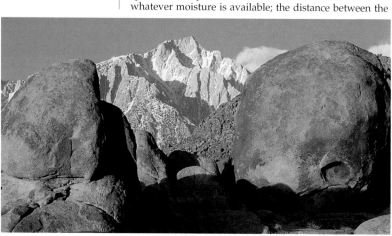

Alabama Hills, near Bishop

pines reduces the risk of forest fires. The most evocative section of the forest is 11 miles farther on and 1,000 feet higher at **Patriarch Grove**▶, where a scattering of bristle-cones bestow a weird beauty on an uncompromising ter-rain—an area selected by NASA for the testing of its lunar rover.

▶ **Bishop**   196B3

Nestling among the motels, restaurants, and adventure sports stores that fill Bishop, 15 miles north of Big Pine, the **Paiute-Shoshone Indian Cultural Center and Museum**▶▶ (2300 W. Line Street; tel: 760/873–4478) shows something of the lifestyles and handicrafts of the valley's native dwellers.

In the Sierra Nevada, as elsewhere in the state, canoeing and white-water rafting are available wherever conditions are right, along with downhill and cross-country skiing, snowboarding, climbing, and mountain biking: the region fully lives up to its reputation as California's most sports-crazy area. There are plenty of schools to help beginners master the basic skills.

Skiing A November-to-May snow covering facilitates some outstanding downhill skiing in the region, although cross-country (or Nordic) skiing is also popular—most area hiking trails (and there are many) can be skied as soon as the snow falls.

Venue of the Winter Olympics in 1960, Lake Tahoe has dozens of ski resorts; the best bet for beginners is Tahoe Donner (tel: 530/587–9444).

Farther south Mammoth Lakes is no less busy, with activity centers on the enormous Mammoth Mountain Resort (tel: 888/462–6668), while the Tamarack Lodge (tel: 760/934–2442) organizes a web of backcountry routes.

In Yosemite National Park, the gentle slopes of the Badger Pass Ski Area are ideal for novices—and the setting is spectacular. Also in the park, the Yosemite Cross-Country Ski School (tel: 209/372–8444) runs overnight and three-day guided cross-country trips to Glacier Point. For skiing with a spectacular view, try Bear Valley (tel: 209/753–2834), where the slopes overlook California's deepest canyon.

Climbing Sheer, near-vertical granite rock faces, such as Yosemite's El Capitan, have forced the world's mountaineering fraternity to devise entirely new techniques to conquer them. The region's climbing schools pass on such skills, and also instruct beginners in the rudiments of rock and ice climbing.

The main climbing schools are Yosemite Mountaineering School (tel: 209/372–8344), based in Yosemite National Park, and Alpine Skills International (tel: 530/426–9108), based at Donner Pass, which arranges classes on all aspects of climbing and runs trips suited to differing skill levels.

Mountain biking Another thrilling way to explore the ups and downs of the Sierra Nevada is by mountain bike. Many sports stores throughout the Owens Valley and around Lake Tahoe rent mountain bikes for a charge of around $30 a day. And in summer, some of the ski slopes around Mammoth Lakes become the **Mammoth Mountain Bike Park** (1 Minaret Road; tel: 800/626-6684), offering 50 miles to suit all levels of experience. Each September the slopes host the passionately contested NORBA Championship Mountain Bike races (see page 202).

WHITE-WATER RAFTING
During April and May, when the melting snow of the High Sierra mountains sends rivers cascading through the foothills, white-water rafting comes into its own along the American and Tuolumne rivers. Most Gold Country towns have companies offering guided river runs, which range from white-knuckle beginners' specials to death-defying experts-only trips. Operators include OARS in Angels Camp (tel: 209/736–4677), and CBOC white-water rafting in Coloma (tel: 800/356–2262).

199

GUIDED TREKKING
An unusual way to soak up the beauty of the Sierra Nevada—and learn a great deal about what you are seeing—is on a pack trip, allowing a mule or a llama to carry your backpack while you ride shank's mare and the guide (usually a qualified naturalist) provides a commentary. Many companies—widely advertised in the area—operate pack trips from the main trailheads. More information is available from the Eastern Sierra High Packers Association, operating through the Bishop Chamber of Commerce (tel: 760/873–8405).

Sierra Nevada

BODIE

Bump over the potholes of Bodie Road, off Highway 395, 20 miles southeast of Bridgeport, and you will enter Bodie Ghost Town State Park. A century ago nearly 10,000 people lived in the Gold-Rush town; several rickety buildings can be entered, including the Miner's Union Hall, which houses a museum. The last three miles of road may be closed in winter.

THE DONNER PARTY

One of the gorier tales of early California concerns the Donner Party of 1846, a wagon train of 89 men, women, and children following the Emigrant Trail into California. A series of errors of judgment by their leader culminated in the party being trapped by snow and forced to spend the winter without supplies in what is now the Donner Pass, just west of Truckee. Only 47 people survived the ordeal, some of them having resorted to cannibalism to stay alive.

Grover Hot Springs State Park in summer. In winter, the area is used for Nordic skiing

▶ Bridgeport   196B4

These days little more than a collection of supply stores, Bridgeport's elegant 1880 **County Courthouse**▶ reflects the community's boom years when, as the county seat, it grew wealthy from nearby Bodie's gold strikes. If you need proof of former glories, explore the **Mono County Museum**▶ (tel: 760/932–5281), which stores artifacts from the halcyon decades.

▶▶ Grover Hot Springs State Park   196A5

Markleeville (tel: 530/694–2248)
Set in a divine alpine meadow, the bubbling waters issuing from the earth at Grover Hot Springs State Park have been credited since California's pioneer days as a cure for whatever ails. More recently, the mineral-rich spring water has meant bliss for aching hikers, who enjoy a soak in one of the park's two temperature-regulated bathing pools.

▶ Independence   196C2

Besides rest and nourishment, Independence, 28 miles south of Big Pine, offers the excellent **Eastern California Museum**▶▶ (155 Grant Street; tel: 760/878–0364), covering the geology, history, and ecology of the region. The museum includes a striking collection of Paiute and Shoshone crafts, and a thought-provoking exhibit on **Manzanar Camp** (Manzanar National Historic Site; for tours, tel: 760/878–2932), where around 10,000 Japanese-Americans were interned following the outbreak of hostilities between the United States and Japan in 1941.

Some of the town's older buildings have been moved to the museum's grounds, together with a large number of aging farming and mining machinery, and assembled as a pioneer village. One that has not been relocated is the former home of author and naturalist Mary Austin (ask directions from the museum), who lived from 1896 in Independence, and described Owens Valley life evocatively in *This Land of Little Rain*, a book of essays published in 1903.

Drive

Sequoia and Kings Canyon National Parks

Enter Sequoia National Park on Highway 198.
Sequoia National Park▶▶ (tel: 559/565–3134) is home to thousands of giant sequoia trees.

Continue on Highway 198, the General's Highway, to Giant Forest Village, turning right onto Crescent Meadow Road.
The road passes famous trees, such as the **Auto Log▶**, and foot trails lead into the groves, one of which contains the largest, the **General Sherman Tree▶▶**.

Turn off Crescent Meadow Road for Moro Rock.
There are fantastic views from the top of **Moro Rock▶▶▶**.

Return to the General's Highway, continuing to Grant Grove.
At **Grant Grove** an excellent **Visitors' Center▶▶** describes the lives of giant sequoias.

Join the Kings Canyon Highway and drive toward Cedar Grove.

❏ California's coastal redwoods may be taller, but in terms of bulk the giant sequoia tree—growing only on the Sierra Nevada's western slopes—is the world's second largest living thing (the largest is an underground-dwelling fungus). The biggest, the General Sherman Tree in Sequoia National Park, is 102 feet in circumference. The largest sequoias have lived for over 3,000 years. ❏

The giant sequoia tree

Part of **Kings Canyon National Park▶▶** (tel: 559/565–3134), the highway makes a spectacular, winding descent through Kings Canyon.

Turn off Kings Canyon Road for Boyden Caverns, signposted near the canyon's floor.
See the fabulous stalagmites and stalactites inside the deep **Boyden Caverns▶▶▶** (Highway 180, 22 miles NE of Grant Grove; tel: 209/736–2708. *Open* May–Sep 9–6, Oct–Apr 10–5. *Admission: moderate*).

Continue along Kings Canyon Highway, passing Cedar Grove Village for Zumwalt Meadow.
A one-mile walking trail winds above and around **Zumwalt Meadow▶**.

Beyond Zumwalt Meadow, only hiking trails enable you to penetrate farther.

You do not need to be in California for long to realize that the state sits on a very fidgety portion of the earth's crust. Not only are earthquakes an almost daily phenomenon (the vast majority of them are too small to cause any concern), but natural forces are still molding what may at first appear to be a solid geographical region: the Sierra Nevada mountains.

MOUNTAIN BIKE RACING
Mountain bikes are ridden at breakneck speed up and down the tortuous terrain for which they were designed in the NORBA Championship Mountain Bike series, in which the machines and their riders are pushed to the limit. The event is held at Mammoth Mountain during September.

202

The formation of the Sierra Nevada Around 200 million years ago, the Pacific plate was gradually slipping under the North American continental plate and what is now California began emerging from the ocean as immense pressures in the earth's crust caused the seabed to buckle and rise. This in turn formed the earliest outline of what were to become the Sierra Nevada mountains.

Between 250 million and 80 million years ago, the surface rock had eroded sufficiently to allow hot magma within the earth's crust to push upward (owing to the reduction of the pressure from above). This magma eventually burst through the surface as volcanoes or, more often, cooled beneath the surface to form huge granite intrusions known as batholites.

Combining with minerals in liquid form on its upward journey, this molten rock provided California with its deposits of gold, silver, and other precious metals.

A subsequent process known as exfoliation, when surface rock expands as a result of underground heat, caused the outer layers of the granite monoliths to fracture and break away, eventually creating the bare domes that are characteristic of the Sierra Nevada ranges. Prime examples are El Capitan and Half Dome in Yosemite Valley.

Around 70 million years ago, the rising of the coastal mountains caused the Sierras to tilt westward, a process that increased the erosive power of its rivers and proceeded to carve great valleys through the hillsides.

FIRST SIGHT
The first white people to see the Sierra Nevada are thought to have been the Spanish military captain, Pedro Fages, and Franciscan missionary Juan Crespi in 1772. Both men had been part of the Portolá expedition which three years earlier made the first European sighting of San Francisco Bay.

During three separate periods, the latest around 30,000 years ago, falling global temperatures caused glaciers to form in the Sierras. The moving ice sheets wore away the weaker rock (leaving spindly towers and pinnacled ridges), smoothed the harder rock surfaces, and chiseled out the rock bowls that later filled with crystal-clear water and became alpine lakes.

Yosemite Valley's U-shape (river-formed valleys have a V-shape) was formed by the action of ice. Lake Tahoe is the country's largest example of a glacial lake, with many smaller ones lying close to Mammoth Lakes.

The Sierra Nevada today The eastern and western sides of the Sierra Nevada are markedly different nowadays. In the west, the forested foothills composed of older rocks rise steadily upward from the immense flat expanse of the Central Valley toward the region's big peaks. In the east, however, the mountains fall off sharply, forming a spectacular wall to the slender corridor of the Owens Valley with a 400-mile-long fault-line along their base considered by many experts to be the most geologically active place in the United States.

An earthquake here in 1872, one of the strongest ever in North America (estimated at 8.3 on today's Richter scale), demolished the town of Lone Pine and instantly added 13 feet to the height of the surrounding ridges. Drive along Highway 395 close to the Alabama Hills and the scarps created by this quake are still clearly visible. More evidence—often bizarre, and often beautiful—of violent upheaval is everywhere, from the columns of cooled lava at the Devil's Postpile Monument to the valley's innumerable hot springs.

Curiously, though, while the Sierra side of the Owens Valley is a comparative infant, the White Mountains, which form the valley's east wall, are composed of some of California's oldest rock and dotted throughout with the world's oldest living things, the bristlecone pine trees, which are thousands of years old.

As geysers gurgle far below, the Palisades Glacier continues to creep steadily through the mountain canyons above Big Pine, a constant reminder of the region's geological extremes—and the fact that the formation of the Sierra Nevada is a process that is far from complete.

203

An alpine lake in the Sierra Nevada. Lakes of this kind result from Ice-Age glaciers leaving indentations in the rock that fill with melting snow

THE PETROGLYPH LOOP TRAIL
Native Americans—some of them predating known tribes—carved colorful figures, or petroglyphs, onto many of California's hillsides. Just outside Laws, a 50-mile Petroglyph Loop Trail through the Chalfont Valley has six marked stops where some of these unusual—and date-less—works can be seen.

Although existing for thousands of years, these tufa formations, reflected in the still waters of Mono Lake, broke surface only when the water level fell, following the draining of tributary rivers to provide drinking water for Los Angeles

▶ Laws   196C3

Being a stop on the railroad line was a blessing during the frontier days, when Owens Valley farm produce needed transporting to the state's mining areas. One such stop was at Laws, six miles from Bishop, which has been partly re-created in its 1880s form as the **Laws Railroad Museum and State Historic Site▶▶** (Silver Canyon Road; tel: 760/873–5950). The train terminal is an impressive restoration, as are several of the town's other early buildings.

▶▶ Mono Lake   196B4

East of Yosemite National Park, Mono Lake Tufa State Reserve, State Road 120 (tel: 760/647–6331)

Almost a million years old and 9,000 feet above sea level, few sights in the Sierra Nevada can match the otherworldly vistas seen at Mono Lake. Gazing across the 13-mile-wide saltwater expanse the eye comes to rest on the bizarre **tufa formations▶▶▶**, mostly on the south side, which sprout above the surface in myste-rious shapes, each one a pillar of limestone created by the alkaline lake water mingling with fresh spring water. The formations have existed for thousands of years, but surfaced when the lake level fell as its tributary rivers were drained to provide water for Los Angeles (see panel, page 206).

The falling water level caused by the Owens Valley aqueduct has greatly affected a finely balanced

ecosystem for which the lake is the linchpin. One consequence was to turn Niget Island, in the center of the lake, into a peninsula, allowing hungry coyotes to reach what was previously a secure nesting place for California gulls, where 90 percent of their population breed. In 1994 decisive action finally began to raise the water levels. One effect so far has been to make Niget Island once again an island. Beside Highway 395, just north of Lee Vining, the **Mono Basin Scenic Area Visitor Center** (tel: 760/647–3044) explains the lake's evolutionary history and the various threats that it is currently facing.

Fringed by thick forests and overlooked by snow-capped mountain peaks, Lake Tahoe holds enough water to flood the entire state. To most Californians the lake means water sports, skiing, or gambling (the eastern third of the lake lies in Nevada, where gambling is legal), but there are many other attractions for visitors.

Rampant tourism threatens the natural beauty of Lake Tahoe, though the commercialism only seriously blights South Lake Tahoe. Here motels and fast-food outlets line Highway 50, which continues into the casino-laden Nevada town of Stateline.

Enjoyable lake cruises These are a more positive feature of South Lake Tahoe, and the **Lake Tahoe Historical Society Museum**▶ (3058 Highway 50; tel: 530/541–5458) gives background on the formation of the lake and its cultures.

The prettiest section of the lake is the southwestern corner, where **Emerald Bay State Park**▶▶ (on State Road 89; tel: 530/525–7277) reaches down to a secluded inlet. Here, a mile-long trail leads to **Vikingsholm**▶▶▶ (tel: 530/525–7232. *Open* weekends only end May–end Jun, then daily until Oct. *Admission: inexpensive*), an approximation of a 9th-century Nordic castle designed in the 1920s by a Swedish-born architect, Lennart Palme. A short trail leads to cascading **Eagle Falls**▶.

Thirty miles north are good sandy beaches at **Sugar Pine Point State Park**▶▶ (tel: 530/525–7982);

the 1903 **Erhmann mansion**▶▶, built of local wood and stone for a San Francisco banker, now serves as the visitor center. Similar properties have been renovated at the **Tallac Historic Site**▶▶ (State Road 89, north of Camp Richardson; tel: 530/541–5227), near Fallen Leaf Lake.

North of Lake Tahoe, **Truckee**▶ appeared with the building of the transcontinental railroad in the mid-1800s, which linked the rest of the nation to Sacramento, 80 miles west. The difficulties that the local terrain presented to travelers prior to the opening of the railroad are outlined inside the **Emigrant Trail Museum**▶▶ (tel: 530/582–7892) at Donner Memorial State Park, a few miles west of Truckee on Interstate 80.

❏ The *Tahoe Queen* (tel: 800/238–2463) operates daily sightseeing trips and, after dark, a dinner cruise. The *MS Dixie II* (tel: 702/588–3508) makes a sightseeing excursion from Zephyr Cove as far as Emerald Bay. ❏

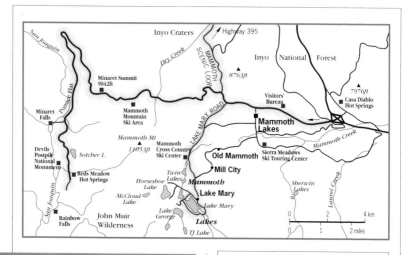

Drive

Mammoth Lakes

Leave Highway 395 between Lee Vining and Bishop, taking State Road 203 until you come to Mammoth Lakes.
With a population of 4,800 and hotel beds for 40,000, **Mammoth Lakes▶▶** is one of the United States' most popular ski areas.

Alongside State Road 203, look for the combined Ranger Station and Visitors' Bureau.
The volatile geology of Mammoth Lakes is explained inside the excellent **Visitors' Bureau▶** (tel: 760/934–2712 or 888/466–2666).

Continue on State Road 203 for eight miles, reaching the Minaret Vista Picnic Area.
Jagged peaks and ridges rise high above the **Minaret Vista Picnic Area▶▶**; far below, flows the San Joaquin River.

Continue on State Road 203 for 14 miles, for the Devils Postpile Monument.
The extraordinary hexagonal basalt columns which make up the **Devils Postpile Monument▶▶▶** (tel:

❏ The Owens Valley Aqueduct was completed in 1913 to siphon water from the Owens Valley to Los Angeles. Despite the harm caused to the valley, the aqueduct was extended to Mono Lake in 1941, and a second built in 1970. ❏

760/934–2289. Vehicles prohibited during the day, take shuttle bus from Mammoth Mountain Inn. *Open* mid-Jun–Oct. *Admission: moderate*) formed as molten lava flow cooled and was polished by passing glaciers.

Retrace your route along State Road 203, after 17 miles turning right onto Lake Mary Road and continuing for six miles to the Lake Mary Loop Road.
The Lake Mary Loop Road circles **Lake Mary▶**, a large glacial lake.

Return to State Road 203 and turn left, after a mile turning right to come onto the Mammoth Scenic Loop.
Constructed in the 1970s as an evacuation route in the event of a major earthquake, the **Mammoth Scenic Loop▶▶** passes several examples of volcanic upheaval, including the water-filled **Inyo Craters▶**, to the left.

Continue on the Mammoth Scenic Loop to rejoin Highway 395 eight miles north of the State Road 203 intersection.

Excellently laid out and well-maintained short trails put some of the Sierra Nevada's most unforgettable scenery within reach even of those people who consider it a major expedition to get out of their cars. The best of the easier walks lie in the Yosemite Valley (described on pages 208–209) and around the giant trees of Sequoia National Park (see page 201). Longer walks (such as the John Muir trail) often branch from simpler foot trails, allowing longer and more arduous forays into the rugged Sierra backcountry.

Exploring on foot Some hikes, traveling far from roads and motels, might take a few hours or a few days (with camping at undeveloped sites), and often connect with longer routes such as the 250-mile **John Muir Trail**, between Mount Whitney and Yosemite Valley, itself part of the enormous Pacific Crest Trail that runs all the way from Mexico to Canada.

Aside from being a starting point for the John Muir Trail, Yosemite National Park has many other hikes that demand fitness and determination. Of them, the most rewarding is the eight-mile route to the summit of Half Dome from the Holiday Isles campsite, steep enough in some sections that hikers are forced to use steel climbing cables fixed to the smooth granite surface.

Many other hikes radiate from Yosemite's Tuolumne Meadows; among them is the High Sierra Loop Trail, which bobs and weaves around waterfalls, meadows, and steep-sided river creeks, for a distance long enough to have six well-equipped overnight huts at eight-mile intervals on its course. Reservations are essential at these.

The High Sierras After viewing the big trees of Sequoia National Park, drive the 100-mile winding road through the secluded southern section of the park and you will reach Mineral King, a hauntingly

quiet valley, 7,500 feet high. Some of the greatest views of the High Sierras—peaceful alpine lakes lined by fir trees and surrounded by forbidding granite peaks—are within reach of Mineral King on short (but often steep) trails. Here, the intrepid walker can also join the 50-mile High Sierra Trail, which affords unmatched high-country views and links with the John Muir Trail.

On the trail in the Sierra Nevada

Guaranteed to stir the soul, Yosemite Valley's granite cliffs topped by tumbling waterfalls and lake-studded alpine meadows all help to make this venerable national park one of the world's most beautiful places.

WATERFALLS
Do not be surprised to find the waterfalls of the Sierra Nevada—and especially those in Yosemite—more closely resembling dripping faucets than the gushing torrents of popular description. The falls are only fully active during the spring, when they are fueled by melting snow.

208

When to visit The park can be visited year-round, but arriving in spring or autumn avoids winter snows and summer's tourist crowds, which have led to plans to ban cars from Yosemite Valley, the park's single most spectacular section. You have not seen Yosemite until you have seen Yosemite Valley, but it is only a seven-mile long section of the 1,000-square-mile park and you should also explore other parts, such as Tuoloumne Meadows on the park's eastern side, and Wawona and the Mariposa Grove, south of the valley.

The numerous accidents caused by distracted drivers prove that there is much to admire even from a car window. Simple foot trails make much more of it accessible, while a network of hiking trails through Yosemite's many undeveloped portions link with marathon trans-Sierra treks (see page 207).

Yosemite Valley A natural sculpture on an infinite scale, Yosemite Valley has been filling arrivals with awe since the first nonnatives entered it in the mid-19th century. After the valley was carved by glaciers, a lake covered its floor. The lake slowly silted up and became today's lush meadow, dotted with fir trees and enclosed by enormous granite peaks.

The spring sunshine catches the face of Yosemite's El Capitan. The steadily rising temperatures cause a gradual melting of the winter snows that will soon lead to the national park's waterfalls being at their most spectacular

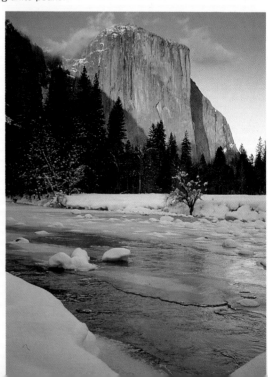

The 8,842-foot **Half Dome**▶▶, its missing half crushed beneath the ice fields, is a vivid reminder of the incredible forces that shaped Yosemite Valley. There is a good view of Half Dome and exceptional views across the valley, from **Glacier Point**▶▶, at the top of a 3,200-foot-high rock wall on the valley's south side, accessible via a winding road and by a steep four-mile trail.

Try to visit Glacier Point at sunset, when Half Dome glows with orange hues, or at night, when moonlight illuminates the valley and millions of stars twinkle above the Sierra Nevada peaks.

From Glacier Point you also get a sense of the mind-boggling scale of **El Capitan**▶▶ at the valley's western end, the world's tallest exposed granite monolith, rising three times higher than the Empire State Building.

A common sight at El Capitan's foot are binocular-wielding visitors, who hope to watch the climbers—almost invisible from the ground—as they seek out the challenging peak's few cracks and fissures.

After enjoying the grand views, explore the walking trails. These reach waterfalls, such as **Lower Yosemite Falls**▶ (the more impressive **Upper Yosemite Fall**▶▶ is at the end of a three-mile uphill hike) and **Bridalveil Falls**▶, opposite El Capitan. With a day to spare, tackle the longer trek to **Vernal Falls**▶▶ and **Nevada Falls**▶▶, reached via the steep but rewarding Mist Trail.

Also on the valley floor, Yosemite Village has shops, services, a visitor center (tel: 209/372–0299) and the **Indian Cultural Museum**▶, giving a brief account of Yosemite's Miwoks and Paiutes.

Close by, the stone-and-concrete **Ahwahnee Hotel**▶▶, the most upscale lodging in the park, has fit neatly into its surrounds since 1927; step inside to peek at the gorgeous dining room and to admire the lounge's mammoth stone fireplace.

Tuoloumne Meadows Close to the park's eastern entrance but better reached from the west by the vista-rich **Tioga Road**▶▶, the vivid green Tuoloumne Meadows—the Sierras' largest alpine meadow—forms a striking contrast to the bald granite peaks all around.

Primarily a base for hardened hikers and experienced climbers, Tuoloumne Meadows is also one of the most quietly beautiful sections of the park, with plenty to reward a day's rambling.

Wawona and the Mariposa Grove After the crowds and visual drama of Yosemite Valley, Wawona, surrounded by dense forests and bordered by meadows and gushing streams, is the picture of pastoral tranquility. The white, wood-framed **Wawona Hotel**▶▶, opened in 1879 to house stagecoach travelers, adds to the rural charm.

Near the hotel, the **Pioneer Yosemite History Center**▶ remembers, with exhibits and restored buildings, the region's early white settlers. One of them, Glen Clerk, is credited with the discovery of the **Mariposa Grove**▶▶, the thickest of the park's three stands of giant sequoia trees. If you are not visiting Sequoia National Park (see page 201), be sure to explore these fascinating trees on the grove's narrated tram tours.

JOHN MUIR'S VIEW
On the way to spending his first summer in the Sierra Nevada, John Muir wrote, in typically lyrical style: "Along the eastern margin rises the mighty Sierra, miles in height, reposing like a smooth, cumulus cloud in the sunny sky, and so gloriously colored and so luminous, it seems not to be clothed with light, but composed of it, like the wall of some celestial city."

209

JOHN MUIR
Scottish-born John Muir arrived in San Francisco in 1868 and allegedly asked for directions to "somewhere wild." Accompanied only by a mule, Muir spent many summers exploring the Sierra Nevada. The eulogistic writings that resulted from these trips, and his tireless efforts to have the Yosemite area put under federal protection, led to the formation of the still-influential Sierra Club, and the creation of Yosemite National Park in 1890 (for more on Muir, see page 81).

GOLD COUNTRY AND FAR NORTH

O R E G O N

BOUNDLESS WEALTH In 1848, the discovery of gold changed California forever. Previously a remote farming outpost, California suddenly became the place to be, and for the first time (and certainly not the last) its very name exuded the promise of instant and unbridled riches. With no easy links to the rest of the country—the Sierra Nevada mountains, whose hillsides held the gold that the rivers had washed to the lowlands, were then as now a formidable natural barrier—it was not until 1849 that the first huge influx of wealth-seekers arrived, the so-called Forty-niners. Three years later, 100,000 people had settled in the hastily built wood and brick towns of what was being called the Gold Country.

Most Gold-Rush fortunes were made by merchants and storekeepers rather than the hopeful prospectors; none became more successful or as influential in shaping the future as the so-called Big Four (see page 221). Many of the prospectors wound up as laborers in the company-owned mines that came to dominate the industry as the stocks of river gold were exhausted.

As mining machinery arrived by ship, port towns such as San Francisco and Sacramento flourished; the latter became the state capital in 1854. The only Gold Country settlement still of appreciable size, Sacramento lost its prestige when California's influential figures departed for the coastal cities. Today it makes the most of its history and is slowly shedding the staid image impressed upon it by its army of state bureaucrats.

EAST OF SACRAMENTO The appropriately numbered State Road 49 links many of the smaller Gold Country towns, which pepper a 200-mile-long strip—known as the Mother Lode—north from Yosemite along the western slopes of the Sierra Nevada mountains. Almost every community here prides itself on preserving its 19th-century buildings that, together with ubiquitous gold-mining museums, evoke a potent sense of rough and ready Gold-Rush days. The down side is that every town seems uncannily like the last.

California's Far North, separated from the North Coast by the Klamath Mountains and reached by Interstate 5 from the Gold Country, provides greater variety, not with its towns, which are forgettable, but with its ravishing scenery: alpine forests, canyons and sparkling rivers, wondrous lava formations at the Lava Beds National Monument, and bubbling mud pits, hot springs, and hot gases issuing furiously from the ground at Lassen Volcanic National Park.

High hopes: panning for gold

Gold Country

GOLD COUNTRY WRITERS
Mark Twain passed through Angel City as part of his grand tour across the western United States, which was recorded—as a mix of fact and fiction—in *Roughing It*, published in 1872. Bret Harte had already gained notoriety as a journalist before taking teaching jobs around Angels Camp, a period that gave rise to sharp, if sometimes whimsical, tales of the lives and lifestyles of the booming Gold Country, the first of which was *The Luck of the Roaring Camp*, published in 1868.

Opposite: a "walk-through" giant sequoia at Calaveras Big Trees State Park, carved before conservation awareness banned such practices

Auburn Old Town's 19th-century elegance

▶ Amador City   210B2

Officially California's smallest city, Amador City is as pretty as a picture and stretches for just one block along State Road 49, holding a handful of cafés, bed-and-breakfast inns, and art and antiques shops.

▶ Angels Camp   210C1

Mines at Angels Camp (named for the two Angel brothers who opened a store here in 1848) yielded $19 million worth of gold between 1886 and 1910, but—bizarrely—it is frogs and not precious metal that have brought the town lasting fame. Every May since 1928, the **Jumping Frogs Jamboree▶**—in which frogs compete over three measured hops for a $1,000 prize (going to the winning owner, not the champion frog)—has brought tens of thousands of spectators to Angels Camp, and accounts for the frog motifs that appear on many of the town's buildings.

The frog fixation is actually an expression of the town's literary claim to fame. Legend has it that writer Mark Twain was relaxing in the bar of the former **Hotel Angels▶** (1287 Main Street) during the 1860s, when he heard the miners' tale about jumping frogs that inspired his first published story. Another writer, Bret Harte, also has links with the town; for more on both scribes, see panel (left).

▶▶ Auburn   210B2

Thirty miles from Sacramento on Interstate 80, Auburn is fast becoming the state capital's favorite suburban community. Down the hill from the nondescript modern town, however, Auburn's cheerful **Old Town▶▶** (Visitor Center, 13464 Lincoln Way, Auburn; tel: 530/887–2111 and 800/427–6463) has many restored mid-19th-century buildings—including an 1892 fire house, the state's oldest continuously used post office, a domed neoclassical courthouse, and a tiny Chinatown district—battling for tourists' attention with restaurants and antiques stores (and some rummageable junk shops).

The highly commendable **Gold Country Museum▶▶** (1273 High Street; tel: 530/889–6500) charts Auburn's past with a collection of gold-mining implements and explanatory displays, backed up with Native American items and intriguing pieces from early Auburn's Chinese community.

Next door to the main museum, the **Bernhard Museum▶** is a complex of late 1800s buildings intended to replicate Victorian life: you will find a period-furnished home, a working blacksmith's yard, and a former winery now housing an art gallery.

▶▶ Calaveras Big Trees State Park   210C1

Near Arnold, State Road 4 (tel: 209/795–2334)

Much less famous nowadays than their counterparts in the Sierra Nevada's national parks, the giant sequoia trees at what became Calaveras Big Trees State Park were the first of their kind to be discovered—by a local settler chasing a bear in 1852—and were first thought to be the only giant sequoias in the world. Widespread disbelief greeted press reports of their size (in terms of bulk, giant sequoias were long considered the earth's

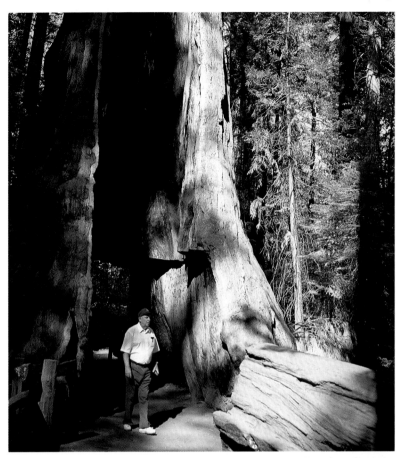

largest living organisms) and there followed a "tree rush" of tourists and naturalists to California. The **Big Trees Visitor Center** provides a thorough grounding on the trees, which lie in two sections of the park. The North Grove is looped by a mile-long foot trail; nine miles south, the less visited South Grove, which requires a bit more walking, shelters more than 1,000 sequoias in atmospheric seclusion.

▶ Chinese Camp   210C1

In 1851, one in ten of California's 250,000 miners were Chinese, and 5,000 of them lived in Chinese Camp, nine miles south of Jamestown at the junction of State Road 49 and State Road 120. Not helped by the "foreigners tax" (described on page 219), few Chinese made a profit from mining and many went on to provide the labor for the transcontinental railroad, before retreating to San Francisco's Chinatown following the government's anti-Chinese Exclusion Act of 1882 and widespread "Yellow Peril" hysteria.

Nothing remains of Chinese Camp except crumbling brick and adobe buildings. It is mainly left to a tourist information office to keep the place's name on the map.

▶▶▶ **REGION HIGHLIGHTS**

California State Railroad Museum *page 221*

Grass Valley *page 218*

Indian Grinding Rock State Historic Park *pages 218–219*

Lassen Volcanic National Park *page 224*

Marshall Gold Discovery State Historic Park *page 219*

Mount Shasta *page 226*

Nevada City *page 220*

Railtown 1897 State Historic Park *page 214*

State Capitol Building *page 221*

Drive

State Road 49: Jamestown to Placerville

See map on page 210.

Begin in Jamestown, at the Railtown 1897 State Historic Park.
Jamestown's **Railtown 1897 State Historic Park▶▶** (5th Avenue; tel: 209/984–3953) preserves the engines, carriages, and equipment of the 1897 Sierra Railway Company.

From Jamestown, drive three miles east on State Road 49 to Sonora.
One of the wealthiest Gold-Rush towns, **Sonora▶▶** continues to thrive, thanks in part to the railway and also to the well-preserved historic buildings in the old section of town.

Continue for four miles on State Road 49 to Columbia State Historic Park.

Panning for gold in Columbia State Historic Park

The outstanding **Columbia State Historic Park▶▶▶** creates an intriguing impression of life in a Gold-Rush town (see page 215).

Continue for 19 miles on State Road 49 to Angels Camp.
Curiously, **Angels Camp▶** is the only Gold-Rush town better known for its frogs than its preserved buildings: writer Mark Twain penned his first published story about them; a Jumping Frogs Jamboree is held each May (see page 212).

Continue for 11 miles on State Road 49 to San Andreas.
In **San Andreas▶**, legendary outlaw Black Bart (see panel on page 223) was tried and sentenced in 1883 at the County Courthouse, an immaculately restored building that is now the **Calaveras County Historical Museum and Archives▶** (30 N Main Street; tel: 209/754–1058).

Continue for 16 miles on State Road 49 to Jackson.
The seat of tiny Amador County, Jackson is home to the **Amador County Museum▶** (225 Church Street; tel: 209/223–6386) which offers a lively examination of gold-mining techniques with working scale models.

Continue for 14 miles on State Road 49, passing Amador City (described on page 212), on the way to Plymouth.
The route passes through Drytown, named for the condition of the local creek, not sarcastically for the 27 saloons that stood here in Gold Rush times. A side road from Plymouth leads to Fiddletown, settled by fiddle-playing Missourians in the 19th century.

Continue for 20 miles on State Road 49 to Placerville.
In **Placerville▶**, once known as Hangtown, the well lit but chilly innards of the **Gold Bug Mine▶** (tel: 530/642–5232) can be toured, and the **El Dorado County Museum▶▶** (104 Placerville Drive (El Dorado County Fairgrounds); tel: 530/621–5865) stores a hoard of miners' tools.

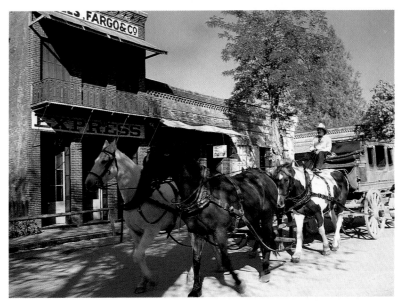

▶▶▶ Columbia State Historic Park 210C1
Parrots Road (off State Road 49) (tel: 209/532–4301)
Open: daily 9–5; closed Thanksgiving and Dec 25
Admission free
In 1854, bustling Columbia was beaten by two votes by Sacramento in the race to become California's state capital. Consequently, as soon as its mines closed so too did the town, leaving the 12 square blocks that now form **Columbia State Historic Park**. Preserved buildings include Columbia's saloon, hotel, schoolhouse, and even its dentist's office, staffed by guides in period dress.

▶ Coulterville 210C1
Coulterville should be on your itinerary because of the engrossing accounts of mining-era life in the **Northern Mariposa County History Center▶** (tel: 209/878–3015) inside the community's former Wells Fargo office. Take a walk, too, along Main Street to view the thick-walled adobe buildings of the 1850s, such as the Jeffrey Hotel and the Magnolia Saloon, and the Sun Sun Wo Co. Store, a survivor of Coulterville's Chinatown district.

▶ Downieville 210B3
Downieville preserves many of its 1850s structures and also keeps a shine on the town gallows. Once a Chinese store and opium den, the **Sierra County Museum▶** (tel: 530/289–3423) on Main Street has photographs and knickknacks.

▶ Folsom 210B2
More than a quarter of Folsom's 29,800 residents are unhappily enduring what Johnny Cash immortalized in song as Folsom Prison Blues. Such is the fame of the town's prison that it has its own museum, devoted to crime and its perpetrators. A more orthodox historical collection fills the **Folsom Museum▶** (tel: 916/985–2707).

A stagecoach is part of the scenery in Columbia State Historic Park

CHINESE "WARS"
The Chinese endured more racism than any other ethnic group during the gold-mining days, and there was much disappointment in the non-Chinese community when a "Tong Wars" battle, which raged in Chinese Camp for several hours in 1856, left only four dead.

GALLOWS HUMOR
The group of public-spirited Downieville citizens who got together in the late 1980s to finance the restoration of their community's most historic landmark—its gallows—rejoiced in the title, The Friends of the Gallows.

The image of the lone prospector standing beside a river sifting through a panful of slush in the hope of finding yellow flakes is somewhat removed from truth. In reality rivers were diverted and dredged, entire hillsides were blown to smithereens, and immense machines hammered quartz to powder. The same technology that made California rich also inflicted scars across its Sierra foothill landscapes that—a century after the damage was done—are only just starting to heal. Many museums in the area showcase the history of gold-mining technology.

216

A gory reminder of the summary justice practiced in the early days of the Gold Country, seen here at Jamestown helping attract attention to a business offering gold prospecting tours

Placer mining Panning was the simplest form of "placer mining" (the term stemming from the idea of the gold being "in place" in rivers and streams), the "placer" scooping up a panload of gravel from the riverbed and carefully removing the lighter material to leave (hopefully) the heavier gold remaining at the bottom. Most of the gold found this way was actually tiny flakes of gold dust nicknamed "color."

A more sophisticated form of placer mining came later with the use of the "rocker," a long box into which one placer shoveled riverbed detritus while a second miner shook the contraption, hoping to capture gold in the cleats at the bottom as the dirt fell through.

A further refinement was the "long tom," a wooden trough about 12 feet long that needed three placers: one shoveling, one mixing, and the third directing a jet of water into the trough. The contents drained out through a "ripple box," which caught any passing gold.

Later, productivity was increased with complex sluice systems, but by the 1850s it was widely accepted that most of the rivers had yielded all the gold they were going to and attention turned to the gold-bearing Sierra rock.

Hydraulic mining During the early 1850s, surface rock was removed from whole hillsides with high-pressure jets of water using adapted fire-fighting equipment and nozzles weighing a ton to expose the seams of gold.

Highly productive (although many tons of rock had to be removed to yield a few ounces of gold) but also highly pollutive, this so-called hydraulic mining wreaked havoc on the natural landscape, destroying wildlife habitats and clogging rivers with so much mud and gravel that the state's farmland came under threat. Because of such damage, "hydraulicking," as it was known, was banned in 1884.

Quartz (or hard-rock) mining Around the time hydraulic mining commenced, it was discovered that gold was embedded in quartz veins, or lodes (hence the term "Mother Lode," applied to the whole Gold Country but misleadingly implying that there was a single large lode), which occurred throughout the Gold Country.

Dynamite, invented in 1860, was used to blast into the hillsides and the first tunnel mines were constructed, often stretching for many miles underground.

Miners descended into the depths and attacked the quartz lodes with pickaxes and shovels, the quartz chunks they hacked out being carried to the surface on mule-drawn wagons. Mules were also used to turn the *arrastra*, a cumbersome machine of Mexican origin resembling a large pestle and mortar, which slowly ground the quartz.

Pulverizing the quartz was greatly speeded up by stamp mills, enormous machines weighing several tons (and now the prize exhibits of many Gold Country museums); hammering day and night, the stamp mills often could be heard in surrounding towns. Gold was extracted from the pulverized quartz through a chemical process, and then, in molten form, it was poured into molds to make ingots.

Dredge mining From the 1890s, dredging machines began gouging up the riverbeds where the earlier placer miners had worked, depositing the resultant material in huge sluicing machines. The tons of waste that this process created were unceremoniously dumped in any available space, often burying vegetation and changing the course of many rivers. Subject to strict controls, limited dredge mining continues today.

GOLD PANNING TODAY
Some people believe the "Mother Lode" has plenty of gold left to yield, and dredge mining and gold panning both have plenty of serious adherents, even today. The pans handed out to tourists at a few spots around the Gold Country, however, are unlikely to produce anything other than minuscule amounts of gold.

Small amounts of gold can still be found by panning California's rivers

The wealth produced by gold mining left its mark in the elegant buildings of Grass Valley

LOLA MONTEZ
Having danced her way across the United States, thrilling audiences with her saucy "spider dance," Irish-born Lola Montez settled in Grass Valley. Flamboyant and glamorous, Lola's was a bemusing presence to miners but not to Lotta Crabtree, a local six-year-old later to become the highest-earning entertainer in the United States, to whom Lola passed on her dancing skills. Leaving Grass Valley after her husband shot her pet bear, Lola underwent a religious conversion and spent the next few years delivering theosophical lectures in Australia and Europe, before dying penniless in New York in 1861, aged 42.

▶▶ **Grass Valley**   *210B2*

The biggest and most lucrative mine in California made Grass Valley one of the state's richest communities by the late 1800s. The buildings, a shaft, and many of the machines of the state's most technologically innovative mine—which ceased operations only in 1956—can be seen at the **Empire Mine State Historic Park**▶▶ (10791 East Empire Street; tel: 530/273–8522), spread across both sides of State Road 174 a mile east of the town.

After the mine closed, Grass Valley kept itself in style through farming and the lumber trade and by exploiting the tourist appeal of its many balconied 19th-century buildings—and the restaurants serving "English-style" food, a throwback to the days when many Cornish miners settled here.

A less likely settler was Lola Montez, a vivacious dancer and a former lover of the King of Bavaria (see panel). A replica of her home (at 248 Mill Street) houses the tourist office and many mementoes of her life.

Elsewhere, the **Grass Valley Museum**▶ (corner of Church and Chapel streets; tel: 530/273–5509) fills an 1865 schoolhouse with historical displays that include reconstructed period rooms and a 10,000-volume collection of antiquarian books, and the **North Star Mining Museum**▶ (intersection of State Road 20 and State Road 49; tel: 530/273–4255) has detailed exhibitions on the development of mining technology.

▶▶ **Indian Grinding Rock State Historic Park**   *210C2*

14881 Pine Grove, Volcano Road (tel: 209/296–7488)
Many generations of Miwok grinding nuts to make flour have left over 1,000 identical *chaw'se*, or mortar cups, indenting a large limestone outcrop at Indian Grinding Rock State Historic Park, between Amador City and Volcano; several hundred petroglyphs also mark the rock. More recent additions to the park are a re-created Miwok Village and a Museum Cultural Center.

▶ Malakoff Diggins State Historic Park 210B3

Lake City Road (tel: 530/265–2740)

Sixteen miles from Nevada City, a massive gash on the side of a mountain caused by hydraulic mining has become a serene expanse of meadows and canyons populated by deer, coyotes, and squirrels. A few restored buildings recall the mining settlement here, but it is the extraordinary regenerative abilities of nature that impress most throughout the 3,000-acre park.

▶ Mariposa 210C1

Most who pass through Mariposa are less interested in the Gold Country than Yosemite National Park, which lies just 30 miles east. If you are one of them, stop off at least long enough to explore the **Mariposa County History Center**▶▶ (5119 Jessie Street; tel: 209/966–2924), a collection revealing plenty about life during the Gold-Rush times with reconstructed period interiors.

Outside, the lawlessness of the old days is suggested much less by the grand **Mariposa County Courthouse**▶ (5808 Bullion Street; tel: 209/966–7081)—finished in 1854 and the state's longest-serving place of justice—than by the nearby Old Mariposa Jail, in use until 1960.

Two miles south of Mariposa, the **California State Mining and Mineral Museum**▶▶ (5005 Fairgrounds Drive; tel: 209/742–7625) proves this region yielded the Gold Country's most spectacular finds, with diamonds and gold nuggets among 200,000 precious pieces.

▶▶▶ Marshall Gold Discovery State Historic Park 210C2

Bridge Street, State Road 49 (tel: 530/622–3470)
Open: 8–dusk. Closed Jan 1, Thanksgiving Day and Dec 25
Admission: inexpensive

California changed forever on January 24, 1848, when James Marshall, building a sawmill for landowner John Sutter, chanced upon flakes of gold beside the American River in the settlement of Coloma, commemorated as the Marshall Gold Discovery State Historic Park.

Within a year, 10,000 people were busy with pickaxes and shovels in the vicinity, although they quickly departed as richer veins were discovered elsewhere, leaving Coloma to decline and a disillusioned Marshall to die in 1879 in his cabin, which still stands here.

Among many restored buildings, the park also has a working model of Sutter's Mill and a museum tracing the colossal effect Marshall's find had on the state.

▶ Murphys 210C1

Named after the two Irish brothers who founded it in 1848, Murphys barely extends beyond its tree-lined Main Street, where the **Murphys Hotel**▶▶ (457 Main Street; tel: 209/728–3444) has stood since 1856, hosting luminaries such as writer Bret Harte and future U.S. president Ulysses S. Grant. The clutter of curiosities filling the **Oldtimer's Museum**▶ (tel: 209/728–1160) attests to the mining community's dislike of throwing things away.

North of Murphys off Sheep Ranch Road, a guided tour of **Mercer's Caverns**▶▶ (tel: 209/728–2101) leads to bizarre limestone formations, discovered in 1885.

219

Raised sidewalks, wooden balconies, and imitation gas lamps are features typical of well-preserved Gold Country communities

The traffic may be modern but many of the buildings in this Nevada City street date from the town's 19th-century prosperity

CORNISH CALIFORNIANS
The Cornish pasty, meat and potatoes wrapped in pastry, is a dish commonly found in Grass Valley and Nevada City, and is a legacy of the Cornish immigrants who brought advanced mining techniques to the Californian gold field from the 1870s. Most had learned their trade in the tin mines of Cornwall, England, and some arrived in California via the lead mines of Wisconsin and Illinois. Many subsequently left California for the silver mines of Nevada.

▶▶ **Nevada City**   210B2

Like neighboring Grass Valley, Nevada City benefited from mining to a much greater degree than most Gold Country communities, and is still comfortably well off, with much from its past lining its narrow streets.

Serving travelers since 1850, the antique-scattered bar and dining rooms of the **National Hotel** (211 Broad Street; tel: 530/265–4551) do much to evoke the past. More evidence of the town's formative days is provided by the **Nevada County Historical Society Museum** (also known as the Firehouse Museum; tel: 530/265–5468), inside the tall, narrow 1861 fire station at 214 Main Street. The museum also features displays of local Native American crafts and outlines the sad tale of the Donner Party (see page 200).

Still more historical exhibits are to be found at the **Miners' Foundry and Cultural Center**▶▶ (325 Spring Street; tel: 530/265–5040), a one-time metalworks turned into a theater and music venue. Adjacent is the **Nevada City Winery**, dating from 1870 but reopened in 1980.

Only two buildings in the old town are not Victorian: the art-deco Courthouse (on Church Street) and the 1937 City Hall (317 Broad Street).

▶▶ **Plumas-Eureka State Park**   210B3

310 Johnsville Road (tel: 530/836–2380)

Enclosed by rough granite peaks and hillsides streaked green by fir and sugar pine trees, pretty Plumas-Eureka State Park sits above 70 miles of tunnels that belonged to the Sierra Buttes Mining Company. The park office and a good **mining museum** fill the miners' former bunkhouse.

▶ **Rough And Ready**   210B2

In an act of drunken bravura and in protest at a miners' tax, Rough And Ready seceded from the United States in 1850 (returning two months later), the only town ever to do so. Today, there is no incentive to pause on your way to the **Bridgeport Covered Bridge**, built in 1862 and spanning 233 feet across the Yuba River—the longest such bridge in the country, in use until 1971.

Today, Sacramento may seem an odd choice for state capital, but in 1854 it was the gateway to the gold mines, and men, machinery, and money were streaming through it. As California's first fortunes were being made, it was here that the Big Four rose to prominence, and established the power base from which they shaped the state's future.

Buildings Eclipsing everything around it, the **State Capitol Building**▶▶▶ (10th and Capitol Avenue; tel: 916/324–0333. *Open* daily 9–5. Closed Jan 1, Thanksgiving, Dec 25. *Admission free*), completed in 1874, is an impressive example of the neo-classical style that defined U.S. public building for decades; it is also, at a cost of $2.5 million, a lasting testament to the incredible wealth of Gold Rush California. Inside, you can see several restored offices and the state legislature in action.

Sacramento's earliest building, the largely adobe **Sutter's Fort**▶▶ (2701 L Street; tel: 916/445–4422), was erected in 1839 by German-born John Sutter as a commercial base for his considerable landholdings. Several reconstructed workshops stand in the fort's grounds, as does the **California State Indian Museum**▶ (2618 K Street; tel: 916/324–0971) making a valiant attempt to chronicle California's 104 native peoples.

Beside the Sacramento River, the wooden sidewalks of the **Old Town**▶▶ (Visitor Center, 1101 Second Street; tel: 916/442–7644) link six blocks of restored 19th-century buildings, and several excellent small museums.

Museums The Old Town also boasts the **California State Railroad Museum**▶▶▶ (125 I Street; tel: 916/445–6645. *Open* daily 10–5. Closed Jan 1, Thanksgiving, Dec 25. *Admission: moderate*), a collection of old locomotives and displays clarifying the crucial role of railways in California's development, and the **Sacramento Discovery Museum**▶▶ (101 I Street; tel: 916/264–7057), which plots the growth of the town.

Outside the Old Town, the **Crocker Art Museum**▶▶ (216 O Street; tel: 916/264–5423) is said to be the West's first art museum.

Continue west along I Street for the Old Town.

❏ The "Big Four"—Charles Crocker, Mark Hopkins, Collis P. Huntington, and Leland Stanford—were Sacramento businessmen who, in the late 1850s, financed the plans of a railway engineer, Theodore Judah, for a transcontinental railway linking California with the rest of the United States. The success of the venture resulted in the Big Four's Southern Pacific Railroad Company enjoying a monopoly of communication links, making them the biggest political power brokers in state history. ❏

The Sacramento River

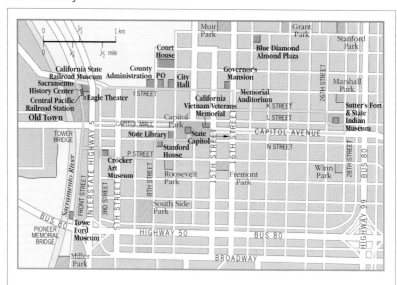

Walk

Sacramento

From the State Capitol, described on page 221, walk east along Capitol Avenue, turning left along 28th Street for Sutters Fort.
Sutter's Fort, the town's earliest building, is described on page 221.

Walk along K Street, turning right into 16th Street for the Governor's mansion.
At 1526 H Street, the 1877 **Governor's Mansion** is now a museum of Victoriana.

Continue west along I Street for the Old Town.
The **Old Town** with restored buildings and museums, is described on page 221.

Walk through the Old Town for the Towe Ford Museum.
At 2200 Front Street, the **Towe Ford Museum** displays gleaming Ford vehicles from 1903 onward.

Walk east along O Street for the Crocker Art Museum.

❑ Born in Germany but living in Switzerland when he went bankrupt, John Sutter arrived in (then Mexican) California in 1839, taking advantage of internecine squabbles to acquire 48,000 acres around the confluence of the Sacramento and American rivers. When gold was discovered on his land in 1848, Sutter's workers became gold prospectors overnight, leaving their boss's possessions to rot. By 1852 Sutter was again bankrupt, and he died impoverished in 1880. ❑

For information on the elegant **Crocker Art Museum**, 216 O Street, see page 221.

Walk east along P Street, turning left along Eighth Street for the Stanford House.

On the corner of N Street, the **Stanford House** (under continuing restoration) was a home of railway magnate Leland Stanford, one of the Big Four (see page 221), from 1871.

Walk east along N Street to return to the State Capitol.

▶ Sierra City   210C3

Evocatively perched in the Sierra foothills beneath towering granite peaks, Sierra City's **Sierra County Historical Park** does a great job of re-creating the homes and illustrating the lifestyles of mining folk. It also does justice to the memory of Ohio-born inventor Lester Allen Pelton, who arrived in California in 1850 hoping to strike gold. Pelton failed in this quest, but did change the face of Californian mining by devising the Pelton Wheel, which enabled the mines' enormous stamp mills to be powered by small jets of water.

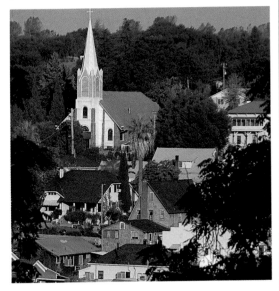

In common with many Gold Country towns, Sonora has grown from 19th-century origins, its early buildings still forming a historic center, into a leafy and pleasant town where contemporary homes dot tree-lined hillsides

223

▶▶ Sonora   210C1

The Mexican miners who founded Sonora were driven away by U.S. settlers before the town became one of the richest Gold Rush towns, and later, thanks to the railway, the commercial hub of the entire region. Even now, Sonora is a coveted address.

The old section of Sonora is extremely well preserved, and many of the town's 19th-century leading citizens lived in opulent mansions that are clustered together along Washington Street. Here, too, you will find the red-and-white **St. James Episcopal Church▶▶**, dating from 1859.

A leaflet detailing the historic homes can be picked up in what used to be the County Jail (188 W. Bradford Avenue), now doubling as a tourist office, and the **Tuoloumne County Museum▶** (158 W Bradford Avenue; tel: 209/532–1317) whose local history exhibits and Old West paintings fill the former cells.

▶ Volcano   210C2

A meandering back road (off State Road 88) gives access to Volcano, named for the crater-like landscape in which it sits. Only a couple of hundred people live here now, and the chief reminder of the halcyon times is the splendid 1864 **St. George Hotel▶** (tel: 209/296–4458).

BLACK BART
Wearing a mask and wielding a shotgun, Black Bart (an alias of one Charles Bolton) relieved 28 Wells Fargo stagecoaches of their gold between 1875 and 1883, often leaving his victims with a self-penned poem. Finally traced by, and captured through, a dropped handkerchief, Bart was tried in San Andreas and served five years in San Quentin prison. Following his release he vanished from the public eye—rumored by some to be receiving a Wells Fargo pension on the understanding that he never robbed from them again.

A sign warns visitors of the dangers of venturing off the trail leading to Bumpass Hell in Lassen Volcanic National Park. Like the county in which it partly sits, the park was named after Peter Lassen, a Danish-born blacksmith and frontiersman who arrived in the area in 1839

224

▶▶▶ Lassen Volcanic National Park 210B4

Northern entrance—take State Road 44 east from Redding; Southwest entrance—take State Road 36 east from Red Bluff then north on State Road 89 (tel: 530/595–4444)
Open all year, weather permitting. Admission: moderate

A seven-year period of intermittent eruptions culminated in 1915 when Lassen Peak, California's only active volcano and the southernmost of the Cascade mountain range, threw a cloud of dust seven miles high, tossed out five-ton boulders, and smothered the surrounding countryside in a 20-foot-deep mud flow.

Lassen Peak, the world's largest "plug" volcano and one unlikely to erupt again for many decades, sits in Lassen National Park, 50 miles east of Redding, the tallest but by no means the only volcanic peak in a geologically very busy region. It occupies a caldera—or crater—left behind by the collapsing dome of a vast prehistoric volcano.

Along State Road 89, which steers a 30-mile course through the park, the major points of interest are indicated by numbered markers corresponding to explanatory descriptions in a leaflet distributed at the park entrance.

A mile-long trail from the road reaches the park's largest hydrothermal area, **Bumpass Hell▶▶▶**, a steaming cauldron of fumeroles—pressured gases hissing to the surface through gaps in the lava rock—hot springs, and bubbling pits of mud.

The same phenomenon on a less imposing scale is repeated at several points throughout the park, but once your nostrils have had their fill of the sulfur gas—and its pervasive rotten-egg smell—you should pay attention to the park's meadows, resplendent with wildflowers in midsummer and sometimes with grazing deer, and pause by a few of the numerous lakes.

Nature's tranquil qualities are also apparent at the **Devastated Area▶▶**, where stands of young trees are beginning to reclaim a landscape razed of all vegetation by the mud flows and gases unleashed by the 1915 eruption.

Hiking trails through the park, and to the summit of Lassen Peak, are described on page 226.

▶▶ Lava Beds National Monument 210B5

South of Tutelake (tel: 530/667–2282)

Few visitors make the effort to reach Lava Beds National Monument, tucked away in the state's northeast corner, but the reward for those who do is an eerie, often foggy plateau ridden with volcanic craters, cinder cones, and lava tubes formed over 1,000 years ago by cooling magma flows.

Many of the hundreds of lava tubes lie a few feet beneath the ground as cylindrical caves, which can be explored with flashlights borrowed from the visitor center beside State Road 139.

Near the visitor center, exhibits inside the illuminated **Mushpot Cave▶▶** aid understanding of the area's geological curiosities, and several unlit caves lie within easy reach on the three-mile **Cave Loop▶**. If you find the darkness daunting, opt for the guided tours that are conducted daily in summer.

THE MODOC WAR
Resisting forcible resettlement, a group of Modocs returned to their ancestral lands (what is now the Lava Beds National Monument) in November 1872, turning the area's volcanic formations into a natural line of defense against the troops sent to remove them. The five-month Modoc War that ensued became the only Native American war fought in California. It needed a two-day mortar attack to finally shift the Modoc, following which their chief, Kentipoos (known to Caucasians as Captain Jack), along with three other Modoc, were tried by a military court and executed.

The single road through the monument's desolate terrain passes many more caves, whose isolation deters all but the most adept explorers (who must get permits from the visitor center), before reaching the area known as Captain Jack's Stronghold. This was named after a Modoc chief who held out here with 52 of his people against 1,000 U.S. soldiers, using the natural landscape as a shield (see panel on page 224).

▶ Redding 210A4

Given the alluring natural wonders all around it and the scores of fast-food joints and motels within its boundaries, it is not surprising that most people use Redding, the Far North's largest town, only for eating and sleeping.

The **Carter House Natural Science Museum▶** (48 Quartz Hill Road; tel: 530/243–5457), provides a moderately successful introduction to the Far North's flora and fauna, and the **Museum of Art and History▶** (56 Quartz Hill Road; tel: 530/243–8801) places temporary local art exhibitions alongside permanent regional historical items, including a large collection of Native American basketry. Both museums are located in Caldwell Park, which sits on the north bank of the Sacramento River.

WEATHER CHECK
Lassen National Park's extremely volatile weather is a more pressing concern than the likelihood of volcanic eruptions. Temperatures range from cool to very cold, with July and August being the only months dependably free of snow. Whenever you plan to come, check conditions before setting out by phoning the park headquarters on 530/595–4444.

Compressed gases burst through crevices in the lava rock at Bumpass Hell

225

It's almost impossible to drive through the Far North without feeling the urge to explore the landscape more closely. In Lassen National Park, and to a lesser extent in the Whiskeytown-Shasta-Trinity National Recreation Area, many miles of hiking trails await—and none requires great strength, although some may be snow-covered even in summer.

CLIMBING MOUNT SHASTA

Mount Shasta can be reached only on very steep trails beginning at Ski Bowl and Horse Camp. You will need to set out at dawn to be sure of returning from the majestic (and mysterious, being a setting for many strange occult tales) mountain before nightfall.

STRANGE SHASTA

Many of the strange tales surrounding Mount Shasta—regarded as a sacred place since pre-European times—focus on the mountain's supposed role as a gateway to Lemuria, an ancient but highly advanced subterranean civilization. The first written account on this theme appeared in the 1880s, and there has been no shortage of alleged sightings of secret tunnels, gold-domed temples, and mysterious entities on its slopes ever since.

Lassen Peak Not surprisingly, the best place for an overview of Lassen National Park is from its highest point, the 10,475-foot-high Lassen Peak, reached by a 2½-mile trail beginning from Marker 22 on State Road 89. A switchback route makes the steep gradient comparatively easy going, but you should allow five hours to reach the top and come back down again, and to savor the sights and the feeling of achievement from the summit.

Other hikes Lassen Peak is a prime objective for many hikers, however, so if you want equally spectacular views and fewer people to share them with, try **Brokeoff Mountain**, the second-tallest peak in the national park, reached along a trail from Marker 2 on State Road 89.

Entering the eastern section of the park on State Road 44 (which, unlike State Road 89, does not cross the park) gives access to the backcountry, where you can hike for several days at a stretch—though the area may well be snowbound even in the summer.

The best hikes The pick of the shorter hikes in this region is the **Cinder Cone Nature Trail**, starting from Butte Lake, a potentially ankle-twisting trek through loose rock, but passing the aptly named Fantastic Lava Beds and Painted Dunes—multicolored lava flows dating from the 1850s.

Much of the **Whiskeytown-Shasta-Trinity National Recreation Area** (see page 227) is geared toward boating rather than walking. The best bets for modest exertion here are the Hirz Bay and Samwell Cave trails, close to Lake Shasta and designed to illustrate local nature and history. Perpetually snowcapped Mount Shasta, 30 miles north of Lake Shasta, is on many hikers' Far North itineraries, but the 14,162-foot-high peak is not to be underestimated, as it is prone to avalanches, rock falls, and constantly changing weather.

For the adventurous hiker For longer and more isolated hikes, make for the Clair Engle (also known as Trinity) Lake area, and the **Salmon-Trinity Alps Primitive Area**, with 400 hikable miles of trails through forests, meadows, and canyons, beside waterfalls, and beneath glaciated peaks. Be aware that local weather is unpredictable and service stations are scarce (for information, tel: 530/623-2121).

► **Shasta** 210A4

Shasta flourished during the late 1800s because of the lucrative gold mines that surrounded it. Remains and detailed reconstructions of Shasta's buildings form the **Shasta State Historical Park►** (tel: 530/243–8194) on State Road 299, 6 miles west of Redding.

►► **Whiskeytown-Shasta-Trinity NRA** 210A4
(tel: 530/242–3400)
Covering nearly 250,000 acres, the Whiskeytown-Shasta-Trinity National Recreation Area divides into three sections, each one adjacent to a dam-formed lake. Sailing, windsurfing, and water- and jet-skiing (supply permitting, most equipment can be rented on arrival) make the lakes, and Whiskeytown especially, intensely busy each summer. Lake Shasta Dam, reached with State Road 155 off Interstate 5, is the area's most spectacular manmade sight and diverts three rivers to irrigate California's Central Valley farmlands. A film describing the dam's construction is shown at the visitor center, while crossing the lake on Interstate 5 takes you over the **Pit River Bridge►**, the world's biggest double-decked bridge.

Turn a visit to Lake Shasta into a day-trip by continuing to the **Lake Shasta Caverns►** (tel: 530/238–2341); guided cavern tours by boat start from O'Brien, on the eastern side of the lake, and feature stalactite and stalagmite formations.

Close to Clair Engle Lake, on the western fringes of the recreation area, **Weaverville►►** has many 19th-century buildings as reminders of its gold-prospecting days. During the 1850s, half of Weaverville's population was Chinese, some of whom contributed to the building of the **Joss House**, a Taoist temple with a 300-year-old altar. Now the centerpiece of **Joss House State Historic Park►►** (Oregon and Main streets; tel: 530/623–5284), the temple has guided tours every half hour.

227

Mount Shasta, 14,162 feet high and usually snow-capped all year, was first climbed in 1854

A WORLD AWAY Far from the affluent cities, crowded sands, and persistent sunshine of southern California, the state's North Coast—between San Francisco and the Oregon border—is heavily forested and almost continually damp, populated by a bizarre mix of lumber workers, marijuana farmers, back-to-nature artists, and radical ecologists.

Despite its size—accounting for almost a third of the state's Pacific seaboard—the North Coast has always been one of California's most sparsely inhabited and least accessible corners; even today, there are only a couple of viable routes through it. The coast-hugging Highway 1 is the most scenic option but covers just half the region before swinging inland to join Highway 101, which links the inland settlements and the northernmost coastal towns before continuing into Oregon and deep into the Pacific Northwest.

CLIMATE The North Coast's summer temperatures can be searing, but fogs regularly block out the heat and, in winter, the area is one of the wettest in the United States. Clearly, this is no place to acquire a tan (and typically, the region's best beaches are slivers of sand enclosed by jagged headlands at the end of winding foot trails), yet it is just this climate that allows the North Coast's most prized feature to flourish: the gigantic coastal redwoods, the tallest trees in the world, found only here.

There are stands of redwoods within easy striking distance of San Francisco at the Muir Woods National Monument, part of the Golden Gate National Recreation Area, and at Point Reyes National Seashore. But travel farther north to Humboldt State Park or the Redwood National Park and you will find these incredible trees—their slender trunks often rising more than 300 feet.

Even without the redwoods, the North Coast would be exceptionally strong on natural spectacle. At almost every turn throughout 200 miles of coastline there is a fresh vista to excite—wave-sculpted rock arches, gale-tormented bluffs, schools of basking seals, and (at the right time of year) migrating whales. The scenery attracts many weekending San Franciscans, as do the region's small, romantic inns and quality restaurants.

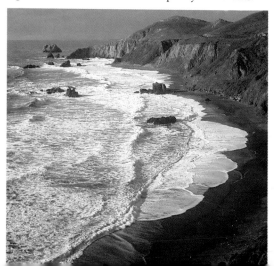

Gull Rock, on the Pacific Coast

TOWN LIFE Small and far apart, the towns of the North Coast generally provide a sedate accompaniment to the wild scenery around them. Most sprang up during the mid-19th century, when their sheltered bays made perfect landing points for men and machinery destined for the Gold Country, and later grew into busy lumber ports as timber became the region's economic backbone.

Several communities—notably Fort Bragg, halfway along the North Coast—are still dominated by the logging industry, despite the fact that depressingly large sections of the North Coast's forests have been reduced to stumps, and pressure from the environmental lobby has stimulated a rethinking of tree-felling methods. This is part of a reassessment of priorities as the region's other staple trades, fishing and farming, face decline.

ALTERNATIVE INDUSTRY From the early 1970s, some landowners in the slumbering agricultural hamlets sought an alternative source of income by cultivating marijuana. This illegal enterprise grew into a highly productive business, particularly in the region around Garberville, nicknamed "the Emerald Triangle." In the mid-1980s, however, the government initiated a clampdown intended to end large-scale cultivation. Despite several high profile raids, however, it is thought that the illegal crop is still a major contributor to many local incomes, whether directly through growing or indirectly through the supply of equipment.

These days tourism is seen as the financial future of the North Coast, something that causes commercial interests and conservationists to lock horns with increasing regularity. The battle is clearest at Mendocino, a lovely artistic town with many restored mid-1800s buildings that is struggling to maintain its charm as gift shops and bed-and-breakfast inns proliferate.

Elsewhere, larger communities such as Arcata and Eureka pack their centers with preserved Victorian homes, and make good bases from which to discover the best of the North Coast's natural pleasures. The quirkiest historical sight is the remnant of a 19th-century Russian fur-trapping settlement at Fort Ross.

One more North Coast curiosity is the notorious San Andreas fault, the line of geological instability that has been responsible for many of California's biggest earthquakes over the centuries. The fault notably scars the landscape with its presence before moving away beneath the ocean.

The North Coast

A North Coast small town: Mendocino

▶ Arcata
228A4

These days a hotbed of student politics and ecological activism, Arcata was founded as a mining supply base and gained notoriety in 1860 by booting soon-to-be-famous writer Bret Harte out of town for publicizing a massacre of Native Americans.

Victorian homes and a lovely central plaza bring character to Arcata, and the small town is kept bubbling by the students of the North Coast's only university.

All the sights worth seeing are natural ones: the **Historic Logging Trail▶** traces the impact of the lumber industry on a section of Arcata Community Forest (tel: 707/822-3619); landfill sites around **Arcata Bay▶▶** such as the **Arcata Marsh and Wildlife Sanctuary** (tel: 707/826-2359) have been turned into a wildlife preserve and bird sanctuary; and azaleas, rhododendrons, and a host of wildflowers blooming at various times throughout the year ensure that some color is always beautifying the 30-acre **Azalea State Reserve▶** (tel: 707/488-2041).

▶ Bodega Bay
228A1

An encouraging first glimpse of the North Coast if you are arriving from the Wine Country, and a good base for exploring the Sonoma Coast State Beach (see page 241), Bodega Bay's tall cliffs and sandy beaches look out over the vessels of a declining fishing fleet, whose plaid-shirted workforce is not overly enamored of the gift shops, bed and breakfasts, and boutiques that are spreading through their village.

If Bodega Bay's immense population of gulls, egrets, pelicans, and herons gets on your nerves, it will come as no comfort at all to learn that it was here (and at the nearby inland town of Bodega) that Alfred Hitchcock shot his 1963 film *The Birds*.

▶ Bolinas
228A1

Just south of Point Reyes National Seashore, Bolinas is so well liked by its residents that they are known to

Oysters being barbecued in a region where the harvest of the sea has traditionally provided a livelihood as well as sustenance

tear down road signs directing traffic to it. As it happens, Bolinas may be a nice place to live but it is entirely uninteresting to visit.

Much more deserving of attention in the area are the birds swooping for fishy snacks at **Bolinas Lagoon**, and the many and various marine creatures inhabiting the tidal pools of **Duxbury Reef**.

▶▶ Eureka   228A3

A glut of Victorian residential architecture has made industrialized Eureka, easily the largest town on the North Coast, into an impressive showcase of turn-of-the-century California living. There is no more eloquent example of the style than the **Carson Mansion▶▶▶** (143 M Street), complete with painted window frames, turrets, and towers, built in 1885 by a builder who did not know when to stop.

Using timber to a different end, the **Romano Gabriel Sculpture Garden▶▶** (325 Second Street) is an intensely colorful collection of people, plants, and symbols carved from disused packing cases with a chain saw. It is either epic folk art or simply a mess—either way, you will kick yourself if you miss it.

Old Town The downbeat bars and flophouses that were once a feature of Eureka's dockside area have been transformed into trendy galleries, boutiques, and eateries. These occupy newly painted restored buildings collectively titled the **Old Town▶**—all a bit contrived and pricey, but nonetheless the area makes for an enjoyable stroll.

Nearby, the **Clarke Memorial Museum▶** (240 E Street; tel: 707/443–1947) keeps the dust off myriad exhibits from Eureka's pioneer times, and maintains a ravishing stash of basketry from the Native American tribes.

By contrast, Eureka's 1853 Fort Humboldt was built to launch attacks on Native Americans. At **Fort Humboldt State Historic Park▶▶** (3431 Fort Avenue; tel: 707/445–6547) only the redwood hospital of the fort's 14 buildings remains upright, and its exhibits—not surprisingly—dwell on logging rather than on genocide.

▶▶ Ferndale   228A3

Almost every one of the thousand or so residents of Ferndale, 20 miles south of Eureka, has a well-looked-after Victorian pile to call home. The few antiques and period furnishings not in daily use are stored inside the **Ferndale Museum▶** (515 Shaw Avenue; tel: 707/786–4466), a collection that sets the seal on this wondrous time-locked community.

▶ Fort Bragg   228A2

You will not find a fort in Fort Bragg, but you will find lumber mills and freight yards that diminish the scenic setting of this hard-working coastal town. The **Guest House Museum▶** (on Main Street; tel: 707/961–2840; *Open* weekends only.) unfurls an uncritical account of the timber industry, but you are better off opting for a stroll along the two miles of trails weaving through the 17-acre **Mendocino Coast Botanical Gardens▶▶** (18220 N. Highway 1; tel: 707/964–4352).

The Carson Mansion, one of over a hundred preserved Victorian homes in Eureka, was built mostly of redwood for wealthy lumber mogal William Carson and is now an exclusive men-only club

231

BOAT TOURS
The cold and choppy waters off the North Coast generally do little to encourage boat tours. An exception is Eureka's sheltered Humboldt Bay, enjoyably cruised on a narrated 75-minute sailing aboard a 1910 ferry, departing from the C Street harbor (for details, tel: 707/ 445–1910). Also in Eureka, the Image Tour includes a boat trip as part of a five-hour guided town tour (details from the Chamber of Commerce, tel: 800/356–6381).

Found only along a slender section of the coast between Big Sur, on the northern half of California's Central Coast, and central Oregon, the tall and comparatively slender coast redwoods (Sequoia sempervirens) *should not be confused with the slightly shorter and much stockier giant sequoias* (Sequoia gigantea) *that live on the western slopes of the Sierra Nevada mountains.*

THE SKUNK TRAIN
Between Fort Bragg and Willits, the Skunk Train—which earned its name from the aromatic qualities of its diesel engine—makes a scenic 40-mile trip, crisscrossing the Noyo River and riding on trestles high above redwood groves. Tourists have replaced timber as the main cargo, although the train still makes unscheduled stops to deliver mail and supplies to the tiny settlements on its route. Operating twice daily in summer, and daily in winter, the Skunk Train should not be missed (tel: 707/964–6371 or 800/777–5865).

The Skunk Train, now mainly tourist transportation

The tallest trees in the world As a species, the redwoods have been around for 60 million years. When dinosaurs roamed the earth, the trees covered large - sections of the North American and European continents. As global weather patterns changed, the redwoods retreated to the United States' West Coast, where the heavy rainfall and regular fogs are much to their liking.

Often growing as high as a football field is long, the coast redwoods are the world's tallest trees—the tallest among them reaching 368 feet—although their life span of up to 2,600 years is less than that of the giant sequoias of the Sierra Nevada, which can live up to 3,400 years. Because of the demands of logging, however, many of the trees you will see along the North Coast are second-growth redwoods and comparative youngsters.

Like the giant sequoias, the coast redwoods absorb rainwater through shallow root systems. Such roots render them unstable in high winds, however, and as a consequence they grow in areas sheltered from ocean breezes and cluster together in tight groves.

With heat-resistant barks, both types of sequoia are able to take advantage of forest fires, dropping their winged seeds to the freshly cleared forest floor, where sunlight is able to reach the sprouting sequoias.

As well as by seeds, sequoias can regenerate in a strange cloning-type process, which enables new trees to grow from fallen branches, stumps, or roots, each one bearing the genetic imprint of its progenitor.

The "harvesting" of the redwoods The dark and damp redwood groves were seldom penetrated by Native Americans, who traditionally regarded such places the domain of spirits. The redwoods' isolation changed when U.S. settlers arrived. The first sawmills appeared in the region during the 1830s, but it was the Gold Rush that turned lumberjacks into lumber barons overnight.

Mining and a fast-expanding population brought a huge demand for timber, the raw material for tunnels, dams, sluices, fences, and flumes, and for the buildings of the new Gold Rush towns. The redwoods' fire-resistant properties made their timber a valued commodity, and as early as 1870 the best of the state's redwood trees had been felled.

With no thoughts of reforestation, commercial logging continued apace for the next 40 years using the highly destructive clear-cutting method. This involved an entire hillside or waterside section of forest being sawed down, leaving a desolate stump-strewn landscape where any remaining groves were exposed to erosion and where local wildlife was devastated.

Saving the trees As the lumber industry made fortunes and kept a large contingent of Californians in work—especially along the North Coast—voices of dissent

Timber became big business when settlers arrived

struggled to be heard. In 1918, the Save-the-Redwoods League was founded and teamed up with the Sierra Club to promote awareness of the dangers faced by California's forests. During the 1930s, the Civilian Conservation Corps increased forest protection against fires, diseases, and pests, and helped pave the way for 18 forests (including Klamath National Forest on the North Coast) to be given National Forest status. This placed them under the control of the U.S. Forestry Commission, which regulated logging activity at least to the extent of providing financial and technical assistance to maximize the forest's commercial potential.

It is only recently that the arguments of environmentalists (some of whom became derisively known as "tree huggers") that continued clear-cutting will eventually destroy the logging business as well as the forests, has struck home with local commercial interests. Sustained-yield timber harvesting—cutting down no more than the amount grown each year—has now become more accepted as the sensible way ahead.

WHO PROTECTS WHAT?
The various categories of natural areas and historic sites in California can be confusing. National Forests, National Parks, and National Monuments are all federally run from Washington, D.C. (forests by the Forestry Service, which is part of the Department of Agriculture; parks and monuments by the Department of the Interior). State Parks, State Recreational Areas, State Historical Parks, and the sole State Historical Monument (San Simeon) are administered by California's State Department of Parks and Recreation, based in Sacramento. But many anomalies exist; for instance, within the Redwood National Park are at least three state parks.

The North Coast

GOOD NEIGHBORS
In marked contrast to the U.S. settlers who followed them, the Russians who lived at Fort Ross enjoyed friendly relations with the area's Native American tribe, the Pomo, who marked the Russians' departure with a mourning ceremony.

MEAT-EATERS' DELIGHT
Particularly in the region's northern reaches, restaurants are likely to offer delectable morsels such as elk steaks, roasted bear, wild boar, and even antelope sausages. Vegetarians who eat fish might console themselves with salmon jerky, a traditional Native American creation that involves drying and smoking the fish.

▶▶ **Fort Ross State Historic Park**   228A1

19005 Coast Highway 1, Jenner (tel: 707/847–3286)
Founded in 1812, Fort Ross was a social center for a colony of Russians, who arrived to grow wheat to supply their compatriots in Alaska and to hunt sea otters for their pelts.

Most of the buildings were destroyed after the Russians' departure in 1841, but many, including the exceptional Orthodox Chapel, have been carefully reconstructed and authentically furnished at Fort Ross State Historic Park, beside Highway 1, 20 miles north of Bodega Bay.

▶ **Garberville**   228A3

When devoted marijuana smokers began forsaking San Francisco for the country, many arrived in Garberville and began cultivating their own patches of the illicit weed.

Discovering a booming market for home-grown hemp, Garberville's pioneers became major dealers, buying up large pockets of land and installing elaborate security systems to guard their crops.

These days, marijuana money contributes much less than it did to the economy of the tiny town, which gets most of its visitors during July, when top musical names from Jamaica perform at the Reggae on the River music festival.

▶▶ **Golden Gate National Recreation Area**   228A1

Headquarters: Building 201, Fort Mason, San Francisco (tel: 415/556–0560)
The Golden Gate National Recreation Area (GGNRA) spreads from San Francisco across the Golden Gate Bridge to the southernmost few miles of the North Coast, rubbing shoulders with Stinson Beach (see page 242) and the Point Reyes National Seashore (see page 241).

A network of foot trails penetrates the GGNRA's Marin Headlands, offering exceptional views of San Francisco and the Golden Gate Bridge while traversing an immense acreage of pristine, scrub-covered hillsides.

Make for Point Bonita and the half-mile trail that negotiates a tunnel—gouged from the rock by hand in 1877—and a spine-tingling rope bridge on the way to **Point Bonita Lighthouse▶**, in itself less spectacular than the views all around it despite being among the West Coast's earliest beacons; or Rodeo Beach, an impossibly slender strip of sand between the ocean and a wildlife-rich lagoon.

Above Rodeo Beach, the **California Marine Mammal Center▶** provides treatment for injured seals and sea lions, and informs the public of coastal environmental issues with hands-on exhibits.

▶ **Green Gulch Farm and Zen Center**   228A1

From Muir Beach (see page 240), a path climbs to the Green Gulch Farm and Zen Center, founded in the early 1970s to further knowledge of Buddhism and meditation techniques. The center's organic farm supplies several of the city's top-ranking restaurants. Get tuned in at the free public meditation session (tel: 415/383–3134.

► Gualala 228A2

Claimed by some to have been named after a Spanish rendition of the Norse myth of Valhalla but actually a derivation of a Pomo word, Gualala is a sleepy former lumber town with little to admire beyond the 1903 **Gualala Hotel** at its center, and a handful of galleries that highlight the work of Mendocino area artists, who are further celebrated by the Arts in the Redwoods festival held here each August.

Just south, **Gualala Point Regional Park** encompasses redwoods and beaches (some of California's few remaining abalone divers do their work here), and has a foot trail to **Del Mar Landing**, a secluded coastal reserve with only the seals basking on the offshore rocks providing company for adventuring humans.

The distinctive onion domes of the Russian-style St. Orres Dining Room rise behind a field of Californian poppies on Highway 1 near Gualala

236

AN ECOLOGICAL STAIRCASE
The five-mile Ecological Staircase Trail at Jug Handle State Park, five miles south of Fort Bragg, makes a geologically fascinating trek across five rock terraces formed by the action of plate tectonics and exposed by wave action. Although only 100 feet separate the terraces, each is 100,000 years older or younger than its neighbor, and covered by entirely different vegetation. A final surprise comes at the top, with the stunted and twisted cypress and pine trees of the Mendocino Pygmy Forest.

BIG FOOT
Drive inland toward the Hoopa Valley and you will be met at Willow Creek by a (supposedly) life-size statue of Big Foot, the large and hairy ape-like creature which is believed by many to exist in North America's least accessible back-country areas. Reports of Big Foot activity have come from almost every state (and the beast has long been known to Native Americans as "Sasquatch," but the majority have originated in this section of California. It was here, too, that the term "Big Foot" was born in 1958, after a plaster cast was made of unexplained 16-inch-long footprints.

The Avenue of the Giants, winding for 33 miles through Humboldt Redwoods State Park

▶ **Hoopa Valley** 228A4

Covering 93,000 acres, the Hoopa Valley Reservation is the largest of its kind in California, but like all reservations it cannot be anything other than a depressing reminder of the wrongs inflicted by white settlers on the country's indigenous peoples. The **Hoopa Tribal Museum**▶ (tel: 530/625–4110) displays the handicrafts of the Hupa and Yurok tribes, but many people make the 60-mile drive from the coast simply to attend the Friday and Saturday night bingo sessions; legally, high-stakes bingo can be played only on reservations. Based inland, the Hupa traditionally exchanged home-grown food and animal skins for the seafood and canoes of the predominantly coastal-based Yurok.

▶▶ **Humboldt Redwoods State Park** 228A3

Visitor center 2 miles south of Weatt
(tel: 707/946–2263; 707/946–2409 for the park)
Illuminated by beams of sunlight breaking through towering foliage, the 33-mile-long **Avenue of the Giants** winds through part of the vast Humboldt Redwoods State Park, a 20-million-year-old forest harboring some of the world's tallest trees. Several short walking trails provide a chance to become an insignificant speck at the foot of these 300-foot-high green giants.

In spring, the park's Eel River, whose course the avenue follows, becomes a torrent that brings out the region's daredevil white-water rafters and kayakers. Slowing in summer to an eminently swimmable emerald-colored stream, the river also has sandy banks.

Hiking trails and long-abandoned lumber roads thread deeper into the park, ascending from the redwood-cloaked lowlands to hillsides covered by stands of fir, where rustic cabins and rough campsites provide for overnight stays.

Drive

The Lost Coast

From the Rockefeller Forest section of Humboldt Redwoods State Park (described on page 236), drive west along Bull Creek Flats Road to join Mattole Road, after 12 miles reaching Honeydew.

The tiny crossroads community of **Honeydew▶**—where the center of activity for the single-figure population is the General Store-cum-gas station—is one of the rainiest spots in the United States, with 200 inches falling annually.

From Honeydew, continue on Mattole Road, after eight miles reaching Petrolia.

At the foot of a thickly vegetated valley, eucalyptus-enshrouded

Petrolia▶ was, in the 1860s, the site of one of California's earliest commercial oil wells; the economic boom that the strike promised was soon thwarted by the remoteness of the region.

From Petrolia, take the bumpy Lighthouse Road to the Punta Gorda headland.

At the **Punta Gorda headland▶**, a jeep track leads to a disused lighthouse.

Return to Mattole Road and continue north, after six miles passing Cape Mendocino.

Bordered by black-sand beaches, **Cape Mendocino▶** is the most western point of the contiguous United States. It is believed to have been named by some 16th-century Spanish seafarers in honor of a Spanish viceroy.

Pass Cape Mendocino and continue on Mattole Road, after 16 miles reaching Ferndale.

An immaculately preserved Victorian village first settled by Swedish dairy farmers, charming **Ferndale's▶** 1,300 inhabitants make the town by far the largest settlement on the Lost Coast; see page 231 for a description.

From Ferndale, continue on Mattole Road for four miles, rejoining Highway 101 10 miles south of Eureka.

237

▶ The Lost Coast   228A3

Black bears and bald eagles are more common than people within the desolate, deserted landscapes of the Lost Coast, a 30-mile portion of the North Coast south of Eureka, whose dense forests, coastal bluffs, and pocket-size beaches are shielded by the sharp inclines of the Kings Mountain Range.

The scenic Lost Coast can be sampled lightly by taking Briceland Thorne Road, off Highway 101 near Redway. This route leads to **Shelter Cove▶▶**, a tiny coast-hugging community adjacent to a beach at the foot of impressive granite headlands, first passing the elk-roamed **Sinkyone Wilderness State Park▶** (tel: 707/986–7711) named after the Sinkyone tribe, who inhabited the Lost Coast from 6000 BC. At that time food, both from the sea and from the forest, was available in plentiful supplies and the Lost Coast region was North America's most densely populated place.

NATIVE AMERICAN RESERVATIONS
One of three Native American reservations in California, the Hoopa Valley Reservation has just 2,000 Hoopa people living on its 93,000 acres. Statewide, an estimated 35,000 of the state's 205,770 native population live on reservations.

In a city of predominantly wooden buildings, Mendocino's volunteer firefighters are an important part of the community

CHARLES F. RICHTER

When Californians declare that they sleep through a mere 2.3, barely notice a 3.6, but know exactly what to do if an 8.9 hits, they are, of course, quoting Richter scale measurements of earthquake magnitudes. Few of them know, however, that the man who devised the Richter scale in 1935, Charles F. Richter, was a 35-year-old seismology professor at the California Institute of Technology in Pasadena.

▶ Manchester State Beach   228A2

(tel: 800/444–7275 or 707/937–5804)
Make reservations well in advance
Stretching for several miles beside Highway 1 south of Mendocino Headlands State Park, Manchester State Beach is a must-see for beachcombers and hikers and for hardy campers who do not mind being buffeted by winds or waking up beside a beach cloaked in fog.

▶▶▶ Mendocino   228A2

151 miles NE of San Francisco, off Highway 1
Mendocino is set on a coastal bluff and has a plethora of well-preserved 19th-century buildings dating from its settlement by New England loggers.

Because of Mendocino's well-deserved reputation as the North Coast's prettiest town, its population of 1,000 permanent residents is frequently outnumbered by tourists, who fill the numerous bed-and-breakfasts and the town's many gift shops and crafts stores.

In decline as a lumber center, Mendocino's unspoiled beauty proved irresistible to a group of San Francisco artists in the 1950s and 1960s, who began renovating and preserving the old buildings and whose influence lingers on, most notably in numerous galleries and in the arts appreciation programs of the **Mendocino Art Center▶** (45200 Little Lake Road; tel: 707/937–5818).

The **Kelley House Museum▶▶**, inside an 1861 residence (45007 Albion Street; tel: 707/937–5791), has written and photographic background on most of the town's early buildings. Among these, the 1868 Gothic-style Mendocino Presbyterian Church (44831 Main Street) is still in use, and Mendocino's oldest residence, the 1854 **Ford House▶** (Main Street; tel: 707/937–5397), functions as a visitor center for **Mendocino Headlands State Park▶▶**, where three miles of footpaths weave around the wind-lashed bluff on which the town sits.

The biggest and most destructive earthquake ever to strike California, the 1906 San Francisco earthquake was caused by the 600-mile-long San Andreas fault, the longest of hundreds of geological fault lines that pass through the state, and one that runs for many miles along the North Coast.

The big shake In fact, the 1906 quake was more powerful along the North Coast than in San Francisco, though the region's moderate level of development meant that damage was limited to displaced cattle fences and slightly skewed roads. Such damage has long since been rectified, but provided you know where to look— and what to look for—the fault line is easy to recognize.

At Point Reyes, which was jolted almost 16 feet north in the few seconds of the 1906 quake, the National Seashores' Earthquake Trail follows a section of the fault, and markers indicate some of its effects.

Where the fault lies From Point Reyes, the fault follows the line of Tamales Bay and continues to Bodega Bay, where it passes between Bodega Head and the mainland. Although it is mostly concealed by sand dunes, the fault's presence here is marked by telltale deposits of mixed and crushed rock. The fault continues under the ocean beyond Bodega Head and returns to land just south of Fort Ross, which lost several of its early Russian buildings in the 1906 quake. Follow the Fort Ross Road inland for a few miles looking for furrows on the hillsides, further evidence of the 1906 quake.

As it travels just inland from the coast, the fault cuts a straight valley through the hills, causing many streams to change their course. This fact explains why the Gualala River flows parallel to the coast for several miles, instead of draining directly into the ocean.

Close to Point Arena, the fault again dips under the ocean. Until recently, experts believed the sharp breaks in the headlands farther north around the Lost Coast were proof of the fault staying close to the shore. A more recent hypothesis, however, suggests that it is only a branch of the San Andreas fault that lies along this part of the coast and that the main line runs some miles offshore, veering west under the Pacific.

239

A sample of the earthquake damage suffered in San Francisco

From the summit of Mount Tamalpais is a dramatic panorama encompassing San Francisco, the Golden Gate, and the East Bay

WILLIAM KENT'S DONATION
It is hard to belive today, but both Mount Tamalpais and the redwood grove that became the Muir Wood National Monument were once in private hands. The land formed part of the family holdings inherited by William Kent, a conservation-minded Congressman who settled in Main County in 1907. His donation asked for the latter to be named after naturalist John Muir, who did much to encourage the preservation of wild California.

▶ Mill Valley 74A5

Full of rural charm despite being a San Francisco commuter base, Mill Valley sits on the eastern slopes of Mount Tamalpais. The town sports a surprising number of coffee bars, and even stages its own film festival.

▶▶▶ Mount Tamalpais State Park 228A1

Panoramic Highway/E Ridgecrest Boulevard (tel: 415/388–2070). Open: daily dawn–dusk. Admission: inexpensive

A switchback road leads almost to the top of Mount Tamalpais, but you will feel you have earned the scintillating views only if you have attained the summit after a day's hike from the redwood-filled canyons of Mount Tamalpais State Park or tackled the network of five roads around the slopes by mountain bike. Weather permitting, concerts and performing arts are staged at the park's **Mountain Theater▶** (tel: 415/383–1100) where more than 3,000 people can enjoy an outdoor show against a stunning natural backdrop.

▶▶ Muir Woods National Monument 228A1

Muir Woods Road, off Panoramic Highway (tel: 415/388–2595)

When San Franciscans feel they are living in a concrete jungle, they head 17 miles northwest to the Muir Woods National Monument (also visited by numerous bus tours from San Francisco), where six miles of trails lead through a dark, cool grove of redwoods. These are not the biggest examples of the North Coast's redwood trees, but at over 250 feet high they are unlikely to disappoint; if they do, push on to the slender semi-circular cove holding **Muir Beach▶**, and mingle with the anglers and bird-watchers.

▶ Point Arena Lighthouse 228A2

45500 Lighthouse Road (tel: 707/882–2777)

Interrupt the lengthy drive between Bodega Bay and Fort Bragg with a tour of the 1908 **Point Arena Lighthouse** and its museum, which details the many ships that have come to grief off this wild and rugged coastline.

▶▶ Point Reyes National Seashore   *228A1*

Highway 1, 30 miles NW of San Francisco (tel: 415/663–1092)
Formed by, and still subject to, seismic activity, the 100-mile coastline of the Point Reyes National Seashore encompasses granite headlands, beaches, dunes, and marshes, and reaches inland to hills topped by pine-fringed ridges. The area's geological background is outlined at the **Visitor Center**, beside Highway 1, and the adjacent easily walked **Earthquake Trail▶▶**.

Longer trails aim to please bird-watchers and beach-combers, and another leads to **Kule Loklo▶**, a re-created Miwok village. If ocean breezes deter walking, drive to the 1870s **Point Reyes Lighthouse▶** (tel: 415/669–1534) on the seashore's western extremity.

▶ Richardson Grove State Park   *228A3*

(tel: 707/247–3318)
A few miles south of Garberville, Richardson Grove State Park has three lush redwood groves and numerous backcountry hikes, in summer the park is one of the North Coast's most popular camping areas.

Close by, the dot-on-the-map settlement of Piercy seeks to lure passing traffic on Highway 1, with the optimistically titled World Famous Tree House, a room built 50 feet up a redwood tree, and Confusion Hill, a collection of visual conceits.

▶▶ Sonoma Coast State Beach   *228A1*

Highway 1, 70 miles NW of San Francisco (tel: 707/875–3483)
Between Bodega Bay and the Russian River hamlet of Jenner, the Sonoma Coast State Beach spans 13 miles of secluded beaches slotted between craggy headlands, many of which have formed sea stacks and arches.

Trails lead to the beaches from Highway 1, and there are connecting paths linking the whole Sonoma coast. Splendid scenery is common to all, yet each beach has its own admirers: fishermen favor **Portuguese Beach▶**; **Shell Beach▶** delights beachcombers, delivering a rich harvest with each receding tide; and the picnic tables at **Rock Point▶▶** provide settings for picture-perfect meals.

SAN ANSELMO
Best known to Northern Californians for its scores of antiques shops, San Anselmo, just north of Mount Tamalpais, lies beneath the hillside stone buildings of the San Francisco Theological Seminary, which in 1992 celebrated 100 years of training Presbyterian Church ministers.

Dark sands, and wind- and wave-lashed rocks, are typical of the Sonoma Coast State Beach

CALIFORNIA GRAY WHALES

Many places along the North Coast make excellent points to observe the migrating California gray whales, which pass by on their 6,000-mile journey between the Arctic sea off Alaska, where they feed, and the warmer waters off Baja California, where the females give birth. The whales are thought to use coastal landscapes to navigate, and can be sighted at any time from December to July, though the largest numbers are usually visible in March.

Old machinery forms part of the historical potpourri at the Mendocino County Museum

▶ **Stinson Beach**   74A5

Unchallenged as the North Coast's finest and busiest strand, the broad and inviting Stinson Beach sits at the foot of Mount Tamalpais within easy reach of San Francisco. Its 3-mile-long crescent-shaped sands stretch north to the Bolinas Lagoon (see pages 230–1).

Because Stinson is spared the strong currents that affect much of the North Coast, swimming is popular here, although many don diver's wet suits before braving the cool waters. If swimming or sitting in the sun does not suit you, try one of the hikes from the beach to Mount Tamalpais State Park or the Muir Woods National Monument.

Three miles north, the wooded canyons of the **Audubon Canyon Ranch**▶▶ (4900 Highway 1; tel: 415/868–9244) are cherished by bird-watchers, especially from March to July, when egrets and blue herons make their nests in the redwood branches and visiting hours to this wildlife research center are extended. Hiking trails here offer amateur ornithologists close-up views of egrets, blue herons, and many other species.

▶ **Willits**   228A2

Taking the Skunk Train from Fort Bragg (see panel on page 232), you will find yourself 40 miles inland at Willits, a likable small country community that conserves its energy for regional rodeos. Other than serving wholesome traditional fare in its diners, it offers only the Native American basketry and pioneer-period artifacts of the **Mendocino County Museum**▶ (400 E. Commercial Street; tel: 707/459–2736) for out-of-towners to pass the time before their journey back.

Provided you are not sick of the sight of the North Coast's redwood trees by the time you reach it, the Redwood National Park, filling 100,000 acres of California's northwest corner and encompassing four state parks, offers an unrivaled chance to delve among the tall trees and their related flora and fauna, and to strike out across 40 miles of California's utterly untrammeled shoreline.

Far from the crowds: Smith River, Jedediah Smith State Park

and fertile by heavy winter rainfall, and its landscapes are at their best at Fern Canyon, a moss-covered floor enclosed by 60-foot-high fern walls. The park also boasts a sizable elk herd; you will see some of them grazing in meadows beside Highway 101.

243

> ❏ Jedediah Smith State Park, and the Smith River which runs through it, are named after Jedediah Strong Smith, a New York-born fur trapper who became a California frontier legend in 1826, after making the first nonnative crossing of the Sierra Nevada mountains. ❏

Redwood National and State Park's Information Center is at the northern gateway, at Crescent City.

Take a hike Dozens of short foot trails lead off Highway 101 (which passes through the park). Longer hiking routes connect the four state parks that form the key sections of the national park.

The southern entrance is close to Orick, where the **Redwood Visitor Center** has geographical orientation and ecological information. Close by, the aptly named **Tall Trees Grove**▶ ▶ contains three of the world's tallest trees, including the 368-foot Howard Libby Redwood; from the ground, though, the tree looks no more enormous than its neighbors.

The park's inland sections Farther on, **Prairie Creek State Park**▶ spans a large tract of grassland between the redwoods and the ocean, with trails leading to tidal pools and coves. The park's inland sections are kept lush

Summer fogs are frequent in the northerly reaches of the national park, especially at **Del Norte State Park**▶ ▶ (south of Crescent City) where the redwood groves reach almost to the shore. Once the fog lifts, seek out the area's main attractions: tide pools, coves, and isolated beaches.

Further inland and less affected by fog, **Jedediah Smith State Park**▶ ▶ (NE of Crescent City) is the least visited section of the national park yet also one of the most enjoyable. Take the meandering Howland Hill Road, a onetime stagecoach route, and stop at Stout Grove to admire the immense girth of the so-called Stout Tree. Salmon fishermen and canoeists are brought to this park by the Smith River, which has many placid sections ideal for swimming and for taking in the rural tranquility from sandy banks.

The Wine Country

244

CALISTOGA'S WINERIES
Though better known for
its spas, Calistoga also
has several notable
wineries. Occupying a
French-style castle,
Château Montelena (1429
Tubbs Lane; tel: 707/
942–5105) produces an
acclaimed Chardonnay
and overlooks Lake Jade,
where formal Chinese
gardens are laid out on
the banks of the lake. The
champagne-making
Schramsberg Vineyards
(1400 Schramsberg Road;
tel: 707/942–4558) were
immortalized in 1880
by Robert Louis
Stevenson's book *The*
Silverado Squatters.

PLEASURES OF THE PALATE You will find wineries all
over California, but only in the Wine Country—
beginning 48 miles north of San Francisco and
encompassing three separate valleys—is the grape the
main attraction of an entire region.

Hot summers, moist winters, fertile volcanic soil—
courtesy of the long-extinct Mount St. Helena—and
heaps of publicity bring hordes of tourists to the Wine
Country, whose wineries range from high-tech modern
plants to century-old family-run operations in stone
buildings. Most of these run tours and tastings and have
become adept at turning beginners into connoisseurs of
California's finest within an hour.

STATE GRAPE Spanish missionaries produced
California's earliest wine, but a take-charge Hungarian
named Agoston Haraszthy was the first to bring choice
European vine cuttings to the state. Their yield of
familiar Mediterranean grapes brought a rush of
European vintners to settle the region from the 1880s.

Decades of patient refining were rewarded in the early
1970s when California wines were acknowledged as
being among the world's best. Everyone from the Coca-
Cola Company to Moët & Chandon began sinking
money into the Wine Country, and the region
underwent an unexpected tourist boom.

Among the 200 wineries in the Napa Valley, on the Wine Country's eastern edge, are the nation's biggest and most prestigious wine producers. Three million visitors annually beat a path through the compact valley, their cars jamming the main route, State Road 29, between the sprawling town of Napa (whose name derives from the Native American word for "abundance") and the historic spa resort of Calistoga, every summer weekend.

SOFTER OPTIONS An alternative to Napa Valley is the less congested Sonoma Valley, immediately west, where apple orchards partner the vines on softly sloping hillsides, and meandering country lanes pass some of the Wine Country's most reputable and longest-established small wineries, while linking amiable rural towns such as history-laden Sonoma, site of the most northerly and last-completed of California's Spanish missions.

On the coastal side of the Wine Country, the Russian River Valley also has its share of smaller wineries. Here, though, the Russian River's sandy banks and thick redwood groves provide appeal beyond wine consuming, and Guerneville, one of the largest communities, fully justifies its reputation as a lively resort town.

Château Souverain in Geyserville is one of the many wineries in this area offering tastings

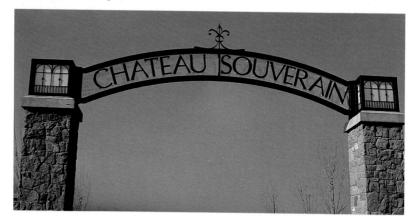

The entrance to Château Souverain, scene of wining and dining and open-air summer concerts

Calistoga see page 247.

▶ Geyserville
244A2

Two towers aping traditional hop kilns on a small hill just outside Geyserville belong to **Château Souverain**▶▶ (400 Souverain Lane; tel: 707/433–3141), whose fame dominates the village. Besides arriving to sample its Chardonnay and Cabernet Sauvignon, most Californians come to Souverain for its widely acclaimed restaurant.

By contrast, the **J. Pedroncelli Winery**▶ (1220 Canyon Road; tel: 707/857–3531) has been producing a good cross-section of low-priced red and white wines since 1904.

▶ Guerneville
244A2

Carefully preserving its rustic charms, turning canoeing and kayaking on the Russian River into growth industries, and keeping its bars and discos jumping into the small hours, Guerneville (pronounced "GURN-ville") is the Wine Country's liveliest resort town and has become the weekend place-to-be for a large gay contingent from San Francisco.

On the edge of town, foot trails penetrate the dark, damp groves of the **Armstrong Redwoods State Reserve**▶, and continue into the bright open meadows of the **Austin Creek State Reserve**▶ (tel: 707/869–2015 for both).

Korbel Champagne Cellars▶▶ (13250 River Road; tel: 707/887–2294) has produced the bubbly—as well as some excellent brandy—since 1862.

▶▶ Healdsburg
244A2

Filled with Victorian homes and prettified by a century-old tree-lined plaza, Healdsburg, at the northern end of the Russian River Valley, also has a dozen wineries.

You can also read about wine at the **Sonoma County Wine Library**▶ (139 Piper Street; tel: 707/433–3772), stocked with more then 3,000 wine-related volumes, or bone up on it in the **Healdsburg Museum**▶ (221 Matheson Street; tel: 707/431–3325). Visit Healdsburg on a summer Sunday and you might well find music in the air—the town stages an excellent series of free concerts in the plaza's park.

THE BOHEMIAN CLUB
Founded in 1872 as a social club for San Francisco newspapermen, and including socialist writers such as Jack London and Ambrose Bierce among its early members, the Bohemian Club is now best known for its Bohemian Annual Summer Encampment, which takes place annually in July. Scores of high-flying (and exclusively male) bankers, industrialists, congressmen, foreign diplomats, and even ex-U.S. presidents, arrive at the club's summer retreat, Bohemian Grove, a Russian River Valley redwood grove near Monte Rio, for two weeks of nefarious activities behind high-security fences.

Bottled and sold throughout the state, sparkling spring water from Calistoga furthers the fame of a Napa Valley town already noted for its mineral-rich spas, which have been earning the respect of dedicated sybarites since the first health resort was founded here in 1859 by millionaire Mormon Sam Brannan.

Take the waters The cheapest way to find out what all the fuss is about is by taking a dip in the mineral pools at Calistoga Springs Hot Spa (1006 Washington Avenue; tel: 707/942–6269) or Golden Haven Spa (1713 Lake Street; tel: 707/942–6793).

A more thorough spa session typically costs $30–$50 ($100 with a massage) and includes a volcanic-mud bath, a soak in a mineral-water whirlpool, a smothering in sweat-inducing blankets, and finally a massage to induce a nirvana-like state of well-being. Purveyors of this relaxing therapy include Nance's Hot Springs (1614 Lincoln Avenue; tel: 707/942–6211) and Indian Springs (1712 Lincoln Avenue; tel: 707/942–4913).

For a serious massage—without the spa treatment—sample the "advanced bodywork" promised at the Calistoga Massage Center, 1219 Washington Street (tel: 707/942–6193), where specialty massage styles include Cranial, Sacral, Jin Shin, Shiatsu and Thai, among others, for around $70 per hour.

Sam Brannan The founder of Calistoga, Sam Brannan arrived in San Francisco from New York with a boatload of fellow Mormons in 1846. Seeking farmland and religious tolerance, they were dismayed to find that California had joined the United States just prior to their landing. The 26-year-old Brannan published San Francisco's first newspaper and quickly became one of the fledgling state's wealthiest, most flamboyant figures. His investment in Calistoga did not pay off, however, and he spent his final years drunk and destitute in Escondido, near San Diego, dying in 1889.

❏ Five miles west of Calistoga, the Petrified Forest (4100 Petrified Forest Road; tel: 707/942–6667) is the result of a redwood grove being uprooted and turned to stone by volcanic mud and ash that was spewed out by Mount St. Helena. ❏

247

Old Faithful Geyser Another way to enjoy the legacy of the area's volcanic activity is simply by looking at it. The Old Faithful Geyser (1299 Tubbs Lane; tel: 707/942–6463), heated by an underground river, sends a high-pressure jet of boiling water 60 feet skyward every 30 or 50 minutes (depending upon seismic activity in the region).

The Old Faithful Geyser, producing natural energy near Calistoga

Drive

Calistoga–Clear Lake Loop

See map on page 244.

Drive 10 miles north from Calistoga on State Road 29 for Robert Louis Stevenson State Park.
Author Robert Louis Stevenson and his wife honeymooned during 1880 in what is now **Robert Louis Stevenson State Park**▶▶ (tel: 707/942–4575), whose 3,000 undeveloped acres include a trail to the summit of Mount St. Helena.

Continue seven miles north on State Road 29 for Middletown.
Middletown marks the halfway point of the former Calistoga–Lakeport stagecoach route, which State Road 29 follows. Immediately east of the town, the **Guenoc Winery**▶ (21000 Butts Canyon Road; tel: 707/987–2385) was once owned by English actress Lillie Langtry.

Continue for 15 miles on State Road 29 to the Anderson Marsh State Historic Park, just north of Lower Lake.
At the **Anderson Marsh State Historic Park**▶ (tel: 707/994–0688) 10,000-year-old sites of Native American habitation

Clear Lake State Park

have been discovered; another section of the 1,000-acre site is a wildlife refuge, protecting bald eagles among many other species.

From Lower Lake, continue on State Road 29 to Clear Lake State Park.
Set on land still bearing evidence of Native American occupation, **Clear Lake State Park**▶ (Kelseyville; tel: 707/279–4293) is popular with anglers, who hunt catfish and perch.

Continue on State Road 29 for 10 miles to Lakeport.
Lakeport's County Historical Museum▶ (255 N Main Street; tel: 707/263–4555) holds a glittering cache of locally grown diamonds.

Continue for nine miles on State Road 29, turning east onto State Road 20 at Upper Lake and driving for 21 miles to State Road 53. Quiet lakeside villages punctuate the drive east from Upper Lake.

From the junction with State Road 53, drive nine miles south on State Road 29 to Lower Lake, continuing for 32 miles to return to Calistoga.

❑ Robert Louis Stevenson spent part of his honeymoon in a miners' cabin on the slopes of Mount St. Helena. He was so impressed that he used it as the model for Spyglass Hill in *Treasure Island.* ❑

▶ Oakville
244B1

Among the Wine Country's best tours are the free and highly instructive offerings available at Oakville's **Robert Mondavi Winery▶▶** (7801 St. Helena Highway; tel: 707/259–9463), which has you winding through the establishment's cool underground passages. A tasting is included as part of the tour.

Along the road, a geodesic dome covers the workings of the reputable Napa Cellars (7481 St. Helena Highway; tel: 707/944–2565), as well as the winery's visitor center.

▶▶ Petaluma
244B1

Long famed for its poultry and dairy farms, Petaluma stages a riotous Butter and Eggs Day parade each April. The colorful procession winds through the center of this riverside town, where carefully maintained 19th- and early 20th-century architecture creates a picture-postcard image of small-town America. In fact, it should be no surprise that Petaluma's streets have served as backdrops for successful nostalgia movies such as *American Graffiti* and *Peggy Sue Got Married.*

The name Petaluma is thought to derive from a Miwok (the indigenous peoples of the region) word meaning "flat bank", probably a reference to a local hill. A great deal about the town's origins and the commercial importance of the Petaluma River on which it sits can be discovered by taking a visit to the **Historical Library and Museum▶** (20 Fourth Street; tel: 707/778–4398), which is housed within the imposing 1906 Carnegie Library Building. Find the time, too, to stroll the riverside footpaths that add greatly to this tiny community's appeal.

Early days There is evidence of still earlier times on a hillside across Highway 101, where the **Petaluma Adobe State Historic Park▶▶** (7 miles east on Adobe Road; tel: 707/762–4871) holds the well-restored 1836 two-story adobe building that was at the center of one of Mexican California's largest land holdings, a vast rancho with which General Mariano Vallejo—the founder of Sonoma—established himself among the province's rich and powerful.

▶ Rutherford
244B1

Several of the Napa Valley's major wine producers lie close to the hamlet of Rutherford and offer novice-friendly tours. The **Rutherford Hill Winery** (200 Rutherford Hill Road; tel: 707/963–7194) is a winery that welcomes beginners and the uninitiated and that, like most of its rivals, ages its wine in caves, though these particular underground tunnels are said to be the biggest such system in the world.

Chateau tasting Wine enthusiasts who happen to be claustrophobic might prefer to visit the ivy-covered stone chateau, complete with stained-glass windows, housing **Niebaum-Coppola** (1919 St. Helena Highway; tel: 707/963-9099), where tastings are complemented by a wine museum and exhibits on filmmaking—your clue that the the property's co-owner is film director Francis Ford Coppola.

CALIFORNIA'S CHEESE
A popular accompaniment to wine drinking, dry and nutty Monterey Jack, California's native cheese, was first produced in 1892 on dairy farms close to Monterey under the control of an unpopular Scottish migrant called David Jacks. Since then, the Sonoma Valley has become a significant cheese-producing area, with the Sonoma Cheese Factory (2 West Spain Street, in Sonoma) giving a slide show on the manufacturing process—and dispensing bite-size free samples.

249

Verdant its valleys may be, but only teetotallers visit the Wine Country for its scenery. For everyone else, a trip through the region begins and ends with a glass in the hand and, given the large number of winery tours and wine tastings offered, it is a glass that you'll know a lot more about by the time you reach the end of a trip than you did at the beginning.

AGOSTON HARASZTHY
Remembered as a pioneering vintner, father of California wine, and founder of Buena Vista Winery in Sonoma, Hungarain aristocrat Haraszthy arrived in California in 1849. A sheriff in San Diego County before moving to the Sonoma Valley, Haraszthy was an impulsive adventurer who later moved to Nicaragua to start a sugar plantation; he disappeared in the jungle, presumed drowned in 1869.

250

A round of drinks Larger wineries have daily tours and tastings for which reservations are sometimes necessary, while smaller wineries may open only for a few hours a week. To avoid disappointment always phone ahead.

Tour one of the major producers first, for a look at the wine-making process and for a broad introduction to the state's wines. Later, move on to the more specialized small wineries, whose products reveal their subtleties only to the initiated.

Grape stuff California's wine types are known by their grape. The main whites include Chardonnay, Chenin Blanc, Gewurztraminer, Riesling, and Sauvignon (or Fumé) Blanc; the main reds are Cabernet Sauvignon, Merlot, Pinot Noir, and Zinfandel.

The extremely versatile Zinfandel also appears as White Zinfandel, actually a "blush" wine, which is pink rather than red because the grapes' skins are removed during the fermentation process.

Sparkling wine (it is bad form to use the term Champagne to refer to a product that does not come from France) is also found in the Wine Country, and some of the more interesting sparkling-wine producers use the traditional Méthode Champenoise, with fermentation carried out in the bottle rather than in casks.

On the train Known locally as the "swine train" for the noise it makes rumbling through the valley, and set up in an attempt to ease traffic congestion, the Napa Valley Wine Train (tel: 800/427–4124 or 707/253–2111) pulls restored Pullman cars on a three-hour trip between Napa and St. Helena, serving pricey gourmet food accompanied by selections from the valley's wineries. The basic round-trip fare does not include meals, but the train, environmental considerations aside, is hard to beat if you have only half a day to see the Wine Country.

Wine-tasting tips It is a good idea to visit no more than three wineries on any single day. Every wine that you sample affects the taste buds, and red wines tend to coat the tongue, so after you've tasted a few, it becomes harder and harder to appreciate a wine's subtleties of flavor.

Also stick to either the whites or the reds at any given tasting. Or at least begin with the whites, move

...and the wine is bottled poetry...

on to the reds and rosés, follow with the dessert wines and, finally, try the sparkling wines.

Young wines Do not feel cheated if your host produces a recent wine to sample. Because the climate varies little from year to year, vintages count for far less in California than they do in Europe, though certain wines are noted as being exceptionally good in certain years (not least the 1973 Cabernet Sauvignon, which won a prestigious European tasting in 1976 and helped put California's wines on the world map). The final verdict on a wine's qualities is for you alone to determine, although there are well-established stages in forming judgments.

Step-by-step tasting First look closely at the wine to judge its color. All wines should be free of clouding; whites should have a yellow to golden shading; rosés should be pink, possibly with an orange hue; reds should have a purple hint and may vary in tone from a light crimson to a rich ruby.

Second, swirl the wine to release its fragrance, or "nose"—something that results from a combination of the "aroma," supplied by the grape, and the "bouquet," which comes from the winemaking process.

Third, sip the wine and roll it around your tongue to determine texture and balance. Flavors are a complex field, and range from a Chardonnay's dry fruitiness to a Zinfandel's zippy spiciness.

At tastings, never feel embarrassed about seeming ignorant. California's vintners are eager for their products to become more widely appreciated, and they respond much better to the genuine interest of a beginner than the witless comments of a wine snob.

Typically, wineries in the Napa Valley charge $2–$8 (usually under $5) for a tasting and a glass, which you may keep; elsewhere tastings are often free.

THE MYSTERIOUS ZINFANDEL

While most Californian grapes are clearly of European origin, the roots of Zinfandel are shrouded in mystery. A Black Zinfandel wine appeared on the U.S. east coast in 1838, and Zinfandel grapes were first grown in California 20 years later, but where the grapes actually come from is uncertain. The son of Agoston Haraszthy, the state's earliest vintner, falsely claimed that his father was the first to import them (but did not say where from), and more recently experts have variously cited southern Italy, Slovenia, and even California itself, as the true home of Zinfandel.

Wine tasting at Oakville's Robert Mondavi Winery, which has one of the region's best introductory tours

The Wine Country

252

▶▶ St. Helena   *244B2*

Ten miles south of Calistoga, St. Helena sits fortuitously at the heart of the Napa Valley, cashing in on its location with its upscale restaurants and crafts shops.

One person who passed through St. Helena was impoverished writer Robert Louis Stevenson who, having married Fanny Osbourne in 1880, honeymooned north of the town in what is now **Robert Louis Stevenson State Park**▶▶ (tel: 707/942–4575). Occupying a special wing of the St. Helena Public Library (1490 Library Lane), the **Silverado Museum**▶▶ (tel: 707/963–3757) celebrates the Stevenson connection with manuscripts and memorabilia.

▶ Santa Rosa   *244B1*

Leveled by the 1906 earthquake, Santa Rosa has made a dramatic comeback. It is now the fastest-growing Wine Country community.

The restored 1920s buildings of Railroad Square and the pre-earthquake railroad terminal in Railroad Park show off their community's roots, but Santa Rosa does a better job at commemorating two former inhabitants.

The **Church of One Tree** (492 Sonoma Avenue)—not the base of a tree-centered religion but built entirely from a redwood felled in 1875—contains the **Ripley Memorial Museum**▶▶ (tel: 707/524–5233) devoted to local man Robert Ripley, whose cartoon strips—recounting strange and exotic phenomena—were hugely popular beginning in the 1920s.

Self-taught horticulturalist Luther Burbank arrived in Santa Rosa in 1875 armed with ten Burbank potatoes, early examples of what was to be a lifetime's devotion to developing vegetable, fruit, and plant hybrids. The **Luther Burbank Home and Memorial Gardens**▶ (415 Steele Lane; tel: 707/524–5445) preserves his Greek Revival-style house and the gardens where his creations evolved.

▶ Sebastopol   *244A1*

Sebastopol is known for its reddish-yellow Gravenstein apples, celebrated by April's Apple Blossom Festival. Otherwise, the area is notable for its dry wines, particularly Pinot Noir. This (and more) can be sampled on weekends at **Sebastopol Vineyards** (junction of Highway 116 and Green Valley Road; tel: 707/829–9463).

In addition to a winery at every turn, the Sonoma and Napa valleys boast a formidable group of state parks. Combining historic and scenic interest, the parks also provide a head-clearing pick-me-up for anyone who has overdone the wine tasting.

Inspirational country A prolific writer, Jack London eulogized the Sonoma Valley in his 1913 book *Valley of the Moon*. At the time he had already put into practice the return-to-nature way of living that its pages advocated, turning a large tract of grassy hillside beneath Sonoma Mountain into an experimental farm, and building the 26-room Wolf House for himself and his wife. His ranch is now **Jack London State Historic Park**▶▶▶ (2400 London Ranch Road (off Arnold Drive); tel: 707/938–5216. *Open Apr–Oct 9:30–7, Nov–Mar 9:30–5. Admission: inexpensive*) in the hamlet of Glen Ellen, just west of Sonoma. Only the ruins of the fire-destroyed Wolf House remain, but the park's House of Happy Walls Museum is well stocked with mementos of London's life (see panel on this page).

At the northern end of the Sonoma Valley Hiking and horseback-riding trails crisscross the 5,000-acre **Annadel State Park**▶ (tel: 707/539–3911) rising from meadows and marshes into steep-sided canyons. Even more rugged terrain fills **Sugarloaf Ridge State Park**▶ (tel: 707/833–5712) 14 miles east of Santa Rosa, where wine-induced lethargy will quickly be forgotten after a brisk hike over chaparral-covered ridges.

Just north of St. Helena in the Napa Valley, a ramble through the **Bale Grist Mill State Historic Park**▶ (3801 St. Helena Highway; tel: 707/942–4575) leads to a restored 19th-century water mill, built for an English ships' surgeon who became a prominent Napa Valley landowner.

Immediately south Greater hiking opportunities are presented by **Bothe-Napa Valley State Park**▶ (tel: 707/942–4575) whose trails pass through stands of coastal redwoods. One leads to the remains of the valley's earliest church and to a pioneer-era graveyard, where several members of the ill-fated Donner party (see page 200) lie buried.

JACK LONDON
The illegitimate son of an itinerant Irish astrologist, Jack London led an eventful life that began in San Francisco in 1876. Largely self-educated, he earned a living variously in Oakland's waterfront canneries, as a harbor policeman, as a sailor, and as a gold prospector before becoming (much to his surprise) a financially secure author, having turned his experiences into a vast body of realist fiction. His *Valley of the Moon*, published in 1913, bestowed a lasting nickname on the Sonoma Valley (resulting from a mis-translation of a Native American word), where London lived until his death—probably by suicide—in 1916.

HITCHCOCK'S RETREAT
Much of the Bothe-Napa State Valley Park occupies the 1,000 acres of creekside land bought by Doctor Charles Hitchcock as a weekend retreat in 1872. An army doctor posted to San Francisco in 1851, Hitchcock was the father of Lille Hitchcock (married name Coit), whose flouting of convention made her the talk of San Francisco society and whose obsession with fires led to the construction of the city's Coit Tower (see page 39).

The Wine Country

FESTIVALS
Guerneville stages the Russian River Jazz Festival every September and the Russian River Blues Festival each June. Petaluma hosts the World Wristwrestling Championships in October; the Sonoma County Fair is staged in Santa Rosa during July; the same city sees the Luther Burbank Rose Parade Festival in May.

▶▶ **Sonoma** *244B1*

With a history far more illustrious than its contemporary importance, Sonoma has many restored adobe buildings that provide an evocative window on the turbulent decades that saw California switch from Spanish to Mexican and finally to U.S. rule. A host of bed-and-breakfasts make the small town a good base for exploring the Wine Country, though Sonoma itself is easily covered by a half-day walk.

Surrounded by historic hotels, Sonoma's eight-acre **plaza** was constructed in 1835 and is the largest in California. In the center is **Sonoma City Hall▶**, dating from 1906 and presenting a symbol of early U.S. authority in the town. The **Bear Flag Monument▶**, on the plaza's northeast corner, commemorates the 1846 hoisting of the Bear Flag, denoting an independent California Republic. Across Spain Street, on the corner with First Street East, is the much-restored **Mission San Francisco de Solano▶**. Founded in 1823, this was the last and most northerly of California's Spanish missions. It also saw service as a saloon, a warehouse, and a barn; a small museum tells its story.

At 285 First Street West, the **Depot Museum▶** (tel: 707/938–1762) across Depot Park from First Street East, mounts changing temporary exhibitions on local heritage themes. The main buildings of **Sonoma State Historical Park▶▶** (20 E. Spain Street; tel: 707/938–1519) are across First Street West: several important structures form this far-flung park, among them two former homes of General Mariano Vallejo—the founder and first mayor of Sonoma—and the Sonoma Barracks, whose storming by the U.S. cavalry in 1846 was part of the Bear Flag Revolt—briefly turning California into an independent republic.

Enjoying a bucolic setting on the outskirts of Sonoma, the **Buena Vista Carneros▶▶** (18000 Old Winery Road;

A stately palm tree stands before Sonoma's City Hall, inside which is a tourist office

tel: 707/938–1266), founded by Agoston Haraszthy (see panel, page 250) in 1857, is the oldest commercial winery in the state.

Although it only opened in 1986, Yountville's Domain Chandon shows off some historic wine-making equipment

▶ Ukiah
244A3

Native American culture keeps a decidedly low profile throughout the Wine Country, a fact that makes the **Grace Hudson Museum and Sun House▶▶** (431 Main Street; tel: 707/467–2836) all the more welcome. It houses lyrical studies of the Pomo by painter Grace Carpenter Hudson and her husband's extensive ethnographical collections, one of the main sources of information on Pomo culture. The layout of the museum is based on the geometry used in Pomo crafts. Remarkably, this outstanding collection crops up in what is a run-of-the-mill lumber town, with only tastings at the **Parducci Wine Cellars** (501 Parducci Road; tel: 707/462–9463) providing other diversion.

▶ Yountville
244B1

A rural counterpart to sprawling Napa, 14 miles south, pleasant Yountville became a stop on the wine tourists' circuit in 1986 following the opening of **Domain Chandon▶▶** (1 California Drive; tel: 707/944–2280) by the top-bracket champagne and brandy producer, Moët & Chandon. Tours describing the sparkling-wine-making process are free, but you have to pay if you would like to sample a glass.

If you like to shop, visit Domain Chandon only after a tour of **Yountville 1870▶** (tel: 707/944–2451) where upscale boutiques, art galleries, and antiques outlets fill an imaginatively restored 19th-century railroad station; the area could seriously lighten the wallet of any less-than-clear-headed browser.

THE SILVERADO TRAIL
Used during the 1800s to carry cinnabar from mines at Mount St. Helena to the river docks in Napa, the Silverado Trail crosses the east side of the Napa Valley and makes for a quieter passage than the busy State Road 29, which it parallels.
Complementing the peaceful mood, several tourable and rarely crowded small wineries line the trail.

Banks

California banks usually open Monday to Thursday 9 or 10–5, Friday 9 or 10–5:30. Major branches may also be open longer hours and on Saturday 10–1 or 2.

Beaches

With almost 1,000 miles of coastline, California is well supplied with beaches. They are endlessly fascinating: you can walk on them, lie and sunbathe on them, watch seabirds and hunt for shells, dig clams or spot seals and sea otters at play. From December through March you can watch the migrations of the gray whales.

What you can't always do is swim. From San Francisco northward, the water is simply too cold for any but extremely hardy souls. Some beaches, even along the southern half of the coast, are too dangerous for swimming because of the undertow.

Park rangers patrol beaches and enforce regulations, such as those on pets (dogs must be on a leash at all times), alcohol, dune buggies, and fires.

Access to beaches in California is generally excellent. The state park system includes many fine beaches, and oceanside communities have their own public beaches.

In addition, through the work of the California Coastal Commission, many stretches of private property that would otherwise seal off the beach from outsiders have public-access paths and trails. Again, the best advice is to look for signs and obey them.

Bed-and-breakfast

California's most atmospheric lodgings, bed-and-breakfasts, are often restored Victorian homes with a small number of antiques-filled guest rooms with private or shared bathrooms. Here, guests are encouraged to mingle, and breakfast itself is normally a hearty affair served around a large table. Prices per room range from $45 to $200, depending on location and facilities.

Reservations can be made through an agency such as Bed and Breakfast California, PO Box 2247, Saratoga,

CA 95070 (tel: 408/867–9662 or 800/872–4500; www.bbintl.com).

Camping

Most of California's 264 state parks have well-equipped campsites costing $10–$24. Places can be reserved up to eight weeks in advance through Reserve America (tel: 800/444 7275). Larger state parks may also have very basic hikers' campsites ($2–$8) in the backcountry.

For information on camping in national parks, such as Yosemite, whose facilities range from large campgrounds with all amenities to rough plots in the wild, contact the National Park Service, PO Box 1600, Cumberland, MD 21501 (tel: 800/365–2267).

In addition, there are many privately run campgrounds throughout the state. One of the larger operators is the **California Travel Parks Association**, Box 5648, Auburn, CA 95604 (tel: 530/823–1076 or 888/STAYCTPA; www.campgrounds.com).

Car rental

All major car-rental agencies serve California, though not all have outlets in every city and airport. Two important suggestions for car rentals: compare prices, and be sure you understand all the provisions of an agreement before you sign it. Often you have to pay extra for the privilege of picking up a car in one location and dropping it off at another; differing requirements for filling gas tanks can change the cost of the rental. Ask questions.

It's always best to know a few essentials *before* you arrive at the car-rental counter. Find out what the collision-damage waiver (usually a $10 to $15 daily surcharge) covers, and know before you leave home whether your corporate or personal insurance already covers damage to a rental car (if so, bring along a photocopy of your insurance documents to have on hand).

More and more companies are holding renters responsible for theft and vandalism damages if they

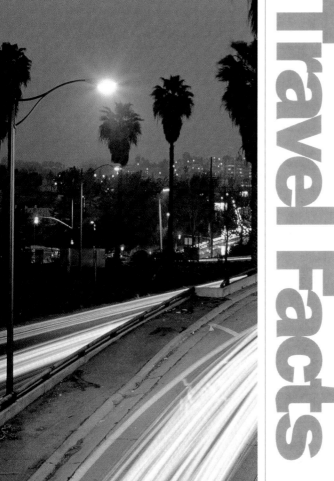

Travel Facts

don't buy the CDW; in response, some credit card and insurance companies are extending *their* coverage to rental cars.

Here are toll-free numbers for some of the car-rental agencies in California:

Alamo, tel: 800/327–9633

Avis, tel: 800/331–1212

Budget Car and Truck Rental, tel: 800/527–0700

Dollar Rent a Car, tel: 800/800–4000

Hertz, tel: 800/654–3131; (in Canada 800/263-0600)

National Car Rental, tel: 800/227–7368

Thrifty Car Rental, tel: 800/367–2277

Children

Rarely in California are children regarded disdainfully. Hotels and motels usually provide a crib or extra bed in the parents' room for kids under 12 at no extra charge, and restaurant servers are likely to appear with games, the children's menu, and—if required—a high chair. If you are renting a car, ask for a car seat when you make your reservation.

The state has much that will amuse children: Disneyland is just the most famous of a number of theme parks; many museums provide hands-on exhibits; and the state's parks and forests (and their wildlife) can make an excellent introduction to the natural world.

For further advice, consult Fodor's *Where Should We Take The Kids? California*, available in bookstores or from Fodor's Travel Publications (tel: 818/846–0400).

Climate and clothing

The common perception of California as a sun-drenched paradise applies only to the southern half of the state, and even here there are variations: humidity-free San Diego ranges from mild to warm; Los Angeles can be hot and sticky in summer, warm but potentially wet during winter; inland, the baking deserts are off-limits to humans throughout the summer and are merely hot during the rest of the year.

In the north, San Francisco's temperatures are mild, but persistent fog can mean a cool start to even the sunniest day; further north along the coast, expect more fog and colder, damper conditions; inland, the Gold Country can be scorching in summer while the higher elevations of the Sierra Nevada region are welcomingly mild—in winter, snow covers the mountains and their immediate surroundings.

If you are traveling widely around the state you should pack with varying climates in mind. California dress is almost always casual, but bare feet and swimsuits are not acceptable in public buildings, and the most elegant restaurants require formal attire. The national and state parks, and much of the undeveloped coastline, are best seen by walking, so bring suitable footwear.

San Francisco's finest—the "Smokey Bears"

Crime

Theft of money and valuables from your room is easy to avoid simply by handing them over to the hotel staff to put in a safe for safekeeping. Being robbed in the street is statistically very unlikely but does happen, usually to people who have been careless enough to make things easy for the robber—by carrying easily snatched handbags or having wallets sticking out of their back pockets.

Lost travelers' checks are relatively easy to replace (read the instructions when you buy the checks), but replacing a stolen passport is much harder and begins with a visit or phone call to your country's nearest consular office (those in San Francisco and Los Angeles are given in the regional gazetteer).

Straying into dangerous areas of cities is another potential hazard. San Francisco is fairly safe (but not completely), San Diego slightly less so, and Los Angeles much less so; get local advice and follow it.

Travelers with disabilities

California leads the United States in providing facilities for travelers with disabilities. All public buildings have to be wheelchair accessible, and wheelchair users will find public transportation equipped with "kneeling" buses, and (in San Francisco) elevators to the BART system. Trains and airlines are obliged by law to provide services for people with disabilities if requested, and **Amtrak** handles this mandate well.

Though less comfortable than trains, Greyhound buses are more frequent and allow a companion to travel free provided you have a doctor's certificate. Car-rental companies are able to arrange vehicles equipped with hand controls provided they receive advance notice; all public parking lots have spaces that are specially marked as reserved for people with disabilities.

For information on traveling in California contact the following organizations:
Society for the Advancement of Travel for the Handicapped, 347 5th Avenue, Suite 610, New York, NY10016, (tel: 212/447–7284; www.sath.org). This is a good source for access information for the disabled. Annual membership is $45; for senior travelers and students, $30.

SATH members receive a color magazine, *Open World*, which provides a wide range of information for travelers with disabilities. Non-members may subscribe to the magazine.

California crabs

Eating

One of the greatest pleasures of the Golden State is eating, which can be done extremely well, and if your budget demands, extremely cheaply. Your biggest problem could simply be succumbing to temptation and overindulging, although the potential for gluttony is balanced by a well-established trend toward healthy eating. Even major fast-food outlets offer low-fat alternatives to burgers and french fries.

To sample what people generally consider California Cuisine, you can venture into any of the haute temples of gastronomy in Los Angeles or San Francisco, or experiment with the myriad bistros that line neighborhood streets. California cooking is light, fresh, and extremely creative (sometimes unappetizingly so). It affords shredded Thai chicken on pizza and goat cheese and sun-dried cherries in salad. Don't be afraid to stretch your palate. You might be surprised to find how delicious some concoctions can be.

Perhaps ethnic food offers the biggest bang for the buck. Both Los Angeles and San Francisco feature large and varied ethnic communities, which have enriched the city's respective restaurant scenes with a full range of eateries—everything from upscale Japanese sushi palaces to down-and-dirty Mexican bogedas. An ethnic restaurant filled with people of that ethnicity is a good sign that the cooking is authentic and very good.

California is also one of the great wine regions of the world, and it would be a shame to experience the food without sampling the best of the barrels. California wines are mostly categorized by varietal, labeled by the grape name rather than the region or producer. The Chardonnays are typically big and oaky while the Cabernet Sauvignon are bold and tannic. They offer a perfect accompaniment to the vibrant cooking of the area.

The relaxed atmosphere of even the most formal restaurants makes dining in California even more

Access-Able Travel Source (www.access-able.com) is an expanding on-line resource offering travel tips and users' travel accounts. It provides links to travel agents and companies, discussion forums, books, magazines, and organizations of interest to disabled travelers.
Mobility International USA, Box 10767, Eugene, OR 97440 (tel: 541/343–1284; www.miusa.org) provides information on accommodations, organized study, and other facilities, around the world. A useful resource within California is the **Center For Independent Living**, 2539 Telegraph Avenue, Berkeley, CA 94705 (tel: 510/841 4776).

Driving

With gas typically costing from $1.20 to $1.60 a gallon and public transportation (see page 262) far from comprehensive, you will save money and time by touring California by car.

California's roads fall into several categories depending on who pays for their upkeep. The Interstates and U.S. Highways are part of the federally run road network; State Highways and State Roads tend to be smaller than Interstates and U.S. Highways, and are financed by the state government; much less frequently you will be traveling on County Roads—most typically winding lanes through isolated rural areas. Gas stations are easy to find in all but the most secluded or inhospitable regions.

enjoyable. A Hawaiian aloha shirt is usually all you need to don to eat in Los Angeles, while a cable-knit sweater will generally suffice in cooler San Francisco.

Traditional Coffee shops and diners are abundant and don't stay in business long if they don't deliver good food at good prices. Most offer gigantic breakfasts for around $6, washed down by as much coffee as you like for the price of a single cup. For lunch, they serve sandwiches (actually a whole hot meal) and salads (actually a whole cold meal) for $6–$9. Some coffee shops and diners close after lunch, but some provide substantial dinners for $10–$15.

At the top end of the scale are the gourmet restaurants, whose chefs are the leading practitioners of California cuisine: an ever-inventive manipulation of local produce to create attractive and nutritionally balanced meals—worth a $30–$80 splurge at least once during your stay.

Festivals and events
From county fairs to frog racing, thousands of festivals and special events take place in California each year. Somewhere, at some time, in California there's bound to be an event celebrating everything you can think of and some more besides. The pick of the bunch is in the regional gazetteer. For a (very long) full list, contact the **California Office of Tourism** (see Maps and Tourist Information).

Gay and lesbian travelers
California in general and San Francisco in particular are welcoming places for gay and lesbian travelers. Gay and lesbian bars, clubs, accommodations, and information centers are well established in the major cities, and gays and lesbians are unlikely to encounter open public hostility.

Health and insurance
The proper insurance is essential to protect you in the event of theft, disrupted travel, or sudden illness.

If you need to see a doctor, find one by looking under "physicians" in the phone book; hospitals have emergency rooms, but if you are dealing with a serious injury call 911.

Supplemental travel insurance can be obtained from several companies. Especially good is International SOS Assistance (8 Neshamny Interplex, Trevose, PA; tel: 215/244–1500 or 800/523–8930), a medical assistance company providing evacuation services, worldwide medical referrals, and medical insurance.

Hotels and motels
The major mid-range hotel chains (usually $70–$90 a night), such as Holiday Inn, Best Western, Travelodge, and Vagabond, are heavily represented in California, offering double beds, color TVs, private bathrooms, and phones in their clean, comfortable rooms.

Such hotels are rarely the best value, however. Many smaller hotels and motels—including budget-priced chains such as Hampton Inn, Days Inn, and Comfort Inns ($40–$70)— often offer the same things as the pricier hotels, minus room service and an on-premises restaurant.

Thousands of small, owner-run motels are likely to have even lower prices ($35–$70), especially during quiet periods when the rooms would otherwise be unoccupied. Although you should always check the room before booking in, bargain-priced motels nearly always offer perfectly acceptable accommodations and include in-room phones, private bathrooms, and TV.

Three people sharing can often add an extra bed to a double room for $10–$15 above the regular rate.

Besides the standard sales tax (see page 263), some areas impose a "bed tax" of 5–15 percent on the standard room charge.

Language
When California joined the Union in 1850, Spanish was spoken as a mother tongue by two-thirds of the state's population. It was only with the influx of English speakers from the east during the gold rush that the language lost its predominance.

Now, after 100 years, Spanish is once again widely spoken in California.

261

Spanish speakers are concentrated in the most densely populated third of the state: over a quarter of the population of Los Angeles, America's second-largest city, are Hispanic Americans. Many face discrimination. Controversy has raged about education provision in Spanish schools and the rights of Spanish speakers. Despite opposition from civil rights groups, Californians voted in a statewide referendum to make English their official language. A Spanish speaker can easily understand Mexican Spanish. The main difficulty is in vocabulary: Mexican Spanish has been much enriched by words from Nahuatl, the language of the Aztec Empire.

On page 263 is a basic vocabulary to help you in Hispanic restaurants.

Various Asian languages are also spoken in pockets around the state.

Maps and tourist information

Almost every community has a Visitors Bureau or Chamber of Commerce equipped to provide free maps and information. The offices are usually signposted and their addresses are always in the phone book. Most keep regular business hours; those in major cities are often open on weekends, too.

Information on and reliable maps of the whole state are provided by the **California Office of Tourism**, based at 801 K Street, Suite 1600, Sacramento, CA 95814 (tel: 916/322–2881 or 800/462–2543; www.gocalif.com). Detailed maps of California national parks are available from the United States Geographical Survey (US65), Box 25286, Denver Federal Center, Denver, CO 80225 (tel: 888/275–8747).

Nightlife

To discover the best of the nightlife—dance clubs, movies, live music, or bars—look for the free local newspapers distributed in bookshops, bars, restaurants, or just piled up on street corners. Each community has at least one and they are dependable (and opinionated) sources of information.

Public transportation

It is possible to see most of California without a car, but it's difficult: public transportation is decidedly thin outside cities and nonexistent in

CONVERSION CHARTS

FROM	TO	MULTIPLY BY
Inches	Centimeters	2.54
Centimeters	Inches	0.3937
Feet	Meters	0.3048
Meters	Feet	3.2810
Yards	Meters	0.9144
Meters	Yards	1.0940
Miles	Kilometers	1.6090
Kilometers	Miles	0.6214
Acres	Hectares	0.4047
Hectares	Acres	2.4710
Gallons	Liters	4.5460
Liters	Gallons	0.2200
Ounces	Grams	28.35
Grams	Ounces	0.0353
Pounds	Grams	453.6
Grams	Pounds	0.0022
Pounds	Kilograms	0.4536
Kilograms	Pounds	2.205
U.K. Tons	Tonnes	1.0160
Tonnes	U.K. Tons	0.9842

MEN'S SUITS							
UK	36	38	40	42	44	46	48
Rest of Europe	46	48	50	52	54	56	58
US	36	38	40	42	44	46	48

DRESS SIZES						
UK	8	10	12	14	16	18
France	36	38	40	42	44	46
Italy	38	40	42	44	46	48
Rest of Europe	34	36	38	40	42	44
US	6	8	10	12	14	16

MEN'S SHIRTS						
UK	14	14.5	15	15.5	16	16.5	17
Rest of Europe	36	37	38	39/40	41	42	43
US	14	14.5	15	15.5	16	16.5	17

MEN'S SHOES						
UK	7	7.5	8.5	9.5	10.5	11
Rest of Europe	41	42	43	44	45	46
US	8	8.5	9.5	10.5	11.5	12

WOMEN'S SHOES						
UK	4.5	5	5.5	6	6.5	7
Rest of Europe	38	38	39	39	40	41
US	6	6.5	7	7.5	8	8.5

many country and coastal areas.

There is a limited train service (Amtrak; tel: 800/872-7245; www.amtrak.com) connecting San Francisco, Los Angeles, and San Diego; a more common form of long-distance travel is Greyhound bus (tel: 800/231-2222; www.greyhound.com); for some this is the classic way to travel, but it can be expensive.

Costs over very long journeys might be reduced with an Ameripass ticket, which offers unlimited Greyhound travel over a fixed period—from four to 30 days. Bear in mind that buses often fall hours behind schedule and that the routes miss much of the state's finest scenery.

With the exception of San Francisco, which has a good public transportation network, getting around cities without a car is also problematic—though again not impossible, provided you study the local schedules carefully.

agua fresca	cold water
arroz	rice
cafe	coffee
cerveza	beer
el guacamole	avocado purée
el jitomate	tomato
el licuado de agua	fruit juice with water
el licuado de leche	fruit juice with milk
el mojo de ajo	fried with garlic in butter
el refresco	soft drink
empanizado	fried in bread crumbs
la botana	appetizer
la carne de res	beef
la cena	dinner
la cochinita pibil	spicy pork Yucatan-style
la comida	lunch
la comida corrida	set menu
la crepa	crepe
la cuenta	the check
la papa	potato
la torta	roll with meat, lettuce, avocado, cream
las puntas de filete	thin slices of beef (sometimes in a sandwich)
las enchiladas suizas	tortilla filled with chicken, covered with cooked cheese and cream
las carnitas	small pieces of grilled pork
las crepas con cajeta	crepes with sweet sauce
las papas fritas	french fries
los tamales	dumplings
los totopos tacos	dips
pan	bread
pescado	fish
pollo	chicken
vegetariano	vegetarian
verduras	vegetables

Mission Beach Broadwalk

tel: 202/434–2277 or 800/424-3410)
has programs for independent
travelers that offer discounts on
hotels, car rentals, and sightseeing,
among other things. AARP members
are age 50 or older; annual dues are $8
per person; a three-year membership
is $20.

Shopping
In California's big cities, opportunities
abound to shop for internationally
famed brands of clothing, jewelry,
leather goods, and perfumes, often in
shops or boutiques set up by French,
Italian, British, or American designers.
There are enough specialty shops and
fine department stores to keep anyone
"born to shop" busy and happy.
(Note: San Francisco and Los Angeles
are centers of clothing manufacture; if
you're a bargain hunter, you'll
want to explore the factory outlets in
both cities.)

If you are shopping for something
unique to California, look at the
output of its artists and craftspeople.
California is home to a great number
of them, and you can find their
creations from one end of the state to
the other in fine city galleries, in small
neighborhood shops, in out-of-the-
way mountain studios, at roadside
stands, and at county fairs. Paintings,
drawings, sculpture, wood carvings,
pottery, jewelry, hand-woven fabrics,
handmade baskets—the creativity and
the output of California's artists and
artisans seems endless. Whatever your
taste and budget, you will probably
have no trouble locating tempting
shopping opportunities.

Another California specialty is wine.
You can visit wineries in many parts of
the state, not only in the Wine Country
north of San Francisco. Wineries and
good wine stores will package your
purchases for safe travel or shipping.

Other possibilities range from
antiques to souvenir T-shirts. If you're
flying home from San Francisco, you
can make one last purchase of the city's
unique sourdough bread at the airport.

Sports
Almost any sport you can think of is
available somewhere in California at

264

When using city buses, take care not
to miss your stop and unwittingly
stray into dangerous areas (this is
especially important after dark); the
driver will be ready to give advice.

Sales tax
The state sales tax is 7.25 percent
plus local taxes.

Senior citizens
Many discounts are available to
older travelers: meals, lodging, entry
to various attractions, car rentals,
tickets for buses and trains, and
campgrounds are among the prime
examples. The age that qualifies you
for these senior discounts varies
considerably. The State of California
will reduce the cost of your campsite
if you are at least 62.

If you are 50, ask about senior
discounts even if there is no posted
notice. Ask at the time you are
making reservations, buying tickets,
or being seated in a restaurant. Carry
proof of your age, and any
membership cards in organizations
that provide discounts for seniors.
Many discounts are given solely on
the basis of age, without membership
requirement. A 10 percent cut on a
bus ticket and $2 off a pizza may not
seem like major savings, but they add
up, and can cut the cost of a trip if you
use the discounts consistently.

**The American Association of
Retired Persons** (AARP, 601 E.
Street, NW, Washington, DC 20049,

some time of the year. A great many sports know no season and go on year round. Skiing, of course, depends on the snow and is limited for the most part to the period between Thanksgiving and April, but golf courses and tennis courts do a thriving business all year.

Swimming and surfing, scuba diving and skin diving in the Pacific Ocean are favorite year-round California pleasures in the southern part of the state. On the coast from San Francisco northward, the seasons play a limiting role.

California has abundant fishing options: deep-sea fishing expeditions, surf fishing from the shore, and freshwater fishing in streams, rivers, lakes, and reservoirs. There are many hunting opportunities as well. For information on fishing and hunting licenses and regulations, check with the California Department of Fish and Game (1416 9th Street, Sacramento 95814, tel: 916/653-7664).

Hiking, backpacking, bicycling, and sailing are popular throughout the state, and rental of equipment can be readily arranged. River rafting, white-water and otherwise, canoeing, and kayaking are popular, especially in the northern part of the state, where there are many rivers; see individual chapters for detailed information.

For skiing, climbing and mountain biking, the Sierra Nevada has a range of resort with stores where you can rent or buy equipment and slopes for all levels of expertise (see page 199).

Taxis
In cities, taxis can be hailed in the street though it is more common to phone for one; many companies are listed (under "taxicabs") in the Yellow Pages. Hotel and motel lobby staff will usually call a taxi for you.

Time
California uses Pacific Standard Time, three hours behind Eastern Standard Time.

Tipping
After using restaurants, bars, or taxis, leave a tip of 15–20 percent of the bill. If a hotel porter carries your luggage, tip 80¢–$1.50 per bag.

Wine and beer
International recognition draws many visitors to sample the produce of California's Wine Country; the state's native beers are also worth investigating. San Francisco's Anchor Steam Beer has gained worldwide acclaim, and there are many micro-breweries creating good brews that blow away the weak and relatively tasteless mass-market beers.

Youth hostels, YMCAs, and YWCAs
Youth hostels and a small number of comparable YMCAs and YWCAs are scattered throughout California and, at $12–$15 a night, are by far the least costly accommodations.

Most hostels have small, shared rooms (usually six to eight beds in each) and a few single and double rooms (around $25), and simple cooking facilities. A three-night limit operates when the hostel is fully booked, as is very likely during the summer. This is an excellent way of planning budget stopovers.

265

Views of California

Accommodations & Restaurants

ACCOMMODATIONS

SAN FRANCISCO

Abigail ($$)
246 McAllister Street tel: 415/861–9728
This delightfully old-fashioned hotel is stuffed with mementos from when it catered to visiting theater companies. It is comfortable and renovated.

Adelaide Inn ($)
5 Isadora Duncan Court tel: 415/441–2261
There are small, pleasant rooms with shared bathrooms and a friendly atmosphere in this hotel, located in a quiet cul-de-sac off Taylor Street.

Alamo Square Inn ($$)
719 Scott Street tel: 415/922–2055
Have bed and breakfast in an atmospheric rambling Victorian building with fabulous views. The inn is located in a fast-improving area near Haight-Ashbury.

Campton Place ($$$)
340 Stockton Street tel: 415/781–5555 or 800/235–4300
Near Union Square, this boutique hotel offers discreet service and surroundings, and is filled with antiques. The rooms are understated and elegant.

Cartwright Hotel ($$)
524 Sutter Street tel: 415/421–2865
With small rooms but comfortable and very competitively priced, this hotel is close to Union Square. Complimentary afternoon tea is served in the study.

Edward II Suites & Pub ($$)
3155 Scott Street tel: 800/GREAT-IN or 415/922–3000
Enjoy four-poster beds and whirlpool baths in the Marina District. The price includes a glass of sherry in the adjoining bar.

El Drisco Hotel ($$$)
2901 Pacific Avenue tel: 415/346–2880
A recently remodeled, elegantly appointed property in Pacific Heights. Continental breakfast, evening wine and personal service such as morning Town Car service to Downtown are provided.

European Guest House ($)
761 Minna Street tel: 415/861–6634
A cozy and low-cost South-of-Market option, this guest house offers an easy-going, youth-oriented mood and a mix of dormitory beds and double rooms.

Fairmont Hotel & Tower ($$$)
950 Mason Street tel: 415/772–5000
This elite hotel in Nob Hill survived the 1906 earthquake. The marble-pillared lobby is just the beginning of the grand opulence that awaits.

Grant Plaza ($)
465 Grant Avenue tel: 415/434–3883 or 800/472–6899
The Grant Plaza is tremendous value in Chinatown. Rooms are small but thoughtfully decorated and there is a stained-glass dome on the top floor.

24 Henry ($)
24 Henry Street tel: 415/864–5686
A five-room guest house on a tree-lined street, the 24 Henry is a friendly and affordable base for gay men. Second house nearby has five more rooms.

Hostelling International San Francisco-Fort Mason ($)
Building 240, Fort Mason tel: 415/771–7277
A massive youth hostel, this has a three-night limit in summer, five nights in winter.

Hotel Union Square ($$)
114 Powell Street tel: 415/397–3000 or 800/553–1900
A well-known 1930s hotel, the Hotel Union Square has been stylishly revamped. Extras include complimentary croissants and herbal teas.

Huntington ($$$)
1075 California Street tel: 415/474–5400 or 800/227–4683
The Huntington offers comfortable accommodations on Nob Hill with excellent service. The rooms are individually decorated.

Inn at the Opera ($$$)
333 Fulton Street tel: 415/863–8400 or 800/325–2708
Opera and ballet stars, classical musicians, and top-billed thespians are likely to be fellow guests. This is a cozy and tastefully decorated hotel.

International Guest House ($)
2976 23rd Street tel: 415/641–1411
Aimed at backpacking students, this guest house has dormitory bunk beds and a few private rooms.

Kensington Park ($$)
450 Post Street tel: 415/788–6400 or 800/553–1900
At this impressively presented boutique hotel, breakfast is included and complimentary afternoon sherry is served to the sound of the resident pianist.

The King George ($$)
334 Mason Street tel: 415/781–5050 or 800/288–6005
This hotel has pleasant if unspectacular rooms in the heart of Downtown. "English-style" afternoon tea is served to a piano music accompaniment.

Laurel Inn ($$)
444 Presidio Avenue tel: 800/552–8735
The Laurel is unspectacular but good value. It is slightly removed from the strongly touristed areas.

Mandarin Oriental ($$$)
222 Sansome Street tel: 415/885–0999 or 800/622–0404
Experience good views of the city from the rooms, all of which are on upper floors. Guests enjoy health club privileges, dining, and gracious service.

Marina Motel ($)
2576 Lombard Street tel: 415/ 921–9406
A motel that is located on a busy street in the largely residential Marina District. A choice of regular and kitchen-equipped rooms is offered.

Mark Hopkins Inter-Continental ($$$)
999 California Street tel: 415/392–3434
An old Nob Hill favorite. The Mark Hopkins retains its individuality and charm.

Mary Elizabeth Inn ($)
1040 Bush Street tel: 415/673–6768
Friendly and low-key women-only accommodations are offered at this inn, established in 1914.

The Miyako ($$$)
1625 Post Street tel: 415/922–3200
This is a discreet, luxurious retreat in Japantown. It is a harmonious blend of Japanese and Western ideas.

Phoenix Inn ($)
601 Eddy Street tel: 415/776-1380 or 800/248-9466
Touring musicians and minor celebrities frequent this tropics-themed two-story motel with a pool. Martinis and sushi are specialties at Backflip, the ultra-hip restaurant/lounge.

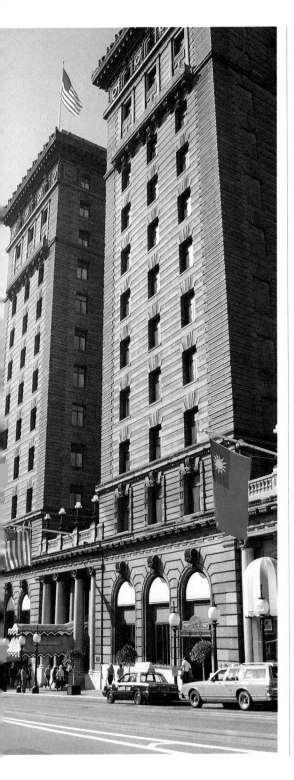

Accommodations & Restaurants

Accommodations & Restaurants

The Pickwick ($$)
85 Fifth Street tel: 415/421–7500
This up-and-coming hotel is in the SoMa district. It is good value despite steadily rising prices.

The Red Victorian ($$)
1665 Haight Street tel: 415/864–1978
Soothing decor, a meditation room, art gallery, and healthy breakfasts—a true San Francisco experience.

Ritz-Carlton San Francisco ($$$)
600 Stockton Street tel: 415/296–7465
A neoclassical landmark building, filled with antiques and paintings. There is a health spa and pool.

San Francisco Marriott ($$$)
55 Fourth Street tel: 415/896–1600
The façade here has inspired great architectural debate. The interior is extremely comfortable.

San Remo Hotel ($)
2237 Mason Street tel: 415/776–8688
Most of the comfortable if spartan rooms, share bathrooms. This is good value in a good location.

Sherman House ($$$)
2160 Green Street tel: 415/563–3600 or 800/424–5777
In the city's most luxuriously restored Italianate mansion, sumptuous rooms with four-poster featherbeds are furnished with Biedermeier, English Jacobean, and French antiques.

Stanyan Park ($$)
750 Stanyan Street tel: 415/751–1000
Elegantly renovated, this hotel faces Golden Gate Park. Rates include light breakfast.

Tulip Inn ($)
480 Geary Street tel: 415/771–1600
Half-priced breakfast and dinner from the first-floor deli are both included in the room rate and make the small but clean rooms temptingly good value for the budget-minded visitor. Free ride to airport.

Tuscan Inn ($$)
425 North Point tel: 800/648–4626 or 415/561–1100
This is the pick of the hotels in touristy Fisherman's Wharf. Rooms are warmly furnished, staff are personable, and there is a complimentary wine hour.

Victorian Inn on the Park ($$)
301 Lyon Street tel: 415/931–1830 or 800/435–1967
Twelve antiques-decorated rooms, some with their original fireplaces, fill a lovely 1897 house. Rates include fruit, croissants and fresh-brewed coffee.

Washington Square Inn ($$)
1660 Stockton Street tel: 415/981–4220 or 800/388–0220
Antiques-laden bed-and-breakfast in North Beach; rates include afternoon tea, and wine and cheese.

The Westin St. Francis ($$)
335 Powell Street tel: 415/397–7000
Nearly 100 years old, this hotel offers old-world luxury and elegance. Services include dining, a beauty salon, shopping, and a health club.

THE BAY AREA

Claremont Resort Hotel and Spa ($$$)
Ashby and Domingo avenues, Oakland
tel: 510/843–3000 or 800/551–7266
This refurbished 1916 mansion is located on landscaped grounds in the Oakland hills. Saunas, swimming pools, and whirlpools are offered.

The French Hotel ($)
1538 Shattuck Avenue, Berkeley
tel: 510/548–9930
There are uncluttered rooms with balconies in this three-story, brickfront hotel just across from Chez Panisse. A coffee house is on the first floor.

The Hensley House ($$)
445 N. Third Street, San Jose
tel: 408/298–3537
A tiny but luxurious 1884 house, the Hensley offers good value bed-and-breakfast.

Hotel De Anza ($)
233 W. Santa Clara Street, San Jose
tel: 408/286–1000 or 800/843–3700
This hotel was built in 1930 and has been thoughtfully restored to its original splendor. The staff is efficient and the rooms are well equipped.

Hotel Durant ($$)
2600 Durant Avenue, Berkeley
tel: 510/845–8981 or 800/238–7268
The Durant is aging but comfortable. It is located within an easy walk of Berkeley campus.

Sanborn Park Hostel ($)
15808 Sanborn Road, Saratoga
tel: 408/741–0166
A former hunting lodge that is now a rustic youth hostel.

CENTRAL COAST NORTH

Carmel Village Inn ($$)
Ocean Avenue and Junipero Street
tel: 831/624–3864
Good value for pricey Carmel. Rooms are comfortable and there are nice grounds in which to relax.

Darling House ($$)
314 W. Cliff Drive, Santa Cruz
tel:831/458–1958
Cozy bed-and-breakfast accommodations are offered in this delightful 1910 clifftop home.

Highlands Inn ($$$)
on Highway 1 four miles south of Carmel
tel: 415/624–3801 or 800/682–4811
One of the Highlands' claims to fame is as the place where singer and actress Madonna honeymooned. Every room offers a lovely ocean view.

Inn at Depot Hill ($$$)
250 Monterey Avenue, Santa Cruz
tel: 408/462–3376 or 800/572–2632
Housed in a 1901 railroad depot building, the sumptuous accommodations are themed—beach, Japanese, railroad baron. This is a sophisticated and unusual choice.

The Monterey Hotel ($$)
406 Alvarado Street, Monterey
tel: 800/727–0960 or 831/375–3184
An elegant, historic hotel, the Monterey Hotel is located in the heart of town.

Motel 6 ($)
2124 Freemont Street, Monterey
tel: 800/727-0960 or 831/375–3184
It is essential to book at this cheapest motel in town. There are plenty of alternatives nearby.

Motel 6 ($)
1010 Fairview Avenue, Salinas
tel: 831/758–2122
The least expensive of the two motels of this bland but dependable motel chain in Salinas.

268

The North Beach area, San Francisco

Super 8 ($)
321 Riverside Avenue, Santa Cruz
tel: 831/464–5100
There are many plain and simple motels located close to the beach and the Boardwalk. This is one of the best.

CENTRAL COAST SOUTH

Adobe Inn ($)
1473 Monterey Street, San Luis Obispo
tel: 805/549–0321
Once a run-of-the-mill motel, the Adobe has been expertly converted. It is now a homely bed-and-breakfast.

Casa Del Mar ($$)
18 Bath Street, Santa Barbara
tel: 800/433–3097
A small Mediterranean-style hotel. Rooms are pleasantly located around a courtyard and spa bath.

Embarcadero Inn ($$)
456 Embarcadero, Morro Bay
tel: 805/772–2700 or 800/292–7265
This serviceable motel has comfortably clean rooms. Find it not far from the water.

Four Seasons Biltmore ($$$)
1260 Channel Drive, Santa Barbara
tel: 805/969–2261
There are breathtaking views of the ocean or the mountains in most of the rooms at this stunning resort-style hotel. Enjoy many outdoor sports, a restaurant, and a full program of children's activities.

Inn at Morro Bay ($$)
60 State Park Road, Morro Bay
tel:805/662–4779
Two-story clapboard structures with pretty rooms surround a landscaped courtyard on the bay. It's near the hiking trails in the state park.

Inn on the Beach ($$)
1175 Seaward Drive, Ventura
tel: 805/652–2000
All rooms have beach-facing balconies. There is a complimentary breakfast, and also complimentary wine and cheese.

Keystone Inn ($)
540 Main Street, Morro Bay
tel: 805/772–7503
The Keystone is the pick of the town's inexpensive motels.

Peach Tree Inn ($)
2001 Monterey Street, San Luis Obispo
tel: 805/543–3170 or 800/227–6396
A quiet and reasonably priced establishment on this motel-lined street.

Simpson House ($$$)
121 E. Arrellaga Street, Santa Barbara
tel: 805/963–7067 or 800/676–1280
Built in 1874, this estate has been restored to one of the area's top hotels. The rooms are elegantly furnished with antiques and fresh flower arrangements.

LOS ANGELES

The Argyle ($$$)
8358 Sunset Boulevard, Los Angeles
tel: 213/654–7100
In this art-deco masterpiece, rooms are individually furnished, many with luxury touches. Former residents have included Howard Hughes and John Wayne.

Banana Bungalow AAIH ($)
2775 Cahuenga Boulevard West
tel: 800/4-HOSTEL
A wonderful backpackers' hostel nestled in the Hollywood Hills. In addition to usual facilities, free transportation is available for residents to the airport and beaches.

Accommodations & Restaurants

Beverly Hills Hotel ($$$)
9641 Sunset Boulevard tel: 310/276–2251 or 800/283–8885
One movie-world legend that everyone has heard of, complete with pink awnings and bungalows. The service may not be great.

The Beverly ($)
7701 Beverly Boulevard tel: 213/931–8100
A clean, tidy, and quiet hotel. It is surprisingly low priced for its fashionable West Hollywood/Beverly Hills location.

Bevonshire Lodge Motel ($)
7575 Beverly Boulevard tel: 323/936–6154
This is an extremely well-priced and well-located small motel.

Cadillac Hotel ($)
8 Dudley Avenue tel: 310/399–8876
Low-cost shared or private rooms are offered here, beside Venice Beach.

Carlyle Inn ($)
119 S. Robertson Boulevard, West Los Angeles 90035 tel: 310/275–4445 or 800/322–7595
A small hotel in a safe neighborhood close to Beverly Hills. There are complimentary buffet breakfasts.

Chateau Marmont Hotel ($$$)
8221 Sunset Boulevard, 90046 tel: 213/656-10110 or 800/242-8328
Well known for its literary connections, Gore Vidal and Dominick Dunne are famous residents. There are cottages as well as suites and rooms.

Crescent Hotel ($$)
403 N. Crescent Drive, Beverly Hills tel: 800/451–1566
You will find comfortable if unelaborate rooms at a good price in this hotel.

Del Capri Hotel ($$)
10587 Wilshire Boulevard, Westwood tel: 310/474–3511 or 800/444–6835
A homey and good value hotel in expensive Westwood. Most rooms have kitchenettes.

Figueroa Hotel ($$)
939 S. Figueroa Street, Downtown tel: 800/421–9092
This relaxed hotel has an appealing Spanish look.

Four Seasons ($$$)
330 S. Doheny Drive, Los Angeles tel: 310/273–2222
A high-rise west of downtown Los Angeles, this is known for attracting rich and famous Hollywood types. The pool and open-air health club are particularly attractive.

Highland Gardens Hotel ($$)
7047 Franklin Avenue tel: 213/850–0536
A hotel with good facilities on a residential Hollywood street, near world-famous Mann's Chinese Theatre. Continental breakfast is free.

Holiday Inn ($$)
1755 N. Highland Avenue tel: 213/462–7181
An unexciting but dependable mid-range chain hotel. It is within walking distance of many of Hollywood's sights.

Hollywood Downtowner Motel ($)
5601 Hollywood Boulevard tel: 323/464–7913
An austere motel, but perfectly placed for exploring Hollywood.

Hollywood Roosevelt ($$)
7000 Hollywood Boulevard tel: 213/466–7000 or 800/858–2244
This hotel is steeped in Hollywood tradition but the rooms are less impressive than the lobby. It is adequate but ordinary.

Hotel Bel-Air ($$$)
701 Stone Canyon Road, Los Angeles tel: 310/472–1211
A beautiful resort-style property situated on 10 acres of garden landscape. The rooms are light and airy. The restaurant and poolside service are exceptional and the staff are extremely accommodating.

Hotel California ($$)
1670 Ocean Avenue, Santa Monica tel: 310/393–2363
Established in 1911 but recently renovated, this cozy hotel is close to the beach.

Huntley Hotel ($$)
1111 Second Street, Santa Monica tel: 800/556–4012
A high-rise near the beach. Aim for a room that has a view of the ocean.

Hyatt Regency Los Angeles ($$$)
711 S. Hope Street, 90017 tel: 213/683–1234
A good place for business functions. All rooms have excellent views of the city.

The Inn at Venice Beach ($$)
327 Washington Boulevard tel: 800/828–0688
An inviting bed-and-breakfast within walking distance of Marina Del Rey and Venice Beach.

Le Parc ($$)
733 West Knoll Drive, West Hollywood tel: 310/855–8888
Quiet, low-key elegance is the key here on a residential street in a fashionable neighborhood.

Le Reve Hotel ($$)
8822 Cynthia Street, West Hollywood tel: 800/835–7997
A pleasant location for these attractively furnished and well-equipped suites.

Loews Santa Monica Beach Hotel ($$$)
1700 Ocean Avenue tel: 310/458–6700
This is an architectural showpiece beside the ocean and Santa Monica Pier.

Los Angeles International Hostel ($)
3601 S. Gaffrey Street, Building 613, San Pedro tel: 310/831–8109
This hostel may be removed from the center of L.A. life but it is handy to South Bay and the airport.

New Otani Garden Hotel ($$$)
120 S. Los Angeles Street, Downtown tel: 213/629–1200 or 800/421–8795
In Little Tokyo, Downtown, try the Japanese-style rooms for maximum value.

Orchid Motel ($)
819 Flower Street tel: 213/624–5855
An attractive budget option in Downtown.

The Peninsula, Beverley Hills ($$$)
9882 Little Santa Monica Boulevard, Beverley Hills tel: 310/551–2888 or 800/462–7899
In one of the top hotels in Los Angeles, every detail is exquisite, including the full service spa, rooftop pool, huge, luxurious bathrooms, and plush lounge. There is an excellent, top-quality restaurant, Belvedere.

Royal Host Motel ($)
1434 Second Street, Santa Monica
tel: 213/626–6255
Refrigerators and minibars are included in the very well-priced rooms. A student discount is avaliable.
Santa Monica International Hostel ($)
1436 Second Street, Santa Monica
tel: 310/393–9913
This large, modern hostel is in a safe and enjoyable area.
Shangri-la Hotel ($$)
1301 Ocean Avenue, Santa Monica
tel: 310/394–2791 or 800/345–7829
An unmistakable art-deco delight that has been carefully restored to its original 1930s style. All rooms overlook Santa Monica Bay.
Shutters on the Beach ($$$)
1 Pico Boulevard tel: 310/458–0030 or 800/334–9000
Santa Monica's latest luxury hotel. It offers every facility imaginable and there are fabulous ocean views from every room.
Wilshire Royale ($$)
2619 Wilshire Boulevard tel: 800/421–8072
A 1920s art-deco hotel that has been renovated, the Wilshire is within easy reach of Downtown. The mini suites are ideal for several people sharing.
Winona Motel ($)
5131 Hollywood Boulevard
tel: 323/663–1243
Small, well-appointed, and in the heart of Hollywood.
Wyndham Checkers Hotel Los Angeles ($$$)
535 S. Grand Avenue, Los Angeles
tel: 213/624–0000
The rooms are particularly comfortable at this historic Los Angeles building. Also featured is a restaurant and health club.

AROUND L.A.

Candy Cane Inn ($)
1747 S. Harbor Boulevard, Anaheim
tel: 800/345–7057
Rooms are pleasantly furnished rooms, and there is a complimentary muffin and coffee breakfast. Transportation to Disneyland is free.
Casa Malibu Inn On The Beach ($$)
22752 Pacific Coast Highway, Malibu
tel: 310/456–2219 or 800/831–0858
A small inn that offers waterfront rooms. It's on a private-access beach.
Channel Road Inn ($$$)
219 West Channel Road, Santa Monica
tel: 310/459–1920
Full breakfast is served at this excellent B&B. Top rooms are expensive; it's one of the best B&Bs in the West. It stands a block from the beach.
Colonial Inn Youth Hostel ($)
421 Eighth Street, Huntington Beach
tel: 714/536–3315
The Colonial Inn is near the busy local beach and L.A. International Airport.
The Disneyland Hotel ($$$)
1150 W. Cerritos Avenue, Anaheim
tel: 714/778–6600
The official Disneyland hotel is every bit as theme-oriented as the famous park itself and with almost as much innocent amusement.

Doubletree Hotel ($$)
191 N. Los Robles Avenue, Pasadena
tel: 626/792–2727 or 800/222–TREE
Chic and stylish, this is ideally placed for seeing Pasadena.
Fullerton Hacienda Hostel ($)
1700 N. Harbor Boulevard tel: 714/738–3721
A tiny hostel, this is just 5 miles from Disneyland. Early booking is advisable.
Howard Johnson's Plaza Hotel ($$)
1380 S. Harbor Boulevard, Anaheim
tel: 714/776–6120 or 800/442–4228
With its plush landscaped grounds, this is an almost unrecognizable link in the nationwide mid-priced chain. It is across the street from Disneyland.
The Inn at 657 ($$)
657 West 23rd Street, Los Angeles
tel: 213/741–2200 or 800/347–7512)
A top-rated B&B, right in the center of Los Angeles. It offers excellent value.
Inn on Mt. Ada ($$$)
398 Wrigley Road, Santa Catalina Island
tel: 310/510–2030 or 800/608–7668
The former Wrigley family home is now a luxurious bed-and-breakfast inn, complete with grand piano and crystal chandeliers in a splendid hilltop setting. Complimentary breakfast, and a deli lunch.
Kawada Hotel ($$)
200 South Hill Street, Los Angeles
tel: 800/752–9232 or 213/621–4455
Choose this hotel for convenience and value. Also it has European charm and many amenities.
Malibu Beach Inn ($$)
22878 Pacific Coast Highway, Malibu
tel: 310/456–6444 or 800/462–5428
A Mediterranean-style hotel just south of the pier. All rooms have private beachfront balconies.
Oxford Palace Hotel ($$)
745 S. Oxford Avenue, Los Angeles
tel: 213/389–8000
A centrally located, first-class hotel with elegant appointments. Ask for a discount when booking.
The Ritz-Carlton Huntington Hotel and Spa ($$$)
1401 S. Oak Knoll Avenue tel: 626/568–3900
A 1907 Pasadena landmark restored to its original grandeur and elegance.
Seacliff Motel ($$)
1661 S. Coast Highway, Laguna Beach
tel: 714/494–9717
An unpretentious motel with oceanview rooms and the best rates in this otherwise very costly town.
Vista Del Mar ($$$)
417 Crescent Avenue, Santa Catalina Island
tel: 310/510–1452
A pleasing 15-room hotel with glorious views over Avalon. The smaller rooms are tremendous value.
Zane Grey Pueblo Hotel ($$)
199 Chimes Tower Road, Santa Catalina Island
tel: 310/510–0966
This is the former home of the western writer and the island's most atmospheric hotel.

SAN DIEGO

Balboa Park Inn ($$)
3402 Park Boulevard, San Diego
tel: 619/298–0823;
reservations: tel: 800/938–8181

271

Accommodations & Restaurants

Twenty-six suites are housed in Spanish-Colonial buildings, around a courtyard. Continental breakfast, newspaper service, refrigerators are provided.

Catmaran Resort Hotel ($$$)
3999 Mission Boulevard
tel: 858/488–1081 or 800/288–0770
A resort hotel, located alongside Mission Bay. It is an ideal base for water-sports fans.

Clarion Hotel, Bayview ($$)
660 K Street, San Diego tel: 619/696–0234
Knockout city and bay views are available at this 22-story hotel. It's also centrally located near 50 restaurants and other entertainment in the San Diego Historical Gas Lamp District.

Hostelling International ($)
3790 Udall Street tel: 619/223–4778
A friendly hostel with small, shared rooms. It is perfectly sited for the local beach but some miles from the city center.

Hotel Del Coronado ($$$)
1500 Orange Avenue tel: 800/HOTEL–DELL
Steeped in history, this is a wooden architectural marvel, .

Inn at the YMCA ($)
500 W. Broadway tel: 619/232–1133
Big and rather soulless, this offers simple rooms for men and women at bargain rates.

Julian Hotel ($)
2032 Main Street, Julian tel: 760/765–0201
A century-old hotel, the Julian is located in the heart of an old mining town. Breakfast is included in the room rate.

La Jolla Cove Motel ($$)
1155 Coast Boulevard tel: 858/459–2621
This motel has no frills but it is a fine base for discovering La Jolla.

La Pensione Hotel ($$)
1654 Columbia Street tel: 619/232–3400
A clean and quiet hotel with a European flavor.

Loma Lodge ($)
3202 Rosecrans Street tel: 619/222–0511
One of the better value hotels on the Point Loma peninsula.

Park Manor Suites Hotel ($)
525 Spruce Street, San Diego
tel: 619/291–0999
An excellent hotel, built in 1926. Located a few short blocks from the west side of the city's popular Balboa Park, it is close to many attractions.

Pickwick Hotel ($)
132 W. Broadway tel: 619/234–9200
An old hotel built on the site of the Pickwick Theater. It is centrally located above a bus terminal.

Ramada Hotel Old Town ($$)
2435 Jefferson Street tel: 800/355–2544
You'll find fine rooms here, adjacent to the Old Town.

Ramada Inn ($$)
830 Sixth Avenue tel: 619/234–0155
This Ramada has classy but not large rooms in an appealingly restored building.

U. S. Grant Hotel ($$$)
326 Broadway tel: 619/232–3121 or
800/237–5028
Full of character, this place has been pampering presidents and celebrities for many years.

Villager Lodge ($)
660 G Street tel: 619/238–4100
Rates are remarkably low for such welcoming rooms.

The Westgate Hotel ($$)
1022 Second Avenue, San Diego
tel: 619/238–1818 or 800/524–4802
A San Diego landmark where the power elite meet. Located in the center of the reinvigorated Gas Lamp Quarter, it's also within walking distance of restaurants, theaters, and other cultural venues.

Wyndham Emerald Plaza Hotel ($$)
400 W. Broadway, San Diego
tel: 619/239–4500
The Emerald Plaza is a distinctive San Diego landmark. It offers many amenities for the business and leisure traveler.

THE DESERTS

Budget Host Inn ($$)
1277 S. Palm Canyon Drive, Palm Springs
tel: 800/283–4678
Rates are very attractive at thid inn. Rooms are simple but clean and comfortable.

Casa Cody Country Inn ($$)
175 S. Cahuilla Road, Palm Springs
tel: 760/320–9346 or 800/231–2639
Choose from a selection of tastefully decorated rooms and suites.

Furnace Creek Ranch ($$)
Death Valley tel: 760/786–2345
Fairly charmless but this establishment is a prime base for touring Death Valley. The large pool is a bonus.

Hampton Inn ($$)
1590 University Avenue, Riverside
tel: 909/683–6000
Part of a nationwide chain noted for its good value.

Hyatt Regency Suites Palm Springs ($$$)
285 N. Palm Canyon Drive, Palm Springs
tel: 760/322–9000
All of the rooms are suites, many with private balconies, at this modern, well-appointed hotel. Main attractions are golf, a pool and whirlpool, and weekend entertainment.

Marriot's Desert Springs Resort and Spa ($$$)
74855 Country Club Drive, Palm Desert
tel: 760/341–2211 or 800/331–3112
The impressive lobby, complete with a waterfall, is the first glimpse of this enormous resort complete with its own lake, beach, five swimming pools, golf, tennis, and a spa.

Merv Griffin's Resort Hotel & Givenchy Spa ($$$)
4200 E. Palm Canyon Drive, Palm Springs
tel: 760/770–5000 or 800/276–5000
Spare no expense and pamper yourself senseless in this top-class facility offering spa treatments.

Motel 6 ($)
660 S. Palm Canyon Drive, Palm Springs
tel: 760/327–4200
The larger of two Motel 6s in town, this one is most likely to have space. Located downtown.

The Ritz-Carlton, Rancho Mirage ($$$)
68–900 Frank Sinatra Drive, Rancho Mirage
tel: 760/321–8282
An exceptional resort with views of both the desert and the mountains. Activities include golf, tennis, and a personal trainer is available. A truly luxurious experience.

SIERRA NEVADA

Ahwahnee Lodge ($$$)
Yosemite Valley tel: 559/252–4848
A 1927 creation in local stone and concrete fitting perfectly into beautiful natural surroundings.

Creekside Inn ($)
725 N. Main Street, Bishop tel: 619/872–3044
Bright, spacious and temptingly priced.

Inn By The Lake ($$)
3300 Lake Tahoe Boulevard, South Lake Tahoe tel: 530/542–0330 or 800/877–1466
Relaxing, well-equipped, and a few strides from Lake Tahoe.

Montecito Sequoia Lodge ($$)
8000 General's Highway tel: 209/565–3388
Comfortable rooms in rustic surroundings within easy driving distance of Kings Canyon and Sequoia national parks. Breakfast is included.

Snow Goose Inn ($$)
57 Forest Trail, Mammoth Lakes tel: 760/934–2660 or 800/874–7368
A welcoming 15-room bed-and-breakfast.

Wawona Hotel ($$)
Mariposa, Yosemite National Park tel: 559/252–4848
This charming Victorian hotel is nicely distanced from the park's busiest sections.

Winnedumah Hotel ($)
211 N. Edwards Street Independence tel: 619/878–2040
A lovely, historic inn. Rooms are very comfortable.

GOLD COUNTRY

Amber House ($$)
1315 22nd Street, Sacramento tel: 916/444–8085
Fourteen individually furnished rooms have marble baths. A hearty breakfast is served each morning.

Coach & Four Motel ($)
628 S. Auburn Street, Grass Valley tel: 530/273–8009
A light breakfast is included in the competitive room rates.

Delta King Hotel ($$$)
1000 Front Street, Sacramento tel: 916/444–5464
Rooms are on a 1927 riverboat, next to Old Town.

Harley House ($$)
700 22nd Street, Sacramento tel: 916/441–5007
A finely furnished Victorian B&B that serves gourmet breakfast. Also try the homemade cookies.

National Hotel ($)
77 Main Street, Jamestown tel: 209/984–3902
Simple, inexpensive rooms are in one of the town's oldest lodgings. The atmosphere is tremendous.

National Hotel ($$)
211 Broad Street, Nevada City tel: 916/265–4551
Believably claims to be the oldest hotel in the west. It has been operating since 1856.

Ryan House ($$)
153 S. Shepherd Street, Sonora tel: 209/533–3445
A competitively priced bed-and-breakfast in a mid-19th-century miner's home.

Stonepine ($$$)
150 East Carmel Valley Road, Carmel Valley tel: 831/659–5160
This ultra-deluxe country inn offers individual suites featuring antiques. There are riding stables, and a full breakfast is served.

NORTH COAST

Albion River Inn ($$$)
3790 Highway 1, Albion tel: 707/937–1919 or 800/479-7944
The inn's contemporary cottages have ocean views, sometimes from private decks, and hot tubs. Decor is a mix of antiques and wicker. Full breakfast is included in rates.

Blackberry Inn ($$)
44951 Larkin Road, Mendocino tel: 707/937–5281 or 800/950–7806
A few blocks from the ocean, this inn is made up to look like a scene from a Western. Single-story units have different decor; some have fireplaces or kitchenettes. Continental breakfast is included in the rate.

Downtowner Motel ($)
424 Eighth Street, Eureka tel: 707/443–5061
The Downtowner is the pick of the town's preponderance of simple, low-cost accommodations.

Eureka Inn ($$$)
518 7th Street, Eureka tel: 707/442–6441
A Tudor-style hotel that offers elegant, spacious rooms. Attentive staff are on hand to make your stay comfortable.

Fairwinds Motel ($)
1674 G Street, Arcata tel: 707/822–4824
This motel is a bargain in this surprisingly expensive town.

Gingerbread Mansion ($$$)
400 Berding Street, Ferndale tel: 707/786–4000
A stunningly restored Victorian B&B studded with carved friezes, gables, and turrets. Here are spacious bedrooms, an English garden, and full breakfast in a town known as a Victorian Village. Spectacular suites on top floors are ultra-pricey.

Hotel Carter ($$$)
301 L Street, Eureka tel: 707/444–8062
A chic, three-story hotel with whitewashed pine floors and contemporary decor. It augments accommodations in the nearby Carter House B&B, and two Victorian cottages, all under the same management. Everyone gets breakfast.

The Lady Anne Inn ($$)
902 14th Street, Arcata tel: 707/822–2797
A gracious Victorian mansion offering bed-and-breakfast accommodations.

MacCallum House ($$)
45020 Albion Street, Mendocino tel: 707/937–0289
This rambling Victorian has a variety of accommodations. There is also a lobby bar and restaurant.

Mendocino Hotel and Garden Suites ($$)
45080 Main Street, Mendocino tel: 800/548–0513
An extremely cozy, antiques-filled hotel dating from 1878. The lounge fireplace is ideal for relaxing on those chilly North Coast evenings.

Accommodations & Restaurants

Quality Inn ($)
*1209 4th Street, Eureka tel: 707/443–1601
or 800/772–1622*
Bland but comfortable, this is part of the popular
motel chain.
Surf Motel ($)
*1220 S. Main Street, Fort Bragg
tel: 707/964–5361*
A simple, clean, and very affordable motel.

WINE COUNTRY

Auberge du Soleil ($$$)
*180 Rutherford Hill Road, Rutherford
tel: 707/963–1211
or 800/348–5406*
This relaxed inn, situated in an olive grove, over-
looks the hills of Napa Valley and has a European
air. The service is top-notch and the restaurant,
bearing the same name, is one of the best in the
area.
Brannan Cottage ($$)
*109 Wapoo Avenue, Calistoga
tel: 707/942–4200*
A highly rated bed-and-breakfast in a cottage
built in 1860 by Sam Brannan, the famous
California pioneer who founded the health resort
here in 1859.
Calistoga Inn ($)
*1250 Lincoln Avenue, Calistoga
tel: 707/942–4101*
A positive bargain deal by Wine Country standards.
This inn offers cozy rooms and a complimentary
breakfast.
Discovery Inn ($)
*500 Silverado Trail, Napa
tel: 707/253–0892*
This motel offers extra value if you get a room with
a kitchenette. Find the inn a mile or so east of the
main drag.
Dry Creek Inn ($$)
*198 Dry Creek Road, Healdsburg
tel: 707/433–0300
or 800/528–1234*
A three-story Spanish Mission-style motel with
attractive rooms. There is a direct bus service from
San Francisco's airport.
The Gables ($$)
*4257 Petaluma Hill Road, Santa Rosa
tel: 707/585–7777*
An atmospheric Victorian home, The Gables serves
a substantial home-cooked breakfast inluded in
your stay.
Gaige House ($$$)
*13540 Arnold Drive, Glen Ellen
tel: 707/935–0237*
This glamorous 19th-century mansion is in a
quaint village and has a mix of traditional and con-
temporary decor. Amenities included are a tasty
full breakfast and a private swimming pool.
Honor Mansion ($$$)
*14892 Grove Avenue, Healdsburg
tel: 707/433-4277*
This pretty, white Victorian building offers deluxe
furnishings. The service is excellent. There are five
tastefully decorated rooms in the main house.
In addition, there is a private cottage with its
own koi pond.

Kenwood ($$$)
*10400 Sonoma Highway, Kenwood
tel: 707/833–1293 or 800/353–6966*
Located in the heart of the Sonoma valley, this
Italianate villa with views of the surrounding vine-
yards is an excellent retreat. All of the rooms have
fireplaces and there is a pool and full service spa
on the premises.
Meadowood ($$$)
*900 Meadowood Lane, St. Helena
tel: 707/963–3646 or 800/458–8080*
This secluded resort has a small spa, excellent
croquet, tennis, and golf facilities. Guests are
housed in bungalows and many rooms have fireplaces and patios.
Motel 6 ($)
*2760 Cleveland Avenue, Santa Rosa
tel: 707/546–1500*
A Wine Country rarity of uninspiring, yet genuinely
cheap, accommodations.
Sonoma Mission Inn and Spa ($$$)
*18140 Sonoma Highway, Sonoma
tel: 800/862–4945*
Stay here to enjoy luxury rooms, gourmet dining,
and a newly expanded, fully equipped health spa in
a scenic setting.
Swiss Hotel ($)
18 W. Spain Street, Sonoma tel: 707/938–2884
This small, atmospheric adobe building is set on
the town piazza.

RESTAURANTS

SAN FRANCISCO

Aqua ($$$)
252 California Street tel: 415/956–9662
Painstakingly prepared and artfully presented
seafood that draws a style-conscious crowd. One
of the city's top restaurants.
Basta Pasta ($)
1268 Grant Avenue tel: 415/434–2248
A late-night North Beach restaurant with fine pas-
tas and succulent wood-fired pizzas. Its large
windows are well suited to people-watching.
Betelnut ($$)
2026 Union Street tel: 415/929–8855
A Pan-Asian affair, this is situated in the heart of
the boutique district. Its offbeat menu incorporates
dishes from virtually every country in Asia.
Bix ($$)
56 Gold Street tel: 415/433–6300
Everything about this lounge-cum-restaurant is cool.
Enjoy the hidden entrance, the jazz music, the dim
lighting, the copious martinis, and the delicious food.
Boulevard ($$$)
1 Mission Street tel: 415/543–6084
Nancy Oaks cooks for adoring fans at this SoMa
hot spot. The food typifies California cooking:
inventive, healthful, and delicious.
The Buena Vista ($$)
2765 Hyde Street tel: 415/474–5044
For good value in the Fisherman's Wharf area, try
the Buena Vista. It's famous for its Irish coffee.
Café Caravan ($)
1312 Chestnut Street tel: 415/441–1168
A locals' diner with fast and friendly service. It is
excellent value.

Café Flore ($)
2298 Market Street tel: 415/621–8579
Salads and other light fare are the way to go at this people-watching paradise.

Caffè Trieste ($)
601 Vallejo Street tel: 415/392–6739
This is a long established Italian coffeehouse, legendary for its espresso and its live opera on Saturday afternoons.

Calzone's ($$)
430 Columbus Avenue tel: 415/397–3600
At Calzone's, wood-fired pizzas are served with inventive and exotic toppings.

Capp's Corner ($$)
1600 Powell Street tel: 415/989–2589
Delicious pasta lunches and three-course Italian dinners will fill you up here.

Cha Cha Cha ($$)
1801 Haight Street tel: 415/386–5758
A small and lively spot that pulls a diverse crowd. Cuban lunches and dinners are offered at reasonable prices. No reservations.

Chaya Brasserie ($$$)
132 The Embarcadero tel: 425/777–8688
A popular restaurant that opened in early 2000. Part teahouse (Chaya), part French brasserie, with a sushi bar and Japanese-inspired French menu.

The Dining Room ($$$)
The Ritz-Carlton San Francisco, 600 Stockton Street tel: 415/296–7465
Elegant French fare by former Le Cirque chef Sylvian Portay is served in an exquisite setting. The service is extremely accommodating and there is also an excellent wine cellar.

Dottie's True Blue Café ($)
522 Jones Street tel: 415/885–2767
The healthful diner food served here is heavy on fresh fruit and cereals. Enjoy it in this good Downtown location.

El Toro Taqueria ($)
598 Valencia Street tel: 415/431–3351
This is a popular fill-up stop for tasty, down-to-earth Mexican food.

The Élite Café ($$)
2049 Fillmore Street tel: 415/346–8668
Good Cajun and Creole fare is served here.

Farallon ($$$)
450 Post Street tel: 415/956–6969
Picture the Little Mermaid meets Jacques Cousteau. The setting is fantasmagorical, the seafood imaginative and delicious.

Fleur de Lys ($$$)
777 Sutter Street tel: 415/673–7779
Hubert Keller's inspired French cooking competes only with the richly appointed dining room. It is draped in hundreds of yards of rich, colorful, batiked fabric.

Flying Saucer ($)
1000 Guerrero Street tel: 415/641–9955
As zany as the Mission neighborhood in which it is located, this is a fun-filled place with a congenial atmosphere. It offers creative, imaginative and tasty food.

Fog City Diner ($$)
1300 Battery Street tel: 415/982–2000
A faux 1950s diner, complete with neon lights and stainless-steel fittings. The California cuisine is creative—and affordable.

Fringale ($$)
570 Fourth Street tel: 415/543-0573
In this contemporary French bistro, the atmosphere is congenial and the cuisine is extremely satisfying.

Gold Spike ($$)
527 Columbus Avenue tel: 415/421–4591
A North Beach institution, Gold Spike serves six-course Italian dinners.

Greens ($$$)
Building A, Fort Mason tel: 415/771–6222
Enjoy rarified state-of-the-art gourmet vegetarian cuisine here. Ingredients are grown on a Zen Buddhist farm across the bay in Marin County.

Hamburger Mary's Organic Grill ($)
1582 Folsom Street tel: 415/626–1985
Great burgers and loud music are on the menu here. The clientele is eye-catching.

Jardinière ($$$)
300 Grove Street tel: 415/861-5555
The elegant contemporary decor is comfortable and inviting. Enjoy chef Traci Des Jardins' sophisticated French-inspired cooking with a California flair.

John's Grill ($$)
63 Ellis Street tel: 415/986–0069
Exceptionally good steak, seafood, and pasta are served for lunch and dinner. John's Grill is mentioned in Dashiell Hammett's *The Maltese Falcon*.

Judy's Homestyle Café ($$)
2268 Chestnut Street
tel: 415/922–4588
Try the hunger-busting omelets and sandwiches. The trendy Marina District crowd eat here.

La Cumbre Taqueria ($)
515 Valencia Street
tel: 415/863–8205
This is a cafeteria-style outlet. Simple but delicious low-cost Mexican favorites are served.

La Folie ($$$)
2316 Polk Street tel: 415/776–5577
Outstanding French food is served in a refreshingly unstuffy setting. Options include a four-course dinner designed to reveal the chef's talents.

Lulu ($$)
816 Folsom Street tel: 415/495–5775
Delicious, fresh food (with an emphasis on grilling) is served at Lulu. The portions are family-sized at this trendy casual restaurant in the increasingly fashionable SoMa neighborhood.

Masa's ($$$)
648 Bush Street tel: 415/989–7154
The inventively prepared and presented French menu is set off by the understated surroundings. The staff is knowledgeable and attentive and the wine selection is admirable. One of the city's best.

MC² ($$$)
470 Pacific Avenue tel: 415/956–0666
The classically trained Japanese chef prepares exquisite seafood in an architectural masterpiece. It is located in a remodeled bricklined warehouse in the old Barbary Coast neighborhood.

North Beach Pizza ($$)
1512 Stockton Street
tel: 415/392–1700
Famous all over town for expertly made pizzas, with a long list of toppings. This place is always busy.

275

Accommodations & Restaurants

Pastis ($$)
1015 Battery Street tel: 415/391–2555
A great French bistro with satisfying food and
friendly service. A sister to Fringale (570 4th Street),
but less expensive and easier to get a table.

Perry's ($$)
1944 Union Street tel: 415/922–9022
This famed Cow Hollow rendezvous serves large
portions of traditional American food.

Postrio ($$$)
545 Post Street tel: 415/776–7825
The Asian- and Mediterranean-inspired California
menu is overseen by superstar chef Wolfgang Puck
at this popular, attractive spot. Enjoy specialties
such as Chinese duck, and excellent desserts.
They also serve a great breakfast.

Rose Pistola ($$)
532 Columbus Avenue tel: 415/399–0499
Try this friendly setting for hearty, contemporary
food. The flavors are bold and the portions large.

Rubicon ($$$)
558 Sacramento Street tel: 415/434–4100
An elegant outpost of New York restaurateur Drew
Nieporent's empire (Nobu, Montrachet). The menu
has inventive Mediterranean fare.

Silks ($$$)
*Mandarin Oriental Hotel, 222 Sansome Street
tel: 415/986–2020*
Enjoy inventive "architectural" cuisine with an emphasis on strong flavors and beautiful presentations.

The Slanted Door ($$)
584 Valencia Street tel: 415/861–8032
Exciting, modern Vietnamese is food served in a
chic, casual setting.

St. Francis Candy Store ($)
2801 24th Street tel: 415/826–4200
This is a wonderful, long-established provider of
sandwiches and famous, frothy milkshakes.

The Stinking Rose ($$)
325 Columbus Avenue tel: 415/781–7673
Every dish, and many of the drinks, makes liberal
use of garlic at this predominantly Italian spot.

Tad's ($)
120 Powell Street tel: 415/982–1718
A good spot for cheap breakfast and lunch. It also
serves tasty burgers, soups, and sourdough bread.

Thai Stick ($)
698 Post Street tel: 415/928–7730
At this Thai restaurant, it's easy to order more than
you can eat and still spend less than you expect.

Ton Kiang ($)
3148 Geary Boulevard tel: 415/752–4440
5821 Geary Boulevard tel: 415/387–8273
An amazing array of dim sum (with over nine types
of shrimp dumplings) are served here.

Yank Sing ($$)
427 Battery Street tel: 415/781–1111
Not cheap but among the best dim sum restau-
rants in the city. Yank Sing is always busy.

THE BAY AREA

Alta Mira ($$)
*125 Bulkley Avenue, Sausalito
tel: 415/332–1500*
Sunday brunch is the time to visit this landmark.
It is loved for its stunning views of San Francisco
Bay from the patio.

Bette's Oceanview Diner ($)
*1807 4th Street, Berkeley
tel: 510/644–3230*
This diner does not really have an ocean view! But
it's a modern diner where you can load up before
shopping on one of the East Bay's best boutique
streets.

The Blue Nile ($)
*2525 Telegraph Avenue, Berkeley
tel: 510/540–6777*
Absurdly cheap East African food is served here.
The Blue Nile is ideal for vegetarians and anyone
looking for a culinary bargain.

Chez Panisse ($$$)
*1517 Shattuck Avenue, Berkeley
tel: 510/548–5525*
The birthplace of California cuisine is as innovative
and popular as ever.

Chez Panisse Café ($$)
*1517 Shattuck Avenue, Berkeley
tel: 415/548–5409*
This offshoot is a chance to sample delectable
California cuisine at a far more affordable price
than the main restaurant downstairs.

Frankie, Johnny, and Luigi's Too ($$)
*939 El Camino Real, Palo Alto
tel: 650/967–5384*
Earns the favor of locals, including many Stanford
students, for its delectable pizzas.

The Good Earth ($$)
*185 University Avenue, Palo Alto
tel: 650/321–9449*
Only healthy, natural ingredients are used to whip
up omelets, salads, and sandwiches. It also has a
counter for muffins to take out.

The Lark Creek Inn ($$$)
*234 Magnolia Avenue, Larkspur
tel: 415/927–7766*
Contemporary American cuisine by award-winning
chef Bradley Ogden is served in an idyllic setting.
Ravioli with shredded ham hocks are among the
many signature dishes.

Oliveto ($$$)
*5655 College Avenue, Oakland
tel: 510/547–5356*
In the restaurant upstairs the cuisine and decor is
Mediterranean. There is a less pricey café on the
first floor.

Palermo Ristorante Italiano ($$)
*394 S. Second Street, San Jose
tel: 408/297–0607*
A popular spot for pasta and pizzas. The
atmosphere is convivial.

CENTRAL COAST NORTH

Dolphin Restaurant ($$)
*Municipal Wharf, Santa Cruz
tel: 831/426–5830*
Several restaurants line the wharf but none is better
than this one, located right at the end and open all
day. It serves a mix of seafood and American
dishes.

India Joze ($$)
*1001 Center Street, Santa Cruz
tel: 831/427–3554*
An inspiring mix of Indian and Indonesian fare is
given the California treatment here.

Kathy's Restaurant ($)
700 Cass Street, Monterey
tel: 831/647–9540
Open for breakfast and lunch, Kathy's is well known for its excellent omelets and sandwiches. There are patio tables.

Pacific's Edge ($$$)
at the Highlands Inn on Highway 1, 4 miles south of Carmel tel: 831/622–5445
Scintillating ocean views and fabulous food are served here. The menu varies according to what is in season.

Rappa's ($$)
Fisherman's Wharf, Monterey
tel: 831/372–7562
Seafood is fresh and tasty at Rappa's. There is a lively, congenial atmosphere.

Rosita's Armory Café ($)
231 Salinas Street, Salinas
tel: 831/424–7039
This Mexican eatery is popular for its low-cost breakfasts, lunches and dinners.

Tuck Box ($)
Dolores and Seventh streets, Carmel
tel: 831/624–6365
Shepherd's pie, Welsh rarebit, and scones are some of the dishes in this shoebox-sized restaurant. It is also open for breakfast.

Zachary's ($)
819 Pacific Avenue, Santa Cruz
tel: 831/427–0646
American breakfasts and lunches are served with delicious homemade breads.

CENTRAL COAST SOUTH

Andria's Haborside Restaurant ($$)
336 W. Cabrillo Boulevard, Santa Barbara
tel: 805/966–3000
Locals and tourists alike come here for the substantial breakfasts. The lunches and dinners are equally filling. At weekends there is entertainment.

Dorn's Original Breakers Café ($)
801 Market Street, Morro Bay
tel: 805/772–4415
Dorn's is unsurpassed for inventive breakfasts. It is also good for lunch and dinner.

Joe's Café ($)
536 State Street, Santa Barbara
tel: 805/966–4638
There is always an eager crowd here. Helpings of meat and fish dishes are large.

Kyoto/China Brown ($)
685 Higuera Street, San Luis Obispo
tel: 805/546–9700
Help yourself to Chinese and Japanese food from a tempting vegetarian buffet.

Paradise Café ($$)
702 Anacapa Street, Santa Barbara
tel: 805/962–4416
Plain but good American cooking is served here. The setting is simple, but comfortable.

Rose's Landing Restaurant ($$)
725 Embarcadero, Morro Bay
tel: 805/772–4441
A deservedly popular seafood restaurant that has a view over the bay and the massive Morro Rock.

Woody's Beach Club and Cantina ($)
5112 Hollister Avenue, Santa Barbara
tel: 805/967–3775
There are barbecued ribs and chicken to bring joy to every carnivore's heart. The menu also includes sizable burgers and spicy chili dishes.

LOS ANGELES

Aunt Kizzy's Back Porch ($$)
4325 Glencoe Avenue, Marina Del Rey
tel: 310/578–1005
Big portions of Southern favorites are prepared with a distinct California style here.

The Belvedere ($$$)
The Peninsula, Beverly Hills, 9882 Little Santa Monica Boulevard tel: 310/788–2306
This quintessential California restaurant is one of the most popular in the area. The decor is exuberant yet formal, and the service is excellent.

Book Soup Bistro ($$)
8800 Sunset Boulevard
tel: 310/657–1072
Enjoy classic American dishes in stylish literary surroundings. The legendary Book Soup bookstore is next door.

Caffe Luna ($$)
7463 Melrose Avenue, West Hollywood
tel: 323/665–8647
Regional Italian fare is consumed by a trendy, fashionable crowd.

Campanile ($$)
624 S. La Brea Avenue, West Hollywood
tel: 323/938–1447
Tasty northern Italian fare is served to a predominantly young and arty clientele.

Canter's Fairfax ($)
419 Fairfax Avenue, West Hollywood
tel: 323/651–2030
A New York-style deli serving generous portions, Canter's has been established for decades.

Chinois on Main ($$$)
2709 Main Street, Santa Monica
tel: 310/392–9025
The flagship of celebrity chef Wolfgang Puck serves astronomically priced but gastronomically perfect California cuisine with Far Eastern touches.

Citrus ($$$)
6703 Melrose Avenue, Los Angeles
tel: 213/857–0034
For food and design, this isthe most creative restaurant in L.A.

Clifton's Brookdale Cafeteria ($)
648 S. Broadway, Downtown
tel: 213/627–1673
Help yourself from the array of steaming trays, then pay at the cash register.

Dar Maghreb ($$)
7651 Sunset Boulevard, Hollywood
tel: 323/876–7651
Morocco is re-created here Hollywood-style, complete with belly dancers. The food is reasonable.

Dining Room ($$$)
9500 Wilshire Boulevard, Beverly Hills
tel: 310/275–5200
California cuisines are served in an elegant setting at the Regent Beverly Wilshire Hotel.

Accommodations & Restaurants

Ed Debevic's ($)
134 N. La Cienega Boulevard
tel: 310/659–1952
This diner is complete with 1950s-style decor and garishly dressed staff. The burgers here are massive.

El Cholo ($$)
1121 S. Western Avenue, Wilshire District
tel: 323/734–2773
Good Mexican food is served in a restaurant once patronized by Hollywood's biggest names.

Fenix ($$$)
The Argyle Hotel, 8358 Sunset Boulevard, Los Angeles tel: 213/848–6677
The Fenix has impressive art-deco style with exquisite views of the city from the outdoor terrace. The French-influenced California cuisine completes the experience.

The Gumbo Pot ($)
at Farmer's Market, 6333 W. Third Street
tel: 323/933–0358
Tempting Cajun and Creole food is served here in an eat-and-run setting.

Hot Wings Café ($)
7011 Melrose Avenue tel: 213/930–1233
Chicken wings, sandwiches, and other snacks at the lowest prices are to be found on this trendy shopping and eating strip.

Kachina Grill ($$)
330 S. Hope Street, Downtown
tel: 213/625–0956
Sizzling Southwestern specialties are served here. Try the classy pasta and seafood.

L'Orangerie ($$$)
903 N. La Cienega Boulevard, Hollywood
tel: 310/692–9770
Elegant French food is served in this fine restaurant, complimented by an extensive wine cellar. It is extremely expensive but, according to most, well worth it.

Matsuhisa ($$$)
129 N. La Cienega Boulevard, Beverly Hills
tel: 310/659–9639
Before there was the show-stopper Nobu in New York City, there was this tiny Matsuhisa in Los Angeles, where Hollywood celebrities come to enjoy extraordinary Japanese food.

Michael's ($$$)
1147 Third Street, Santa Monica
tel: 310/451–0843
Michael McCarty virtually invented California cooking at this favorite haunt of Los Angeles' glamour scene.

Mon Kee ($$)
679 N. Spring Street, Chinatown
tel: 213/628–6717
A justifiably busy Chinese eatery that specializes in seafood.

Patina ($$$)
5955 Melrose Avenue tel: 213/467–1108
Inspired modern-French cooking issues forth from Joachim Splichal's kitchen. Sparse, elegant dining room and casual but efficient service.

Ocean Café ($$)
1700 Ocean Avenue, Santa Monica
tel: 310/458–6700
Located in the fashionable Loews hotel, this café is excellent for people-watching.

Original Pantry Café ($)
877 S. Figueroa Street, Downtown
tel: 213/972–9279
This famous but unprepossessing coffee shop is the best value in Downtown. It is always open.

Pacific Dining Car ($$)
1310 W. Sixth Street, Wilshire District
tel: 231/483–6000
Succulent ribs and steaks are served in a luxury railroad dining car setting. The restaurant is open 24 hours; breakfasts are worth sampling at any hour. The Pacific Dining Car is known for its excellent beef.

Philippe's the Original ($)
1001 N. Alameda Street, Downtown
tel: 213/ 628–3781
Wholesome American food has been served here since 1908. Diners share wooden bench tables.

Pinks Famous Chili Dogs ($)
711 N. La Brea Avenue, Hollywood
tel: 323/931–4223
Burgers, hot dogs, and chili dishes are served from a giant hot-dog shaped stand in what is (inexplicably) an L.A. fast-food legend.

Pinot Bistro ($$)
12969 Ventura Boulevard, Studio City
tel: 818/990–0500
An off-shoot of Joachim Splichal's Patina, this less-expensive bistro features satisfying fare such as crispy whitefish with roasted garlic sauce.

Spago ($$$)
8795 Sunset Boulevard, West Hollywood
tel: 310/652–4025
With exotic pizzas and mouthwatering pasta dishes, Spago has been setting L.A.'s culinary standards for years—reserve weeks ahead.

Spago of Beverly Hills ($$$)
176 N. Canon Drive, Beverly Hills
tel: 310/358–0800
Rub elbows with who's who of Los Angeles at the latest addition to Wolfgang Puck's legendary chain. The California cuisine is as good as ever.

Valentino ($$$)
3115 Pico Boulevard, Santa Monica
tel: 310/829–4313
World-class Italian food is served here. There is a long and diverse list of exceptional daily specials.

Water Grill ($$)
544 S. Grand Avenue, Downtown
tel: 213/891–0900
Delicious seafood is stylishly served in a light, spacious, and modern art-filled dining room.

Ye Olde Kings Head ($)
116 Santa Monica Boulevard tel: 310/451-1402
A pseudo-English pub serving top-notch fish-and-chips alongside several well-known imported British beers.

Yorkshire Grill ($)
610 W. Sixth Street tel: 213/623–3362
This long-serving and highly rated deli is ideal for low-cost breakfast or lunch.

AROUND L.A.

Armstrong's Seafood Restaurant ($$)
306 Crescent Avenue, Santa Catalina Island
tel: 310/510–0113
Freshly caught swordfish and mahi-mahi are among the mesquite-grilled delights at Armstrong's.

Café Del Rey ($$$)
4451 Admiralty Way, Marina del Rey
tel: 310/823–6395
Inventive French/Japanese cooking by Katsuo Nagasawa offers delectable dishes. Try spicy black pepper-crusted hamachi and pan-fried sea tower.

Cajun and Grill ($$)
395 Santa Monica Boulevard, Santa Monica
tel: 310/393–2088
Good seafood and meats are cooked Cajun-style, usually blackened. The service is fast.

The Epicenter Restaurant ($$)
200 South Hill Street, Los Angeles
tel: 213/625–0000
This restaurant is housed in a charming building with an earthquake motif. Its innovative cuisine has Asian and California influences.

Fresco ($$$)
514 S. Brand Boulevard, Glendale
tel: 818/247–5541
Draws fussy eaters from all over L.A. to its world-class Italian menu.

Gladstone's 4 Fish ($$)
17300 Pacific Coast Highway, Malibu
tel: 310/573–0212
Fine, fresh sea fare with ocean views and, at dinner, memorable sunsets.

Hometown Buffet ($)
1630 Katella Avenue, Anaheim
tel: 714/539–2234
Huge buffet certain to satiate the most ravenous of appetites.

Inn of the Seventh Ray ($$)
128 Old Topanga Canyon Road, Topanga Canyon tel: 310/455–1311
California flower power lives on in this long-running and rightly popular health-food restaurant.

Mrs. Knott's Chicken Restaurant ($)
8039 Beach Boulevard, Buena Boulevard
tel: 714/220–5200
The chicken dinners that begat the Knotts Berry Farm theme park, plus tempting fruit pies.

Parkway Grill ($$)
510 S. Arroyo Parkway, Pasadena
tel: 626/795–1001
Scintillating fresh salads and mouthwatering pizzas and pastas are served here. A well-stocked wine cellar compliments quality fish and meat dishes.

Ruby's ($)
Balboa Pier, Newport Beach tel: 949/675–7829
This pier-end, art-deco diner has a great location and superb milkshakes. Other food is average.

Tommy Tang's ($$$)
24 W. Colorado Boulevard tel: 818/792–9700
Thai cuisine is exquisitely prepared and presented with panache here.

White House ($$)
340 S. Coast Highway, Laguna Beach
tel: 849/494–8088
The impressively diverse menu is uniformly good. You can shake a leg on the dance floor after dinner.

SAN DIEGO

Anthony's Star of the Sea Room ($$)
1360 Harbor Drive tel: 619/232–7408
An extensive range of succulent seafood is served in this restaurant overlooking the harbor.

Blarney Stone Pub ($)
502 5th Avenue, San Diego
tel: 619/233–8519
A popular San Diego Irish pub and restaurant in the Gas Lamp District.

Broken Yolk ($)
1851 Garnet Street
tel: 858/270–9655
Try the immense range of omelets at tempting, next-to-nothing prices.

Café 222 ($)
222 Island Avenue, San Diego
tel: 619/236–9902
Popular with the business people in the downtown area, Café 222 serves an eclectic variety of traditional American fare. Only open for breakfast and lunch, it provides excellent dining in a casual atmosphere.

Carnitas Uruapan ($)
8035 Broadway, Lemon Grove
tel: 619/462–0704
A Mexican restaurant with an authentic menu; deep-fried pork is a specialty. It's owned by the same family that operates the original, in Tijuana, Mexico.

Dick's Last Resort ($)
345 Fourth Avenue tel: 619/231–9100
Enjoy the lively atmosphere and generous portions of American favorites.

Dobson's Bar & Restaurant ($$$)
956 Broadway Circle, San Diego
tel: 619/231–6771
Dobson's has long been a popular spot with the city's political and business power brokers. Its signature dish is a mussel bisque, crowned with puff pastry.

Filippi's Pizza Grotto ($$)
1747 India Street, San Diego
tel: 619/232–5094
Located in the center of Little Italy district, this restaurant serves excellent, authentic Italian food at a very reasonable price.

George's at the Cove ($$$)
1250 Prospect Street
tel: 858/454–4244
George's is justly acclaimed for its creative seafood dishes and divine pastas.

La Gran Tapa ($$)
611 B Street tel: 619/234–8272
Mesmerizing tapas are served here. The paella is excellent.

La Jolla Brewing Company ($)
7536 Fay Avenue tel: 858/456–2739
House-brewed beers are the main attraction here. Delicious soups, salads, and burgers help the ale go down.

La Provence ($$)
714 4th Avenue, San Diego
tel: 619/544–0661
Go for the excellent southern French cuisine. It's without the usual heavy sauces.

Laders of La Mesa ($$)
5654 Lake Murray Boulevard, La Mesa
tel: 619/463–9919
An excellent place to find out that traditional Italian cooking does not always have a tomato sauce. Find it about 15 minutes from downtown San Diego.

279

Accommodations & Restaurants

Las Parrillas Mexican Restaurant ($)
555 Montrose Court, El Cajon
tel: 619/444–3955
A good family style restaurant that serves typical Mexican food in the East County area. It has an adjoining cantina with evening entertainment and karaoke singing. Sunday brunch includes an all-you-can-eat Mexican buffet.

Nob Nob Hill ($)
2271 1st Avenue, San Diego
tel: 619/239–8176
A few blocks from downtown, this place has operated under the same management since 1944. It is well known for its fresh-baked muffins and breads.

Old Columbia Brewery & Grill ($)
1157 Columbia Street tel: 619/234–2739
Meat and seafood dishes are served here in satisfyingly large portions. The beer is brewed on the premises.

Old Town Mexican Café y Cantina ($$)
2489 San Diego Avenue tel: 619/297–4330
Always packed, but worth the wait for the best Mexican food in Old Town.

The Spot ($$)
105 Prospect Street, La Jolla
tel: 619/459–0800
Sample fine affordable food, including steaks, seafood, and pizzas here.

Trattoria Mama Ana ($$$)
644 5th Avenue, San Diego
tel: 619/235–8144
Sicilian food is a specialty of this trattoria, highly recommended for its food and atmosphere. Other Italian cuisine is also offered.

THE DESERTS

Cuistot ($$$)
73111 El Paseo, Palm Desert
tel: 760/340–1000
Experience the excellent California-French cuisine that pleases the desert communities' wealthiest diners.

Elmer's Pancake and Steakhouse ($)
1030 E. Palm Canyon Drive, Palm Springs
tel: 760/327–8419
Pancakes and waffles galore are served at prices to incite gluttony.

Flower Drum ($$)
424 S. Indian Canyon Drive, Palm Springs
tel: 760/323–3020
Classy cuisine from five regions of China is served alongside an indoor waterfall.

La Casuelas Terraza ($$)
222 S. Palm Canyon Drive, Palm Springs
tel: 760/325–2794
Consume well-prepared, authentic Mexican food here. As the name suggests, there is a patio, which is micromist cooled.

Le Vallauris ($$$)
385 W. Tahquitz Canyon Way, Palm Springs
tel: 760/325–5059
Sample top-notch, French–California cuisine here.

Louise's Pantry ($)
124 S. Palm Canyon Drive, Palm Springs
tel: 760/325–5124
Simple coffee-shop favorites are served in a shed-sized diner.

Nate's Delicatessen ($)
100 S. Indian Canyon Avenue, Palm Springs
tel: 760/325–3506
A deli seemingly transplanted from New York, offers unlikely desert fare such as chicken soup and corned beef sandwiches.

SIERRA NEVADA

Ahwahnee Dining Room ($$$)
Yosemite Valley tel: 209/372–1489
Formal dining in a grand setting.

Giant Forest Lodge Dining Room ($$)
Sequoia National Park tel: 559/561–3314
Indulgent dinners to finish off an exhausting day exploring in the forest.

Jack's Waffle Shop ($)
437 N. Main Street, Bishop tel: 619/872–7971
Solid nourishment 24 hours a day.

Rosie's Café ($)
571 N. Lake Boulevard, Tahoe City
tel: 530/583–8504
Sandwiches, soups, and burgers served with a smile.

Village Cafeteria ($)
Giant Forest Village, Sequoia National Park
tel: 209/ 561–3314
Unpretentious, filling fare for dedicated hikers.

Wolfdale's ($$)
640 N. Lake Boulevard, Tahoe City
tel: 530/583–5700
An ideal venue for scrumptious vegetarian meals.

Yosemite Trails Inn ($)
Highway 395, Lee Vining tel: 619/647–6369
Great food is served in big portions all day.

GOLD COUNTRY

Biba ($$$)
2801 Capitol Avenue, Sacramento
tel: 916/455–2422
Classy Italian dining draws a stylish crowd.

City Hotel Dining Room ($$)
Main Street, Columbia tel: 209/532–1479
French-California cuisine is served in a Gold-Rush era setting.

Greta's Café ($)
1831 Capitol Avenue, Sacramento
tel: 916/442–7382
Try the soups, sandwiches, and substantial salads in this excellent café.

Murphys Hotel Dining Room ($$)
Main Street, Murphys tel: 209/728–3444
Specialties here include veal scallopini.

Rubicon Brewing Company ($)
2004 Capitol Avenue, Sacramento
tel: 916/448–7032
Try the home-brewed beer and wholesome meals.

Wilma's Café ($)
275 S. Washington Street, Sonora
tel: 209/532–9957
Earthy, coffee-shop staples are served from 6 AM till late.

Stokes Adobe ($$)
500 Hartnell Street, Monterey
tel: 831/373–1110
This historic 1823 adobe is transformed into an elegant series of rooms. Dine here for cutting-edge French, Italian, Spanish and vegetarian cooking.

NORTH COAST

Café Beaujolais ($$$)
961 Ukiah Street, Mendocino
tel: 707/937–5614
An excellent place to try French-based eclectic cooking with Thai and Mexican accents.

Café Waterfront ($$)
102 F Street, Eureka tel: 707/443–9190
Fresh fish and sandwiches are served in a casual eatery. Find it across from the marina.

Egghead Omelettes ($)
356 N. Main Street, Fort Bragg
tel: 707/964–5005
A cozy, relaxed diner that delivers plenty of what its name suggests—and much more.

Lost Coast Brewery ($$)
617 Fourth Street, Eureka tel: 707/445–4480
Fantastic soups, stews, and sandwiches accompany the beer brewed on the premises.

Restaurant 301 ($$$)
391 L Street, Eureka tel: 707/444–8062
Regional seafood and produce and an award-winning wine list make this a not-to-be-missed restaurant. Located in the best hotel in town, this outstanding restaurant is run by a native Eureka family.

Samoa Cookhouse
Cookhouse Road, Eureka tel: 707/442–1659
A ramshackle joint on the outskirts of town that serves three square meals a day.

Samraat
546 Main Street, Fort Bragg
tel: 707/964–0386
Dine in a serene setting with soothing pastels and recorded sitar music. Tandoori, curries, and seafood are all on the menu.

WINE COUNTRY

Auberge du Soleil ($$$)
180 Rutherford Hill Road, Rutherford
tel: 707/963–1211
Delectably prepared and presented nouvelle French and California cuisine is served in a rural location.

Bistro Giovanni ($$)
4110 Highway 29, Napa tel: 707/523–4814
The closest to Tuscany you can get in California, this roadside favorite mixes fish and game with seasonal produce, offbeat ingredients and a vineyard setting to die for. Very good any time of year, it's unbeatable during the fall harvest season.

Bistro Ralph ($$)
109 Plaza Street, Healdsburg
tel: 707/433–1380
A small restaurant with a big attitude. A no-holds-barred kitchen is willing to mix and match regional and international ingredients.

Boskos ($)
1364 Lincoln Avenue, Calistoga
tel: 707/942–9088
The freshly made pasta is followed up by some very tempting desserts.

Bouchon ($$$)
Washington Street, Yountville
tel: 707/ 944–8037
This sleek and shimmering restaurant is a French bistro. Onion tarts, entrecôte avec frites and sole meunière star on the menu du jour.

Calistoga Inn and Brewery ($$)
1250 Lincoln Avenue tel: 707/942–4101
A varied range of classy meat and seafood dishes is on the menu. Eat outdoors in summer.

Dempsey's Ale House ($)
50 E. Washington Street, Petaluma
tel: 707/765–9694
A sociable spot overlooking the Petaluma River. Good food is complimented by great beers.

The French Laundry ($$$)
6640 Washington Avenue, Yountville
tel: 707/944–2380
This hard-to-book unassuming restaurant is one of the best in the country. The food is contemporary French, perfectly executed, and delicious, served by extremely knowledgeable and attentive staff.

The Girl & The Fig ($$$)
13690 Arnold Drive, Glen Ellen
tel: 707/938–3634
Figs are just the half of it at this country town restaurant beloved for its innovative wine flights and cheese plates. Unpretentious yet daring, this place will serve you a meal to remember.

Juanita Juanita ($)
19114 Arnold Drive, Sonoma
tel: 707/935–3981
Make a colorful roadside stop here for fabulously fresh Americanized Mexican food and dozens of types of hot sauce to put on top. It's popular with local vintners.

Meritage ($$)
522 Broadway, Sonoma tel: 707/938–9430
Enjoy a fusion of southern French and northern Italian cuisine in a souped-up storefront restaurant. The wine list is dynamite. The Meritage is only steps away from an historic plaza.

Mustards Grill ($$)
7399 Highway 29, Yountville
tel: 707/944–2424
Sample the delicious grilled morsels served here. The style is California cuisine.

Sonoma Cheese Factory ($)
2 W. Spain Street, Sonoma tel: 707/996–1931
Deli sandwiches, condiments and homemade cheeses can be purchased here. Find the ingredients perfect for including in your picnic basket.

Terra ($$$)
1345 Railroad Avenue, St. Helena
tel: 707/963–8931
A casually elegant setting in a renovated foundry, and a menu serving California, French, and northern Italian fare. Try specials such as broiled *sake*-marinated sea bass. Leave space for the excellent and tempting desserts.

Tra Vigne ($$$)
1050 Charter Oak Street, St Helena
tel: 707/963–4444
A large, fun, contemporary restaurant that feels like an Italian trattoria crossed with a French bistro. The satisfying menu is informed by the regional cooking of Italy.

Willowside Café ($$)
3535 Guerneville Road, Santa Rosa
tel: 707/523–4814
This is an unprepossessing café, off the beaten path. But it is well worth visiting for its highly original, very short menu, and a sought-after bohemian ambience.

Index

Index

Index

287

Picture Credits and Contributors

288

Picture credits

The Automobile Association would like to thank the following photographers, libraries and associations for their assistance in the preparation of this book.

CALIFORNIA DEPT OF PARKS AND RECREATION 97 Monterey area beach, 200 pools across the meadows; **CORBIS/Richard Cummins** Front cover (a); **J PAUL GETTY TRUST** 154; **IMAGE BANK/David Vance** Front cover silhouette; **IMAGES COLOUR LIBRARY LTD** 19a zodiacs; **MARINE WORLD** 87 elephants, dolphin; **MARY EVANS** 22 Native Americans and Jesuit missionaries, 23 Mission San Diego, 26 prospector, 28 earthquake, 29 cartoon; **POPPERFOTO** 16 Charles Manson, 30 gentlemen of Paramount, 32–33 police and demonstrator; **REX FEATURES** 132 Beach Boys, 133 The Doors; **ROYAL GEOGRAPHIC SOCIETY** 20 map; **SPECTRUM COLOUR LIBRARY** 75 fireworks, 97 fruit, 102 oil platforms, 128–129 Hollywood sign, 137 University of California, 202–203 Sierra Mountain lake, 207 Kaweah River, Mount Whitney Trail, 239 earthquake damage, 243 Smith River; **WALT DISNEY CO.** 160 Sleeping Beauty's Castle; **ZEFA PICTURE LIBRARY (UK) LTD** 136 LA Westwood village, 144 Hard Rock Cafe, 145 Sunset Boulevard, 148 LA airport, 149 Yellow cabs, 162 Catalina Island, 164 L.A. freeways and skyline, 175 Mission Bay, 201 Sequoia tree, 228 Gull Rock, 257 L.A. harbour.
The remaining pictures are held in the association's own photo library (**AA PHOTO LIBRARY**) and were taken by **ROBERT HOLMES** with the exception of the following pages which were taken by **HAROLD HARRIS** 15, 35, 78, 80, 245; **KEN PATERSON** 8, 13b, 14b; **BARRIE SMITH** 38, 39, 51, 52, 53, 60, 62, 63, 68, 70, 72, 73, 88, 125, 259, 265, 266, 267, 268, 269; **JAMES TIMS** 19b, 19c; **PHIL WOOD** 4, 5, 6-7.

Contributors

Revision editors: Donna Dailey, Irena Hoare, Julian Rowe   **Original editor**: Diana Payne
Revision verifiers: Mick Sinclair, Carole Harley, Marty Olmstead